Better Homes and Gardens®

New Baby Book

by Carol Keough

Medical Reviewer: Donald W. Schiff, M.D.
Past President of the American Academy of Pediatrics and
Professor of Pediatrics at the University of Colorado School of
Medicine in Denver

Better Homes and Gardens® Books

An imprint of Meredith® Books

Better Homes and Gardens® New Baby Book

Author: Carol Keough
Product Development Editor: Benjamin W. Allen
Copy Chief: Angela K. Renkoski
Contributing Copy Editor: Becky Danley
Contributing Proofreader: Sharon L. Emmons
Contributing Illustrator: Rita Lascaro
Electronic Production Coordinator: Paula Forest
Editorial and Design Assistants: Susan McBroom, Jennifer Norris, Karen Schirm, Barbara Suk
Production Director: Douglas M. Johnston
Production Manager: Pam Kvitne
Assistant Prepress Manager: Marjorie J. Schenkelberg

Meredith® Books

Editor in Chief: James D. Blume
Design Director: Matt Strelecki
Managing Editor: Gregory H. Kayko
Executive Health Editor: Alice Feinstein

Director, Sales & Marketing, Retail: Michael A. Peterson
Director, Sales & Marketing, Special Markets: Rita McMullen
Director, Sales & Marketing, Home and Garden Center Channel: Ray Wolf
Director, Operations: Valerie Wiese

Vice President, General Manager: Jamie L. Martin

Better Homes and Gardens® Magazine

Editor in Chief: Jean LemMon

Meredith Publishing Group

President, Publishing Group: Christopher M. Little
Vice President, Consumer Marketing & Development: Hal Oringer

Meredith Corporation

Chairman and Chief Executive Officer: William T. Kerr

Chairman of the Executive Committee: E.T. Meredith III

Cover photograph: Andy Lyons

All of us at Better Homes and Gardens® Books are dedicated to providing you with the information and ideas you need to ensure your family's health. We welcome your comments and suggestions about this book. Write to us at: Better Homes and Gardens® Books, Health Editorial Department, RW–206, 1716 Locust St., Des Moines, IA 50309–3023.

Note to the Reader: This book is intended to provide you with information about health and baby care. It is not intended to be a medical guide or to serve as a substitute for advice from your doctor. Every woman's health needs are unique. Every baby's health needs are unique. Diagnosis and treatment must be done through a health care professional. Please consult with your doctor for all your health care needs.

Board of Advisors

Jan Barger, R.N.
Board certified lactation consultant, in private practice with The Breastfeeding Connection and for Wheaton Pediatrics, Wheaton, Illinois. Program director and instructor for Breastfeeding Support Consultants, Wheaton, Illinois, and nationwide.

Suzanne LeBel Corrigan, M.D.
Spokesperson for the American Academy of Pediatrics. Associate clinical professor, University of Texas Southwestern Medical School/Dallas. Private practice, pediatrics, Irving, Texas.

Theodore Croll, D.D.S.
Clinical professor, Department of Pediatric Dentistry, University of Pennsylvania School of Dental Medicine, Clinical Professor, Craniofacial Growth and Development (Pediatric Dentistry), University of Texas, Health Science Center at Houston (Dental Branch), Adjunctive Assistant Professor of Pediatric Dentistry, University of Iowa College of Dentistry, and author of *The No Boring Science Take Care of Your Kid's Mouth Book* (American Society of Dentistry for Children, 1993.) Private practice, pediatric dentistry, Doylestown, Pennsylvania.

Matthew Davies, M.D.
Assistant professor of obstetrics and gynecology and associate director of the residency program at Pennsylvania State University in Hershey.

Anita Hirsch, R.D.
Nutritionist, registered dietitian, member of the International Association of Culinary Professionals

James Martin, M.D.
Director of Obstetrics and Maternal/Fetal Medicine at the University of Mississippi Medical Center and professor of obstetrics and gynecology at the University of Mississippi in Jackson.

Celeen Miller
Director of The Childbirth Connection/The Wellness Connection, and health educator for Bucks County Department of Health in Doylestown, Pennsylvania, and certified childbirth educator for Doylestown Hospital.

Donald W. Schiff, M.D.
Past president of the American Academy of Pediatrics and professor of pediatrics at the University of Colorado School of Medicine at Denver Children's Hospital.

Rebecca Shaw, M.D.
Private practice, obstetrics and gynecology, Des Moines, Iowa.

Deborah Tolchin, M.D.
Associate professor of pediatrics, Albert Einstein College of Medicine in the Bronx, New York, and past president of New York Chapter Three of the American Academy of Pediatrics.

Contents

having a baby

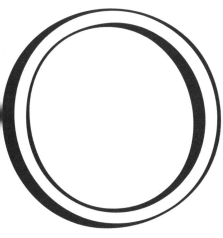

ne morning it just happens. You open your eyes to the same familiar bedroom, the same view from the window, the same you in the mirror. But somehow you know that everything is different, and from that day on, you will be living a new life.

You've been supposing all along that the tingling in your breasts is a signal that your late period is finally arriving. And the fact that all you want to do is slee-ee-eep … well, you chalked that up to over-work. But today, you just know that it's not your period, and it's not your job. In fact, there's only one thing it *could* be—a baby. Does this sound like your story? It's a fairly common scenario.

Every pregnant woman, however, has her own personal story about how she first tuned in to the awareness that she is going to have a baby. For some, it comes as a hint of nausea or dizziness or an unusually full feeling in her breasts. For others, it's simply a missed period after months of hoping and praying for a child. Some women even have a flash of intuition that they've conceived a child after an evening of lovemaking.

No matter how you found out, if you're pregnant (whether this is your first time or your seventh), you're probably bursting with joy. And fear. And every feeling in between. And why shouldn't you experience a full range of emotions? The mere thought of bringing a new person into the world is nothing short of overwhelming.

Life Changes 101

You wouldn't be human if you didn't wonder what your pregnancy will be like. And will the baby turn out healthy? And labor?! Can all those horror stories be true? Every bad story you've ever heard tries to replay itself in your mind.

On another level, you may be concerned about how you will pay for your coming child's needs—the clothes, furniture, toys. *The college education!*

And how can you manage a baby on top of all your other responsibilities? And what in the world is this new baby going to do to your marriage?

But then you think of bringing a new being into the world and of the awe-inspiring creative act that's going on inside you. You think of holding your own little baby to your breast, touching those impossibly tiny hands. You begin to sense that your life will never again be quite the same. And you know what? You're right!

Suddenly, you and your husband are no longer just a couple. You're soon-to-be parents. You're starting a family. No matter how deep and true your love for each other is today, it is about to become deeper. From now on, you will share a concern for your baby and rely on each other's special abilities to raise that child to be a happy, healthy human being.

This is a good place to note that this book is intended for single mothers as well as married women. Whether you have the man you love by your side as you go through your pregnancy or you are embarking on this adventure on your own, this book will serve as a friendly support and guide— right through your delivery and up until your little one reaches 3 years of age.

Your new family is poised to become a small, unique universe of your own making. Every family has its own flavor and character. Some families are cast in the traditional mold—perfect models for Norman Rockwell paintings. Others are made up of wisecracking practical jokers, or bookish intellectuals, or circus clowns. (Yes, even circus clowns get married and make wonderful parents.)

The important thing to remember is that you don't have to be a certain type of mother or father to be a good parent. You don't have to have a lot of money or a fancy car. You do have to be loving and caring to be a good parent. In fact, all you really need is love and the will to do the right thing for your baby.

Test for Pregnancy At Home

Once you have pretty good reason to suspect that you're pregnant, your next step is to verify your suspicions. Most women do this at home with a pregnancy test kit. You can pick up a kit at your local drugstore and know within the hour whether or not you're really going to have a baby. The tests are extremely convenient, reasonably accurate, and fairly inexpensive.

They work by detecting a hormone called human chorionic gonadotropin (HCG), which is produced by the developing placenta and fetus. (The placenta is the structure that attaches to your womb and delivers oxygen and nutrients to your baby.) A home test kit can detect HCG as early as two weeks after your first missed period.

The test contains a solution that you mix with a small sample of your urine. If a dark ring forms, the test is positive. If no ring forms, the home pregnancy test is negative. But you can't assume you're not pregnant and forget about it. It's not that simple. It's still possible that you may be pregnant, but you simply made the test too early in your pregnancy. Doctors advise trying the test again in a couple of weeks.

You also should be aware that a test may register falsely positive if you are near menopause, taking antidepressant medications, or having irregular menstrual periods. In these circumstances, you'll want to see your doctor for further confirmation of your pregnancy.

You could also forgo the home test completely and let your doctor determine whether you are pregnant. A pregnancy test done in your doctor's office measures the levels of HCG in either your urine or your blood. Blood tests are more sensitive than urine tests. In fact, the most sophisticated blood tests are almost 100 percent accurate and can give you results within several days after conception.

Once you believe you are pregnant, you should see your doctor as soon as possible. Once you are certain of your pregnancy, you'll have to select an obstetrician and start prenatal care. Prenatal care is extremely important to the health of both you and your unborn child, and the sooner you start your regular visits the better.

Safe and Healthy From the Word "Go"

At your first visit, your obstetrician (or the doctor's assistant) will ask you about your reproductive history, whether you've ever been pregnant before, and if you have any inherited disorders. You'll be asked about your current and past illnesses. Finally, you'll have to estimate the time of conception so you can plot a fairly accurate due date. Don't worry if you're not quite sure when it happened. Your doctor will help you pinpoint the date as accurately as possible.

If you've been healthy all your life, your first visit to an obstetrician can be disconcerting. You'll be getting a lot more tests than you're used to. The doctor will start by measuring your height and weight. Next, he or she will record your blood pressure and pulse, then perform a general physical examination, paying special attention to your heart, lungs, abdomen, and pelvis. The pelvic examination will include a Pap smear and allow your doctor to estimate the size of your uterus and pelvis. You will

Choosing Your Obstetrician

The first step in choosing your obstetrician is to decide on the hospital where you want to deliver your baby, according to Matthew Davies, M.D., assistant professor of obstetrics and gynecology and associate director of the residency program for Pennsylvania State University at the Milton S. Hershey Medical Center in Hershey.

Visit local hospitals to examine their labor or birthing rooms and to review what sort of prenatal classes are offered, advises Dr. Davies.

"Next, like asking about good restaurants, ask your friends for their recommendations," Dr. Davies says. "You'll soon find out which doctors in your community have good reputations." Make sure you also ask your gynecologist.

"Then," he adds, "make sure of two things. One, be sure the doctor you are considering has privileges at the hospital you've chosen. Two, be sure he or she is fairly close, geographically, to the hospital." You don't want to have to wait for the doctor when your delivery gets underway.

It's also advisable, he says, to be sure the doctor is board-certified or has board eligibility. It's easy to find out: S11imply call the doctor's office and ask these specific questions. Also check with the doctor's office to see if it will accept the health coverage plan you have.

Finally, make an appointment to meet the doctor.

"It's important for doctor and patient to be of like mind," Dr. Davies says. "For example, if you want one of the more unusual birthing methods, make sure your caregiver is comfortable with that, and that he or she has time in the practice to accommodate less common procedures."

"It's also important to be flexible about time," he says. "If you like to spend a lot of time with your doctor at each visit, asking questions and seeking information, that's fine. But a patient has to understand that such long visits lead to a long wait time for the next patient. On following visits, she may be that next patient." If you really feel you need to spend a good deal of time with the doctor on each visit, you need to find a doctor who can take that kind of time with each patient. You may have to do some searching, as doctors are increasingly under pressure to see more patients per hour.

"On the other hand, if the expectant mother just likes to get in and out of the office quickly, she may be more comfortable with an obstetrician who has a different style," Dr. Davies says. "It's important they be of like mind."

also undoubtedly be asked to supply a urine sample.

Finally, a sample of your blood will be tested in a lab for syphilis and gonorrhea. It will also be used to do a complete blood count, blood chemistries, and blood-typing. The doctor probably will order a blood test known as a rubella titer to see if you are already immune to rubella (German measles). You are immune if you were exposed to the disease at some point in the past, and that's good. If you discover that you are not immune, ask your doctor what steps to take to keep from being exposed to this disease. Contracting rubella in the first three months of your pregnancy can lead to serious birth defects. The amount of risk goes down later in your pregnancy, and after the first three months, the risk is extremely small.

Some states also require a test for phenylketonuria (PKU), a rare metabolic defect. Mothers with PKU may give birth to mentally retarded infants if they do not follow a special diet. In addition, some states require tests for blood levels of a type of protein—alpha-fetoprotein—that can help predict whether or not a fetus has a defect in growth or a condition such as spina bifida that affects the development of the spinal cord or brain.

If you are descended from Ashkenazi Jews, you can be checked for Tay-Sachs disease, a birth defect that causes death in early childhood. (Doctors prefer that, if this is your heritage, you have the test done before you become pregnant.)

During the first visit, your doctor may want to schedule you for monthly appointments right up until your 28th week. After 28 weeks, you'll need a checkup every three weeks for several visits, then every two weeks. And after the 36th week, you'll be seeing the doctor every week until the baby is born.

Why is it important to see your doctor so often? At each office visit, your doctor will chart your weight and blood pressure and will ask for a urine specimen to measure your protein and sugar levels. Excess sugar can signal a type of diabetes that is triggered by pregnancy. Your average blood pressure probably won't change during the course of your pregnancy except for a mild drop sometime during the second trimester. Your doctor will monitor your blood pressure carefully to watch for a condition known as pregnancy-induced hypertension, or preeclampsia. Other signs of this dangerous condition include protein in the urine and sudden swelling. (This swelling or bloating is caused by water retention and is known as edema.)

If your checkups reveal any unusual symptoms, or a failure of the uterus to grow, your doctor may order an ultrasound or sonogram examination to confirm the age of your unborn baby and to make sure that the fetus and placenta are developing as they should.

Your Changing Body

So, now it's official. You are pregnant. For the next 280 days or so you will be growing another human being inside your body.

Within the darkness and warmth of your womb, the great alchemy of transformation is now taking place. Two single cells—one provided by you and one provided by your husband—have joined and mingled their genetic material and are now growing into a complete human being.

Your baby will be an intriguing blend of physical characteristics—your husband's chin, your mother's eyes, your nose, your sister-in-law's hairline. Wait! The vision is too grand, or maybe too comical, to contemplate.

Your body is providing the safe environment for this miracle of new life to take place. You're also feeding your little one. You eat and digest the food, but your body has created a nutrient delivery system—the placenta—to share the nutrition in the food you eat with your unborn baby.

As the fetus grows within you, you'll experience

Special Tests: Making Sure Things Go Smoothly

Here is a rundown of the most common tests performed during pregnancy, what the tests are for, at what time in your pregnancy they are likely to be done, and how they are performed.

Alpha-fetoprotein test: This blood test can screen for problems such as spina bifida—a congenital malformation of the spine. The test is usually performed between the 15th and 18th week of pregnancy by measuring a specific protein, alpha-fetoprotein (AFP), in your blood. If the AFP levels are high, a second test usually is performed to rule out error. If a high level occurs in a second test, the doctor usually will recommend an ultrasound test.

Amniocentesis: This test of the fluid surrounding your baby detects genetic disorders, such as Down's syndrome, hemophilia, and sickle cell anemia. It usually is performed on women older than 35 when they are 15 to 16 weeks pregnant.

Blood tests: At your first visit, your doctor will draw blood from your arm for a number of tests. These include one to determine your blood count, in case you are anemic, and one to determine your blood group, in case you need a transfusion at some point during your pregnancy or delivery. Other tests check your blood sugar levels, look for immunity to rubella (German measles), and check for sexually transmitted diseases, such as syphilis and HIV (AIDS virus). (If you are at any risk, your doctor will eventually perform tests on your baby to identify genetic diseases, such as sickle cell anemia, thalassemia [a rare blood disorder], or Tay-Sachs disease.)

Cervical swab: If you've had genital herpes, your doctor will do this test to determine whether the herpes virus is active. If so, your doctor may suggest a cesarean delivery to prevent the baby from becoming infected.

Chorionic villus sampling (CVS): This test samples the developing chorion for genetic and chromosomal disorders. (The chorion is the outer membrane surrounding the fetus early on in the pregnancy. It later develops into the placenta.)

Diabetes screening: A blood test to look for diabetes is done at 28 weeks.

Embryoscopy: This relatively new test can view the fetus in the uterus. Your doctor will do this test only if he or she suspects a problem that can be verified only by getting a look at the fetus.

Pap smear: In this test, your doctor scrapes a few cells from the surface of the cervix to check for early signs of cervical cancer.

Rhesus (Rh) antibody-level test: Most people have a specific protein in their blood called the Rh factor. Those who have the protein are considered to be Rh positive, those who don't are Rh negative. If a woman tests Rh negative, the father of the child also must be tested for his Rh factor, because problems arise when an Rh-negative women conceives a baby with an Rh-positive man. The tests are done fairly early in the pregnancy or at once if the woman has a bleeding problem.

Sonography (ultrasound): This test uses high-frequency sound waves to look at your unborn baby inside your womb. The technology has been used for more than 25 years and appears to be safe for both mother and fetus.

The majority of today's obstetricians have the capability of performing ultrasound tests in their offices. When you have this test done, your obstetrician will coat your abdomen with mineral oil or gel. The doctor will then move a device known as a transducer gently and smoothly over your tummy, allowing sound waves to pass painlessly through your abdominal cavity. The waves will bounce back to the transducer, forming an image that's displayed as a picture on a monitor.

With a vaginal ultrasound, the transducer is placed in your vagina to allow the doctor to see the early pregnancy sac and to detect any abnormalities. This technique is also used to guide the doctor in doing a CVS test.

An ultrasound examination can detect a pregnancy as early as six weeks after your last menstrual period and can show the baby's movements at approximately 12 weeks of gestational age.

This test carries with it a little plus—it will let you know well before delivery whether you're carrying a boy or a girl. If you don't want to know until you give birth, make sure you let your doctor know before this test is performed. (Your doctor will know, but doesn't have to divulge the secret if you want it to be a surprise.)

Triple marker (or serum marker) screening: This blood test is offered prior to amniocentesis. It tests for Down's syndrome and helps you decide whether or not to undergo amniocentesis.

Urinalysis: This test measures the protein and sugar in your urine. It will detect excess protein, which can be a warning sign of preeclampsia, a condition involving high blood pressure and water retention. It also can detect excess sugar, which can signal diabetes, a disease sometimes triggered by pregnancy. Urinalysis also may be used to detect drug use.

Let There Be Life!

First Trimester:
13 Weeks

Your tummy doesn't really show yet. Your baby is now approximately 2 ½ inches long and weighs a half ounce or less. He or she (gender is established right from the start) looks a bit alien, with a big head and a tiny body. Your baby's heart is beating and he or she has hands and feet smaller in size than your own thumbnail.

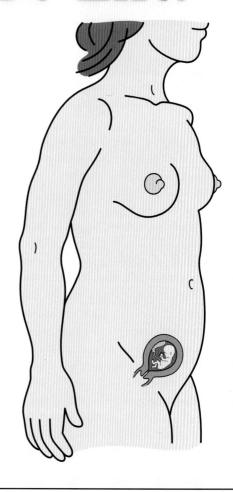

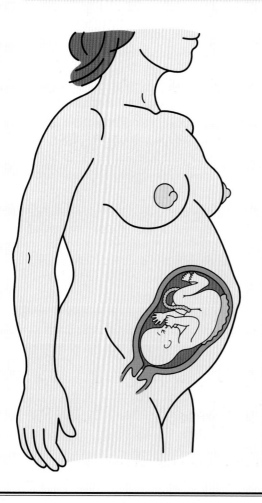

Second Trimester:
27 Weeks

Your breasts are a little larger and feel heavy and tender.
Your tummy is definitely bulging (but will get much bigger).
Your baby is now about 10 inches long, weighs a little more than a pound, and looks like a fully formed, but very small baby, with eyes, ears, and a face that changes expression.

Third Trimester:

40 Weeks

(Just before the birth of your child)

Your tummy is about as big as it's going to get (and bigger than you'd ever thought possible).

Your baby weighs somewhere in the neighborhood of 6 to 10 pounds. He or she can see, hear, and change position to try to get more comfortable, but no longer has the space to be comfortable. He or she will have to come out into the world to continue to grow.

Your Changing Breasts

Once you become pregnant, your breasts become significantly larger and fuller. That's because the milk-producing glands in your breasts are primed and ready to produce food for your baby. Once you're nursing regularly, your breasts will be at their maximum size and fullness. They may also feel warm to the touch and be more sensitive.

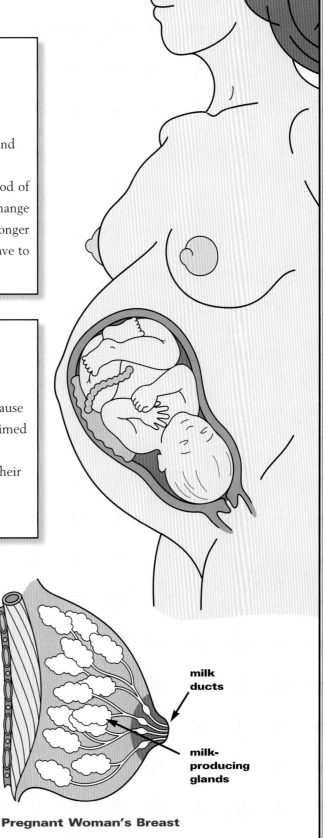

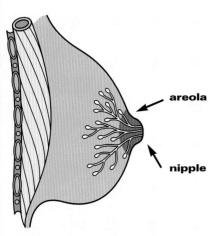

areola

nipple

Adult Woman's Breast

milk ducts

milk-producing glands

Pregnant Woman's Breast

In December 1994, my grandmother became very ill and was hospitalized. We were told she would not live long. While she was conscious most of the time, she often became confused and nonsensical. One day while I was visiting her, she asked, out of the blue, "Are you pregnant?" Little did she know that my husband and I had been trying for several months, unsuccessfully. My response had to be, "No, I'm not pregnant."

In January 1995, she passed away and, because of the stress, my periods became irregular and my husband and I stopped trying for a baby. One day in May, I realized I was quite late and called my doctor's office to make an appointment for a pregnancy test. Unbelievably, it came back positive. I would be due on the first anniversary of my grandmother's death.

I know that she had something to do with this, because although my daughter was actually born two days after this anniversary, we were so busy anticipating her birth that we could not possibly be sad on that day. I believe my grandmother sent our daughter, Sarah Rose, to us on that day so we would rejoice, rather than mourn.

Ruth Spiro
Skokie, Illinois

some profound changes—emotionally as well as physically. Some women who are sardonic and flippant can find themselves uncharacteristically gushy over Paddington Bear or a pair of tiny high-tops. Sweetly shy women can become imbued with the kind of wild courage that once served to protect the unborn from marauding tigers and woolly mammoths.

And that little growing baby, not even the size of a lima bean to begin with, will have its effects on your body, too. Your looks will begin to change, and the change is not limited to an expanding abdomen.

Here's a look at the changes that will take place at the milestones of your pregnancy.

Enlarged Breasts

Even if you're just a few weeks into your pregnancy, you've probably already noticed that your breasts are becoming larger and heavier. They change during pregnancy to produce milk, developing a network of milk-producing glands and ducts.

Here's how to deal with it:

☞ **Go shopping.** It's now time to fold away those little wisps of nylon and lace you've been wearing and search out a bra that will give you firm support. Remeasure your bustline to see if your size has changed, then go out and shop for a well-constructed bra. Look for one that has wide, comfortable shoulder straps. Try it on to make sure the fit is right. But don't buy more than a couple at this time. Your bra size is likely to change and change again before you give birth.

☞ **Alert your doctor to changes.** Later in your pregnancy you may develop a nipple discharge. It is considered normal, but you should mention it to your doctor at your regular visit.

Frequent Urination

When you're pregnant, you'll find yourself spending a lot more time in the bathroom. Especially during the first three months, you will need to urinate frequently. Doctors think the increased flow is the result of hormonal changes and also from the pressure the enlarging uterus exerts on your bladder. Sometimes, when you laugh or cough, you may lose a little control. Sure, it's troublesome, but don't worry; it's all perfectly normal.

Be aware, however, that urinary tract infections are more common during pregnancy than before. If you experience burning when you urinate, get prompt medical attention. Do not wait until your next scheduled visit.

Morning Sickness

You'll also be visiting the bathroom a lot if you have morning sickness. A lucky few have only brief, occasional upsets. Others may have to endure frequent or chronic sickness that lasts all day and is triggered by simple things, such as the smell of food cooking or driving over a pothole.

Be reassured. Even though morning sickness seems as though it will go on forever, it will most likely stop—abruptly and without the sound of trumpets—as you reach the end of your fourth month.

But, what do you do in the meantime?

☞ **Munch in the morning.** It's a good idea to stash some graham crackers or melba toast on your nightstand. Have a couple of these crackers first thing in the morning before you get out of bed—or even before you lift your head off the pillow. Have a light snack, too, before you go to sleep. One theory is that low blood sugar levels may trigger nausea, and since they are lowest when you first wake up, you're more likely to feel sick then.

☞ **Graze all day.** Doctors recommend that you eat small, frequent meals to help keep your blood

Warning Signs

If you experience any of the following symptoms, call your doctor immediately.

Uterine cramping—which may feel like a mild lower abdominal cramping, a rhythmic pelvic pressure, or low back pain—is a symptom that may signal the onset of labor.

Vaginal bleeding is an emergency at any point during your pregnancy.

Rupture of the membranes also is known as the water breaking. You'll know when this happens either by a trickle or a sudden gush of clear fluid coming from your vagina.

Headache, one that does not respond to the usual remedies, may be one of the first signs of preeclampsia, a condition involving pregnancy-induced high blood pressure.

Rapid swelling of the feet and ankles is also a sign of preeclampsia.

Prolonged vomiting. It's cause for concern if you cannot keep anything down, not even water, for more than five or six hours.

Dehydration accompanied by failure to urinate.

Weight loss.

If you have any symptom at all that concerns you, you should contact your doctor. Your doctor will not think you are worrying foolishly. He or she will think you are being a responsible pregnant woman, someone who will turn out to be a caring and careful mother.

sugar levels on more of an even keel.

☞ **Be prepared.** If morning sickness tends to strike when you're away from home—commuting to work, for example—develop a strategy. If you drive, scout out places where it will be safe to pull over. Put together a little kit in a plastic bag, including tissues, disposable wipes, and breath spray or mints and tuck it into your purse.

☞ **Don't let smoke get in your eyes.** Stay out of smoky rooms and avoid other strong odors, if possible.

☞ **Reach for the ginger.** If your nausea is severe, try this natural remedy—suck on a small slice of gingerroot. Or sip small amounts of flat ginger ale. Some studies have shown that ginger has the ability to settle a fluttery stomach even better than some medications.

☞ **Try a little herb tea.** You might want to brew up some mint or raspberry leaf tea. Herbalists maintain that either of these old-fashioned, pleasant-tasting beverages will calm an upset stomach. Pregnant women have used both of these herbs safely for centuries for just this purpose. You can drink the tea either hot or iced.

Do not try other herbs without mentioning them to your doctor. This is not the time to be experimenting with new herbs.

☞ **Take solace from women's wisdom.** Remember, morning sickness doesn't last forever, and many mothers believe it's a sure sign that the baby is holding firm and that the pregnancy is progressing as it should.

Heartburn

Heartburn usually surfaces in the last months of your pregnancy, when your growing baby can put pressure on your stomach. There are a number of things you can do to keep the problem at bay:

☞ **Eat often and keep it light.** Instead of eating three big meals, try eating five or six small meals a day. Limit fatty, fried, or spicy foods.

☞ **Stay loose.** Don't wear tight belts or any clothing that binds you at the middle. If ever there were a time for comfort, this is it.

☞ **Get elevated.** At night, it helps to elevate the head of your bed by putting some small blocks of wood under the legs at the head of the bed. Note: You might think it would be easier to just elevate your head with an extra pillow. Not so. You want gravity to work in your favor by helping to keep stomach acid—the stuff that gets up into your esophagus and causes the "burn" in heartburn—down in your tummy where it belongs. If you elevate just your head or just the upper portion of your body, the acid can still bubble up.

Backache

As your baby grows inside you, you'll discover that it becomes increasingly difficult to haul yourself up out of a chair or to get out of bed. Then, one fine day you may also feel an achy pressure in your lower back. Usually this discomfort doesn't appear until late in your pregnancy, when the weight of your baby throws your body off balance. It seems to be an extremely common problem.

Fortunately, there are lots of simple strategies you can employ to ease the ache:

☞ **Get a little padding.** When sitting in your most comfy chair, tuck a firm, little cushion behind the small of your back. If high-tech stuff appeals to you, buy a product called a lumbar roll from a medical supply store. It's a tube about 5 inches long, designed to fit right into the small of your back. Either will give you support and help to relieve the feeling of pressure you experience after you've been sitting for a while.

☞ **Rest more frequently.** If you have a job for which you sit all day, take regular breaks. Get up and walk around. Conversely, if you stand a great deal, take a break by sitting with your feet up.

☞ **Wear low-heeled shoes with good support.** Slip some shock-absorbing inner soles into your shoes to cushion the stress that walking can transmit to a bad back.

☞ **Watch those extra pounds.** Don't gain more than the recommended amount of weight. It will put even more pressure on your aching back muscles.

☞ **Get coddled.** Ask the Dad-to-be to give you a gentle back rub.

Varicose Veins

The veins in your legs transport blood back toward your heart and lungs, where it is cleansed of carbon dioxide and other impurities, and reoxygenated.

The volume of blood you have in your body increases naturally with pregnancy. This increased blood volume, along with hormone changes and the expanding size of your uterus, can cause unsightly varicose veins.

Veins have to work hard to transport blood to the upper part of your body because they're working against the pull of gravity. As blood moves up through the veins, a series of valves closes to keep the blood from flowing back down again. However, when the valves become overwhelmed, blood can collect, stretching the veins' walls out of shape. The result? Varicose veins.

Varicose veins can make your legs feel achy or heavy. Sometimes they can cause severe pain. Even the skin over the swollen veins can become painfully irritated.

Here are a number of preventive actions you can take:

☞ **Get a leg up.** Put your feet up whenever possible. Try to raise them above the level of your heart to minimize gravitational pull whenever you can. If you can, put your feet up under your desk at work. At night, watch television with your feet propped up on a pillow.

☞ **Avoid prolonged standing.** If you must remain on your feet, try to move around. The action of your leg muscles will help keep the blood moving through your veins.

☞ **Ease out of that squeeze.** Do not wear socks or stockings with tight elastic that cuts off your circulation. You shouldn't be wearing a girdle at all during pregnancy, unless your doctor tells you to for some reason.

☞ **Get moving.** Go for a 20-minute walk every day.

☞ **Keep the pounds down.** Talk to your doctor about how much weight you should gain during your pregnancy, and don't exceed that amount. Ask your doctor for advice on keeping extra pounds at bay.

☞ **Get a little support.** Wear support panty hose. And put them on before you get out of bed in the morning.

☞ **Get a lot of support.** If preventive measures fail, your doctor may have you fitted for elastic stockings. These are considerably more expensive than regular support hose and not very attractive. But, underneath them, your legs will remain pretty, and you'll feel more comfortable.

Hemorrhoids

If you develop hemorrhoids, you certainly have lots of company. This itchy, irritated, swollen anal tissue is a common condition among pregnant women. What to do?

☞ **Eat lots of fiber.** The easiest way to get more fiber in your diet is to eat lots of fruits and vegetables and switch to whole grains. These are dietary changes you should be following anyway for the health of your baby. For a more complete list of fiber-rich foods, see "Foods High in Fiber" on page 18.

☞ **Don't overdo the bran.** Cereals containing bran are the fastest route to getting more fiber, but whatever you do, if you're not used to a high-fiber diet, don't buy a box of bran cereal and eat a great big bowl the first day. It will cause you immeasurable discomfort. If you want to travel the bran route, start small, on the order of a couple of tablespoonfuls, and gradually increase the amount each day.

☞ **Drink lots of water.** Without fluid, fiber can be quite constipating. And that's exactly the opposite effect from the one you're looking for.

Weight Gain

You'll probably gain only 2 to 4 pounds in the first trimester, but you can count on adding nearly a pound a week after that, for a total of 25 to 30 pounds during the course of your pregnancy.

Doctors have found that when a pregnant woman maintains the appropriate weight, she is less likely to experience certain kinds of complications (preeclampsia, for example) and is more likely to have a normal vaginal delivery.

Remember, you may be eating for two, but the other one is not Arnold Schwarzenegger. On the

Foods High in Fiber

Have hemorrhoids? As if pregnancy weren't uncomfortable enough! To keep hemorrhoids from getting any worse, doctors routinely recommend eating lots of foods that are high in fiber. This table will help get you started. To find out about the fiber content of processed foods, check the label on the package.

Food	Serving	Fiber (in grams)
Vegetables		
carrots, raw	1	3.7
celery, raw	2½ stalks	3.0
kidney beans, cooked	1 cup	3.6
lentils, cooked	½ cup	4.0
potatoes, cooked	⅔ cup	3.1
Fruits		
apple	1 small	3.1
grapefruit	½	2.6
orange	1 small	1.8
peaches, canned	½ cup	1.3
strawberries	½ cup	2.6
Grain products		
All-Bran	1 cup	23.0
graham crackers	2 squares	1.5
Grape Nuts	⅓ cup	5.0
whole wheat bread	1 slice	2.4

other hand, pregnancy is not the time to be following a weight-loss diet. Seek your doctor's advice about how to stay within appropriate weight limits. Also refer to "Your Pregnancy Diet," which begins on page 21.

Food Cravings

You've surely heard about women who develop a sudden, ravenous midnight hunger for kosher dills and hot fudge, or some other outrageous combination of foods. Is there anything to these bizarre dietary cravings? In a word, yes. If you find yourself lusting for weird food combos, should you be concerned? Not necessarily. Here's what doctors advise:

☞ **Go ahead and indulge.** Doctors tell us that most food cravings are not dangerous and are not a sign of some sort of nutritional deficiency. So, if you want to eat cornflakes topped with sliced tomatoes, then go ahead and enjoy.

☞ **Don't overindulge.** Make sure you don't go overboard on cookies, candy, or other junk food. Remember, you're also feeding a growing fetus. Make sure your calories are well chosen and pack a nutritional punch. You want what you eat to contribute to your well-being and that of your unborn child—not to the girth of your thighs.

☞ **Let your doctor know about nonfood cravings.** There is a condition known as pica, which causes a pregnant woman to crave substances—clay and laundry starch, in particular—with little or no nutritional value. For some unknown reason, pica appears to be more common in the South. The National Research Council has noted that as many as 75 percent of the pregnant women visiting health department clinics in the South reported eating starch, and 50 percent ate clay at some point during their pregnancy.

Doctors worry about this practice for several reasons. First, eating clay or starch may take the place of eating nutritious food. Second, some substances, such as starch, that women with pica crave are high in calories and may cause too much weight gain. Third, some so-called pica substances—charcoal, air fresheners, and moth balls, for example—can be toxic. Finally, the chemical make-up of some pica substances can interfere with the way your body absorbs minerals.

The bottom line. If you find yourself with a craving for any nonfood item, make sure that you tell your doctor about it. If you are anemic, the craving may go away once that condition is corrected. Do not let yourself give in to the craving, no matter how tempted you are.

Swollen Ankles and Feet

It's pretty common for your ankles and feet to swell somewhat during pregnancy. If you drink a quart of lemonade, iced tea, or any other fluid before you go to bed on a hot summer night, don't be surprised to discover that your ankles are puffy the next day. Now, there's certainly nothing wrong with drinking lemonade when you're thirsty. It's just that almost anything can trigger this response when you're pregnant.

Swollen ankles are not serious unless they develop suddenly, in which case they can be a sign of preeclampsia, a condition characterized by sudden weight gain, an increase in blood pressure, and swelling of the hands, face, and ankles. Call your doctor immediately; the usual treatment is bed rest. It's reassuring to know that preeclampsia is not very common, and for unknown reasons occurs most often during a first pregnancy.

Stretch Marks

Your unborn baby grows. Your abdomen grows. Your skin doesn't grow. It stretches. And stretches. And stree-ee-eetches. Not surprisingly, most pregnant women develop stretch marks. Stretch marks take the form of red or pink striations that appear on the abdomen, hips, and/or breasts.

If you have inherited extra-good skin tone, you may escape the problem altogether. But the best option most women can hope for is prevention. Here's how:

☞ **Watch your weight.** If you can avoid a large, rapid weight gain, your skin will go through a more gentle, leisurely stretch, thus minimizing the marks.

☞ **Get the right vitamins.** Eat plenty of foods high in vitamins A and D. (For a list of these foods see "Your Vitamin Requirement" on page 25.) These particular vitamins nourish your skin from the inside and help keep it supple. Do not take supplements of these vitamins without consulting your doctor, however. Large amounts of these vitamins are toxic.

☞ **Be lavish with lotion.** You also can try rubbing lotion on your tummy to keep the skin soft.

☞ **Be patient.** Don't waste time worrying about how you'll look in a bikini next year. The color will fade from any stretch marks after you have your baby. The marks become pale and infinitely less noticeable.

Headaches

Do not, repeat *not*, take two aspirins and call the doctor in the morning. If anything, call the doctor first to see if your headache is serious enough to warrant taking two aspirins.

As common and ordinary as aspirin is, it is still a drug. Taking frequent doses of aspirin during pregnancy has been related to fetal development problems. What's more, this seemingly benign medication can prolong labor. It also lessens the blood's ability to clot, thereby creating the potential for hemorrhaging during delivery.

If you've taken aspirin before you confirmed your pregnancy, don't panic. The problems created by aspirin occur mostly in the third trimester. Even so, be sure to get your doctor's OK before you pop those pills.

Switching to an acetaminophen pain killer isn't a good idea, either. This drug brings a separate set of problems, most associated with liver damage caused by excessive doses. Once again, get your doctor's approval before taking any kind of pain killer.

So what should you do if you have a pounding headache? To begin with, let your doctor know. Headaches are a possible sign of high blood pressure or elampsia.

☞ **Take a mental vacation.** Try lying down in a quiet place. Cover your forehead with a warm, damp washcloth. Close your eyes and massage your temples. Now visualize a beautiful scene that you find particularly restful. Picture the ocean, for example. Get all of your senses involved in this mental scene. Smell the salt air. Listen to the gulls cry. Get yourself totally into the scene. Look at the way the waves roll in. Imagine each one touching you gently and carrying your headache out to sea.

☞ **Walk away from stress.** After you feel better, try to sort out the cause of your headache. For most people, most of the time, it's stress. After a tiff with your mother or deadline pressure at work, the muscles in your scalp knot up so that you feel you have a narrow band tightening around your head. A certain amount of stress is, of course, unavoidable. One of the best nondrug ways to cope with stress is to exercise. At the first sign of a tension headache, head out the door for a walk and see if that helps.

Along with all the changes you can see taking place in your body, there are numerous changes you can't see as your pregnancy progresses. In fact, your whole body is involved in the process of creating a new human being. For the full duration of your pregnancy, things like eating right and getting the right kind of exercise are more important than ever.

Exercise During Pregnancy

If you've been a reluctant exerciser—or even a sofa spud—all your life, you may well think that pregnancy is the best excuse of all for taking it easy. Wrong. Doctors recommend that most women exercise regularly throughout their pregnancies. Moderate exercise is good for both you and your baby. It will make you feel better, reduce stress, ease backache, relieve insomnia, help prevent constipation, and, when the time comes, make labor a little more bearable. In addition, exercise will help your heart handle the extra work that comes with pregnancy. A toned-up heart muscle will be better able to pump the increased volume of blood circulating through your body for the nine months that your baby is growing inside you.

Note, please, that we are talking about *moderate* exercises such as walking, swimming, and special low-impact aerobics classes for pregnant women. Pregnancy is not the time to start weight training or long-distance running. This kind of vigorous exercise is out, doctors say, because much of the blood that normally would flow to the uterus is diverted to the muscles. If you've been fairly athletic up until the

Exercise Safety

To get all the benefits of exercise without any of the drawbacks, it helps to follow these guidelines:

☞ **Wear athletic shoes and a support bra.**

☞ **Always warm up and cool down.**

☞ **Avoid sudden changes in direction that could cause you to topple.**

☞ **Don't get overheated and avoid exercising when it's hot or humid.**

☞ **Keep your pulse rate at less than 140 beats per minute.**

☞ **Stop as soon as you feel tired.**

☞ **Drink water to replace the body fluids you've lost in perspiration.**

☞ **After the first trimester, do not do any exercises while lying on your back.**

time of your pregnancy, your doctor will probably give you the go-ahead to continue a fairly strenuous exercise program. But you should be candid with your doctor about the details of your current program and be aware that you'll undoubtedly need to modify your program as your pregnancy progresses.

Doctors also frown upon participating in sports that require a lot of dexterity, such as horseback riding or skiing. Even if you're an expert at one of these sports, it's possible for weight gain to affect your coordination. The last thing you want to do while pregnant is take a tumble on an icy mountain trail.

It's a good idea to consult your doctor before taking up *any* kind of exercise. With your doctor's permission, try one of these often-recommended exercises:

☞ **Go for a 20-minute walk** three times a week.

☞ **Stop off for a swim** on the way home from work. (You'll feel like a new person!)

☞ **Spend 20 minutes on a stationary bike** three times a week.

Stop Exercising If...

☞ **You experience vaginal bleeding or other discharge of fluid**

☞ **You have abdominal pain**

☞ **You experience dizziness, nausea, or numbness**

☞ **You become short of breath**

There are, however, a few exceptions to the regular exercise rule. The American College of Obstetricians and Gynecologists advises that women should not exercise while they are pregnant if they have the following risky conditions:

• **pregnancy-induced hypertension** (high blood pressure)

• **ruptured membranes before term**

• **incompetent cervix** (one that lacks elasticity)

• **persistent bleeding** in the second or third trimester

• **a history of premature labor**

• **slow fetal growth**

• **other conditions** that require medical evaluation, such as heart or lung disease

Many gyms offer the use of hot tubs and saunas. Doctors say that you should totally avoid using either one during the first 12 weeks of pregnancy. Enjoying a session in a hot tub or sauna during the second and third trimesters is probably not a problem, they say, as long as you limit your stay to 10 minutes or less to avoid excessive elevations of body temperature. The water temperature should be no greater than 100 degrees Fahrenheit.

Your Pregnancy Diet

If you're like most women, you were paying careful attention to diet and nutrition even before you became pregnant. The occasional lapse from healthy eating to enjoy your favorite treats was no big deal. Now suddenly, your health and your baby's whole future seem to be riding on your nutritional savvy. Yesterday, it was enough to know which wine to serve with fish. Today, you're responsible for developing the perfect menu to grow the perfect baby.

If you ask your doctor about diet, you'll undoubtedly be told to make sure you're eating a combination of foods that are high in protein and foods high in the fat-soluble vitamins A, D, E, and K, and the water-soluble vitamins C, folic acid, thiamine (B-1), riboflavin (B-2), vitamin B-6, niacin, and vitamin B-12. (Whew!) You might even get a list of recommended foods and recommended portions.

All this nutritional advice may well leave you feeling a little overwhelmed. Where are you going to put all those foods on that list that's as long as your arm? How will you keep from gaining too much weight? And what's your figure going to look like when this whole pregnancy thing is over?

Your Eating Guide

You're not eating for just you anymore. On the other hand, you don't want to look like you've been eating for two. How do you create a healthy baby without creating hefty thighs in the bargain? The trick is to make sure that everything you eat counts as good nutrition. This chart should help.

Food Group	Major Nutrients	Servings Per Day	Serving Sizes	Food Sources
Meat (and other protein foods)	Protein	3	2–3 ounces meat 1 egg or ½ cup peas or beans	Beans, eggs, fish, nuts, peanut butter, pork, poultry, split peas, tofu, tuna fish
Milk products	Calcium	4	1 ounce cheese 1 cup milk or yogurt	Cheese, evaporated milk, low-fat milk, powdered milk, skim milk, whole milk, yogurt
Vegetables and fruits	Vitamin A and fiber	1	½ cup	Apricots, broccoli, cantaloupe, carrots, mangos, nectarines, peaches, pumpkin, peppers, spinach, sweet potatoes, tomatoes, watermelon, winter squash
	Vitamin C and fiber (not in juice)	1	½ cup	Cabbage, cantaloupe, cauliflower, grapefruit, grapefruit juice, orange juice, oranges, peppers, strawberries
	Other vitamins, minerals, and fiber	3	½ cup	Apples, bananas, berries, celery, cherries, corn, cucumbers, grapes, green beans, lettuce, melons, pears, peas, turnips
Breads and Cereals	Carbohydrates, B vitamins, iron, fiber	6	1 slice bread or roll; 3–4 crackers, ½ cup rice, pasta, or hot cereal; ¾ cup cold cereal	Bread, cereal, macaroni, noodles, rice, rolls, spaghetti, tortillas
Fats and sugar	Provide calories with few nutrients			Bacon, butter, cake, candy, chips, jam, margarine, pie, salad dressing, soda pop, sugar, syrup

This chart is adapted from "A Good Beginning: Eating for a Healthy Pregnancy," compiled by the Nutrition Section of the Idaho Department of Health and Welfare.

Don't worry. Eating well for both you and your baby is a matter of paying careful attention to some basic guidelines. Here's what you need to know.

Your Protein Requirement

Protein is one nutrient you really *must* get more of. Why? Because you need protein to build tissue. And tissue building is exactly what's going on inside your body right now. You are building the tissues for a whole new person.

Most doctors agree that you should be consuming about 75 grams of protein a day. That's a really big increase over the recommended 44 grams for women who are not pregnant. Yet, your protein requirement is easy to satisfy, because the standard American diet is loaded with it.

Here's a sample menu that contains almost 100 grams of protein, yet you'll notice that it's not particularly heavy on meat or meat products. What it does have is a great deal of milk—which helps you meet your calcium requirement at the same time you fill your protein requirement. Skim milk, by the way, is a far better option than whole milk, which contains a lot of fat. With skim, you get a better nutrition-to-calorie ratio.

Breakfast:

6 ounces orange juice (1.27 grams)

1 cup cornflakes (2 grams)

8 ounces skim milk (8.4 grams)

1 slice whole wheat toast (2.3 grams)

(You've already consumed 13.97 grams of protein, and the day has only just begun.)

Midmorning snack:

Carrot sticks made from one carrot (.7 grams)

Lunch:

A sandwich made with 1 ounce of tuna canned in water (8.36 grams) on a bun (3.4 grams)

8 ounces skim milk (8.4 grams)

1 orange (1.4 grams)

(You are now up to 36.23 grams, more than halfway home.)

Midafternoon snack:

1 banana (1.2 grams)

Dinner:

½ chicken breast, roasted (26.7 grams)

1 baked potato (4.9 grams)

½ cup spinach (2.7 grams)

A salad of romaine lettuce and tomato (1.05 grams)

8 ounces skim milk (8.4 grams)

(You're now up to 81.18 grams.)

Bedtime snack:

2 squares graham cracker (1.0 grams)

8 ounces skim milk (8.4 grams)

(Food values from *Bowes & Church's Food Values of Portions Commonly Used*, 15th edition, by Jean A. Pennington, J.B. Lippincott & Co.)

Without even trying, you've managed to consume an over-the-top total of 90.58 grams of protein. The message of this sample diet is that you don't have to go out of your way to meet your protein requirement.

If you are a vegetarian, it's entirely possible to maintain your protein quota with just a little planning. After all, you can get nearly half the amount you need by drinking a quart of skim milk a day. A hard-boiled egg will give you 6.1 grams. Order your pizza with extra cheese and grate some low-fat cheese on top of your favorite salad.

If you eschew all animal products, focus on the vegetable proteins found in grains, beans, legumes, and seeds. Because vegetable proteins are incomplete—they do not contain the full complement of amino acids that make up a complete protein—be sure to include both grains and legumes (such as peanuts or kidney beans) in your daily menu. Look to soy products such as tofu and soy milk as well.

Your Calcium Requirement

Filling your calcium needs can be difficult, especially if you don't particularly like milk. The reason? Your body's need for calcium increases by 50 percent when you are pregnant. You need to consume

Your Vitamin Finder

Getting enough of the right kinds of vitamins is extremely important while you're pregnant. Here's a brief rundown of what you need and the specific foods high in each of the major vitamins.

Vitamin	RDA for Pregnant Women	Good Food Sources
Vitamin A	4,000 international units	Broccoli, carrots, spinach, sweet potatoes
Vitamin E	10 international units	Almonds, cereal, vegetable oils, wheat germ, whole grain bread
Vitamin K	65 micrograms	Asparagus, broccoli, fresh strawberries, raw spinach, rolled oats
Vitamin C	70 milligrams	Apples, blackberries, blueberries, broccoli, brussels sprouts, cabbage, cantaloupe, corn, okra, oranges, papaya, parsley, plums, potatoes, radishes, raw sweet peppers, strawberries, tomatoes, turnips, watermelon
Folic acid	400 micrograms	Asparagus; dried beans; dark green, leafy vegetables (such as spinach or kale); orange juice; wheat germ
Thiamine (Vitamin B1)	1.5 milligrams	Lima beans, oatmeal, oysters, peas, pork, wheat germ, whole grain and enriched bread and cereal
Riboflavin (Vitamin B2)	1.6 milligrams	Dried beans and peas; dark green, leafy vegetables; eggs; meat; milk; mushrooms; whole grain and enriched breads and cereals
Vitamin B6	2.2 milligrams	Avocados; bananas; chick peas; fish; green beans; green, leafy vegetables; meats; potatoes; poultry; prune juice; spinach; whole grain breads and cereals
Niacin	17 milligrams	Dried peas and beans, eggs, meat, poultry, tuna and other fish, whole grain and enriched breads and cereals
Vitamin B12	2.2 micrograms	Eggs, fish, meat, milk, oysters, nutritional yeast
Vitamin D	10 micrograms	Egg yolks, fortified milk

1,200 milligrams a day of calcium throughout your pregnancy.

In reviewing the sample menu on page 23 you probably noticed that it included four 8-ounce glasses (a quart) of skim milk. That's what you should be drinking each and every day. There are 255 milligrams of calcium in each glass, totaling 1,020 milligrams. You can easily raise that amount to reach your goal with a little cheese or by eating nondairy foods high in calcium, such as broccoli, soybeans, turnip greens, almonds, and canned sardines and salmon (it's in the bones).

If you have lactose intolerance—an inability to fully digest milk and dairy products that causes gas and bloating—try acidophilus milk instead. This milk, which contains bacterial cultures that make it easy to digest, can be purchased at many health food stores. Or, add a product such as Lactaid to regular milk. This product contains an enzyme that will help you digest the milk.

If you simply can't stand drinking plain milk, there are any number of ways you can manage to get more of it into your diet. Try making soup with milk: cream of tomato, New England clam chowder, or cream of chicken, for example. Eat pudding made with milk for dessert. Try putting a splash more in your mashed potatoes and morning cup of coffee. At the same time, step up your consumption of low-fat cheese and yogurt.

Your Vitamin Requirement

There's no need to get technical about water-soluble and fat-soluble vitamins. All you really need to know is that the water-soluble vitamins—the B vitamins and C—are not stored in your body. What your body doesn't use today winds up in the porcelain bowl tomorrow. Therefore, it's important to make the effort to eat foods high in these nutrients every day.

Getting enough of one particular B vitamin—folic acid—is extremely important. Medical researchers have found that adequate amounts of folic acid help prevent birth defects in the developing neural tube. These serious birth defects, such as spina bifida, affect the spine and brain. These defects develop within the first four weeks of pregnancy, usually before a woman even suspects she is pregnant. That's why the U.S. Centers for Disease Control and Prevention recommend that every woman of childbearing age get 400 micrograms a day of folic acid.

Beginning in early 1996, the U.S. Food and Drug Administration required that folic acid be added to certain foods, specifically, most enriched bread, flour, corn meal, rice noodles, macaroni, and other grain products. The government agency notes that without this fortification program, most women between the ages of 10 and 50 get only 0.2 milligrams of folic acid a day, and that's simply not enough. Folic acid intake should be kept to less than 1 milligram a day, so do not take a supplement unless your doctor tells you to do so.

Fat-soluble vitamins, on the other hand, are stored in the body, so it's not a problem if you don't eat foods high in these nutrients every day. But you do need to include these foods in your diet on a fairly regular basis. The fat-soluble vitamins include A, D, E, and K.

Many doctors recommend that you not only eat a healthy diet but also take nutritional supplements during pregnancy. They often prescribe a multivitamin supplement containing iron. It's especially important to get enough iron, since many young women have depleted iron stores when they become pregnant. *Warning:* Do not select supplements on your own; let your doctor do the prescribing to meet your individual needs. Any vitamin or other nutritional supplements that you take while you are pregnant should have your doctor's approval.

Make Some Positive Changes

Eating the right foods and getting enough exercise are important during your pregnancy, but your health concerns can't stop there. There's more for you to be aware of and concerned about.

Protect Your Baby from Smoke

If you've been meaning to give up smoking "one of these days," that day has arrived. No more putting it off. No more excuses. If you smoke, your fetus smokes. Now, there's a picture!

Research has shown that women who smoke are more likely to have low birth weight babies than nonsmokers. Researchers have also found that babies born to smokers grow slowly. So, put out the cigarette and put together a plan for quitting. You've never had a better reason.

Nobody says that giving up smoking is easy. It's not. Nicotine is considered to be extremely addictive, and you'll undoubtedly feel crummy for the first week or so. Further, you can't count on using a nicotine patch or even nicotine gum to ease you

A Change of Kitty Litter

Here's one change you won't find hard to make: You must stop cleaning your cat's litter box for the duration of your pregnancy.

You'll have to pawn off the job on your husband or some other family member, because you can get a disease called toxoplasmosis from cat feces. It's caused by a protozoan that's also found in uncooked meat, particularly lamb, pork, and goat.

Adults with the disease generally feel just a little under the weather. The disease is not uncommon, and a lot of us have had it without knowing it. As a result, our bodies have formed antibodies to it, and so the chances of transmitting the disease to the fetus is small.

However, researchers have estimated that the chances of getting toxoplasmosis for the first time while you are pregnant are about 1 in 1,000. The problem, doctors say, is that without antibodies to the disease, the organism can cross the placenta and severely damage or even kill the fetus.

So, get your sweetie to empty the cat box—preferably every day, to reduce the risk of exposure. Make sure you wear rubber gloves when handling raw meat and be sure to clean any kitchen surfaces that the meat has touched. That's good advice for preventing food poisoning, such as salmonella, too.

---

through the transition. Researchers maintain that nicotine in any form is bad for a developing fetus.

The first two days of withdrawal are the hardest, but after about 48 hours, your body will be clear of nicotine. You may feel a bit light-headed as your body adjusts. And, here's an ironic twist, you may develop a cough. But think of it as a nonsmoker's cough, because it signals that your lungs are doing their own form of spring cleaning.

At first you may be sorely tempted to light up. It may help to know that these potent urges usually last less than a minute, and they always go away on their own—whether you light up or not. The trick is to distract yourself during that short time. Try this: Take a big, deep breath. Expand your diaphragm fully. Hold your breath for a few seconds. Now slowly exhale.

If you believe you just can't give up smoking, maybe the problem is that you can't do it alone. Take advantage of one of the many smoking cessation programs. If you want to find the one closest to your home or work, call the American Cancer Society at 800-227-2345, the American Lung Association at 800-586-4872, or Smokenders at 800-828-4357.

If you join a group, you'll have the advantage of moral support from a group of other would-be nonsmokers. And over a few weeks' time, you will receive professional counseling to help you get through the physical and psychological changes involved in quitting.

Say No to Alcohol

You might want to hide the key to the wine cellar for the duration of your pregnancy. There's been a lot of talk in the media about the heart-healthy benefits of having a drink a day and about the seemingly magical properties of red wine. But they're not talking about pregnant women. In fact, many obstetricians now frown on drinking any alcohol at all while you're pregnant. A champagne toast at your sister's wedding probably won't do any harm, but regular drinking has been linked to a condition called fetal alcohol syndrome. It's the most common prenatal cause of mental handicap in the United States.

Put a Cap on Pesticides

Pesticides are products used to kill household pests such as ants, roaches, and termites, as well as assorted bugs in the lawn and garden. The U.S. Environmental Protection Agency (EPA) warns that exposure to pesticides may cause irritation to the eyes, nose, and throat; may damage the central ner-

Holding your child for the first time is a moment you will never forget. This is one moment in the grand scheme of things that I can recall instantly, and it makes me happy to be a woman and a mom. There's no feeling like it in the world.

LuAnn Hart,
Scotia, New York

vous system and kidneys; and may increase the risk of cancer. All of this raises an important question: Is there any danger to the developing fetus?

According to the EPA, scientific studies to date have not produced any evidence that exposure to pesticides during pregnancy can cause adverse health effects in the fetus. Even so, the agency cautions that pregnant women would be wise to reduce or eliminate exposure to all pesticides as a precaution.

And that may not be an easy task! The agency's preliminary research shows a widespread presence of pesticide residues inside our homes. Surprisingly, the biggest offenders are not bug-killing sprays. If these are used strictly according to directions and disposed of properly, they meet federal standards for safety. (That's not to say that you should allow them to be used in your home. Remember, govern-

ment research is still looking into this whole area.)

The real troublemakers, according to the EPA, are these:

- **pesticide bombs**
- **no-pest strips**
- **flea collars**
- **shampoo for head lice**
- **Diazinon** (a common pesticide spread in granular form to control cockroaches, ants, and other crawling insects)

The EPA suggests that the best way to deal with insects is to prevent them from getting into your home in the first place. Keep your home clean, dry, and well-ventilated. Many problems can be prevented by keeping cabinets clean; by removing lint, hair, and food particles; and by sweeping and vacuuming on a regular basis. Also, caulking cracks and crevices around windows and in your foundation can help keep critters outside.

All of these things are a routine part of house-cleaning in most homes. What exactly are you supposed to do if (or when) bugs bypass your cleanliness barriers and move in with their families and start multiplying?

If you simply must use a pesticide in your home while you're pregnant, follow these guidelines:

☞ **Recruit a substitute.** If you can at all avoid using pesticides yourself, do so. Ask your husband, another family member, a friend, or an understanding neighbor to do the actual mixing and applying. Consider hiring someone if you have to. And make yourself scarce while the pesticide is being applied. Now's a good time to go for that long walk or do your shopping. (If you have other children, take them with you.)

☞ **Let there be air.** If you are absolutely the only one who can do the chore, mix or dilute the pesticide outdoors.

☞ **Follow the rules.** Apply pesticides only in recommended quantities. Resist the urge to really blast the pests.

☞ **Throw out what you don't use.** Do not store unneeded pesticides anywhere in your home.

Avoid Pesticides in Foods

When strawberries and asparagus appear in the produce aisle just in time for Christmas dinner, you know they didn't spring from the frozen earth of your hometown. Instead, they probably came from South America, Mexico, or almost any country in the world—perhaps even one that still allows the use of pesticides that were banned in the United States years ago.

Because you don't know what safety standards have been enforced in growing imported food, it's wise for the duration of your pregnancy to minimize your potential exposure to the chemicals on what you eat.

Here are some suggestions from the U.S. Food and Drug Administration (FDA) on how to do this:

☞ **Buy organic.** Organic produce is ever more widely available. Although the organic label is still not an absolute guarantee the produce is completely pesticide-free, new certification programs for organic growers make it more likely that that's what you're getting.

☞ **Buy from local sources.** Ask the supermarket or store manager what produce is imported and buy the seasonal produce that was locally grown. In other words, you may have to skip the asparagus and buy winter squash instead. Buy at local farmer's markets whenever possible and ask the grower about pesticide use. Let the grower know that you are concerned because you're carrying a baby.

☞ **Grow your own.** Gardening is healthful exercise, and if you grow your own carrots and tomatoes, you'll know for sure they are pesticide-free.

☞ **Scrub those veggies.** Many pesticides can be washed off with a mixture of warm water and a little vinegar or detergent, which helps dissolve the chemicals. Make sure you rinse well.

☞ **Peel and toss.** Peel all your fruits and vegetables. Even if you normally eat the peels of foods such as carrots, toss the peel while you're pregnant. (Unless you know for sure that it's organic.) You'll lose some nutrients, but the food will be safer to eat. Remove and toss the outer leaves of lettuce and cabbage, and discard celery leaves.

Avoiding Lead

Lead poisoning can affect a pregnant woman by reducing her baby's birth weight and possibly causing premature birth, according to the EPA. It can also delay physical and mental development in children. Here's how to avoid this deadly poison:

☞ **Cover, don't strip.** One of the main ways lead can enter your body is via lead-based paint. If you're thinking of remodeling or painting the nursery, don't sand or strip away old paint. If it's lead-based, you will inhale lead dust and possibly harm your baby. You can leave the old paint where it is and cover it up with a fresh coat of paint.

☞ **Flush your pipes.** It helps to flush out your household plumbing each morning. Lead from soldered joints can leach into your drinking water, accumulating overnight. First thing in the morning, let the water run five minutes or more before you use the water for drinking. Lots of women do this by taking their morning shower first thing, then drawing water for coffee or frozen juice.

For information about protecting your baby from lead poisoning and other toxins in the environment, see pages 110–118.

Eliminate Organic Gases

Organic gases are given off by household products such as paints, paint strippers and other solvents, wood preservatives, aerosol sprays, cleansers and disinfectants, moth repellants, air "fresheners," stored fuels and automotive products, hobby supplies, and dry-cleaned clothing. They're also given off when natural gas or wood is burned for fuel.

According to the EPA, these pungent gases, although organic, can irritate your eyes and nose, as well as cause damage to the liver, kidneys, and the central nervous system. Some organic gases cause cancer in laboratory animals, and some are suspected or even known to cause cancer in humans. This is not the kind of stuff you want to bring into contact with a developing fetus. The following suggestions from the EPA will help you reduce exposure:

☞ **Follow directions.** Use all household products strictly according to manufacturer's directions. Never mix one household product with another, unless it specifically says on the label that it's OK.

☞ **Ventilate.** Don't let yourself breathe any kind of fumes. Open the windows and provide lots of fresh air as you go about your work. Take dry-cleaned items out of the plastic bag and let them hang outdoors or in a well-ventilated room before you wear them or hang them in your closet.

☞ **Toss those cans and jars.** Once you or someone in your household finishes a household project involving chemicals that give off fumes, get rid of the containers and the unused chemicals.

☞ **Use natural gas wisely.** Keep any gas appliances properly adjusted. (If you're not sure whether yours are properly adjusted, call your gas company and ask for advice.) Install and use an exhaust fan that vents outdoors over your gas stove.

☞ **Take care with how you heat your home.** If you have an unvented space heater, replace it with a vented model. Choose the right-size wood stove for your home, one that is certified to meet EPA emission standards, and make sure the doors fit tight. And never, ever use a gas stove to heat your house—not even for a short time.

☞ **Make sure your heating system is properly serviced.** Have a trained professional inspect, clean, and adjust the furnace, flues, and chimneys annually. Repair any leaks promptly.

☞ **Avoid wood smoke.** Open the flue as soon as you light the fireplace. Do not barbecue indoors, not even in the fireplace.

☞ **Respect gasoline fumes.** Do not idle the car inside the garage, and do not use any gasoline-powered engines in an enclosed space.

☞ **Monitor your monos.** What about using a carbon monoxide monitor? They may be helpful, according to the Consumer Product Safety Commission (CPSC). However, these monitors are simply not as reliable as smoke alarms. The commission warns that some carbon monoxide monitors are too sensitive, setting off a series of false alarms; others fail to react when they should. If you do have one installed in your home, you should still follow all the precautions listed above.

Sleep Right

Here's one final change: your sleep position. Doctors say that lying on your back all night impedes circulation, so your developing baby might be short-changed of oxygen. The weight of the baby pressing down on your blood vessels cramps the circulatory system's efficiency. Try sleeping on your side, nesting like a spoon inside your husband's protective frame. (As your pregnancy progresses, he'll be able to feel the baby kick, too.)

At some point in your pregnancy, some well-meaning individual will tell you that "pregnancy agrees with you," that "you've never looked better," or that "you have that certain glow about you." Pay special attention to this moment. It may be your first real taste of what being a mother is like. We're talking self-sacrifice here.

It's you who has given up smoking and taken up veggies. It's you who's been exercising conscientiously, going to bed early, and taking your vitamins. But who gets the credit for your "glow"? That's right. Your little angel. You might as well get used to the feeling of basking in the glow of your child. From this moment on, whenever someone says something positive about your offspring, it will make you feel good, too.

Hello in There!

While you've been busy glowing, your unborn child has been busy growing. Often your first concrete sign of your little one's existence will come when you get to hear the fetal heartbeat. Doctors can hear it at about 12 weeks by using an electronic amplifying device called a Doptone that's placed on your abdomen. This instrument is safe and can be used right in the doctor's office. The heartbeat can't be heard with a regular stethoscope until approximately 20 weeks. What you'll hear at 12 weeks through the Doptone is a little heart beating at about 140 beats per minute.

Then, some three months later, you may detect a little signal from within. Some women say their baby's first hello feels like a little gas bubble popping somewhere deep inside. Others describe the sensation as a flutter, a little butterfly moving its wings. If you've never been pregnant before, you will find that distinguishing these baby movements from digestive burbles is just about impossible. But, when you are about 20 weeks along and feel the same sensations in the same spot for two or three days in a row, you can be sure that you're beginning to feel the movement of your child. Mothers who have previously been pregnant may be able to feel life somewhat earlier.

Please understand that your baby has been wiggling and jiggling for quite a while. You just haven't been able to feel it yet. At only six or seven weeks, the baby starts to make occasional whole body movements. At about 14 weeks, the baby can extend both arms and legs, open his or her mouth, and make grasping motions with the hands. At 20 weeks, when you first notice the fluttering field goal attempts, your baby also can move lips, eyelids, and fingers. At 27 weeks, your baby will jump at loud noises.

Doctors say that by the 24th week, you should feel movement at least once every day, and by the 28th week, you should feel movement off and on throughout each day.

Many doctors require that you keep a kick chart, noting the time of day you felt life. They also require that you call if you have not felt a kick within a 12-hour period.

A lot of mothers say that nighttime is the most active time. Just when you're all snuggled under the blanket and ready to sleep, Little Angel will decide it's the perfect time for a romp. The reason, some experts think, is that glucose, a natural sugar in food, can trigger fetal activity. So, if you've eaten a meal at about 7 o'clock, you can expect some action at about 10.

These late jaunts, for the most part, are not too disrupting. In fact, many women find them deeply satisfying. Some mothers say they could not fall

The New Father

Back in "the old days" all a father was expected to do was rush his wife to the hospital and pass out cigars later to family and friends. Whether or not he wanted to be more involved in the labor and pregnancy wasn't even open for discussion.

Today's new fathers often have a deep desire to be part of the childbirth experience. Rather than pacing the waiting room chain-smoking cigarettes, a father is more likely to be helping his wife through labor and delivery. Some men coach their wives to perform special breathing techniques and may even cut the baby's umbilical cord.

Men who participate in the childbirth experience describe it as profoundly beautiful. They describe feeling a tenderness and deep respect for their wives and an overwhelming sense of joy when the baby arrives.

Being there at that special time can accelerate the bonding between father and child and intensify the love that has been waiting for this moment.

It's not surprising, then, that this new kind of father turns out to play a much bigger role in his child's upbringing than his father before him. It's been estimated that some two million men have left their outside-the-home jobs to be full-time caregivers for their children. Some continue to work, but from home offices. Others have given themselves over totally to child care and home management.

Many fathers set aside a special time to be with their babies—maybe giving the little one a bath or singing silly songs while spooning in the pureed carrots. The closeness pays big dividends to both father and child.

A father's desire to spend time with a baby is natural, despite the myth that a baby belongs totally to Mom. Historians say that up until the beginning of the 20th century, fathers spent a great deal of time with their children at home.

Back in the 18th century, for example, children in America worked and played alongside their fathers in the shop, at the forge, or on the farm. Fathers were responsible for a significant part of their children's moral and spiritual upbringing and for their education.

The book you're holding in your hand right now, in fact, has an entire companion volume related to this subject—*The Better Homes and Gardens® New Father Book* by Wade F. Horn, Ph.D., and Jeffrey Rosenberg, M.S.W., both leaders in the National Fatherhood Initiative. This is a great book for men who are struggling with that all-too-common feeling of being sidelined during their wives' pregnancy and the months following the birth.

---

asleep without these reassuring movements. One such mother said, "I would feel so lonely having only me inside of me."

Speaking of lonely, sharing baby kicks is a wonderful way for the expectant father to feel more a part of the process. It is also a wonderful time for Dad to talk to the baby because you know for sure that if the baby is jogging, the baby is awake. Now is the time for your husband to nuzzle up to your tummy and start talking, singing, or reciting nursery rhymes. Whatever. It's the contact that's important.

Most women relate to their babies verbally without even thinking about it, carrying on whole one-sided conversations with their unborn child. Many men, given even the slightest encouragement that it's OK, will be more than willing to participate. Doctors say that bonding between babies and parents can't start too soon, so a lullaby sung to a swollen tummy is, in a way, just what the doctor ordered. Will the baby really benefit from this kind of playful and loving interaction? There are some small studies hinting that during the last couple of months in the womb, babies do indeed hear and respond, to a degree, to what's taking place in the outside world.

Motherhood. How do you truly define an emotion that touches every part of you? I'm a second-time mom, but the news of my second child was as great a thrill to me as my first. Just to know that you carry within you a tiny life that you will raise someday to contribute to our society and to fill your home with joy and laughter. The joys of motherhood are endless.

Jody Martin
Kingsland, Georgia

Preparing for Care: Choosing a Pediatrician

Along with taking good care of yourself, you're going to have to start now to think about taking good care of your baby after the delivery. That means you're going to have to have a pediatrician all picked out well before your little one arrives.

A pediatrician is more than a baby doctor. He or she is also your partner in baby care. As with all successful partnerships, the individuals involved must share the same goals and also the same way of looking at things.

Maybe that statement sounds a little heavy. But picture a laissez-faire set of parents teamed up with an authoritarian doctor who issues strict guidelines. It just wouldn't work. It's important that you and your baby's pediatrician are *simpatico*.

Here are some steps you can take to make sure you find the right doctor to meet the needs of both you and your baby:

☞ **Ask around.** Solicit recommendations from your obstetrician, friends, and family members. Or, call the nearest teaching hospital and ask the head of the pediatrics department which pediatricians in your area have the best reputations.

☞ **Set up face-to-face meetings.** To ensure a good match between you and your baby's doctor, set up interviews with likely candidates before your baby is born. Most pediatricians welcome couples expecting a baby, and they are more than happy to answer any questions about their medical practices and their approach to child care.

☞ **Get answers to your questions.** Ask the doctor about hospital affiliation and whether that hospital is set up to provide proper treatment if your child becomes seriously ill.

Ask if he or she has been certified. Ask whether the doctor works alone; ask who serves as backup. Is the substitute physician also board-certified? If it's a group practice, will you be able to request to see a specific doctor?

Ask if the doctor has telephone hours, during which you can ask questions without having to pay for an office visit.

Before leaving, ask the receptionist if the office has evening or weekend hours. Also ask about insurance plans the doctor participates in and about payment plans.

☞ **Case the joint.** Now look around. Are there two separate waiting rooms: one for sick children and one for well children?

Is the office child-friendly? Are there books or toys appropriate for young children available? Is there a fish tank, for example, or some other diversion to help pass the time while waiting? How does the receptionist interact with incoming parents and children?

Based on these get-acquainted calls, you should have a strong preference for one doctor and can feel more comfortable working with him or her from the start. Your time looking will have been well spent.

Planning Your Leave

As the day draws closer for your delivery, you'll have to give some thought to taking time off from your job. It's understandable to be more than a bit nervous about the impact your pregnancy will have on your career. Be assured that the law is on your side.

The Federal Pregnancy Discrimination Act, which is an amendment to Title 7 (the Civil Rights Act), prohibits job discrimination based on pregnancy, childbirth, or related medical conditions. The law says that you cannot be penalized, demoted, denied a promotion, or forced to resign simply because you are pregnant.

Even in the unlikely event that you become partially disabled by your pregnancy, you need not resign. If your employer regularly assigns light work to other partially disabled employees, he or she is obligated to offer you light work as well. If you are temporarily unable to work, you have the same rights as other employees who are temporarily disabled by accidents or illnesses, including the same medical insurance benefits. You should be permitted to return to your job or one that is equal in pay and status without loss of seniority, just like other employees who have been temporarily disabled.

The Family and Medical Leave Act of 1993 provides 12 weeks of guaranteed but unpaid leave for women who work for companies with 50 or more workers. In order to be eligible, you must have worked a minimum of 1,250 hours in the previous year. This, of course, means that part-time workers are not eligible. The act also states that your employer must maintain your benefits. You may be asked to pay part or even all of the cost, but benefits cannot be eliminated. When you return after 12 weeks, your employer must provide you with a comparable job within the company.

"An employer is in no way obligated to go beyond the 12 weeks that are federally mandated," says Maripat Blankenheim, director of public relations for 9 to 5, the National Organization of Working Women.

Some employers are more than happy to make accommodations for extra time off for a valued employee, especially if she reaches an understanding up front about the various ramifications of missed time. Other employers are not quite so tolerant and may go so far as to use the need for extra time off as an excuse to change a woman's job responsibilities while she's not there to defend her territory or even to terminate a relationship.

"I recently became aware of a woman who had been working for a law firm for more than 10 years," recalls Blankenheim. "She had an extremely difficult pregnancy because she had a heart condition and was 40 years old. As a result, she was in the hospital for a long time. After 12 weeks, on the first day after her leave expired, she received a certified letter at the hospital firing her. Needless to say, she also lost her benefits."

Extending Your Time Away

So how do you make sure you're financially covered and protect your career if you find that 12 weeks is simply not enough time? Blankenheim suggests you negotiate with your employer for additional time. Your company, for example, may have a short-term disability policy that you can take advantage of by working it into your unpaid leave.

"The most important thing," says Blankenheim, "is to do your homework first. Plan out your leave so that it's not only to your advantage but also to the company's. Investigate the possibilities within your company or explore the use of temps. Then explain to your employer how the various aspects of your job will be covered while you're on leave and recommend how the rest might be covered. You are under no obligation whatsoever to work out who will do your job, but it's to your advantage. Being prepared in this way will give you more leverage in negotiating."

You should also be aware that some states have mandated leaves longer than 12 weeks, and that the better law prevails. California, for example, allows for 16 weeks.

Because maternity leave is generally unpaid, many women return to work long before 12 weeks are up. It's a simple matter of economics, according

to Karol Rose, a partner in the benefits consulting firm Kwasha Lipton, in Fort Lee, New Jersey.

Flexing Your Options

Rose also suggests that you investigate the possibility of alternative or flexible work arrangements for when you return to your job. These can include:

• **part-time work**
• **job sharing**, which is a type of part-time work
• **flex-time**, which involves core hours that you must work but allows the flexibility of coming in earlier or staying later
• **a compressed work week**, during which you still work 40 hours, but perhaps as four 10-hour days
• **flex-place**, where you work at home and by telephone, computer, or fax machine

"Lots of times it's possible to return on a flexible schedule," says Rose. "If you don't take the full 12 weeks—and most people don't—you may not want to come back to work full-steam. So suggest an alternative schedule to your boss that you believe will work for you and for your company. When you approach your boss with the idea, think business. The mistake most often made is to come to the manager with an emotional request. But the bottom line is that they are businesspeople. So what women need to do when negotiating is to think about the business advantages of flexibility. That usually boils down to productivity and morale."

Take the case of proposing part-time work. Research consistently shows that part-time employees are "way more productive" than their full-time counterparts, says Rose. Why? "Because," she says, "they cut out all that kibitzing in the hall and getting more coffee and chatting on the phone. When people work part-time, they work!"

Increased productivity also can serve as an argument in favor of flex-time. "If you come in earlier or leave later, you can provide more coverage for your group or department," says Rose. "That's especially true if your business is one that works with people in other time zones, or if machinery or equipment stands idle before or after normal working hours."

Consider proposing your alternative suggestions for small periods of time. "A manager might be a little scared of the idea, thinking you're going to do it forever," says Rose. "So make the idea more acceptable. Say something like, 'Let's try it for two weeks and see if it works for you and me.'"

With good planning and a little luck, you should have the leave you want and the job you love when you're ready for it.

Before we move on to other things you'll have to do to get ready for your baby's arrival, we need to visit the special challenges faced by older women who are pregnant. If you're in your teens or 20s, you can skip directly to Chapter 2, "Buying for Baby," which begins on page 37.

The Older Mother: Joys and Risks

In 1970, the number of women ages 20 to 24 giving birth was 167 per 1,000. That number dropped to 116 in 1990, according to the U.S. Census Bureau. But during that time, the number of women ages 30 to 34 giving birth jumped from 73 per 1,000 to 80.8 per 1,000. This trend toward giving birth later in life shows no sign of letting up.

So, if you're older than 30 and you're pregnant for the first time, take comfort from the fact that you have plenty of company.

"Older women having babies today is a more common event," says Matthew Davies, M.D., an assistant professor of obstetrics and gynecology and associate director of the residency program for Pennsylvania State University at the Milton S. Hershey Medical Center in Hershey. "It is not the exception it once was, but is becoming more of the rule. And the outcome of an older woman's preg-

nancy is as good as that of a younger woman's—as long as there's no underlying health problem." (Dr. Davies notes that an increase in health problems often comes along with an increase in age.)

What exactly is different about an older woman's pregnancy versus that of a younger woman?

"It's a little more difficult throughout the entire pregnancy," Dr. Davies says, "beginning with the fact that an older woman usually finds it harder to conceive."

Most older pregnant women tire more quickly and more often, he notes. Other routine problems, including nausea, are more pronounced. Morning sickness can be more severe, sometimes to the point of debilitation. And at the end of the pregnancy, labor tends to be more tiresome. "It just takes more out of the older mom," says Dr. Davies.

The Need for Vigilance

If you're an older woman expecting a baby, you can expect to get closer scrutiny from your doctor than a younger woman would experience. You will be watched more closely for problems that may—but probably won't—arise.

One potential problem specifically related to a mother's age is giving birth to a child with Down's syndrome, a congenital disorder characterized by mental retardation. A 21-year-old woman has a 1 in 1,500 chance of having a baby with Down's syndrome, a 35-year-old woman has 1 chance in 400, a 40-year-old woman's chance is 1 in 100, and a 45-year-old has a 1 in 30 chance.

In addition to the genetic risks, doctors have discovered that an older woman is more likely to have a baby whose weight at birth is low. In one study, researchers found that women 40 or older were more than twice as likely to have low-birth-weight babies than those 20 to 24 years old.

Prenatal care is exactly the same for older moms as it is for their younger counterparts, with two exceptions.

First, because they have an increased risk of cardiovascular diseases, for all the immune diseases, and for renal or kidney disease, older women tend to be monitored more vigilantly.

Second, women older than 35 are offered genetic testing. "Blood screening is used for the younger women," says Dr. Davies, "but not for those over 35. Instead, they are offered amniocentesis or CVS."

Notice that the doctor said you are "offered" these tests. The purpose of these two tests is to detect serious birth defects so that, should one be discovered, you can terminate your pregnancy early. If you would never consider having an abortion under any circumstances, there is really no point in having the tests.

Testing for Genetic Defects

Amniocentesis is designed to detect chromosomal defects and other genetic disorders in your unborn baby. The test is done when you are about 15 or 16 weeks pregnant. This test is not usually done on pregnant women younger than 35.

To perform the test, the doctor inserts a long, hollow needle through the abdomen and into the uterine cavity to remove amniotic fluid (the fluid that surrounds the fetus in the womb and contains cells that have been excreted by the fetus). An analysis of the fluid shows not only the absence or presence of defects such as Down's syndrome, hemophilia, sickle cell anemia, and Tay-Sachs disease, it also reveals the baby's sex.

The biggest risk from amniocentesis is miscarriage; there's a 1 in 200 or 300 chance of this occurring as a result of the test.

There is also a blood test called triple-marker or serum-marker screening that can reasonably predict the chances of having a baby with Down's syndrome. This test can help you make an informed decision about whether to undergo amniocentesis or CVS.

One scientific study of more than 5,300 women suggests that the need for amniocentesis could be reduced if pregnant women 35 and older are given a blood-screening test for Down's syndrome that is typically performed on younger women. The test, done between the 15th and 20th weeks of pregnancy, can detect levels of hormones and other substances in the blood that indicate a woman's risk of having a baby with Down's syndrome.

The number of amniocentesis tests performed could be decreased by about 75 percent by combining the age factor with the blood test results, rather than going by the woman's age alone, according to James E. Haddow, M.D., medical director for the Foundation for Blood Research in Scarborough, Maine, and a principal author of the study. The blood test identifies 9 out of every 10 cases of Down's syndrome and provides more information about each woman's individual risk. The blood test is not meant to replace amniocentesis, which is nearly 100 percent accurate. Instead, Dr. Haddow suggests, the test can give women who are concerned about the risk of amnio-related miscarriage an option. He estimates that the blood test could prevent as many as 1,400 such miscarriages each year.

Chapter Two

buying for baby

When you're about six or seven months pregnant, it's time to begin shopping for both the nursery and your baby. At this point you still have the energy to do a great job, and you're far enough into your pregnancy to have real motivation. If you're pinched for cash, you still have time to comparison shop or cruise the yard sales and thrift stores. The little shopping trips that will help you get ready for your baby's arrival sweeten the anticipation, too.

But where to begin? Actually, the place to begin is in a quiet corner, armed with pencil and notebook. Start by making these lists: The Nursery, The Layette, Feeding, Outings, and Playtime. Any and all baby gear will fit under one of these headings. As you go through this chapter, take note of what you already have and list the things you think you'll need. These lists will help you plan your shopping trips.

Baby Comes First

Before you get into shopping for the basics, there's one thought that needs to be held in mind. You'll be buying things that meet your needs when it comes to caring for your baby. But your baby will also have needs that must be met.

Are you perhaps thinking of decorating the nursery with fuzzy white lambs gamboling across a mint green meadow, for example? Or maybe you have in mind a pattern of little pink kittens cuddled in a white wicker basket? You may want to put those fantasies aside. You are not thinking the way your baby will.

If babies could do their own decorating and select a wallpaper border for their nursery, what would it look like? Would you believe a simple black-and-white cartoon strip featuring, say, Moe, Curly, and Shemp? It's not that babies are born fans of the Three Stooges (heaven forbid!). It's that researchers have discovered that newborns prefer a high-contrast look, especially black and white, because their eyes are not developed enough to distinguish color. At about 2 months of age, they also love to look at faces.

But don't dash out to the wallpaper store just yet. An infant's needs change quickly, and there are lots of attractive ways to provide stimulating designs and colors, ways that are easily changed as your baby grows.

Babies love the black-and-white scheme only during the first few weeks of life when they are just beginning to practice looking about. To meet that passing fancy, you could fashion a mobile made of black-and-white circles and squares. Once your child is about 6 weeks old, you might toss out the homemade mobile and install a crib mirror so your baby can be amused by watching his or her own fascinating face.

Visual stimulation is important for the baby's growth, but a nursery must provide a whole lot more than that. A report from the Carnegie Corporation's Task Force on Meeting the Needs of Young Children maintains that newborns usually have a capacity to adapt to their surroundings, but that creating the right kind of environment can help them develop properly.

"The unfolding of the developing brain," the report says, "is not inevitable. It depends on a fostering environment that is reasonably stable while at the same time, stimulating, responsive, protective, and loving." The report maintains that it's really important to create the right kind of environment for a new baby. The nurturing qualities of a baby's first room can have "decisive, long-lasting impact on a child's well-being and ability to learn."

With your lists and your baby's needs uppermost in your mind, you're ready to shop.

Nursery Basics

The nursery doesn't necessarily describe a separate room. It just identifies the place where you put the baby to sleep and change the diapers. It's the spot where you store your baby's clothes and other essentials. The nursery can be a corner of your bedroom (which many mothers prefer in the early weeks) or a screened-off area in any relatively quiet area of your house.

You have a tall order to fill: putting together a nursery that is attractive, functional, adaptable, safe, protective, and stimulating. Here are some suggestions that may help.

Walls

Instead of giving in to the appeal of cute nursery wallpaper, consider painting the walls with a latex paint that's scrubbable. You'll be glad you did for the easy cleanup and flexibility. Although baby patterns do have a sweet appeal, you might want to consider skipping them altogether. There's nothing wrong with little bunnies and teddy bears on the walls, of course, but they do become dated rather quickly as your child ages. You can always use the baby patterns in other areas of the nursery besides the walls, such as on the crib sheets, bumper pad, blankets, and curtains.

Floors

Make sure the floor can be easily cleaned. Here function rules over form. Rugs can give a room warmth and feel cushy under bare feet, but they don't stand up well to projectile vomiting or a leaky diaper. (Yes, you will be dealing with both of these things on a regular basis.) Avoid throw rugs, too, because they can skid and bunch up. You don't want to trip or fall when you're carrying your newborn.

Vinyl flooring may not be cozy, but it is easy to clean. It comes in bright colors (your baby starts to like bright colors within the first couple months), pretty patterns, and a shining finish.

A bare wood floor is an acceptable alternative, provided it's in good condition and free of splinters. A coat of polyurethane will make it nearly impervious to spills. (You, Mom, are not to do the refinishing while you're pregnant because of the toxic fumes you would breathe. In fact, be sure the work is done at least a month before your baby is born, so that all the fumes will have dissipated.)

Making the Nursery Safe

Question: When is a room not just a room? Answer: When it's a nursery, of course. When you're setting up a nursery, you have to look at the space with a new set of eyes—those belonging to a very young, very active, very curious baby. It's a given that anything that can be pulled down, toppled over, poked into, torn up, broken up, or tampered with in any way, will be.

You've heard of the proverbial accident waiting for a place to happen? Your job now is to figure out what kind of accidents could happen and see that they don't. This chart should help get you started. But don't stop here. You must look at every single aspect of the room in which you are about to place your baby and ask yourself two questions: Is it safe? How can I make it safer?

1-The crib. Place it away from windows, heaters, lamps, wall decorations, electrical cords, and climbable furniture. Keep the drop side up and locked. When your baby can pull up to standing, remove the bumpers (which can be used as a step) and keep the mattress in its lowest position.

2-Heaters. Make sure heaters such as radiators are enclosed to prevent burns.

3-Windows. Avoid drapes and blinds with cords. Buy window guards or locks that allow windows to be opened just a crack. Keep all furniture away from windows.

4-Bureau. This should be deep rather than high to prevent tipping over. If corners are sharp, install corner guards.

5-Electrical outlets. These should be covered with safety caps.

6-Changing table. Use the restraining strap. Keep toiletries out of a baby's reach.

7-Walls and woodwork. If your home was built before 1978, the paint may contain lead. For information about how to get a paint chip analyzed, call 800-LEAD-FYI (800-532-3394.)

8-Floors. Get rid of area rugs. You don't want to slip while you're carrying your baby.

9-Door gate. Use one that has a straight top edge and a rigid mesh screen or an accordion type with extra-small openings.

39

Windows

You'll need curtains, shades, or blinds to help block out the light for daytime naps. But be careful about what you buy. Any blinds that have a cord are not appropriate for a nursery. The Window Covering Safety Council says an average of one death per month involving pull cords has been reported since 1981. The problem is that babies become entangled in the cord, perhaps when they yank them into the crib or try to look out the window.

Blinds you can open and close by twisting a rod are safer. The Consumer Product Safety Commission (CPSC) calls these rods "safety tassels" and notes that the store where you purchased the blinds should be able to supply them to you. If they cannot, call the CPSC at 800-506-4636. They will tell where you can get safety tassels.

Lighting

Overhead ceiling fixtures give you the best overall lighting. If you have a dimmer switch installed, you'll have both the bright light you need to trim those tiny fingernails and the soft glow that enhances a lullaby.

Avoid floor lamps, because a baby can tip one over trying to pull up into a standing position. A table lamp is fine, provided it is placed away from the changing table (where the baby can grab it), away from window shades or curtains (where it can start a fire), and away from the crib. Wind up the electric cord so it is fairly taut from the lamp base to the outlet and doesn't pose a hazard by looping down to the floor.

Shelving

Install a shelf in a location visible from the crib to display stuffed toys at first, then picture books and perhaps models of dinosaurs or a doll collection. A shelf is easy to repaint in a fresh color whenever you change your decor, and it's inexpensive.

Furnishing Baby's Room

Now that you have considered nursery basics, let's talk about furnishings. The list of furnishings will vary from mother to mother, because one person's must-have item is optional for another. Some mothers feel they absolutely need a cradle or bassinet, for instance, and that the baby can graduate to a crib later. Other mothers start off with a crib. Some moms couldn't get through the day without a changing table; others are most comfortable changing diapers on a waterproof pad on their own bed. The following rundown of common baby products will help you decide which items will work best for you.

Bassinets

A bassinet is a thing of fairy-tale beauty. It's generally fitted out with a fluffy, floor-length skirt and a lovely hood. It looks charming and totally impractical, but it actually is quite functional. It's a snug little bed for a newborn. Usually made of wicker, a bassinet is set on wheels so it's easy to move from room to room. The hood keeps out drafts and light, protecting the baby's sleeping place. (However, it also gets in the way whenever you pick up or put down your baby.)

If you opt for a bassinet, be sure its folding legs lock into place, that it is sturdy, and that it has a wide base to keep it from tipping over. Even the sturdiest bassinet, however, must be put away once your baby is big enough to pull up or roll over.

Cradles

The idea of a cradle rocking your baby gently to sleep is appealing, but the reality is something altogether different. You place the baby in the cradle and give it a little push. What happens? One side of the cradle lifts up and baby rolls helplessly "downhill" to the other. Then that side lifts up and there goes baby again, risking injury and discomfort. It's entirely likely that babies find cradles to be truly annoying. If someone gives you a cradle or if you simply can't resist the appeal, you can give this piece of furniture a try. Just don't be disappointed if it doesn't quite work for you and your baby. The next option may be more to your liking.

Rocking Chair

Yes, babies do like to be rocked, but they like a head-to-toe rocking motion—the kind that you provide in a rocking chair. If you don't already have a comfortable rocking chair, you might consider getting one. It will provide endless hours of comfort for both you and your baby.

Moses Baskets

These portable infant beds are extremely popular in Europe and are becoming trendy in the United States. The Moses basket is long and narrow, with a hood at the head and two sturdy leather straps for carrying. It's outfitted with a thin, waterproof mattress. Often, it's decorated with a froth of ruffles and frills. Moses baskets are suitable beds for only two or three months.

The Crib and Mattress

If you are buying a new crib, you're buying a pretty safe product. Even so, check it out carefully.

☞ **Look for the Juvenile Products Manufacturers Association (JPMA) seal.** This organization sets safety standards, and the seal indicates that the manufacturer has met those standards.

☞ **Measure the slats.** They should be no more than $2^3/8$ inches apart.

☞ **Check to be sure the drop side works easily.** Raise the side and lock it in that position. You will be performing this action hundreds of times, so be sure you can do it easily with one hand, because you'll probably be holding your baby in the other. Shake the side to make sure the lock holds it

up. Unlock the side and drop it. Make sure the side slides smoothly.

☞ **Check the teething rails.** Make sure they are securely attached.

☞ **Keep it simple.** The crib should not have ornamental corner posts. The CPSC has reported numerous strangulation deaths because a baby's shirt or pacifier string caught on a post. (Pacifiers worn around the neck on a string are a bad idea in any case—with or without corner posts on the crib.) The corner posts should be nearly flush with the headboard and footboard.

☞ **Look for a snug-fitting mattress.** It should fit tightly inside the crib. You want the barest minimum of space between the edge of the mattress and the side of the crib. Too wide of a space can entrap some part of your baby's body, and babies have suffocated when caught in such gaps.

What kind of mattress should you buy? As long as it fits snugly, there are a wide variety of mattresses, from expensive innerspring models to less expensive polyurethane foam. An innerspring mattress will give your baby good support, but it may be heavy for you to lift and maneuver when you change the sheets (and you will be changing sheets frequently). Foam mattresses are easier to handle. Just be sure the mattress is thick and sturdy. Thinner foam mattresses may break down at the edges and allow that dangerous gap to form between the mattress and crib.

Crib Bedding

You will want to buy a bumper pad to protect your baby from direct contact with the hard sides of the crib. The bumper should have at least six straps to hold it in place. If the straps tie to the crib rather than snap together, trim excess ends to keep the baby from becoming entangled in them or from chewing and gagging on them. The bumper should fit around the entire inside of the crib, leaving no area where the

My husband was sure we were having a daughter, because he wanted one so bad. He started calling her Kaylee when I was about 3 months pregnant. The tears flowed from his eyes as he held his daughter for the first time. I will never forget that day or that look of love in my husband's eyes.

Julie A. Ells
Port Orford, Oregon

baby could bang his or her head or get it wedged between the bumper and the side of the crib.

Along with a bumper, you will want to purchase several new, fitted sheets. They should be new so you don't have to worry about them bunching up and ensnaring the baby because the elastic edging is shot. Examine them for loose or pulled threads.

Do not buy crib pillows or puffy comforters and quilts. They look attractive and cozy, but the CPSC reports that they can suffocate babies. When a baby is put to sleep face down on top of a pillow or quilt, the baby's breath can become trapped in the fiberfill or batting. The baby then may re-breathe exhaled carbon dioxide and suffocate.

According to an extensive study done by the CPSC, the practice of placing a baby face-down in a crib that has soft bedding may be associated with as many as 1,800 deaths a year, or about 30 percent of the 6,000 deaths attributed to Sudden Infant Death Syndrome (SIDS).

Baby Bathtub

The small plastic tub makes a comfortable bath environment for your baby. You can buy one to fit either a single or double sink. Some come with reclining seats. Many have compartments to hold supplies or a rinse pitcher. You also can bathe your newborn right in the sink. Just be sure it's absolutely clean and the faucet is out of the way. Line the sink with a soft towel before you lower your child into the water.

Changing Table

A changing table is a real back-saver because it puts the baby at a comfortable height when you have to change diapers. The table should have a restraining belt to keep your little one in check while you wield the washcloth. It also should have a safety railing around the top.

Some tables fold, some roll on wheels, some are made of wicker, and some are wooden, so you can pretty much go by your personal taste when purchasing one. The most important thing in terms of safety and convenience is that the table be solid. Babies are not always still when getting a diaper changed, so the table should not wobble or shake even when your child is wriggling.

Diaper Pail

A diaper pail is just a big pail, right? What, you might wonder, must one know about buying such a simple product?

Strange as it might seem, the CPSC reports that diaper pails can be dangerous. The greatest problem is with children eating the deodorizing cake inside them. The commission also reports that children occasionally fall into the pail and drown.

When shopping for a diaper pail, look for one that has a locking lid. Some models even have a child-resistant deodorizer compartment. Also buy one that has a foot pedal, which will enable you to keep your hands free for your baby.

Clothing Storage

A dresser, new or used, will help store your child's wardrobe right through high school and beyond, so it's a good investment. Look for one that is wide and deep, rather than tall. The problem with tall dressers is that some toddlers pull out each drawer a few inches, in effect creating a flight of steps. When they try climbing up, the dresser can fall on top of them.

If you're not ready to purchase a dresser, consider storing your baby's clothing in bright-colored plastic crates, in pretty baskets, or even in cardboard cartons you can cover with adhesive shelving paper that has an attractive design.

Soft Carrier or Backpack

A soft baby carrier lets you "wear" your baby when he or she is little. The soft pouch cuddles your baby against your body and is supported by straps over your shoulders. Babies usually love the warmth and soothing motions of being worn, and parents love it, too, because the pouch leaves their hands free for other activities, such as cooking and shopping. Cranky babies often relax and cheer up when they're snuggled in carriers.

Backpacks are carriers with frames that are meant to hold babies who can sit up unsupported. The frame helps to distribute your baby's weight over your entire upper body rather than just on your shoulders. Because of that stiff metal frame, however, it won't feel quite as snugly and cuddly for either you or your baby.

Bathing Safety Warning

A bath ring seems like such a good idea. This is a small inner-tube-like device that is supposed to cushion and support a baby during a bath (and baby's are wiggly when they're in the water). The latest and best advice: Do not use one of these rings. The Consumer Product Safety Commission (CPSC) has received more than a dozen reports of accidental drownings involving bath rings. It notes that the rings are particularly dangerous for infants 5 to 12 months old. The baby can slide under the ring and drown in very little water. Bath seats and rings "may make caregivers believe a baby is in a relatively safe environment," says CPSC chairperson Ann Brown. "Any such belief can have a devastating consequence because these products, regardless of how sturdy they look, cannot prevent drowning."

Thrifty Shopping?

What's Safe and What's Not

It's so tempting to buy used baby items at your local thrift shop or at garage sales. The price is certainly right when you're getting hand-me-downs from friends and family. After all, your little one uses so many of these things for such a short time before outgrowing them. Why spend a fortune when you don't have to? It comes down to safety. Is it safe to use stuff that comes from other babies? Yes and no.

Thrift shops and garage sales are great places to find a bottle sterilizer, bottles (buy new nipples), a baby bath tub, a warming dish, a nursery lamp, clothing, and lots of other odds and ends for a fraction of what they originally cost. All these items are safe.

However, some products—cribs, playpens, car seats, and baby gates—are best bought new so they meet today's strict standards. Many an old crib is offered for resale, for instance, but safety standards for cribs went into effect only in 1973, and have become more stringent since then. The crib from Grandma's attic may look great but have features that fail to meet today's safety standards. For this type of equipment, it's better to play it safe and opt for new products.

What about clothing? Most of it is just fine, with a couple of important exceptions. Drawstrings on clothes can catch on crib rails and other objects and have caused at least 12 deaths and 27 serious accidents in the last decade. In recent years, more than 20 leading manufacturers of children's clothing have agreed to voluntarily eliminate the use of drawstrings.

Hand-me-downs may have been manufactured before that time. The Consumer Product Safety Commission (CPSC) recommends removing all drawstrings. You should also be aware that older clothing and bed linens may not be made of flame-retardant materials.

Diapers

Experts estimate that a baby will need about 6,000 diaper changes in the first 2½ years, so it's an important decision to make. Disposable diapers are extremely convenient. They contain an absorbent gel, so they really keep the baby dry and almost never leak. They're available in many sizes, and most now come in boys' and girls' models. There is even a new type of disposable for newborns that has a notch at the waistband so there's no diaper touching the healing belly button. You will pay for the convenience. At 25 cents a disposable diaper, the cost adds up (total is $1,500 based on 6,000 diapers).

Cloth diapers are far less expensive because they're reusable. They are also kinder to the environment. (A good portion of the landfills across the nation is given over to used diapers.) Unfortunately, cloth diapers tend to be less absorbent than disposables and are more likely to leak. If you do opt for the cloth diaper route, you'll need about four dozen. You'll also need some diaper wraps to protect your furniture and baby's clothing from leaks.

Lots of parents use disposables in the first months, when—working through a fog of fatigue—their convenience seems more like a necessity. Later they switch to cloth diapers and save the disposables for traveling and visiting.

Yet a third option is a diaper service that sends a delivery person to your home to pick up a week's worth of dirty diapers and, at the same time, drop off a freshly laundered batch. Diaper services were more common before disposables became so popular, but you may be able to find one serving your area. Generally, the diapers belong to the service, so you will not have to buy any. You may want to keep a package of disposables on hand for emergencies and travel.

The Layette

A layette is a complete outfit of clothing for a newborn. You may be tempted to buy lots of those tiny outfits simply because they're so darned cute and you can't wait for the day you'll be able to dress your little darling.

The best advice: Restrain yourself. It's a waste of money because babies grow awfully fast.

It's best to buy only a few of each basic layette item, because you won't be using newborn clothing for all that long. Besides, the people who love you probably will show up with armloads of clothing, either new outfits or ones their babies have outgrown.

Clothing manufacturers offer this tip for the shopping you'll do after you have your baby: Select the size based on a child's actual weight and length rather than the age listed on the label.

Baby Clothes

Here's a list of clothing that will provide a modest layette. If you do not have easy access to a washing machine, you should buy at least one more of each item.

- **2 or 3 one-piece stretch suits**
- **2 sets of matching pants and tops**
- **4 or 5 shirts**
- **1 machine-washable sweater**
- **4 nightgowns or sleeping sacks**
- **1 hat**
- **6 pairs of stretchy cotton socks**
- **6 receiving blankets**

Getting Ready For Feeding

If you're planning to bottle-feed your baby, you'll need some basic equipment. As a matter of fact, it's a good idea to have these items on hand even if you're breast-feeding.

Bottles

You'll be using at least six bottles (complete with nipples, rims, and caps) each and every day. It seems sensible to buy a dozen.

Bottles are available in glass or plastic. There is a type with an angled neck that keeps the nipple filled with liquid, so the baby doesn't suck down air. The shape also encourages feeding the baby in a semi-upright position, which keeps liquid from flowing into the middle ear. (Pediatricians have found liquid trapped in the middle ear to be a common cause of ear infections.)

If you are breast-feeding, you'll need fewer bottles, but you will want to have a few on hand for relief feedings. Three or four should do for a start. They can be washed in the dishwasher, but the nipples must be sterilized in boiling water for five minutes.

Sterilizer

A sterilizer will process a full day's bottles at one time. In the past, a sterilizer was considered a necessity, but today many doctors say that, if your home drinking water is safe, bottles can be sterilized in the dishwasher. You'll have to check with your doctor for individual advice. Nipples should be sterilized in a pan of boiling water for five minutes.

If you do sterilize a day's worth of bottles at a time, store them in the refrigerator. For easier, faster heating, you may also want to buy an electric bottle warmer.

Breast Pump

If you plan to keep nursing after you've returned to work, you'll need a breast pump. You can choose from manual, battery-operated, or electric models. (See "Mastering the Basics" on page 91 for more information on buying and using a breast pump.)

Pacifier

Pacifiers must now meet federal standards that require a mouth shield to keep the nipple where it can't choke the child. The shield must have two breathing holes just in case the pacifier somehow gets caught in the baby's throat. A pacifier also must withstand a test that shows the two pieces will not come apart.

High Chair

When your child is ready for solid food—and that's what it's called no matter how mushy it is—you'll need a high chair.

Look for a high chair with a JPMA label. The JPMA certifies high chairs that meet certain safety standards. The chairs bearing the group's label have been tested and found to be stable, to have no sharp edges or protrusions, to employ caps and plugs that a child cannot remove, and to have a good restraining system. To make your life easier, buy one that has a tray with good spill capacity and that can be positioned with one hand.

The best high chair in the world, however, cannot prevent an accident if the parent doesn't observe certain precautions:

•**Use the seat strap.**
•**Watch the child carefully.**
•**Make sure the tray is firmly locked.**
•**Use the chair in a level spot.**

Each year, nearly 9,000 children end up in hospital emergency rooms as the result of an accidental falls from high chairs, according to CPSC. The problem, reports the commission, usually arises when the parent does not fasten the safety strap and the tray accidentally unlatches.

Infant Seat

Infants are neither comfortable nor safe in a high chair, so many parents buy an infant seat that will cradle the baby in a semi-upright position. The chair provides a nice place for feedings, chatting, and playing. After all, you cannot always hold the baby in your arms, and this kind of seat is a pleasant alternative to the cradle or crib. You can place the baby right in the middle of things so he or she can see what's going on.

Look for a seat that has a broad rear support, rubber grips on the base to keep it from sliding, and a good seat strap.

Outings

Yes, it is possible to get out and about with a baby. It simply takes the kind of planning that puts a circus on the road. For all but the briefest of errands, you'll probably be toting food, diapers, extra clothing (just in case), and a safe place for the baby to sit and sleep.

Car Seats

The most important purchase for most parents is the car seat. All 50 states require that parents restrain babies and children while they are traveling in a car. The federal government has developed specifications for car seats to ensure a high level of protection for your child.

Two basic types of car seats are available: One is specifically for infants weighing less than 20 pounds; the other is a convertible model that adapts to infants and toddlers up to about 40 pounds.

The infant seat faces the child backward so that, in case of a crash, the back, which is the strongest part of a baby's body, takes most of the impact. These seats feature an adjustable harness system that grows with your baby.

If your car has air bags, it is important to place your baby's car seat in the back seat. Air bags inflate violently, and the velocity and force of air-bag inflation have caused the deaths of dozens of children (and some adults). Automobile manufacturers are working on the problem. Until it is solved, keep your child out of harm's way, tucked safely in the back seat while you drive.

Infant car seats usually come with a handle so they are portable. Many fit tightly into the seat of a grocery shopping cart. Some can be rocked when placed on a flat surface. Some models allow you to leave the base of the seat in the car and pop out just the seat itself.

The convertible car seat is rear-facing for infants

then adjusts to allow an older baby to face front. Some have a removable back support and pillow. All have highly engineered harness systems to secure the baby safely in the seat.

A five-point harness system provides maximum restraint. In this version, straps go over the baby's hips and shoulders, more straps go between the legs. All the straps are latched in front with a buckle.

Other versions have cushioned bar-shields that lower in front of the child and lock in place. Still others have a T-shield, with the vertical part of the T latched to the seat between the child's legs and the crossbar reaching across the chest.

The Stroller

The stroller has a softly padded seat that reclines to accommodate your little baby and a hood to protect the seat from the elements. Here's what to look for: A stroller should have a wide wheel base for stability, good brakes, and a good restraining system that will prevent your baby from slipping (later, from climbing) out.

Lightweight Stroller

When the umbrella stroller was introduced, parents instantly fell in love with it. It was lightweight and extremely convenient. You could close it quickly and hang it from your arm, just like an umbrella. You could, literally, toss it into the car. Unfortunately, the stroller was not comfortable for the baby, the unit was not durable, and several models were recalled for safety problems.

As a result, the umbrella stroller has evolved into today's lightweight stroller, which weighs in at about 10 pounds. All lightweights fold into a tidy package. All have some type of fabric sling seat, most have brakes on at least two wheels, and some have shock-absorbers.

Portable Play Quilts

Unfold the padded package, and it turns into a small quilted rug. The raised sides sport brightly colored animal shapes. Some have toys, such as a rattle or a button to push, sewn to the padding. Some zip up into wearable bunting. The idea is that you have an easily portable place to put your baby down on any floor, from a department store dressing room to your doctor's waiting room. You don't need to get one of these, but they are convenient.

Playtime

The most fun you'll have shopping for your baby may well be buying those first toys. It's good to remember that in a real sense playing is the work that children do. Even the simplest toys can encourage learning and enhance motor skills. Here are a few good toys to get you started.

A Mobile

Babies are entranced by watching a mobile turn and dip. You can make your own inexpensive mobile with bright-colored craft paper in a variety of

The Walker of Doom

Baby walkers resulted in 23,000 emergency room visits in 1993, making walkers the number one cause of juvenile product-related accidents, according to the Consumer Product Safety Commission. As a result, the commission has called on walker manufacturers to develop safer designs.

Instead of buying a walker, the commission recommends purchasing either a bouncer or a jumper. If you do use a walker, your baby should be closely supervised and the walker always should be used where there is no access to stairs.

shapes. Or you can buy one at almost any price, from inexpensive plastic butterflies hanging from a simple crossbar to embroidered, quilted, miniature farm animals that twirl mechanically while a wind-up music box plays "Farmer in the Dell."

Mobiles are great for quieting fussing babies and helping their visual powers grow.

Play Yard

These baby-holding areas used to be called playpens, but they have been renamed play yards.

Generally speaking, play yards now have tightly woven mesh sides with a strip of solid vinyl running along the bottom to prevent drafts. The floor usually is made of hardboard and folds in half when the play yard is stored. The floor is covered with a vinyl pad. The top rail usually is padded as well.

The only serious danger with play yards, according to the CPSC, is that a baby can become entrapped and suffocate in the material that's supposed to provide protection from drafts. To keep this from happening, the enclosure material must be fully up and secured.

Play yards provide a safe enclosure when a parent must be distracted by cooking dinner, for example. Many play yards, however, simply become giant toy boxes.

Swings and Jumpers

An alternative to a play yard is a swing that will hold your baby safely while providing a steady, pleasant rocking motion for about 30 minutes. Some swings wind up by hand; others use batteries.

A more action-oriented seat, called a jumper, attaches to the top frame of a doorway. It has an enclosed seat that hangs on sturdy straps from a spring. When your baby touches his or her feet to the floor, the seat bounces.

Ten Great Toys to Get an Infant

If you walk into a toy store thinking you'll "just pick something up," you could easily be overwhelmed. The choices are so mind-boggling that it's a good idea to have something specific in mind before you cross the threshold into Toyland. You might share this list with anyone who wants to buy a toy for your baby but doesn't have a clue about what is appropriate:
- a plaything with a bell that the baby can bat and make ring
- a rubber ducky to float in the tub
- a music box for bedtime
- a plastic crib mirror
- a rattle
- a mobile
- a play mat with toys that dangle from it
- a teddy bear or some other stuffed animal
- a tape player for music appreciation
- a jack-in-the-box

Part II

a new
life

Chapter Three

the birth of your child

Turn the page on the calendar and there it is, circled in red: The Big Day. The Birth Day. Of course, you don't need a calendar to tell you that your baby's on the way. Your body sends you that message loud and clear.

Most babies don't arrive exactly on the due date. But, clearly, you're now in the home stretch. Congratulations to you even before the baby makes the first move toward daylight. You're soon to be rewarded for all your diligence and care.

It is perfectly natural to be a little nervous. Your head is probably full of "what ifs." And you know deep in your heart that labor is going to be (how shall we put this?) *challenging* to your body, mind, and spirit.

How challenging? A few years ago, scientists at McGill University used a questionnaire to ask a variety of people to rate any pain that they had experienced in the past on a scale of 0 to 40. When the answers were tabulated, guess which one came out on top? That's right, labor pain. Arthritis pain was rated at about 15, cancer pain at 25, and labor pain for a first-time mother at about 35.

Today you hardly ever hear the term "labor pains." Instead, doctors and other health care providers speak of "contractions," which is technically correct, and even of "abdominal discomforts." Their thinking, apparently, is that the words "labor pains" will scare the daylights out of women. But labor is a process that is well-named: It's physically, emotionally, and mentally taxing and often painful. Denying that fact also denies a woman her claim to courage, it denies the reality that every mother is a hero.

Yet consider this: Women often say that the pain of their labor was soon erased by the euphoria of seeing their newborn.

And know this: Anesthesia is available that will help you and not harm your baby, and that will allow you to participate fully and consciously in the birth.

Remember this as well: Your mother gave birth, as did her mother, and her mother before her, and they most likely went on to have even more children.

Household Checklist

Once your baby is born, housework will be the furthest thing from your mind. That doesn't mean it will go away, however. Certain chores need to be done whether you have a baby demanding every single moment of your attention or not. Is there anything you can do ahead of time to make sure those first several weeks at home with your new baby go more smoothly? You bet!

☞ **Cook and freeze.** Prepare and freeze as many meals as you can manage. You'll appreciate not having to make dinner when your hands are busy taking care of your baby (or when you'd rather take a much-needed nap!).

☞ **Clean the house thoroughly.** Of course, you don't feel like cleaning house when you're pregnant. You'll feel even less inclined after you deliver. Here's the perfect place for your husband to lend a helping hand.

☞ **Disinfect.** Wipe all "baby" surfaces with a cleaner that kills germs.

☞ **Set up the nursery.** Set up the nursery. Organize the baby's diapers, clothing, and other supplies. You'll find a complete overview of everything you need in "Buying for Baby," which begins on page 37.

☞ **Prepare to be skinny.** Put together your own post-baby wardrobe and hang it in the closet. (Yes, as hard as it is to believe right now, you *will* fit back into your favorite jeans, even if this doesn't happen right away.)

☞ **Anticipate sibling jealousy.** Buy and wrap little gifts for any older children that you have and hide them until you return home.

☞ **Call for reinforcements.** Line up a relative or friend, or hire a mother's helper, to assist you during the first week or two.

Preparing for Childbirth

Given the physical and mental challenge you're facing, is there anything you can do ahead of time to get ready? Indeed there is—you can go to school.

Most women these days attend some kind of childbirth classes, usually with their husbands or with someone else who is close and will offer loving care and unstinting support.

Celeen Miller, certified childbirth educator at Doylestown Hospital and health educator with the Bucks County Department of Health in Pennsylvania, has been teaching childbirth education classes for 10 years. She says there are some good, solid reasons for signing up for these classes: "Statistics show that women who attend prepared childbirth classes need less pain medication. Consequently, there are no—or fewer—side effects from anesthesia."

Two things are at work here, she explains. One is that women who use the techniques taught in these classes actually feel less pain, and the other is that the pain they do feel is perceived differently.

"There's something called the gate theory of pain," Miller says. According to this theory, certain sensations, such as heat and touch, can get to the brain before pain sensations do. So, the right kind of loving touch can sometimes help override perceptions of pain. That's why instructions on how to give a back massage are included in so many childbirth preparation classes.

"Not so long ago," she says, "women used to think they wouldn't have pain in labor, and if they experienced pain, they'd think something was wrong with them." Even today, she notes, many couples still want a pain-free birth.

"I think that desire reflects living in a society that wants everything to be done quickly and without pain," Miller says. "You want wate? Turn on the tap. Feel chilly? Turn up the heat. Labor must be one of the most physically difficult things in life these days for most women. Maybe women don't have to go out and harvest vegetables in the fields anymore, but they *still* have to work hard during labor. Some things don't change."

"Childbirth classes also are confidence-building," says Miller. "Women are filled with curiosity and concern about childbirth. Think about it. Today's

Natural Birthing Methods

Why go to school to learn how to have a baby? After all, isn't this something that women do naturally anyway? Well, yes. But after years of study, scientific research has demonstrated that women who take childbirth education classes generally have shorter labors, less need for pain killers, and even a more positive attitude toward their babies—all good reasons for signing up.

If you opt for childbirth classes, there are quite a few to choose from. The most common method used in the United States today is a combination of the Bradley and the Lamaze methods. Here's the lowdown on what each of the different methods has to offer.

The Bradley Method

The aim of the Bradley method is to reduce the mother's need for anesthesia by teaching her to relax through abdominal breathing. A woman is taught specific exercises for muscle development. In addition, she is shown how to synchronize her breathing with uterine contractions. At the same time, she is urged to focus on pleasant thoughts. The father plays a major role in the delivery by acting as the labor coach.

The Lamaze Method

The Lamaze method is based on the theory that if a woman understands the nature of labor pains, she will be less afraid. Instead of dreading each contraction, the laboring mother is taught to think of them as necessary bodily functions that bring about dilation of the cervix and the eventual birth of the baby.

This method theorizes that if the negative aspects of labor pains can be neutralized, a woman can be taught to respond to them as a signal for a special type of breathing. The breathing patterns, which are taught in a series of classes, act both as a distraction from labor pains and as a way of easing the pain.

The Leboyer Method

Frederick Leboyer introduced this method in 1975 with his book, *Birth Without Violence*. With this method, the focus is on the baby as well as the mother during labor. Leboyer attempts to reproduce the environment within the womb as the baby is being born.

The warmed delivery room is bathed in a dim light, so the baby is not traumatized upon leaving the womb. The infant is placed immediately on the mother's abdomen, so the little one instantly feels warmth and comfort. The umbilical cord is not cut until it stops pulsating, allowing the maximum amount of oxygen to pass into the body. Finally, the baby's back is massaged, and he or she is placed into a body-temperature bath.

Babies have been scalded in the "body temperature bath," leading some obstetricians to rule this approach unsafe. They also feel that it's not necessary to postpone cutting the umbilical cord because the baby is already getting all the oxygen needed by breathing.

The Reed Method

The goal of this method of natural childbirth is to overcome the fear of pain associated with labor. The method tries to achieve this goal by teaching mothers about their anatomy and physiology and what is involved in labor and delivery.

Expectant mothers receive relaxation training and learn breathing exercises. They also get a general physical fitness program. This method asks the baby's father to become involved in labor and delivery.

Some doctors—and some mothers—have criticized this method for putting too much emphasis on the importance of a drug-free delivery. If a woman runs into trouble delivering and requires medication, she often feels a bit of a failure for not living up to the Reed method's high standards.

women do not even have the advantage of having seen their mother or sister have children."

One of the other aims of childbirth classes, she adds, is to alert women to a simple fact: "You can do this even though you never have done it before." The classes help both mother and father conquer the fear of the unknown.

The typical childbirth class stresses breathing and relaxation techniques to break the tension/pain cycle. Both fathers and mothers can benefit from using these techniques in areas other than childbirth, says Miller. That's because some of the techniques are identical to those taught in some stress management workshops and can be employed on the job.

Happy Birth Day

Because labor can be so different from one woman to the next, and because its initial phase can vary considerably, you may not be sure when to call the doctor or go to the hospital. It's important to be able to recognize the early signs of labor.

Labor is within days when:

• **You see an increased and thickened vaginal discharge.**
• **The mucous plug that has sealed off the opening of the uterus is expelled.**
• **You feel an intensification of Braxton Hicks contractions (mild, irregular uterine contractions that you may perceive as spasms in your lower abdomen).**

You know it's time to call the doctor when:

• **You see a "show," or blood-tinged mucus discharge from the vagina.**
• **The water breaks, which you experience as a gush or a trickle from the vagina.**
• **You feel contractions at regular intervals.**
• **The intervals between the contractions gradually shorten.**
• **The intensity of the contractions gradu-**

ally and steadily increases.
• **You feel increased discomfort in your back and abdomen.**

Timing Contractions

As eager as you undoubtedly are to get to the hospital, it won't do you any good at all to head out the door before you're actually ready. If you arrive at the hospital too early in your labor, or if you are in false labor, you probably will be sent home. The medical staff will check your progress, listen to the fetal heartbeat to make sure the child is not having early difficulties with even mild contractions, then send you packing.

"We can do a disservice to patients with very early labor by admitting them to the hospital, when sedating them and sending them home for bed rest in a familiar environment might be better," says James N. Martin, Jr., M.D., director of obstetrics and maternal/fetal medicine at the University of Mississippi Medical Center in Jackson. "It's really part of a waiting game, where you wait to see if the contractions dissipate or if you are in true labor."

He says, "We usually counsel women to come in and be checked when they are experiencing repetitive uterine contractions five to six minutes apart that have persisted for an hour or more. If a woman's contractions are rapidly getting stronger and stronger, or if she also has bleeding or has begun to leak fluid, she is advised to come in for assessment."

An hour is a fairly good length of time to self-monitor contractions, according to Dr. Martin. How long you monitor your contractions depends on factors such as the distance you have to travel to the hospital and your previous labor history. This is something you should discuss with your doctor well ahead of time.

Sometimes women experience a phenomenon known as false labor. If you want to know whether your labor pains are the real thing, Dr. Martin suggests the following:

Packing Your Bag

Going to the hospital to deliver your baby is like no other trip you've ever taken. It's a good idea to pack your bag ahead of time, because when you're having labor pains and are worried about getting to the hospital on time, there are more important things on your mind than remembering to take your toothbrush. Besides the toothbrush, here are the other items you might want to include in your bag:

• **Some makeup** (remember, you'll be photographed for eternity), a hairbrush, and a comb
• **A nightgown** (one that opens in the front if you plan on breast-feeding your baby)
• **Slippers and warm socks**
• **A book or a deck of cards** (You may think you won't want to read or play cards, but labor can stretch out for long hours with nothing but an occasional labor pain to grip your attention.)
• **Materials from your childbirth classes**
• **An outfit to wear home** (Select some clothing that fit you in mid pregnancy. You definitely will be slimmer than you are now, but nowhere near as slender as you were nine months ago.)
• **Clothing for the baby:** a stretch suit, undershirt, booties, and a receiving blanket (And be sure the new car seat is installed before the trip home.)

There are also a few optional things your husband might want to bring:

• **A camera and film** (Note that photography is prohibited in some delivery rooms, but photos can be taken after mother and child have had a chance to recover.)
• **A tape recorder** to capture your baby's first sounds or a video camera, which will take care of both pictures and sounds.
• **Something to eat** (Your husband might want to brown-bag a sandwich and a couple of juice boxes for himself).
• **An armload of fresh flowers** (for you)

"Get up and be active when the contractions start, because activity tends to decrease false labor. With false labor, you are having what are called Braxton Hicks contractions, which are not the productive contractions of true labor and don't result in uterine or cervical changes. Braxton Hicks contractions usually go away when the mother is active. This is the tried and true test."

Finding Comfort and Support

Once at the hospital or birthing center, you may discover that your childbirth experience is more similar to your grandmother's than to your mother's. The environment will be homier than your mother's sterile labor room, and your husband will likely be there to comfort and labor with you. Your mom labored alone, attended by nurses and doctors but without a family member present.

Why the big change? Today's hospitals have responded to women's demands for more comfort, more emotional support, and more flexibility in the medical approach to labor and childbirth. It is no longer unusual for a hospital to offer one, or even several, alternative birthing rooms called LDPRs. The letters stand for labor, delivery, postpartum, and recovery. Walking into one of these rooms is like walking into a suite in a fine hotel. You're likely to find beautiful draperies, paintings on the wall, a cozy afghan spread across a large, comfortable bed, and lots of chairs for visiting family members. The surroundings are usually lovely.

And why not? For ages, women gave birth at home, surrounded by family and aided by an experienced midwife. (The downside was that mother and child could not receive appropriate care in an emergency.) It wasn't until after the 1920s, when advances in anesthesia and medical technology allowed women who were ill to give birth safely, that women began giving birth in hospitals.

Over the years, even perfectly healthy women with absolutely normal pregnancies were admitted to the hospital for the births of their children. In fact, today 95 percent of births in the United States take place in a hospital.

It's a natural evolution for hospitals to offer a home-style delivery area, now that maternal and fetal mortality are not such big problems, says Dr. Martin. "It is a far preferable solution than to return to home births, where the mother and practitioner have limited resources to respond to unforeseen problems."

Most women appreciate the security of a hospital environment—not only for themselves, but for their babies—if a problem develops. On the other hand, there are a number of things that happen routinely in a hospital setting that a woman might not appreciate. These include things like taking the baby away to a nursery or limiting the new father's visits to specific hours. At least most hospitals have discontinued certain procedures connected with the childbirth itself after so many women objected—shaving the pubic area and requiring an enema, for example.

Hospital procedures, after all, were developed to protect the ill. But women recognize that having a baby is not an illness. Indeed, what could be healthier than bringing a new life into the world?

And so, after 25 years of listening to a growing percentage of new mothers grump about their unsatisfactory birth experiences, doctors and hospitals have eased the rules. They've come to understand what mothers have always known: Families belong together right from the start. And they've created birth centers that are right in the hospitals.

These relatively new hospital birth centers attempt to offer you the best of both worlds. You'll be in a homelike room to labor, have the baby, and recover. But at the same time, you will be near the hospital labor and delivery rooms, where serious complications, should they arise, can be handled efficiently and effectively.

You also may want to develop what's known as a birth plan or birth script to be sure you have the baby the way *you'd* like. The plan is a written document that you and your husband create, working with the doctor who is going to deliver your baby. So before you ever give birth, you've come to an understanding about your choice of anesthesia, who you want present during delivery, and whether or not you'll breast-feed. The hospital's medical staff will adhere to the plan if the birth is a normal, uncomplicated vaginal delivery.

Labor Intensive

When you arrive at the hospital to have your baby, you and your unborn baby will be assessed, probably by a receiving nurse who reports the findings to the doctor or other health care provider.

You'll be checked for vital signs, including blood pressure, temperature, pulse, and respiration. The doctor or nurse will note the frequency and strength of your contractions, how far your cervix has dilated, whether the membranes are intact or not, and whether there is any evidence of bleeding. The doctor or nurse also will determine the baby's position inside the pelvis and whether the fetal heart is beating at a normal rate and rhythm.

Three Stages of Labor

The birth of a baby occurs in three stages.

The first stage of labor is the longest of the three. You will probably already be well into the first stage when you arrive at the hospital. In the first stage, several changes take place within you. One is that your uterus and cervix, which together look like a great big pear, are going to change from pear-shaped to more of a keg shape. The cervix (the neck of the "pear") will shorten—a process known as effacement. As the cervix shortens, it begins to dilate (open) so the baby's head will be able to pass through.

During this stage, you will feel uterine contractions that become rhythmic, stronger, and longer. At first, they may last only 30 to 40 seconds and occur every 5 to 15 minutes. As labor becomes more active, however, they will last 60 seconds and come every 3 to 5 minutes.

Before the birth of my baby, when I'd see someone who might be viewed by most as a "menace to society," I'd question, "How could God love that person as much as He loves me?" Now, after having my little boy, I understand God's unconditional love for all his children. Regardless of what happens during my son's life, I'll always remember the rocking and cuddling at 2 a.m.! I love him unconditionally. I'm glad I now understand and have felt this kind of love. I feel much less guilty about my imperfections—because I now understand that God loves me—no matter what!

Dana McKelvain
Fair Oaks Ranch, Texas

The first stage of labor ends with a transitional phase, during which your cervix dilates from 7 to 10 centimeters (2¾ to nearly 4 inches), and the contractions are occurring at a rate of one every 2 to 3 minutes. Each contraction lasts approximately 60 seconds.

In the second stage, you will begin to feel the urge to push with each contraction. When your cervix is fully dilated to 10 centimeters, it is out of your baby's way, and pushing is both safe and desirable. Your childbirth preparation classes have taught you how to breathe and bear down to make each contraction more effective. Now is the time for your husband (or designated coach) not only to coach but also to cheerlead. His energy will help give you more energy.

Your doctor may use a fetal monitoring device to detect any signs that your baby is under stress or in distress and to measure the strength of your contractions.

"Fetal monitoring is commonly employed," says Dr. Martin, "particularly when the baby may be at more risk for problems than usual—if the birth is premature, for example, if the mother has high blood pressure, or if the heart rate is abnormal. Some maternity units routinely use fetal monitoring for all labors. Others do not, but instead use what is called intermittent auscultation, where they are committed to a schedule of monitoring during and after a contraction, every five to 15 minutes, depending on the stage of labor."

An external monitor involves a device placed on the mother's abdomen over the uterus, with a belt to measure contractions.

Pain Relief

With all the options for pain relief available these days, there's no reason why you need to suffer unduly through labor.

In many parts of the United States, an epidural is the most commonly used anesthetic for labor and delivery. An epidural is a local anesthetic, given by injection in the lower back, that numbs the lower half of the body.

"The newest development is the epidural anesthetic that is continuous," says James Martin, M.D., director of obstetrics and maternal/fetal medicine at the University of Mississippi Medical Center and professor of obstetrics and gynecology at the University of Mississippi in Jackson. "In the past, we would give relatively large amounts of anesthetic every hour or so. The epidural served as a motor and sensory blockade."

Women tended to like this form of epidural because they lost all sense of feeling from the waist down. But when it came time to deliver, they could not feel their contractions and therefore couldn't help to push at the right time, says Dr. Martin.

"With the continuous epidural," adds Dr. Martin, "the anesthetic is fed in small amounts by pump, so that there is a continuous bathing of nerve fibers, rather than a large amount administered every 30 to 60 minutes.

"The woman retains her ability to push. The epidural can be fine-tuned to the patient, so there is less risk of blood pressure dropping, interrupting a normal labor."

The continuous epidural is available in most hospitals, he says. If the anesthesia staff is small, however, this form of pain relief may not be available to everyone because the number of anesthetics in use can exceed the staff's ability to manage them. If 10 women are in labor, someone would have to decide who gets the continuous epidural.

Another kind of epidural is also coming into use. This one is known as the walking epidural, and it allows a woman to receive pain relief and still maintain her mobility.

Analgesics like Demerol or Stadol also are used to take the edge off painful contractions. They work by depressing the nervous system and raising the pain threshold. They are given as part of an IV drip or as an injection, usually in the hip.

Drug-free pain control methods such as self-hypnosis also work, according to a preliminary study published in the *Journal of Women's Health*. In this study, one group of women was taught the technique, and another group was not. Women in both groups had their babies using the same family doctor. The group that had learned self-hypnosis had shorter labors, an 11.4-percent reduction in epidurals, and a 15.9-percent reduction in episiotomies (an incision made from the vagina to the anus to enlarge the vaginal opening and enhance delivery).

You'll learn a good deal about pain relief techniques during your childbirth classes. You should also discuss pain relief options and the potential effects of the drugs on your baby with your doctor well before your delivery time.

"When there is concern about a baby's status, an internal monitor is usually placed on the baby's scalp," says Dr. Martin. "An electrode will be attached to the baby's scalp and sometimes a catheter also is inserted into the uterus to measure strength of contractions. The internal monitoring is used more commonly in high-risk pregnancies, and is less common in straightforward situations."

Before long, you will achieve crowning, where the top of the baby's head can be seen during and after a contraction. At this point, you are ready to deliver.

The third stage of labor involves expelling the placenta (the afterbirth) following the delivery of your baby.

The Episiotomy Debate

During your delivery, your doctor may want to do an episiotomy, which is a shallow incision made in the lower vagina downward toward the anus to prevent the tissue from tearing. Until fairly recently the operation has been considered routine, but it is now becoming somewhat controversial.

"The thinking on episiotomies is in transition," says Dr. Martin. "An episiotomy is meant to help a woman in several ways. The procedure prevents an uncontrolled tear, and a well-done episiotomy might prevent the tissue from overstretching, and thereby prevent the later development of pelvic relaxation."

The result of such overstretching can lead to uterine prolapse, a condition in which the muscular and tissue supports of the uterus give out, and it drops down into the vagina, sometimes even protruding outside the body.

Routine episiotomies are being looked at more critically, however, with many doctors questioning whether they are really necessary, says Dr. Martin. However routine it may be, an episiotomy does leave a surgical wound that takes time to heal.

The British medical journal *Lancet* reported on a study of 2,600 women delivering in public maternity units. The women were divided into two groups: those who delivered their babies and received a routine episiotomy and a selected group who were given the episiotomy only if specific indications of a need for the surgery were present.

Episiotomies were done in 82.6 percent of the group receiving routine episiotomies, but in only 30.1 percent of the group having the procedure done when certain indicators were present. Severe damage to the vaginal area was "uncommon" in both groups, *Lancet* reports. But it was slightly *less* frequent in the group that did not receive routine episiotomies. The researchers who conducted the study concluded that the procedure is "widely done despite poor scientific evidence of its benefits." They also concluded that "routine episiotomy should be abandoned, and episiotomy rates above 30 percent cannot be justified."

If you're concerned about having an episiotomy, you should discuss the pros and cons of the procedure with your doctor ahead of time.

Saying Hello

One thing's for sure: No matter where you decide to have your baby, or who your doctor is, or what it says on your birth plan, your baby will be born. First the head slides out slowly, usually with the face down. Then the baby turns so he or she can emerge one shoulder at a time. The doctor helps the rest of the baby into the world.

At that moment your heart, Mother, will shatter with joy, and an unbelievably strong, pure, perfect love will pour from you into your child.

Your doctor will probably place your new baby directly on your bare abdomen for skin-to-skin contact, provided the baby is in good condition and not in need of resuscitation. The baby will be face down so fluid can drain naturally from the nose and mouth. The newborn may take a first breath at that moment, or you may have to gently massage the little one's back. Sometimes the doctor will do a little suctioning to be sure the baby breathes freely. Then, you will have a few quiet moments to admire and perhaps even nurse your newborn.

The first contact is all too brief, but so sweet. Now your baby's umbilical cord will be cut (perhaps by your husband, if that was in your birth plan). Your baby's eyes will be treated to prevent gonorrheal infection, as required by most state laws. The doctor and nurses will evaluate your baby's condition using what is known as the Apgar score. Then your little one will be footprinted and given an ID bracelet. You will get a matching one.

While all those details are being attended to, you will complete your third stage of labor, which is delivering the placenta. This stage is comparatively easy after what you've just been through.

You learn about it in elementary school. You watch it in films. You read about it in books. And for nine months you learn it all again. There is no doubt in your mind that a life is growing inside you. You have even watched your unborn baby on film. You know that the day will come when your child will be ready to enter the world, and you will hold this new life in your arms. And then, that moment arrives. And all the preparation, all the knowledge and understanding, still leaves you amazed. How did this happen? You have witnessed a miracle. Words cannot describe how you're feeling.

But in your arms, you hold a true gift from God. A perfect baby clings to you, wailing. Instinctively, you comfort him, putting him to your breast, and he does what comes naturally. The world fades around you. You cannot take your eyes off this beautiful child, as you proudly realize that your body created and delivered this life.

Julie Schmidt
Rocky Hill, Connecticut

The Cesarean Birth

In a cesarean section (also known as a C-section) the baby does not emerge through the vagina. Rather, an incision is made in the abdominal wall and uterus to deliver the baby. Nearly one in every four babies in the United States is delivered by cesarean section, according to the Centers for Disease Control and Prevention, giving this nation one of the highest cesarean rates in the world.

In the early 1970s, only about 5 percent of all births were done by cesarean section. What happened in the meantime?

Better anesthesia methods, better antibiotics, better blood-banking, and better surgical techniques made cesarean sections less dangerous to perform, according to Dr. Martin. Further, he says, the use of fetal moni-

tors made it easier to keep track of the babies' well-being. The steady rise in use of fetal monitoring was accompanied by a similar rise in C-sections.

There are several valid reasons for delivering a baby by C-section. A woman is likely to need a cesarean if her baby is in distress, say, with a compressed umbilical cord that limits the blood and oxygen flow. Or, she might need the operation if the placenta has separated before the baby is born. A woman with active herpes will need a C-section to spare her baby the infection. A baby too large for the mother's pelvis, or too small and frail to withstand the rigors of a vaginal birth, also may require a cesarean delivery.

Too Many C-Sections

Medical experts say the number of cesarean deliveries is too high, and that a rate of one in six births

The Apgar Score

To get a quick read on whether your newborn baby may require medical treatment, doctors employ a uniform system known as the Apgar score. It is used to evaluate the baby's color, heart rate, breathing, reflex response, and muscle tone on a scale of 0 to 10.

The Apgar scoring is done one minute after the birth and again at five minutes after the birth.

A score of 7 to 10 means the baby is in excellent condition; a score of 5 to 7 indicates that one or more of the systems is not working at full efficiency yet; a lower score may indicate the need for resuscitation.

Do not be alarmed if your baby doesn't score a perfect 10. Many healthy babies do not, perhaps because their hands and feet are not yet pink, or because they are quietly alert rather than noisily alert. Often the scores measured after five minutes are better than those taken at one minute.

(rather than one in four) is a reasonable goal.

The rate is high despite the fact that doctors began to reconsider the frequency of using a cesarean delivery in the 1970s, when, according to the National Institutes of Health (NIH), the cesarean birth rate began to soar.

A consensus statement issued by the NIH in 1980 reported that cesareans increased about threefold between 1970 and 1978. It said the jump occurred as people began to rely more on medical specialists, such as obstetricians, rather than on general practitioners or midwives.

Because studies suggested that a C-section improved the outcomes of various complications of pregnancy, obstetricians came to favor them when confronted with, for example, abnormal fetal position that formerly required a difficult forceps delivery.

One of the factors most responsible for the rise in numbers, says the NIH report, was the increased diagnosis of a condition called dystocia. The term refers to either of two kinds of abnormal labor. The first is problems of fetal position or size. The second, however, simply can mean that the labor is not progressing well.

The consensus report suggested that, instead of performing a cesarean on a woman whose labor is not going well, doctors might look to less invasive methods—provided the fetus is not in distress. The report recommended that doctors rely more on rest, hydration, walking around, sedatives, or the use of a drug such as Pitocin to bring on productive contractions.

Studies that compare women attended by midwives or giving birth in nonhospital settings to women attended by physicians in hospitals reveal that the nonhospital/nondoctor group has considerably lower C-section rates.

The studies indicate that midwives consider some problems that might prompt a doctor to do a cesarean to be "pseudo- problems" that could be handled with less drastic measures.

Doctors admit that reading a fetal monitor can be a subjective process. A monitor is helpful because, when it shows a normal heart rate, the baby is most likely fine. But when a monitor reveals something different about the heart rate, it may pinpoint a baby who is not really in trouble. Doctors tend to put it this way: "The baby may be stressed but not in distress."

Doctors may perform a cesarean for a variety of reasons, but they would would rather chance doing an unnecessary cesarean than put a child at risk.

C-sections are now falling out of favor with both doctors and patients. HMOs are now evaluating doctors on their rate of C-sections, and those with high rates of 30 or 40 percent are in danger of being excluded from the HMO.

The bottom line here is that if your doctor recommends that you deliver your baby by cesarean section, you should know the reasons behind that decision. There are lots of good reasons for having a

C-section, and if you're going to undergo this procedure, you need to know what those reasons are in your case.

Vaginal Birth After a C-Section

What about the mother who already has had a cesarean? Is she destined to have a repeat cesarean for any subsequent pregnancy? Not necessarily. Here's the good news: Today, 60 to 80 percent of the women who attempt a vaginal birth after a cesarean have normal deliveries. One reason is a change in the location of cesarean incisions.

The belief that "once a C, always a C" originated in the early 1900s, when doctors sought to avoid the risk of uterine rupture at the scar site during labor.

In those days the scar was the result of the classic C-section incision, which was made in the thick, muscular upper body of the uterus. There was a very real risk that this kind of scar might rupture during labor. Today's cesarean incisions are usually in the lower segment of the uterus, which is thinner, tougher, and has fewer muscle fibers. These newer incisions heal more strongly and are less likely to rupture.

If you want to try for a vaginal birth after having had a cesarean, your chance of success is greater if you seek out an obstetrician who is willing to give labor a try.

Alternative Birthing

A small but growing movement toward giving birth at home developed in the 1980s and early 1990s. This is a movement that seems to fly in the face of progress and turn its back on the life-saving benefits that come from all the recent the technological advances in birthing methods.

Behind this movement is home birth's emphasis on "normalcy and nonintervention," according to a report put together by the Medical College of Pennsylvania's Department of Community and Preventive Medicine.

Women who opt to give birth at home simply want to have a baby "naturally" and to allow nature to take its course without any interference. They argue that a healthy woman who has had a normal pregnancy should be able to give birth safely at home, assisted by a doctor or midwife and supported by her family. The ideology that fuels the movement, the report says, is one that "promotes individual authority and responsibility for health and health care."

Most doctors do not support the home birth movement. They contend that a birth can be considered risk-free only in hindsight. These doctors argue that if a women runs into complications, valuable time would be lost transporting her to the hospital for emergency care. They argue that choosing a home birth can endanger both mother and child, and that the conditions of a home birth are beneath the standards of care in the United States. Some doctors (and hospitals) who have rescued mothers when a medical disaster occurs during a home birth have even been sued for malpractice.

Along about the time that interest in home birth began to grow, a similar interest developed in giving birth in out-of-hospital birth centers. Some studies conclude that birth centers offer a safe and acceptable alternative for certain pregnant women.

One such study compared the experiences of 2,000 women with low-risk pregnancies who delivered in a hospital with data from the National Birth Center's study on freestanding birth centers. The study was done by researchers at the Department of Community and Family Medicine, University of California, San Diego School of Medicine in La Jolla.

The study concluded that hospital care "did not offer any advantage for women at lowest risk," and

Water Birthing

If you think the idea of giving birth in water is just a passing fad, you're mistaken.

The idea of spending part of your labor in a hot tub or spa and maybe even delivering there "has taken off like wildfire," says Dianne Moore, Ph.D., director of the Birth Center of the Beth Israel Hospital in Newark, New Jersey, and a midwife.

"Hydrotherapy has been used for centuries in a variety of ways to help people feel better," Dr. Moore says. "People have always sought out spas, like those in Hot Springs, Arkansas, for example, to help them feel better. Today people use hot tubs, but the concept is the same: using water for therapy."

It was a natural leap for women to think of using a hot tub to ease labor pains. And that's how it started. Some women in labor became so comfortable and relaxed in the warm water that they simply wouldn't get out of the tub, and they ended up having their babies in the water, says Dr. Moore. "The first babies born in water were actually born there accidentally," she says, "but the babies did just fine."

Don't women have to worry about their babies drowning? Apparently not, says Dr. Moore. To a baby, the water in a hot tub or spa feels just like the warm fluids inside the uterus. The baby continues to "breathe" in the same way as before the birth, by taking in oxygenated blood through the umbilical cord. A baby won't try to breathe while still in the water, and as long as the umbilical cord is not cut, will continue to get plenty of oxygen, explains Dr. Moore. "The gasp reflex doesn't take place until the baby is out of water," she says.

There are a number of reasons why a woman might want to consider a water birth. "Women using the tub appear to have fewer lacerations and do not need episiotomies," says Dr. Moore. "We think it's because the skin softens and stretches more easily after being in the water."

The water in the tub is essentially body temperature and certainly no warmer than 100 degrees.

It should be noted that while water birthing is more widely available, many mainstream doctors do not favor this method. Discuss it with your doctor before making a decision.

it was associated with increased intervention.

So what do you do if you want the safety net that a hospital birth provides but long for a warm, homey, natural atmosphere for your delivery?

Giving birth in a hospital's homelike birthing unit—known as an LDRP (Labor, Delivery, Postpartum, and Recovery) unit—is a satisfactory compromise to make the birthing experience as homelike as possible for women with low-risk pregnancies, suggests Dr. Martin. A woman can feel at home "and yet enjoy the immense benefit of rapid access to emergency management of unforeseen problems" that can only be provided by a hospital obstetric unit, he says.

If you would like information about home births, here are some organizations you can contact:

• **American College of Home Obstetrics,** P.O. Box 25, River Forest, IL 60305. This organization will provide information for physicians who cooperate with couples opting for home birth.

• **Association for Childbirth at Home International,** 116 South Louise, Glendale, CA 91250. This group provides information, including publications, and support for home birth.

• **Informed Homebirth/Informed Birth and Parenting,** P.O. Box 3675, Ann Arbor, MI 48106. This group trains and certifies home-birth teachers and attendants, offers classes in home-birthing, and publishes books and newsletters on the topic.

If you would like information about out-of-hospital birthing centers, you can contact:

• **American College of Nurse-Midwives,** 1522 K St., NW, Suite 1000, Washington, DC 20005. This group provides a number of referrals and information in the form of fact sheets and brochures.

• **National Association of Childbearing Centers,** 3123 Gotschall Rd., Perkiomenville, PA 18074. This organization will provide referrals to birthing centers in your area. Send $1 for postage and handling.

Pain Relief with Hydrotherapy

To get the pain-relieving benefits of a hot tub, you don't have to actually have your baby in the water. Many women are offered the use of a hot tub when their labor becomes intense.

"A woman in labor has a need to relax," says Dr. Moore, "and the tub is simply another tool to help her relax and to ease the pain in labor."

Women say they are comfortable in the tub, where the water helps to support their weight and allows their muscles to relax. When it's time to deliver, the woman is helped out of the tub.

"We have gotten many, many inquiries from hospitals that are thinking of putting in tubs just for water therapy," says Dr. Moore.

If you want to deliver your baby in the tub, you'll have to have this understanding with your doctor ahead of time. Not all doctors favor this method of delivery, and many have no experience with it.

Meeting Your Baby

Most hospitals now allow your baby to stay in the room with you 24 hours a day. During those first precious hours, you can snuggle your baby in your arms as much as you want and place your baby in a crib when you feel the need to nap.

Another option is a system called modified rooming in, which involves keeping the newborn in the mother's room during her waking hours and putting the newborn into a nursery at night. When night-feeding time rolls around, the baby is brought to the mother's room to be fed, then returned to the nursery until morning.

A third approach is to have the baby spend all of the time, except for feedings, in the nursery, where he or she is cared for by the hospital staff. This is a good approach for a mother or child who is ill.

If you have strong preferences about how much time you want to spend with your newborn at the hospital, make sure this is part of your birth plan. You don't want to be surprised and upset when a nurse who is just doing her job whisks your newborn away to the nursery when you'd rather cuddle and coo into the wee hours of the morning.

The hospital stay is brief for most women. Your grandmother probably spent 7 to 10 days in the hospital after giving birth. Your mother probably had a 5-day stay. You'll probably go home after only 24 to 48 hours.

Here's a word of advice about what to do with your time in the hospital: Take advantage of it. This is the time to bond with your child, to stare into each other's eyes, smell each other's skin, and touch each other's hearts. It is a time sheltered from all other responsibilities, all other cares. It is your special time together.

During this time, the staff will give you a crash course in the care of your stitches and the baby's umbilical cord, diapering, and breast-feeding. Take it all in and, by all means, ask questions.

Your Beautiful Baby

Your newborn is probably absolutely gorgeous, with huge eyes and silky hair and plump little cheeks. But ... what if this little being is not exactly what you expected? Newborns are often red

I have learned many lessons in my short stint as a mother, the most important being patience and selflessness. I am no longer able to do what I want, when I want, and most of the time I am OK with that. I am a mother, and my job is to raise my son. I marvel at the new skills my son is learning. In seventeen short months, my wunderkind has learned to walk, run, and speak! Even more amazing is that he recognizes the value of smiling coyly at his parents to get his way. How did he learn this trick?

Joyce D. Neely
Grayslake, Illinois

and wrinkled, have funny little-old-man expressions (girls, too), and don't look like pretty little Gerber-perfect babies. What should you do if the first time you look at your child you see a homely little alien creature instead of the gorgeous baby you were dreaming of? Don't panic. Most of the little imperfections you may be concerned about will soon disappear on their own.

• **Spots.** About half of all newborns have little white spots called milia on their faces. These are caused by plugged pores and soon go away by themselves. African-American, Indian, and Asian babies commonly have Mongolian spots, or bluish-black spots on the buttocks, genitals, and back. These fade away, too.

• **Funny-shaped head.** Your newborn's head may be a little misshapen, having been "molded" to fit through the birth canal. The head will return to normal shape in a few days.

• **Flattened nose.** Does your newborn's nose look like it belongs to a boxer who has taken too many punches? Babies' noses often get flattened by the pressure of being born. Don't be concerned. That pancake nose will fill out within a couple of days.

• **Gunky white stuff.** Before entering the world, your newborn's skin was coated with a slippery white substance known as vernix. Some mothers call it "angel cream." This natural substance protected the skin while the baby was surrounded by amniotic fluid. It also provided lubrication, which helped during the birth. Once born, your baby will not produce any more vernix, so when it's wiped off, it's gone for good.

• **Fur.** You expect fur on your puppy, but it's quite another thing to find it on your baby. You'll probably find little furry spots on your baby's back, shoulders, earlobes, and cheeks. The fine baby hair is called lanugo. It sheds (thank goodness!) within a few months.

- **Birthmarks.** These are quite common and usually disappear by themselves. The most likely are red spots on the neck or eyelid, known as stork bites or salmon patches. Less common are the cafe-au-lait spots, which are light brown patches. Not all birthmarks disappear, however. You should discuss larger birthmarks with your doctor. These may fade later or could be removed when the child is older if they are in an unattractive location.

The Circumcision Decision

If you give birth to a son, should he be circumcised? Many doctors now hold that routine circumcision is unnecessary. Yet, because of religious beliefs or for other personal reasons, most parents still decide to have their baby boys circumcised. If you're uncertain, you should have a frank discussion of the pros and cons with your baby's pediatrician.

Without circumcision, the baby's foreskin will be tightly attached to the head of his penis during the first year. The foreskin naturally retracts in time. Eventually, your son will learn to clean the area under the foreskin when he bathes or showers. If you opt for circumcision, be assured that the operation is generally safe.

Ask your doctor about using a local anesthetic so your baby does not feel much pain. (Frequently, the surgery is performed without any anesthetic.)

After the circumcision, apply a little petroleum jelly to the incision each time you change the baby's diaper. It will keep the wound from sticking to the diaper as it heals.

What's in a Name?

The Victorians liked to name their daughters after flowers, so Rose, Daisy, Lily, and Violet were popular names at the turn of the century. Boys' names were more seriously considered. Consequently, sons were named after the father or grandfather, or given a family name to use as a first name.

Times and fashions change. Violet and Harrison eventually gave way to Tiffany and Chip, which surrendered to Ashley and Joshua.

Choosing a name is one of the most important decisions you make for your child. A name can affect your child's self-esteem and have a major impact on the way other children respond to your child. Naming a girl Dorcus, for example, is just asking for trouble.

These guidelines can help you avoid the pitfalls:

- **Avoid names that rhyme.** A child named Tracy Lacey or Richard Pritchard is in for teasing.
- **Watch those acronyms.** Skip any first and/or middle name where the initials would form an unflattering combination, such as Barbara Mitchell (BM) or Daniel Owen Goldman (DOG).
- **Don't be too cute.** Cross off any name that combines with your last name to produce something bizarrely cute, such as Penny Candy or Hank O'Hare.
- **Respect spelling rules.** Don't indulge in an offbeat spelling, such as Soozie or Phrank. It will needlessly complicate your child's life.
- **Take your time.** Don't give in to pressure to name your child before you're ready. Some parents put off the final selection of a name until they actually see baby, to be sure there's a fit.

the fourth trimester

What's this about a fourth trimester? Some kind of joke? Every mother knows that pregnancy is measured in three-month periods known as trimesters, and that there are, in fact, only three of them. So the phrase "fourth trimester" is more than a bit humorous. But at the same time, it does reflect a certain reality: An entire pregnancy, including recovery, actually takes about a year.

When you consider all that a pregnant woman experiences, a year is a brief span in which to move through a remarkable series of peaks and valleys: that first hint of something happening, morning sickness, the feelings of life stirring within you, the big belly and the backache, the labor and delivery, nursing your baby, your body returning to normal size, resuming your sex life …

So let's take a close-up look at this postpartum "trimester"—the fourth trimester, if you will. Let's consider the events, problems, and opportunities you and your family will face during the first three months following the birth of your baby. Then let's look at ways to handle them successfully.

Planning Your Recovery

Unless your delivery was complicated, you probably spent just 48 hours in the hospital before being sent home with your new baby. That's the average these days. For a healthy mother and child, spending just two days in the hospital is usually safe. And most medical problems that develop can be handled well at home with the right kind of support, says Rebecca D. Shaw, M.D., an obstetrician with an active practice in Des Moines, Iowa.

The big challenges for most new mothers are not medical. They have to do with the basic skills of caring for a newborn. In some communities, a nurse or lactation consultant visits a new mother at home within 48 hours after she is discharged from the

Do You Need a Doula?

The word "doula" is Greek, meaning "one who serves." But you don't have to go to Greece to find one. There are more than 2,000 doulas now serving pregnant women and new mothers in North America.

Once upon a time, a woman could count on her mother or sister to lend a hand, offer advice, and provide support, says Debra Pascali, president of MotherLove Inc., a home-care service for new mothers based in Ridgewood, New Jersey. But for many women those days are gone. That's where the doula comes in.

"A doula will provide nonmedical and mother-to-mother support," says Pascali. "This helper will teach the mother about caring for her baby and provide information and support for breast-feeding."

Much of the instruction given by the hospital staff can simply be lost on a woman who is still reacting to one of life's most profound events.

"A woman who comes home within 24 hours of birth is still processing the experience, so that information provided by the hospital is not really absorbed," explains Pascali. "On day two or three, a mother is more able to absorb information, and the doula will be there to provide it. Further, a doula validates that the parents can trust their instincts about caring for their baby, and that they can relax a little more. Often times they really are afraid—afraid that they'll do the wrong thing. A doula can help them listen to the baby and interpret the cues, and to trust themselves to do a good job."

Doulas can be particularly helpful in the area of breast-feeding, says Pascali: "Sometimes a mother's milk hasn't even come in yet when she is sent home, and she simply doesn't know what to do. What a mother really needs is some follow-up, as there is in Europe, where someone comes into the home to provide instruction and support, or where the family structure is still intact. The United States is one of the few countries without this kind of support."

A doula can have expertise in one of three areas: prenatal care, birth assistance, and postpartum care. Postpartum doulas usually provide their helping hands for two or three weeks after delivery, spending three to five hours a day at a home. They are trained in breast-feeding, postpartum care, CPR, and first aid. They also will cook, do laundry, and run errands while the mother tends to the baby or rests.

Doulas are paid between $15 and $25 an hour, with the East and West coasts paying the higher salaries. If you would like a referral, you can call the National Association of Postpartum Care Services in Edmonds, Washington, or write to Doulas of North America (DONA), 1100 23rd Ave. East, Seattle, WA 98112.

---

hospital. During the visit, both mother and baby receive a physical assessment. The nurse may use the visit as an opportunity to teach and reinforce parenting skills such as feeding, bathing, diapering, and caring for the baby's umbilical cord.

The problem is that not every community provides these services, and some new mothers are left to handle everything on their own.

"I would recommend having help available at home," says Dr. Shaw. "I can't say that it's essential, because it depends on a woman's individual circumstances and her prior experience. If a woman has other small children at home to care for, she probably does need help."

Beyond having an extra set of hands helping you around the house, there are a number of things you can do to get through those challenging first days:

☞ **Be a bit selfish.** For the first week or so after giving birth, you can make life easier if you simply put yourself and your baby first. (Doing so is not self-indulgent pampering; it's a matter of survival.)

☞ **Put your feet up when you can.** "Take frequent rest periods for the first few days," suggests Dr. Shaw, "and avoid playing the hostess."

☞ **Forget about doing housework.** The rug won't disintegrate if it isn't vacuumed for a week. You should put off doing anything but tasks that are absolutely essential—feeding and cuddling your baby, for example.

☞ **Be specific about the kind of help you want.** Remember, the people who love you probably are more than willing to help, but may not know what you need. Don't wait for them to figure it out: Give them direction. It's not taking advantage to ask someone to pick up the items you need from the supermarket or drugstore. It's OK to ask for help with the housework. And your mother or husband probably is in better shape now to change the bed linens than you are.

☞ **Dress the part.** Some mothers recommend that you stay in your pajamas and bathrobe for a week. This is a strategy that helps remind those around you that you are not yet back to normal and require a little extra loving care.

☞ **Put out a call for casseroles.** If you were clever enough to prepare and freeze several meals ahead of time, you'll be patting yourself on the back right now. If you never had the time for cooking in advance, ask your family and friends to bring casseroles or other prepared meals. You can also collect take-out menus from local restaurants or check the phone book for places that deliver.

The Bumpy Road Back

You're a young, strong, healthy woman. So you want and expect to be back to normal in short order. And you will be. But the road to recovery has a few potholes and bumps you should be aware of. If you are prepared for these minor problems and can sort out the normal aches and pains from the potentially dangerous ones, you'll feel more secure and confident. Here are several common problems and what to do about them.

After-Pains

Some women swear they are still having labor pains in the days following delivery. Are they imagining these pains? Is something wrong inside? The answers are: No and no.

These uterine contractions are known as after-pains. Although uncomfortable, these contractions actually help the uterus return to its normal size and stop bleeding. Women who have already had children and those who are breast-feeding are more likely to experience after-pains than others. If there is such a thing as "good" pain, this is it.

Action: After-pains usually subside in the week after delivery. If you experience these contractions longer than a week, or if they are so strong they disrupt your sleep, call your doctor or midwife. Otherwise, just think of them as involuntary uterine fitness exercises.

Pain in the Ribs

If you feel a pain in your ribs when you laugh, cough, or twist your torso, you may have strained a muscle during childbirth. (It's not called labor for nothing!)

Action: Don't concern yourself with this kind of pain. It will go away by itself in two or three days.

Bleeding

Your uterus is returning to normal size; in the process it is releasing a fluid called lochia. This fluid, which comes from the vagina, is a combination of blood, mucus, and tissue. In the first two or three days after delivering your baby, the flow will be fairly heavy and consist mostly of blood. In time, the flow will diminish and change in color, becoming pink, then brown, then finally yellow. After five or six weeks, the flow of lochia should be over. In fact, at six weeks you may again begin to menstruate.

Action: In the postpartum period, use sanitary pads rather than tampons, which can block the flow and create conditions that foster infection.

It's time to contact your doctor if:

• **The lochia smells bad.**

• **The flow of lochia lasts more than six weeks** (a sign of possible infection).

• **The flow consists of bright red blood after the fourth day following delivery.**

• **Large blood clots appear in the lochia.**

If you are bleeding heavily—filling two or three sanitary pads an hour, for several hours—call the doctor and have someone take you to the nearest emergency room. If you are alone, call 911 or request an ambulance from the hospital. Meanwhile, place a bag of ice cubes directly over your uterus. (In a pinch, you can always use a bag of frozen vegetables.)

Fever

If your temperature is above 100.4 degrees for more than six hours, you must call the doctor. The fever could well be a sign that you have a uterine infection.

"A small number of recently pregnant women will develop an infection in the uterus following vaginal or cesarean delivery," says James Martin, M.D., director of obstetrics and maternal/fetal medicine and professor of obstetrics and gynecology at the University of Mississippi in Jackson.

Action: If the temperature persists or worsens, especially if it is associated with chills, seek immediate medical attention and treatment.

Fatigue

You are deeply tired. You do a zombie walk from bedroom to bassinet and back, going through the process of feeding, burping, and diapering the baby. Your physical and emotional resources are depleted, and you really need to rest. But how can you rest when the baby needs you so frequently?

Most new mothers feel that their biggest postpartum problem is fatigue, resulting from the rigors of childbirth and being awakened by a hungry baby as often as every two hours throughout the night.

Action: How do other new mothers cope with such profound fatigue and still meet the needs of a helpless newborn? Some say a couple of catnaps throughout the day take the edge off tiredness.

Your baby is sleeping most of the time, and you can take advantage of that schedule. As soon as you put your baby down after breakfast or lunch (or both), turn on the answering machine, wheel the baby into your room, and close the door. Then go to bed. (By the way, you can turn your answering machine message into a birth announcement. It's

Finding Yourself, Restoring Perspective

Your universe now revolves around a helpless, screaming little bundle of flesh. Sure, you love your baby, but what about *you*?

Some mothers can become completely absorbed in meeting the needs of that helpless little infant—so much so that they forget they have their own lives and their own needs. Granted, the responsibility is great, but everyone needs a break now and again as a way of retaining a sense of self and a healthy perspective on life.

After the first week or so, it's a good idea to get out of the house at least once a week for a brief excursion *without* the baby, according to Rebecca Shaw, M.D., an obstetrician and gynecologist in private practice in Des Moines, Iowa.

"A woman who has been active suddenly finds herself confined with a newborn and dependent," says Dr. Shaw. "Further, her schedule is demanding and not one she is used to. A brief outing with the father, or even alone, will prevent cabin fever. Going out without the baby is a recognition of your own personal needs. And it's OK to have your own personal needs."

Some mothers are hesitant to leave their baby with someone else. "I tell the mother that it's a good idea to do this, because your marriage is very important to your baby," says Dr. Shaw. She recommends that you set up some baby-sitting arrangements before the baby is born, so that it's not so hard to find help. See "The Working Mother's Survival Guide," which begins on page 119, for advice about hiring a baby-sitter.

fun, and it gets out the news without too much effort on your part.)

If you'll baby yourself in this manner for a week or so, you'll make up some of your sleep deficit and start to feel like yourself again.

Eating well is another way to fight fatigue. Now is not the time to diet. Your body needs the full complement of protein, vitamins, and minerals to rebuild and heal itself. You need energy-producing foods to keep going. So make sure you are eating a healthy breakfast, lunch, and dinner. Keep fresh fruit and raw vegetables on hand for nutritious snacking.

If you are breast-feeding, you'll need some extra calories. See "The Wonder of Breast-Feeding," which begins on page 77.

Soreness

Most likely you've had an episiotomy, and your stitches hurt. Even if you weren't cut, your entire vaginal area is sore, swollen, and bruised from the pressure of giving birth. And, thanks to the weight and pressure of carrying a baby to term, maybe you have hemorrhoids, too. Your whole bottom is a throbbing nest of pain.

Action: Try the following ideas to ease the pain and advance the healing.

☞ **Take painkillers.** Reach for ibuprofin for pain relief.

☞ **Get local relief.** Ask your doctor to prescribe a local anesthetic spray or cream.

☞ **Keep bacteria away.** Change sanitary pads five or six times each day to keep the area clean. Always remove the pads from front to back, so that bacteria from the rectal area are not introduced into the vaginal area.

☞ **Spray and dab.** After going to the bathroom, clean the genital area using a squirt bottle filled with warm water. Dry by dabbing gently.

☞ **Flip over.** Lie on your side to relieve pressure on your bottom.

☞ **Cushion your bottom.** Whenever you spend any time sitting, put a bed pillow on your chair.

☞ **Take a warm sitz bath.** Fill the tub with just enough water to cover your hips and sit with your legs open and elevated. With your doctor's permission, you might try this technique to ease both episiotomy and hemorrhoid pain.

☞ **Avoid constipation.** If you have a tear that extends into the rectum, you should take special care not to become constipated. Your doctor may recommend stool softeners to keep you more comfortable.

Breast Pain

Unfortunately, more than your bottom may hurt. Some women also experience breast pain, particularly if they are not nursing the baby. "If you are not breast-feeding," says Dr. Shaw, "your breasts may become engorged or swollen and be somewhat painful."

Action: A good-fitting (almost tight) bra is helpful. Applying ice packs and taking small amounts of ibuprofin to ease the pain are also helpful, says Dr. Shaw. She further counsels that you avoid expressing breast milk. Breasts produce as much milk as a baby demands, and although expressing the milk may give you some temporary relief, you'll only fool your breasts into producing more.

Postpartum Blues

Have you been singing the blues ever since you had your baby? If you are, you're part of a gigantic chorus. About 70 percent of all new mothers feel somewhat blue. Why should an event so joyous trigger unhappiness?

•**Hormones.** Following childbirth, the levels of estrogen and progesterone in your body take a sharp downturn. As a result, the "baby blues" (like premenstrual syndrome, which is also caused by hor-

Call the Doctor If ...

If you are a first-time mother, you may be worrying over some of the things your body is doing right now. What is normal and what signals trouble?

Rebecca D. Shaw, M.D., an obstetrician with an active private practice in Des Moines, Iowa, says she frequently gets phone calls at night from women concerned about vaginal bleeding.

What happens, she says, is that when a woman has been lying down, the blood pools in the vagina. Then, when she stands up, the blood drains out all at once, giving the appearance of a heavy flow.

"You can experience a large amount of drainage for several minutes, and that is perfectly normal," says Dr. Shaw. "However, the heavy flow should not continue."

Call your personal physician, suggests Dr. Shaw, if you experience any of the following:

- **heavy bleeding** (needing a fresh sanitary pad every 20 to 30 minutes)
- **episiotomy stitches that are becoming more tender rather than less tender** (a sign of possible infection)
- **fever**
- **severe breast pain**
- **redness of the breast**
- **severe abdominal pain** (not just cramping)
- **burning when you urinate**
- **severe leg pain, especially if the pain is only in one leg** (may signal a blood clot)

---

mone swings) may bring you to tears for no real reason at all.

•**Fatigue.** If you're exhausted, nothing seems to go right.

•**Stress.** Let's face it. You've just started a stressful new job. You are doing the absolute best you can as a new mother, but you may feel overwhelmed by the responsibility you have for this precious life and be unsure of your parenting skills.

•**Physical appearance.** The gorgeous mane of hair you grew with the help of pregnancy hormones is probably thinning out. You may look tired and drawn, and your tummy is puffy. You don't quite fit back into your prepregnancy wardrobe. You just don't feel pretty at all, and that's depressing.

If you *are* singing the blues, here are a few ways you may be able to help yourself:

☞ **Try a change of scenery.** In nice weather, sit outdoors in the sunshine for a few minutes each day. Go for a brief walk outdoors. Ask someone to take you for a short, scenic drive.

☞ **Wait it out.** Surf through the weepiness by reminding yourself that these emotions are normal and the mood will pass in about a week.

☞ **Distract yourself.** Rent an absorbing video tape. Read a gooey romance novel.

☞ **Pass it on.** Cry on your best friend's shoulder; that's what it's for. She'd do the same for you.

☞ **Reach out and have someone touch you.** Ask your husband for cuddling hugs and kisses. Men often feel sidelined when there's a new baby in the house. Besides helping you around the house and with caring for the baby, he needs to be demonstrating his affection for you. Let him know how much you need this, and you'll undoubtedly be amazed at the response you get. If you're a single mom, ask friends and family members for hugs. You need physical expressions of affection at this sensitive time in your life.

☞ **Catch some z's.** Make sleeping a priority. Slip in an extra nap whenever you can.

You should call your doctor or midwife if you

experience frequent crying spells after the first week or two, or if you have anxiety or panic attacks, cautions Dr. Shaw. These symptoms may signal a more serious depression than the blues that commonly follow childbirth.

"About 10 percent of all women who have recently given birth can suffer from this more serious depression," says Dr. Shaw. "Other symptoms include negative thoughts about the baby or even a desire to harm the baby, and having difficulty sleeping or concentrating. Don't wait until your postpartum checkup to talk to your doctor about these feelings. Call your doctor, midwife, or nurse now. A woman with this problem probably will need professional help if it goes on for more than two weeks, but the condition usually is not a permanent thing."

Reclaiming Your Figure

You get on the scale and feel a surge of satisfaction at the new lower weight. Then you look at yourself in the mirror and the sense of satisfaction wilts away. You may ask the mirror, "What have you done with my waist?"

Don't panic. And, whatever you do, don't diet. If you're nursing your baby, you need to be getting top-quality nutrition. Anyway, dieting is not necessary, says Kenneth G. Keppel, Ph.D., a statistician and researcher at the National Center for Health Statistics in Hyattsville, Maryland. If you have gained the appropriate amount of weight during pregnancy, you should lose most of it within 10 to 18 months after delivering. If you've gained significantly more than the appropriate amount, now is the time to discuss it with your doctor.

The real problem with your waist probably isn't weight. It's more likely to be muscle tone—or, more accurately, *lack* of tone. Only exercise will bring back that firm, flat abdomen you once were so proud of.

No, You're Not Going Bald

You run a brush through your beautiful mane, and out comes a big hank of hair. What's going on here? Is this nature's way of adding insult to injury? Bad enough you're a tad paunchy, so now you're going bald, too?

Yes, indeed, your hair really is falling out. You're not imagining it. But what you may not realize is that it's all extra hair. That luxuriant mane grew because of the extra hormones your body produced during pregnancy. No more pregnancy, no more extra hormones. No more extra hormones, no more extra hair.

Sure it was nice while it lasted, but you'll be no "balder" than you were the day you became pregnant. Try not to dwell on the amount of hair you find in your brush and comb and plugging up the shower drain. Instead, treat yourself to a new hairstyle.

You can begin exercising right after the baby is born, but limit it to walking, suggests Dr. Shaw. Swimming is an excellent exercise once the vaginal bleeding has subsided, usually in three to six weeks. "And you can begin some mild abdominal exercises within the first two weeks, but the timing really depends on whether you've had a vaginal birth or a C-section," she says. "After a C-section, the doctor may not want you to do anything abdominal in the six-week period after delivery, because it may impair healing."

Mild abdominal exercises include curl-ups (shoulder and head lifts), pelvic tilts, and leg slides. Dr. Shaw does not recommend sit-ups, which she says are not a good exercise for anybody. (Most fitness experts these days recommend the curl-up in place of the old-fashioned sit-up for everyone.)

The Right Moves

Here are a few abdomen-flattening exercises to get you started. Begin modestly and listen to your body for signs of fatigue or pain. Begin with a set number of repetitions, and when the exercise begins to feel less demanding, increase that number. Ten reps is a good starting number, but if you can do only five or six, that's OK, too. Do the complete set of exercises every other day.

The pelvic tilt:

Stand with your back against the wall with your knees slightly bent. Your feet should be about 6 inches away from the wall and about 18 inches apart. Contract your abdomen and buttocks while pressing your lower back against the wall. Hold the contraction for a count of one-and-two-and-three. Repeat a total of 10 times.

Wall pushaway:

Stand facing the wall, more than arm's length away. Your feet should be parallel and about 18 inches apart. Place your hands on the wall, just slightly below shoulder level, with palms down and fingers pointing toward the center. Allow your body to move forward, keeping your back straight and your arms bent. Now push your body away from the wall by straightening your arms. This exercise will tone your upper arms and chest. You'll also feel a stretch in the back of your legs. Repeat 10 to 20 times.

The diagonal curl-up:

Lie on your back with your knees bent and your feet flat on the floor. Your arms are at your sides. Bring your chin toward your chest, being careful to keep your lower back pressed to the floor. Continue the motion, curling up with your arms reaching toward the outside of your left knee. Slowly return to the starting position. Repeat the curl, this time reaching toward the outside of your right knee. Repeat the exercise 10 times, and as you gain strength and vitality, increase the reps to 20.

The straight curl-up:

Lie on your back with your knees bent and your feet flat on the floor. Your arms are resting at your sides. With your lower back pressed to the floor, bring your chin to your chest, at the same time lifting your arms. Try to raise your upper back 6 to 8 inches off the floor. Do not raise yourself to more than a 45-degree angle. Ease back to the starting position. Repeat this exercise 10 times, gradually increasing the number to 20.

Leg slides: Lie on the floor

with your knees bent and your feet flat on the floor. Your arms are at your sides, and your lower back is pressed to the floor. Slowly stretch both legs out straight by sliding your heels along the floor. If your back arches, return to the starting position. Extend your legs only to the point where your back can remain pressed to the floor. Exercise in this range until your abdominal muscles increase in strength and you can slide your legs out fully while retaining your position with your back in contact with the floor. Repeat this exercise 10 times, gradually increasing to 20.

1

2

Resuming Relations

From a strictly physical standpoint, you can resume having sexual intercourse three weeks after delivering, provided you have stopped bleeding and the episiotomy (if you had one) has healed. Many new mothers may feel the need to wait a bit longer, and that's OK. You and your husband can express your love for each other in many ways other than vaginal intercourse. Some women wait until after their six-week checkup to be sure they are completely healed and to get a prescription for birth control before resuming sexual relations.

If fatigue or anxiety has made you less than eager to engage in sexual intercourse, talk to your mate frankly about the reasons behind the delay. He may be interpreting your lack of sexual response as a personal rejection. Further, he may already feel somewhat ignored because of your focus on the baby. Talk to him. Explain honestly and clearly what you are feeling. Perhaps you can plan a romantic evening together that will renew that special feeling you have for each other. Order a take-out dinner, put some candles on the table, wear your best perfume, and get someone to mind the baby for a couple of hours.

At first, intercourse may be a little painful, especially for women who are breast-feeding, says Dr. Shaw. "This occurs," she explains, "because nursing mothers have less estrogen coming from the ovaries. So the tissues in the vagina are less elastic and also thinner." She recommends using a commercial lubricant such as K-Y Jelly and/or a hormone cream, which the doctor must prescribe. (Do not use petroleum jelly. It can harm birth control devices and also contribute to infection.)

Hormone creams will not interfere with breast-feeding, and neither will birth control pills, although they may diminish the milk supply a little, says Dr. Shaw.

If you find intercourse uncomfortable, try various positions to see which one works best for you. Some women find that being on top of the man allows them to have more control of the amount of pressure on the pelvic area.

Postpartum Checkup

About six weeks after giving birth you'll see your doctor for a checkup. He or she will examine your cervix to make sure it's returned to normal following your delivery. The site of an episiotomy or C-section incision will be checked. Your doctor will determine whether your uterus has returned to its normal shape and location. He or she will also take your blood pressure and weigh you.

Now is the time to ask all the questions about your recovery and baby care that you've been storing up. This also is a good time to clear up any questions you still have about birth control methods.

Chapter Five

the wonder of
breast-feeding

Suppose you met up with a good fairy, and the two of you really hit it off. Suppose, as a result of your magical meeting, she granted you the use of a potion, one that magically would help restore your body to its former shape and fitness without either diet or exercise. Further, the elixir would serve as an all-natural, chemical-free aid to birth control, with no harmful side effects. It might even reduce the risk of developing breast cancer in the future.

Sound good so far? Well, the good fairy is generous with her gift and explains that you are merely the secondary beneficiary: The potion is intended primarily for your baby. This magic drink will provide complete nourishment, will ward off viruses and bacteria that might bring harm, and will prevent the onset of allergies.

This potent potable is indeed magic, for it appears—ready to consume—at the very moment that your child is hungry. What's more, it doesn't cost you a thing.

Breast-feeding indeed can sound like magic. And the act of nursing your baby can cast a love spell on you both. Back when your growing baby was still cradled inside you, you fed your little one with nourishment from your body. Now you can make a cradle of your arms and thrill as the gift of food and love flows from your body into the tiny, hungry body of your baby.

How to Begin

One might think that nursing a baby is the most natural thing in the world. Yet a fair number of women who attempt to nurse run into problems. They are willing, but thwarted by pain or circumstance. To breast-feed successfully, you must acquire the right technique. At one time, a young girl did that by watching her mother nurse younger siblings or by sitting at her sister's side as she put the newest niece or nephew to the breast. A girl watched and learned.

Now ask yourself this: How many women have

Nursing Your Baby

There is no one best position for nursing your baby. Depending on the time of day, where you will be nursing, and your baby's preference, you can try any of the following positions and nurse successfully:

Sitting: Place a pillow on your lap to raise your baby high enough to comfortably reach your breasts. You should be tummy-to-tummy with your child, with his or her lower arm around your waist. Your nipple should be right at your baby's mouth so your little one doesn't have to turn to reach it.

The football hold: Place your baby at your side, with your forearm supporting his or her back and your hand cradling the head. This hold is easier if you use a pillow to support your arm. Bring your baby directly to your nipple. This hold is especially good for mothers who have had a cesarean-section delivery.

Lying down: Lie on your side, with one arm bent behind your head and resting on the pillow. Offer the lower breast to your baby, then the upper breast. (You do not have to roll over to change sides.)

you seen—up close and personal—nurse a baby?

Please understand that your baby has what it takes to nurse instinctively. Touch your finger to a baby's cheek and his or her head will turn toward the finger, mouth opening, looking for the nipple. The movement is instinctual and is known, rather inelegantly, as the rooting reflex.

It might take a little practice and a little coaxing, but babies are programmed to nurse. Often a young father will be amazed to find that the baby he's holding is trying to suckle on his shirtfront.

Therefore, the learning is pretty much one-sided. Mom is the one who has to learn how to nurse. This requires a certain amount of patience and good humor. Most mothers who quit tend to do so in the first two weeks. But that may be just the amount of time you'll need to acquire and refine your technique.

If you intend to breast-feed, be sure to tell your hospital staff and your health care provider. Many hospitals have lactation specialists who are trained to help breast-feeding mothers. Their job is to assist you both in the hospital and after your discharge. They'll provide information and counseling to help you nurse your baby comfortably.

The First Feedings

The best time to begin breast-feeding is within the first hour or so after birth, when the baby is wide awake. This is really what your baby wants. "If a mother hasn't been medicated during labor, and if the baby isn't taken away from her, the baby will literally crawl up her abdomen, find the nipple, latch on, and start suckling—without help," says Jan Barger, R.N., a lactation counseling instructor in Wheaton, Illinois.

If babies are allowed to nurse in the first hour, says Barger, "they often go into a deep sleep that can last for several hours."

The first few times your baby nurses, he or she may seem more interested in nuzzling your breast than in getting down to serious business. That's perfectly normal, and the nuzzling will give your child comfort and pleasure.

During the first two days or so after giving birth, your breasts are not producing milk yet. Instead, they are producing colostrum, the perfect nutrient for a newborn. Colostrum is a rich, yellowish fluid that provides everything your baby needs in the first days of life. It is full of substances produced by your immune system—antibodies and immunoglobulins—to protect your baby from illness.

The naturally low volume of colostrum when you first begin nursing gradually increases as you continue to breast-feed, which helps your baby's tiny tummy adapt slowly to taking in larger

One of the most wonderful aspects of motherhood has got to be breast-feeding. Aside from the sheer convenience of never having to worry about whether the milk is warm, or whether you've brought enough bottles with you, or whether the bottles have spoiled, or trying to mix a bottle in the middle of the night, there is just something about holding a newborn to your breast and watching him/her nurse for the first time. Watching your baby grow and thrive because of your milk is a wonderful feeling!

Stacey LeDoux
Baton Rouge, Louisiana

amounts of fluid. You may not experience the sensation of your breasts emptying suddenly (often called the let-down reflex) but your body is doing just what it is supposed to do. Your milk will come in between the second and fourth day after delivery.

Nurse your baby on cue, probably every 1½ to 3 hours. What's known as "cue-based feeding," explains Barger, is done whenever your infant shows signs of hunger. These signs include sucking motions, rooting, mouthing, making fists, and bringing the fists to the mouth or around the head.

"Babies will do this for 20 to 30 minutes before they start to cry," says Barger. These are golden moments when your newborn is less likely to have difficulty taking the breast and will settle down easily for a good feed.

Sometimes your newborn may want to nurse for only 3 or 4 minutes. Other times, the nursing may last for 15 to 30 minutes. Be patient and enjoy the experience whether it's short or long. In a few weeks, your baby's system will mature so that the two of you will fall into a feeding schedule that works for both of you.

Getting Ready

Nursing is something you're going to be doing for a long time, usually for several months. It helps to pay attention to your technique right from the start.

One of the most important factors in successful breast-feeding is the way the baby takes the nipple and areola (the colored portion of the breast sur-

Positions for Nursing

Lying down: You'll probably be more comfortable nursing while sitting up, but nursing while lying down can be an nice alternative if you need to put your feet up for a while.

Football hold: Some women find it more comfortable to more or less tuck the baby under one arm.

Sitting down: This classic nursing position is probably the one you'll use most often. Remember, there's no one correct position. Do what feels right for you.

Hint: To tell if your baby has latched on properly, look at his or her face. If dimples appear in the cheeks, your baby is not properly latched on, and you will have to start the feeding again in the correct position. Also, if nursing is painful to you for more than 20 to 30 seconds, you'll have to start over. If your baby has latched on properly, his or her ears will be moving in time with the muscle action of the jaws and cheeks. As your infant sucks, the pressure on your milk sinuses in the areola releases the milk, which then flows through the nipple.

Problems with Your Nipples

When it comes to providing milk, not all nipples are created equal. Sometimes a baby has trouble latching on if Mom's nipples are flat, dimpled, or inverted.

Flat or dimpled nipples: The problem can become worse if the breasts become engorged with milk. With engorgement, even normal nipples may flatten. However, you can overcome the problem with a little patience and a little effort.

First, try to nurse your baby as soon after birth as possible. Often the baby will latch on during these first hours and continue to do well.

Flat nipples can be made to stand out if you gently roll them between thumb and forefinger, or if you apply ice to them just before nursing.

You also can gently compress the breast behind the areola, thereby creating a little wedge at the tip of the breast that the baby can latch onto.

Inverted nipples: This problem usually requires more aggressive treatment. Try using a breast shell that is designed specifically to draw out the nipple. These are available in maternity shops or from your hospital's maternity unit.

The shell consists of two sections: a bottom part with an opening for the nipple and a top that holds your bra away from the emerging nipple.

Shells can be worn during the last stage of pregnancy or after birth between feedings.

When nursing, help the baby to latch on by placing your thumb above the areola and your fingers below. Then gently push your breast back toward your ribs. This action will clear the nipple and areola so the baby can latch on.

rounding the nipple) into his or her mouth to suck. This is known as latching on.

To get your baby to latch on properly, nestle into a comfortable spot such as a rocking chair or a chair with arms. You'll need the arms to help you hold the baby properly without fatigue. Put a big bed pillow on your lap to raise your baby up to the level of your breasts. By using a pillow, you don't have to stoop over, and your baby doesn't have to stretch to reach you.

Hold your baby so that his or her head is supported by the crook of your elbow. Your baby should be facing you, and your baby's body should be in a straight line with ear, shoulder, and hip all in a row.

Bring your baby to your breast. Take your breast in one hand, with four fingers underneath and your thumb on top forming the letter C. Your hand will direct the nipple and areola, and mold it into a more compact shape. Make sure your fingers are behind (not on) the areola.

Tickle your baby's lower lip with the nipple until the mouth opens as wide as a yawn. Once the mouth is open, quickly pull your baby closer, positioning your areola in the center of his or her mouth. As feeding begins, your baby's nose and chin should be touching your breast, but should not be obstructed.

Latching On With Precision

To ensure a successful nursing session, there are a few things you should pay attention to. Be sure that:

• Your baby's lower lip has not been drawn into his or her mouth along with the areola.

• You do not bend to your baby, but your baby is drawn to you.

• A good portion of the areola is in your baby's mouth.

• Your baby's head is not turned to the side, but faces your breast fully and comfortably.

• Your areola and nipple are positioned

I often wonder why women do not choose to nurse their children. With my first child we lived in a cozy cabin in Montana, without running water or electricity. Even though I worked part-time, nursing was the only option! Just think: No bottles to wash or warm. You always have the right mixture, right amount, right temperature... and it's on tap! Life was easy in those days!

Kris Carlson
Somers, Montana

above your baby's tongue, not below or to the side.

If your baby sucks on just your nipples, the constant pressure of the gums and rubbing of the tongue will cause your nipples to crack and bleed. With proper positioning, however, your areola fills your baby's mouth, and your nipple is positioned at the back of the mouth, well away from the chewing action of the gums

You may feel some momentary discomfort in the first week or two as your baby latches on to your breast and begins to suckle, but as your milk starts to flow, your nipples should not hurt. Once your baby has successfully latched on, your nipples will not hurt, but you may feel a little tugging. In fact, nursing is an enjoyable sensation for most women.

Lactation counselors maintain that a good many cases of nipple soreness—one of the main reasons a woman is likely to give up nursing—are caused by improper positioning.

Other problems, such as bleeding, infections, plugged ducts, low milk supplies, and fussy babies, also may be caused by improper positioning. Occasionally, however, these problems crop up for other reasons. If improving your positioning technique does not seem to help, you'll need to consult with a lactation counselor to explore the cause.

New mothers "need to realize sometimes there are problems that, despite positioning 'right,' are beyond their immediate control and for which they may need help," says Jan Barger. She worries that mothers may think that problems, should they arise, are "their fault" because they were not nursing "the right way."

82

The bottom line is, if you're having problems with nursing your baby, don't fret about it. Get help. Your doctor can put you in touch with a lactation counselor who will help answer your questions and get things going in a way that is comfortable and satisfying for you and your baby.

Getting Enough Nourishment

When your baby has nursed for as long as he or she wants to, your breast will be fairly empty. By allowing your baby to empty the breast, you assure that the baby has taken in two kinds of milk: foremilk and hindmilk. *Foremilk* flows when you begin nursing. It's high in protein, low in fat, and digested quickly. "Because it is digested so quickly, it can cause the baby to have some cramping, especially if the mother's breasts are overfull," says Barger. *Hindmilk*, on the other hand, is rich in fat, loaded with calories, and takes longer to digest.

One thing you don't want to do is switch your baby to the other breast before the first one is empty, says Barger. "A common mismanagement concept that is still in most of the books" calls for switching the baby over after 10 minutes or so. The problem in doing that is that the baby never gets the super-rich hindmilk.

Instead, allow your baby to feed as long as he or she wants to on the first breast. "When the baby starts to doze at the breast, then mom can take him off, burp him, and offer the second side," she says. "There is no rule that babies must take both breasts at each feed. Sometimes they will and sometimes they won't."

Before you can remove your baby from your breast, you'll have to break the suction. (The first time you nurse, you'll be amazed at how strong the suction is.) To do this, insert your finger into the

Your Nursing Wardrobe

Several times a day you need to bare your breasts so your baby can nurse. What should you wear?

Think convenience. You'll want to wear clothing that allows your baby to have easy access to your breast. Line up any blouses you own that button down the front. Dig out any loose sweaters or sweatshirts. Wear half-slips if you wear a dress or skirt.

These clothes allow not only for easy nursing, but also discreet nursing. If you open the flap of your nursing bra then move your baby into position, a bulky sweater or sweatshirt will cover the breast and the baby's face. To the casual observer, you're simply cuddling a baby.

An open blouse front can be disguised by positioning a receiving blanket or diaper over your shoulder, blocking your nursing baby from view. Again, all the world will assume that you are simply holding your baby.

It's a sad situation, when a nursing mother feeding her baby has to scurry for cover, while the public accepts billboards, television shows, and movies that exploit breasts as objects of sexuality. Go figure.

corner of your baby's mouth between the gums and wait to feel the release. Now burp your baby gently by holding him or her upright, facing your body and cuddled against you. Pat your baby's back gently until the burp comes. You might want to drape a clean cloth over your shoulder to catch the almost inevitable spit-ups.

Repeat the whole nursing procedure on the other breast. Your baby may not nurse as long or as vigorously at the second breast because of a full tummy. Therefore, this breast will not produce as much milk as the first because there is less demand on it. To ensure that both breasts are making as much milk as your baby needs, it's necessary to alternate the breast that is offered first. To be sure you remember, put a safety pin on the shoulder strap or flap of your bra on the side of the breast that should go first at the next feeding.

You also can keep track by offering the breast that feels heaviest. That breast is the one that's most full of milk, whether it was offered at the last feeding or not.

Once you've finished nursing, there's no need to wash your nipples or swab them with an antiseptic to sterilize them. The fact is, you have your own built-in nipple sterilizer. While your baby was nursing, glands surrounding your nipple, called Montgomery glands, secreted a substance that kills bacteria. Too vigorous or too frequent washing, or using something such as alcohol, will lead to dry, sore nipples. In fact, you should clean your nipples only with clear water when you shower or bathe.

Some Common Mommy Problems

Sometimes a nursing mother will run into a few glitches, little problems that are more annoying than they are serious. You can handle most of them by yourself.

Sore Nipples

At one time women were encouraged to toughen their nipples with massage before the birth of the baby in an attempt to prevent soreness. But this technique is no longer considered a prerequisite to successful breast-feeding now that the experts have discovered the importance of proper positioning.

Proper positioning will go a long way toward preventing soreness. In the correct position, your nipple will be at the back of your baby's mouth, protected from the pressure of gums and tongue. But even if you do everything right, you may occasionally have a bit of soreness to contend with.

Here are a couple of other techniques that may prove helpful:

☞ **Save the painful side for last.** Begin nursing on the side that is least sore. Your baby nurses more vigorously on the first breast offered.

☞ **Ice and rinse.** Put ice on your nipples before nursing and some breast milk on them after you are finished. Allow them to air-dry.

☞ **Get help.** If your nipples remain sore, call your doctor, who will check for infection, and a lactation consultant. Support groups such as the International Lactation Consultants Association can recommend a certified lactation consultant in your area. Or, consult your phone book for the number of the LaLeche League.

Leaking

Almost all new mothers leak milk at some time. Depending on circumstances, leaking can be excruciatingly embarrassing or completely inconsequential. Here's how to deal with it:

☞ **Soak up the excess.** If you do not want any leaking to show in public, use disposable nursing pads. They fit into your bra and absorb wetness. You also can use clean handkerchiefs or scraps of soft flannel—any absorbent material that will not irritate your nipples. If you use folded pieces of cloth as padding, be sure to wash them as needed.

☞ **Ban plastic.** If you use disposable nursing pads, avoid those with plastic liners. They hold in the moisture, which can lead to sore nipples. If you are going somewhere special and wearing something special, however, you won't hurt yourself by using a pad with a plastic liner on those occasions.

☞ **Push your off button.** Sometimes a mother will begin to leak while she is nursing, when the breast not being suckled begins to flow. In that case, simply press the breast gently toward the chest wall to stop the leaking.

Mothers also can begin to leak when they hear another baby cry. If this happens, just follow the same procedure, pressing the breast toward the chest wall.

How to Buy the Perfect Nursing Bra

A nursing bra isn't absolutely necessary, of course, but it sure is convenient. Here's what to look for:

•**Easy access.** You'll want a nursing bra that has flaps on the cups that can be opened easily with one hand, so you can hold your baby in one arm as you get ready to nurse.

Make sure the cups are made of a smooth, comfortable fabric, one that will not irritate your skin or your baby's sensitive face. Buy at least three bras, so you'll always have a clean one on hand.

•**Comfort.** Once you have selected a bra, make sure it fits properly and isn't too tight or binding. It should be comfortable to wear when the hooks are fastened in the middle set of eyes.

The bra should support you securely under each breast, but be roomy on top so there is room for your breasts to expand when your milk comes in. You also may want to allow sufficient room for an absorbent breast pad or shield.

•**Proper fit.** To determine your nursing bra size, you will need two measurements: your body size and your cup size. Take the measurements while you are wearing your most comfortable bra.

For the body size, measure under your bust around the bottom band of your bra, then add 5 inches to this measurement. The total is your body size. If that measurement is an uneven number, add 1 inch.

Determine your cup size by measuring around the fullest part of your breasts. Subtract your body size. The difference determines your cup size. Each inch of difference represents one cup size.

For example, if your body size is 36 and your bust measurement is 40, subtract 36 from 40. The difference is 4 inches, indicating a cup size D.

Difference in size	Cup size
1 inch	A cup
2 inches	B cup
3 inches	C cup
4 inches	D cup
5 inches	DD cup

Wash your nursing bras often, because milk leakage is common. Do not wear the same bra more than one day without washing it. Nursing pads also should be changed as they become damp.

Engorgement

Occasionally milk can build up in your breasts so they feel uncomfortably full. If your breasts are hard to the touch and warm, they may be engorged with milk. Don't confuse engorgement with the normal fullness you feel in the first weeks of nursing.

The engorgement of the first few weeks, which is known as primary engorgement, happens when the colostrum changes to milk. The breasts naturally get full, firm, and heavy at that time from all the extra blood and lymph that they contain. Here's what to do to deal with primary engorgement:

☞ **Nurse your baby.** Once your baby has learned to latch on so you can nurse in comfort, the condition resolves itself.

☞ **Get rid of some milk.** If your breasts are so swollen that the nipple has flattened and latching on is impossible for your baby, you need to express some to soften the areola. Only then will the baby be able to nurse.

☞ **Use cold compresses.** You can try applying ice packs to your breasts to reduce the swelling.

☞ **Relax in the shower.** Take a warm shower with the water running on your back. After you've relaxed a bit, gently massage your breasts to release some milk.

If your breasts become engorged after your milk is established, this condition is called secondary engorgement. It happens if the baby sleeps through a feeding, for example, and your breasts become overfull with milk. Here's how to deal with secondary engorgement:

☞ **Give your baby the breast.** Nursing the baby will help take care of the problem.

☞ **Get warm.** Put a warm washcloth on your breasts or take a warm shower to help the milk flow and thereby relieve the pressure. You also can massage your breasts to release a little milk before feedings. To prevent engorged breasts in the future:

☞ **Don't skip feedings.** Nurse at least 8 to 12 times a day with both breasts.

☞ **Be a night owl.** You need to nurse frequently at night as well as during the day.

☞ **Check your technique.** Be sure your baby has latched on properly and is nursing in the proper feeding position.

Breast Infection

If you have a fever or feel like you have the flu, and if one of your breasts is red and tender to the touch, you probably have a breast infection. Here's how to cope:

☞ **Warm your breast.** Put wet, warm compresses on the sore breast for a few minutes before nursing. A disposable diaper run under warm water will hold the heat for about 15 minutes and makes a convenient, effective compress. (The secret is in the water-holding gel.)

☞ **Do not stop nursing.** In fact, you may feel considerably better if you nurse more often. It may help to offer the painful breast first.

☞ **Get medical help.** Call your doctor, whether or not you have a temperature. You may need antibiotics to knock out the infection. It may help to stay in bed for a day.

Not Enough Milk

Successful breast-feeding works on the supply-and-demand principle. The more milk your baby demands, the more milk your body supplies. If you think you don't have enough milk, here's what you can do:

☞ **Nurse more frequently.** Allow your baby to remain at the first breast as long as you can hear

Is Your Baby Getting Enough to Eat?

You can be sure your baby is getting enough milk if you answer YES to the following questions:

1. Does your baby have six or more wet diapers a day?

2. Is your baby content after feedings?

3. Are you nursing eight to 12 times each day?

4. Does your baby have soft, yellow stools? (Two a day or even one after each feeding is normal. After two months, however, a totally breast-fed baby may have a bowel movement only once a week.)

5. Has your baby gained enough weight by the second week of life to equal or exceed birth weight?

6. Is your baby gaining at least a pound a month?

7. Does your baby feed vigorously, with a good sucking motion?

If your answer is NO to any of these questions, discuss your concerns with your doctor (first choice) or lactation consultant. You might try nursing your baby more frequently and letting your baby nurse longer each time. Don't offer water or formula. Increased nursing will produce more milk.

swallowing. Then switch to the second breast, again listening for swallowing. Repeat the process at least once. Some mothers time nursing intervals, but Barger says that watching the length of time your baby spends nursing at each breast is not as effective as listening for swallowing. Sometimes a baby can spend 20 minutes at the breast, with much of the time used for nuzzling rather than eating. You need active feeding to increase milk flow. After about 48 hours, your milk supply will increase.

☞ **Double your milk delivery.** Allow your baby to feed actively on each breast, then repeat the process immediately.

☞ **Nurse on demand.** Don't follow a feeding schedule. Allow at least one hour between feedings, but then offer your breast to your baby whenever he or she shows signs of being hungry.

☞ **Limit your baby's menu.** Don't offer your baby formula, water, or other food.

☞ **Take care of yourself.** Always drink when you feel thirsty, eat sensibly, and get plenty of rest.

☞ **Check your medications.** If you are taking any medications, check with your doctor to see if they might be interfering with milk production, or if they will have an adverse effect on your baby. Aspirin, for example, can lower your milk concentrations. Antihistamines can cause your baby to become so drowsy and irritable he or she may refuse to feed. Certain antimigraine drugs can cause your baby to vomit, have diarrhea, or even have convulsions.

Tender Breast Lumps

If you find a tender lump in one of your breasts or in the areola, you may have a plugged milk duct. The area around the lump may be red, and you may feel achy. Here's what to do about it:

☞ **Try warmth and massage.** Apply a warm compress on the lump before feedings and gently massage the area to help release the plug.

☞ **Let your baby do the unplugging.** Offer the affected breast to your baby first and try to position your baby so his or her chin is close to the sore spot. After a few feedings, the plug will dislodge, eventually coming out of the nipple. It may look like a strand of thin spaghetti.

☞ **Take it easy.** This is easier said than done with a new baby in the house, but if you're feeling achy, try to get as much bed rest as you can.

☞ **Get medical help.** Call your doctor if you have a fever or if the plug is not moving toward the nipple after several feedings.

Here's what to do to prevent plugged ducts:

☞ **Nurse often.** It's important for you to be feed-ing your baby a good 8 to 12 times a day.

☞ **Vary your technique.** Change your nursing positions often by sitting, lying down, or using the football hold (see page 80.)

☞ **Give your breasts some room to work.** Position your baby so you don't have to compress your breast to make an airway for your baby's nose.

☞ **Check your bra.** You should be wearing a good nursing bra that is not too tight. Avoid bras with underwires, push-up pads, or other features that compress the breasts.

☞ **Check your baby carrier.** Do not use a front baby carrier if it fits tightly. Your breasts should not be compressed between nursings.

Cosmetic Breast Surgery

Breast enlargement surgery usually does not interfere with breast-feeding. Breast reduction surgery, however, may interfere, if the nerve endings or ducts around the areola were severed during surgery. If you've had cosmetic breast surgery, you should let your doctor know about any nursing problems you are experiencing.

Some Common Baby Problems

Often it takes a little while for your baby to settle into a nursing routine. Some babies would rather sleep through their feedings, others become so excited they cry frantically, and a few attempt to squirm away from the breast. Here's an overview of the more common problems and what to do about them.

The Sleepyhead

You're trying to feed your baby. Your baby soon seems more interested in visiting the Land of Nod. Here's how to handle it:

Feeding the Preemie

Evidence suggests that breast milk protects premature infants from potentially life-threatening infections. The problem is that premature babies seem to have trouble bulking up on breast milk. There does seem to be a way of getting around that particular problem, however.

Reports from researchers at the Children's Nutrition Research Center in Houston say that preemies show a significant increase in weight when they are fed exclusively on hindmilk. Hindmilk is that breast milk that comes in two or three minutes after the initial flow, or foremilk. Hindmilk is three to four times richer in fat and calories than foremilk.

Because premature babies cannot suck or swallow, they must be fed regulated amounts of breast milk through a tube. When that breast milk is hindmilk, they receive more calories in each feeding.

The researchers followed 15 infants at Texas Children's Hospital who were 8 to 12 weeks premature. Lactation consultants taught mothers to divide their milk during routine expressions. The hindmilk was delivered to the hospital each day and fortified with protein and minerals.

If you have a premature baby and want to nurse, you might ask your doctor about following this procedure to help your baby gain weight quickly.

☞ **Don't try to interrupt a deep sleep.** If your baby's arms show resistance to being moved, and if you see mouthing movements, your baby is in a light sleep. In a deep sleep, your baby's limbs will be completely limp and unresponsive. If your baby's in a deep sleep, save the feeding for later.

☞ **Try a little cool air.** Gently pick up your little dozer and take him or her to the changing table. Remove all the clothing but the diaper. Still asleep? Change the diaper—yes, even if it's still clean. Cool air on the bottom usually does the trick. Still sleeping? Pat your baby's legs with a cool, damp cloth or rub his or her back.

The Town Crier

A baby who cries when you attempt to nurse may simply be upset by being awakened or may be really, really hungry and not able to understand that you are trying to remedy the situation.

☞ **Go full speed ahead.** Working quickly and with confidence, wrap your baby securely in a receiving blanket and pull him or her into the nursing position. As soon as your baby smells your breast and feels your skin, understanding will dawn and your little one will get down to business.

☞ **Try the finger trick.** You also can put your finger into your baby's mouth, pad side up, to elicit the sucking response. This trick usually works to calm the baby so you can offer your breast.

The Squirmy-Wormy

Don't take it personally if your baby tries to pull away from you at feeding time.

☞ **Be patient.** Maybe your little one just needs to settle down. Swaddle your baby tightly in a receiving blanket. Gently cuddle your baby for a few minutes, then bring him or her to the breast.

☞ **Do a health check.** If your baby is refusing to eat, check his or her mouth for thrush, a condition that may be causing oral discomfort. (See pages 201–202 for a description of this condition and what to do about it.)

☞ **Review your diet.** Have you been eating highly spiced food? Some experts maintain that many food flavors affect the taste of breast milk. You may have to forgo the garlicky salad dressing.

☞ **Get medical help.** If your baby refuses to eat two times in a row, you'll need to alert your pediatrician. The problem may be thrush, an ear infection, or even something more serious.

Minor Physical Impairment

Occasionally a baby may be "tongue-tied," which means the little stringlike tissue known as the frenulum that anchors the tongue to the bottom of the mouth may be too short or attached too closely to the tip of the tongue. With this very rare condition, the baby may not be able to latch on. If you suspect this problem, try the following:

☞ **Take the tongue test.** Touch your baby's tongue with your finger. Most babies react by sticking out their tongues. If your baby cannot do this, be sure and tell the doctor.

☞ **Seek medical attention.** If your baby is tongue-tied, the frenulum must be clipped to free the tongue. The simple procedure takes only a minute. Some physicians, however, are reluctant to perform this procedure because studies have shown that being tongue-tied does not lead to speech difficulties. Explain that the nature of the problem is inability to breast-feed.

Back to Work

If you are dedicated to breast-feeding but have to go back to work and leave your baby for long periods of time, take heart. You can continue to nourish your baby with breast milk only. But you'll have to be both organized and creative to succeed. If you determine that offering just breast milk creates more stress than joy, you can always offer your baby formula along with your breast milk.

If you want to continue feeding your baby breast milk only, follow this road map to success:

☞ **Have a plan.** Two to four weeks before you return to work, begin to stockpile breast milk in the freezer. Express your milk a few times each day. (Try nursing your baby on one side and expressing the other at the same time.) Consider what your schedule for nursing will be when you return to work and try to approximate that schedule.

When your baby is about a month old, begin to offer a supplemental bottle of breast milk. This practice will help the baby get used to nursing from

The Nursing Father

Your husband may feel great joy at watching his very own madonna and child. But let's face it, he wouldn't be human if he isn't feeling just a little left out. It's not at all unusual for a man to feel sidelined when watching his wife nurse their new baby.

What can you do to make sure your husband feels more a part of this cozy family picture? Consider making nursing more of a communal activity by occasionally nursing your little one at night in bed with your husband. Your husband can cuddle both of you while you nurse. Up close and comfortable, he can listen to your baby's contented breathing and the energetic sucking and swallowing.

Once your baby's done nursing on one breast, let your husband hold the baby for a while, maybe even going for a burp, before you offer the other breast.

Once your milk comes in and your baby has become adept at breast-feeding, you can express enough to fill an occasional bottle for a relief feeding. Your husband can feed the baby while you take a nap, go shopping, or head out for some fresh air and recreation.

a bottle. Your baby may accept the bottle more readily when someone else offers it.

☞ **Schedule bottle feedings.** When you return to work, nurse your baby early in the morning, then again at the sitter's house or day-care center just before you leave the baby. Provide the sitter or center with the feeding schedule you have developed, as well as the proper number of bottles of breast milk. Ask the caregiver to feed the baby at or near the scheduled times. Stress that you do not want the baby to be given a bottle just before you arrive from work.

☞ **Try for a lunch nursing.** Your life will be a lot easier if you can find a caretaker at or near your work, because close proximity may allow you to breast-feed your baby during your lunch hour.

☞ **Use a breast pump at work.** You will have to find a time and a place to express your breast milk for the next day. You also will need a cool place to store the milk until you leave work. You can pump or hand-express your breasts every three hours. Most women prefer a pump for speed and efficiency. Lactation consultant Jan Barger recommends using a one that can pump both sides at the same time. These efficient pumps can be rented almost anywhere in the United States, she says.

☞ **Keep your milk safe.** Store your milk in a sterile bottle or disposable nurser bag. Put enough milk for one feeding in each bottle or bag. If you plan to freeze the milk in a bag, use double bags or put several into a larger freezer bag that seals.

Label the bottle or bag with the date, so you can be sure you are using up the older milk first. Your milk will last three days in the refrigerator and three months in the back of a freezer set at zero degrees. If your place of work does not have a refrigerator or freezer available, bring an insulated cooler and pack the milk on ice.

☞ **Take advantage of your time with your baby.** Your baby may want to nurse more often when you are together. This increased frequency is a good opportunity to ensure that you will continue to produce sufficient milk.

☞ **Consider the formula approach.** If you want to supplement your breast milk with formula while you are at work, ask your pediatrician to recommend a formula. Make it clear to the doctor that you're talking about supplemental bottles.

Two to four weeks before you return to work, begin to offer the bottle of formula at one of the feedings you will miss when you are at your job. Each week, replace one additional breast-feeding with one formula feeding.

Don't feel you are letting your baby down if you choose this method. Any amount of time you spend nursing is good for your baby and for you, too. And remember, your baby will be much happier and calmer if you are happy, calm, and not feeling guilty.

When Nursing Is Impossible

Sometimes it happens that a woman cannot or should not nurse her baby. And there are all kinds of reasons why that might happen.

Some women experience a condition known as low-milk syndrome, meaning that their breasts do not produce enough milk to nourish the baby.

Contrary to lore, a bottle of beer (or any other alcohol) will not increase milk flow. According to a Tufts University nutrition newsletter, infants drank 22 percent *less* milk when their mothers consumed alcohol before nursing.

Low-milk syndrome is not common, but doctors are seeing more of it in recent years. In the past, the condition usually was detected while mother and child were still in the maternity ward.

With today's quick discharge, women with the syndrome go home from the hospital without ever knowing a problem may exist. (If you are concerned that your baby may not be getting enough milk, please see "Is Your Baby Getting Enough to Eat?" on page 86.

If you have a debilitating illness, a serious infection, or if you are extremely underweight, your health care provider may advise you not to nurse. Anyone with AIDS should definitely not nurse, because the disease can be passed along to the baby in the breast milk.

If you must take medicine every day to control a health problem such as high blood pressure or anxiety, and if that medication will pass into your breast milk, you may be advised that you should not nurse.

If you're planning on nursing, your doctor should know about any drugs you're taking.

Chapter Six

mastering the basics

Just look at your little baby, lying there so helpless and frail. Handling such a fragile being can make some first-time parents approach their newborns with trepidation.

Well, here's a news flash. That "fragile being" is programmed for survival. One prime example is known as the rooting reflex, which enables a newborn to know exactly where to find food. This is an innate response that causes the baby to turn toward anything touching him or her around the mouth. In theory, Mom could be completely unaware, but if her breast happened to be near her baby's mouth, the little one would root around, find it, and suckle.

A baby also has protective reflexes that help in threatening situations. Say, for example, that an object such as a blanket accidently covers the newborn's nose and mouth. These reflexes will kick in, and the little one will try to nuzzle the item away.

If mouthing doesn't work, the baby will turn his or her head vigorously from side to side to get free of the object. And if that doesn't work, the baby will fling his or her arms about in an attempt to bat it away.

This is not to suggest that your baby is indestructible. Not at all. But neither is an infant made of spun glass. Babies, generally speaking, are tough enough to withstand any well-intentioned, new parent mistakes you may make. So try to relax. Trust that you will learn and grow as a parent, and that the love you feel for your child will guide you.

It's not difficult to master the basics of baby care. Maybe you feel as if you're all thumbs in the first days at home with your child, but awkwardness will quickly disappear as new routines become familiar, as you grow in understanding of your baby's signals, and as your baby settles down.

The following rundown of some of the basics—from how to hold your baby to ways to recognize and respond to emergencies—will help add to your confidence.

The Security Hold

The first day back from the hospital, you walk across your threshold with your little bundle in your arms. You carry your baby to the wonder-

Inborn Talent:
Your Baby's Reflexes

If your doctor taps your knee with a rubber mallet in just the right spot, your foot will jump. You're undoubtedly familiar with that particular reflex. But did you know that your infant came equipped with a number of built-in reflexes?

Many of these reflexes are protective. Not only are they interesting to observe, but understanding them can help you know why your baby does some of the wonderful—and even wacky—things that can leave you wondering. Here's what babies can do:

Moro reflex: When babies feel a sudden change of position, they act startled, throwing out their arms and legs. Their heads drop backward and their necks extend. Then they cry briefly and rapidly bring their arms together and flex their bodies as if to grasp something while falling. Once this reflex action has passed, they'll settle down if they get a little security. They need to be held firmly for a few minutes. Swaddling (wrapping snugly in a blanket) works, too.

Rooting reflex: In an attempt to find a nipple to suck, babies will turn toward any object that touches their mouths or cheeks.

Sucking reflex: Should anything touch a baby's soft palate (the roof of the mouth toward the back), he or she will suck on it.

Grasp reflex: If you touch the palm of a baby's hand, the baby will grasp your finger. If you touch a baby's foot at the base of the toes, the toes will curl in a grasp-like reflex.

Babinski reflex: If you stroke the sole of a baby's foot, the toes will spread out, and the big toe will point upward.

Hand-to-mouth reflex: When babies' cheeks or palms are stroked, their mouths will open. At the same time, their arms will bend and their tiny hands will go right into their mouths. This particular reflex usually ends in babies learning how to suck on their own fingers.

Protective reflex: In addition to the protective reflex that responds to objects covering a baby's nose and mouth, a baby will try to flee from a painful stimulus or force the stimulus to flee. For example, if your baby were pinched on one foot, your baby would flex a knee to pull that foot away. If flexing didn't work, your baby would take the opposite foot, cross it over the body and use it to bat away the painful pincher.

Also, if placed face down, your baby will lift up his or her head and turn it to the side to aid in breathing freely.

Amphibian reflex: Your baby can propel forward under his or her own power by extending and flexing the arms and legs and swinging the trunk of the body from side to side. Using this reflex, your baby moves a bit like an alligator.

Stepping reflex: When your baby is held upright with feet touching any flat surface, he or she will lift one foot then the other, stepping along as though having already mastered the art of walking.

ful bassinet you outfitted with the greatest of care and place the little one on the tiny mattress to rest. And your baby screams. Why? What happened?

Often, the way you handle your baby can determine whether he or she will settle down contentedly or become upset and cry. When babies are jostled, they react instinctively by flailing their arms and legs and crying. This reaction is called the Moro reflex, and it can set off a chain of crying and flailing that leaves the baby (and you) completely exhausted and miserable.

To keep this from happening, hold your baby securely. When you pick up your baby, tuck one arm under the baby's back with your hand under the head. Now bend down to your baby, and rise slowly, with the baby gently pressed against your chest. When you put your baby down, simply reverse the procedure, holding your baby to your chest until he or she just about reaches the mattress. If it's necessary, gently pat or stroke your baby until he or she is settled.

Before you leave your baby for naptime, check the room's temperature. Babies can become chilled easily. Be sure your baby's bed is out of any drafts. Be sure your baby is covered by a blanket—a light one in summer if the temperature is below 72, a quilt or heavier blanket in cooler weather or if your home is air-conditioned.

The Formula for Success

What about feeding your baby? If you're nursing, you've got a built-in, ready-made food supply. (For nursing basics, see Chapter Five on page 77.) If you opt for bottle feeding, you have a number of decisions to make and a bit of shopping to do.

Many infant formulas are available. Some are sold ready to serve, some come in the form of liquids that need to be mixed with water, and still others come in powder form. As a rule of thumb, the more convenient the formula, the more expensive it is.

Most likely your pediatrician has suggested that you choose an iron-fortified formula. Breast milk is naturally rich in iron, but bottled milk and milk products are rather low in that mineral. That's one reason you can't just open a bottle of cow's milk and use that to feed your baby on a regular basis before age one. You also can't use cow's milk as an acceptable substitute because it may cause bleeding of the stomach lining.

You'll need to buy formula especially prepared for infants. In fact, the American Academy of Pediatrics says that iron-fortified infant formula is the only acceptable alternative to breast milk. When you prepare the formula, follow the package instructions carefully. Each day, a formula-fed baby should drink 20 to 32 ounces, depending on the baby's age and size.

Breast milk or formula with iron is the only food your baby needs for the first four to six months of life. After your baby starts eating solid food, you should continue to give breast milk or formula until the end of the first year.

No Need to Sterilize

Your mother, if she used formula to feed you, undoubtedly spent a good deal of time sterilizing everything. However, doctors have not recommended sterilizing baby bottles for nearly two decades, according to Donald W. Schiff, M.D., professor of pediatrics at the University of Colorado Medical School in Denver and past president of the American Academy of Pediatrics. Sterilization isn't necessary, but thorough cleanliness is, he says.

Even if you live in a rural area where you draw your water from a well or other private source, bottles do not have to be sterilized if the water has been tested and found to be pure, says Dr. Schiff. "But if you are concerned about your water supply, use bottled or boiled water."

Rinse the bottles right after each feeding so the milk film doesn't cement itself to the glass. Then run them through the dishwasher or wash them in hot, soapy water using a bottle brush. Be sure the nipples are thoroughly cleaned.

Warming the Bottle

Microwaving a bottle is a no-no. But the temptation to heat the formula that way is ever-present. (When your baby is crying with hunger, you do feel some sense of urgency to get the bottle ready quickly.) Baby-care experts will tell you that microwaving is not a good idea, because the process heats the formula unevenly. The bottle may feel comfortably warm to your hand when you remove it from the microwave, but it can have hot spots of scalding milk at the center. In addition, high temperatures can destroy necessary vitamins.

To warm a bottle of formula, stand the bottle in a pan of water and heat it on the stove for five minutes or until it reaches a comfortable temperature. (Test a drop on the inside of your arm.)

Feeding Your Little One

When giving your baby a bottle, hold him or her in a semiupright position. If a baby drinks while lying

When I was pregnant, everyone told me how much my life would change. Late night feedings, dirty diapers, no more social life, dirty diapers, no time for myself, more dirty diapers. The list went on and on. I honestly thought, "Oh gee, what am I getting myself into? Do I really want to give up all of that for some kid?"

Now that I've had my baby, the answer to that question is, "Absolutely." What they didn't tell me was how wonderfully my life would change. Who cares about the dirty diapers! When you hold and nurse your baby, when you see his sweet smile, when you come home from work, when you see him reach milestone after milestone ... nothing is better. A mother's love for her child is truly profound.

Mary Lynne Ashley
Reston, Virginia

down, swallowed milk can enter the eustachian tube—the tiny tubes that connect the back of the throat and the ears. Milk in the eustachian tubes can lead to ear problems.

Use this time while your baby is feeding to cuddle and comfort your little one, making the most of this chance for closeness. A bottle-fed baby can be every bit as secure and serene as a breast-fed child if you always hold him or her during feeding. (Propping a bottle may be efficient, but it's neither warm nor comforting.)

Make sure the milk is not flowing too quickly from the nipple. If your baby sucks too fast or swallows a lot of air, he or she will suffer with gassiness. Which leads to fussiness. Which leads to crying. Which leads to a cycle of misery for everyone.

Hint: To tell if milk is flowing through the nipple properly—that is, whether the hole in the nipple is too large or too small—hold the bottle upside down. If the formula flows fast enough (about one drop per second) but not so fast that it is a steady stream, the flow is just right.

You can keep formula at room temperature for up to an hour, or save it in the refrigerator if it's been out less than an hour, says Dr. Schiff. This is helpful to know if your baby takes only part of a bottle and then wants more in a few minutes. Formula left out longer than an hour must be discarded without fail.

Once you've fed your baby a few times, you'll soon fall into a regular routine. At least you can *hope* for something resembling a regular routine. Your baby may have other plans. If your baby develops gas and diarrhea, constipation, chronic congestion, or a rash, you may worry that he or she is allergic to the formula.

"The issue of milk sensitivity or allergy is a complex one," says Dr. Schiff. "The incidence of true milk allergy is probably less than 1 percent. But the incidence of babies who have some distress—such as loose stools, hard stools, or spitting up—is very common. Probably 50 percent of all babies have one or more of these problems, and in most cases it has nothing to do with milk.

"Some people switch to a soybean formula, or from one kind of milk to another, and most of the time the switch is probably both unnecessary and unhelpful. But the problems are so common that people feel forced to try to do something to relieve the baby."

You should mention any symptoms to your pediatrician so your baby can be checked to eliminate any other possible cause of problems.

Although at the beginning your baby's diet will consist solely of formula, it's perfectly OK to offer your baby a bottle of water from time to time, says Dr. Schiff, but not at feeding time.

Warning: Never, ever give your baby water with honey. Honey may contain bacteria that adults easily can handle. Babies younger than 1 year old, however, cannot. In fact, consuming honey can lead to botulism, a potentially fatal disease.

Burps and Bubbles

Babies tend to swallow some air as they feed, and that little bubble in the tummy makes them feel full before they have actually eaten as much as they need. Here's how to deal with this problem:

☞ **Encourage frequent burps.** It is really important to burp your baby halfway through each bottle. Some babies may have to be burped more frequently, especially if they appear uncomfortable or are not interested in feeding. So they can rest comfortably, all babies must be burped after every feeding is over.

☞ **Bring up those bubbles.** How do you get a baby to burp? To bring up a bubble, hold your baby against your upper chest with his or her head resting on your shoulder. Gently pat your baby's back until you hear the burp. It's a good idea to protect your shoulder with a clean diaper or a napkin, because often a little milk comes up with the bubble of air.

☞ **Try a change of position.** If your baby has difficulty squeezing out a burp, try sitting the baby on your lap. Support his or her chin in your hand and pat the back gently with your other hand.

Spitting Up

A little regurgitation is normal and doesn't indicate that the formula disagrees with the baby or that you should switch to formula if you are breast-feeding. Spitting up can be a nuisance, but it's not a big problem.

Feeding Schedules

The clock simply is not a factor in an infant's desire to eat. The baby cries out because of hunger pangs, certainly an uncomfortable, new sensation. After all, before birth, the placenta provided nutrients steadily around the clock. Your baby never knew hunger until after birth. Here's how to deal with feeding schedules:

☞ **Don't make a newborn wait.** It's hardly reasonable to make your child wait for an arbitrary dinner hour in the face of his or her distress. Feed your baby when he or she is hungry. Don't think you are spoiling your child; you simply cannot spoil a newborn.

After two to three months, your baby may be ready to settle into a feeding schedule. But at the beginning, it's best to feed on cue. By letting your baby know that food—as well as comfort and safety—is available around the clock, you are helping him or her develop a sense of security, a feeling that the world is an OK place after all.

☞ **Be flexible.** At the beginning you will be feeding your infant at unpredictable intervals—sometimes every hour, sometimes once in four hours.

As your baby matures, the intervals between feedings will become more widely spaced and more predictable. Flexibility and patience are the words of the day.

Bowel Movements

Of course, with all this feeding going on, something's got to come out at the other end. Your baby's first bowel movement may surprise you.

Usually, that very first bowl movement is a sticky greenish-black substance that doesn't look like anything you would expect. It is called meconium, and it's a substance that accumulates in your baby's intestines before birth and is usually passed in the first day or so.

After three to four days, your baby will begin to pass normal stools, which vary in color and consistency depending on whether the baby is breast-fed or formula-fed.

A breast-fed baby's bowel movements are loose and a dark mustard color. After your breast milk is in, the baby may have a bowel movement after every feeding.

Bottle-fed babies have bowel movements in almost any color, from buttery yellow to olive green. In addition to these colors, there is one other difference: These babies usually have fewer bowel movements than breast-fed infants.

A healthy baby who is getting enough to eat will make at least one substantial bowel movement a day and wet at least six diapers. (Some healthy infants have bowel movements every other day, but all healthy infants should be wetting at least six diapers a day.)

And that's a lot of diapers to change.

The Fine Art of Diapering

Most mothers these days use disposable diapers. They are a little expensive, but many parents feel their convenience makes up for the extra cost. If you opt for disposables, you have a few choices to make. You will find diapers designed for boys or girls, diapers with pleats, with expanding waistbands, and with cut-outs for healing umbilical cords. They all contain a gel to absorb urine.

If you are using cloth diapers, you can fold them in a special way for a boy and another way for a girl.

For a boy: Place the diaper flat on the table. Bring one long side toward the center, then overlap that side with the other. Bring the bottom end up to the middle. The thickest part of the diaper will be in front, where it will more effectively absorb the urine.

For a girl: Place the diaper flat on the table. Bring one long side toward the center, then overlap with the other. Fold the top end down, a bit past the middle of the diaper. The thickest part of the diaper will be in the center/back, where it will more effectively absorb the urine.

Tender Bottoms

Newborns have remarkably delicate and tender skin. You'll touch it in awe and probably cuddle your baby just so you can sniff the sweet, soft smell of your baby's skin. You'll also be amazed at how easily your newborn's skin can become red and irritated. Here's how you can protect your little one's skin:

☞ **Watch those pins!** If you are using diaper pins, be sure to place your fingers under the diaper so that you avoid sticking the baby with the pin. If you have difficulty pushing the pin through the folds of fabric, it helps to slide the pin through your hair. It will pick up just enough oil to make the going a bit easier.

☞ **Try to limit the use of plastic pants and diaper wraps.** These can foster the development of diaper rash. Save the plastic coverings for when you are away from home. Instead, place a waterproof pad under your baby in the bassinet, crib, or carriage. Replace the wet pad with a dry one when you diaper your baby.

☞ **Become a quick change artist.** The best way to prevent diaper rash is to change wet diapers often. Changing a wet diaper isn't the big production number that some people turn it into

You really don't need to use all those sweet-smelling lotions or powders. In fact, talcum powder can be downright dangerous if the baby inhales it. And you don't need baby wipes if the diaper is only wet. Just ditch the soggy drawers for dry ones. You're done in a wink.

☞ **Reach for the ointment.** If you see some red spots on your baby's bottom, apply a little barrier protection to keep the urine away from contact with the skin. Good products include Vaseline, A&D Ointment (the letters stand for the vitamins A and D), Desitin, and zinc oxide.

Remove diapers and plastic pants as frequently as possible until the rash clears up to allow air to reach your baby's bottom.

☞ **Wash when necessary.** When your baby has a bowel movement, you will have to wash his or her bottom. You can use baby wipes, if you want to, but a warm, wet washcloth will do just as well. If you're using cloth diapers, after changing, flush out the contents of the soiled diaper in the toilet. Hold onto that diaper, or you'll be calling the plumber. Store the diaper in a diaper pail with a tight lid.

Washing Diapers

If you are washing the diapers yourself, buy a laundry detergent that is fragrance-free and dye-free.

This is so much kinder to your baby's tender skin. You can use chlorine bleach to lighten or eliminate any stains, but you'll have to rinse the diapers twice to be sure no residue remains in the fabric to irritate the skin.

Residue from detergent can cause a rash that is dry and red, and usually develops where the diaper rubs against the baby's skin. This sort of contact dermatitis isn't very common, but it can be avoided completely with commonsense laundering.

While using a fabric softener may seem like a good idea, it isn't for infants. Generally these products contain a fragrance—as do those special "gentle" soaps made for hand-washing delicate fabrics. Softener sheets you toss into the dryer also may leave a residue that can irritate baby's skin.

One final word on laundry: Don't combine the baby's diapers with other clothing. Do them as a separate wash load to avoid spreading bacteria.

Baby's Sleep Patterns

You are very involved in what your baby eats and what your baby wears. When it comes to sleeping, however, your baby is pretty much going to be in charge. Sleep patterns are extremely variable. Each baby seems to have his or her own internal rhythms.

In the first week after delivery, your baby will be considerate of you, perhaps sleeping 16 to 17 hours a day. Take advantage of the quiet by resting whenever your baby rests.

After the first week, and up to about the age of 3 months, your baby may doze about 15 hours a day. During this time frame, sleep periods are broken up for feedings throughout the day and (yawn) night.

Obviously, you cannot tiptoe around the house for 15 hours a day in an attempt to provide your baby with quiet time for sleeping. In fact, you

When my 15-month-old son suddenly became afraid of the "big" bathtub, and he had outgrown the bath seat for the bathtub, I was in a panic! Bath time had become a terrible experience for him, until one day I put the laundry basket inside the bathtub and gave him a bath inside the basket. It worked! He was once again enjoying his bath time! He needed the security of a smaller space inside the large tub. We continued this for a couple months until he was ready to explore the rest of the bathtub.

Bonnie Ohren
Blaine, Minnesota

shouldn't. The experts say that if you create an unnatural silence as your baby drifts off, he or she will become accustomed to it and eventually will awaken at the slightest sound. Instead, they recommend you continue making your usual household noises, running the vacuum and dishwasher, talking on the phone, watching television, and so forth.

Preventing SIDS

Years ago mothers were told to put their babies to sleep on their tummies. The reason, and it seemed to make good sense, was that if the baby spit up while sleeping, he or she wouldn't choke. Research in the past few years, however, has shown that this danger is insignificant when compared to the risk of sudden infant death syndrome (SIDS). For some reason that doctors do not yet understand, infants are more likely to die from SIDS when sleeping on their tummies.

In the past decade, studies in several countries have shown that putting a baby to bed in the proper sleep position can cut the risk of SIDS in half. The proper position—the safe way to put your baby down—is now known to be on his or her back.

Just how much of a danger is there of SIDS? A truly healthy baby actually is at low risk of SIDS— less than 2 in 1,000

Yet, several thousand newborns in this country still die of SIDS each year. Nobody knows for sure what causes the sudden death of an infant who seems to be perfectly healthy.

Researchers are just now beginning to think that

possibly these babies only *appeared* to be in perfect health, but, in fact, were not healthy.

They suspect that at least some of these newborns had an underlying, undiagnosed condition. One prime suspect is a brain stem abnormality that doesn't allow the baby to wake up if he or she begins to suffocate.

Researchers also have begun to think that SIDS may have several distinct causes and, in fact, may be several different diseases.

What they do know is this:

- **Babies between 2 and 4 months old are most at risk.**
- **Ninety percent of SIDS cases occur by the age of 6 months**.
- **Boys are more at risk than girls.**
- **Premature or low-birth-weight babies are more at risk.**
- **Those whose parents smoke are three times more likely to die.**
- **SIDS most often occurs in cold weather.**
- **SIDS most often occurs between midnight and 8 a.m.**

Fortunately, you can take action to lessen the risk of such a catastrophe happening in your home.

☞ **Think firm, not soft.** First, be sure to provide your baby with a firm mattress. Keep the snuggly pillows and puffy quilts out of the crib—at least for now.

These seemingly harmless, even comforting, items are dangerous. If your baby snuggles into them, exhaled carbon dioxide can get trapped in the folds. With each breath, the baby will draw in less oxygen and more carbon dioxide. This can lead to suffocation and death.

☞ **Put your baby to sleep on his or her back.** If your baby forcefully resists the position, you can try using a pillow to prop your little one on his or her side. Doctors do recommend having an infant sleep on his or her back as the best choice for preventing SIDS, however.

Swaddling Your Infant

"**A**nd they wrapped him in swaddling clothes and laid him in the manger..." You have no doubt heard of swaddling a baby. Ever wonder exactly what this process involves, and why it's done?

In the first few weeks after birth, babies' nervous systems are still pretty immature. They sometimes make little jerky motions with their arms and legs. These involuntary movements are perfectly normal. However, they may wake up your child. Some mothers have found that swaddling the baby constrains the arms and legs so that they do not flail. The baby also may feel more secure wrapped in a tight bundle; after all, he or she was living in pretty close quarters for the last few months. Here is how to swaddle your child:

☞ **Spread out a receiving blanket.** Fold down one corner about halfway down the blanket.

☞ **Lay your baby on the blanket diagonally,** with his or her head on the fold.

☞ **Draw the right corner of the blanket over your baby,** tucking it in under the baby's arm and behind his or her back.

☞ **Lift the bottom corner of the blanket** and tuck it into the section covering your baby's chest.

☞ **Now take the left corner,** draw it across your baby's body so that it envelops both arms, and tuck it snugly into the blanket behind the baby's back.

Be sure the lower arm is extended, so if the baby wiggles around, he or she will be forced onto the back rather than rolling onto the stomach.

☞ **Don't smoke.** Don't allow anyone else to smoke in your home either.

☞ **Protect your baby from respiratory illness.** Keep your baby out of crowds during cold and flu season and ban any visitors who have a cold. Be sure your baby is regularly checked by a doctor or clinic.

☞ **Think cool.** Don't let your baby get overheated. If the room is comfortably warm for you, it should be comfortable for your baby, as well. And make sure you don't overdress your baby on warm, summer nights.

Giving a Sponge Bath

New parents often approach their baby's first bath with a good deal of fear and trepidation. After all, newborns are so tiny and seemingly fragile. The good news is that, for the first few days anyway, newborns don't need much in the way of a bath. After all, they only get dirty in a couple of spots. And so, washing your baby's face with clear, lukewarm water after feeding easily takes care of one of the spots. And cleaning your baby's bottom when you change diapers takes care of the other.

After about two or three days, however, you may want to give your baby a sponge bath. Tub bathing must wait until after the umbilical cord falls off, and, for boys, after the circumcision has healed.

Here's how to give a sponge bath that will be satisfying and comfortable for your baby:

☞ **Set the atmosphere.** Be sure the room is warm and there aren't any drafts.

☞ **Lay out your supplies.** Place cotton balls, a soft washcloth, baby soap, a pan of warm (not too warm) water. Test the water's temperature by pouring some over your own wrist. You'll also need a towel.

☞ **Start at the top.** Keep your baby's diaper on at first. Start by rinsing your baby's hair with clear water and patting it dry with a towel.

Wipe each eye with a damp cotton ball. Use cotton balls to clean gently all around your baby's mouth and ears.

☞ **Move it on down.** Using a soapy washcloth, clean your baby's neck, chest, and underarms, especially where there are creases or folds. Then rinse and dry your baby's upper torso.

☞ **Move it on further down.** Wash your baby's legs and feet, paying attention to creases and folds at the ankles and knees. Rinse and pat dry.

☞ **Save the bottom for last.** Remove the diaper and clean your baby's bottom from front to back, turning the washcloth frequently. Now rinse and dry your baby's bottom and rediaper.

☞ **Stay focused.** Once you have begun, don't turn away from your baby. Do not leave your baby—wet and getting cold—for any reason. If the phone rings, let it ring. It's amazing how fast a slithery, wet baby can move and how quickly trouble can develop, even if you are standing only a few short feet away.

Belly Button Care

You really can't give your infant a bath until what's left of the umbilical cord turns black and falls off. That will happen all by itself about two weeks after the birth (resist the temptation to pick at it).

A cord clamp may be still attached when you bring your baby home. Don't worry about it. It doesn't hurt your baby.

Here's what you should pay attention to while the cord remnant is still attached:

☞ **Air it out.** The more the cord is exposed to the air, the better it will heal. The air will also help it dry out faster.

☞ **Use special diapers.** Diapers designed for newborns have a scoop cut out at the front of the waist, which allows for air circulation. If you use cloth diapers, fold them so they don't cover the belly button.

☞ **Help the drying along.** When you change the baby, dab the cord and the base of the cord with a little alcohol on a cotton ball. It will help speed the drying and work to prevent infection. A small amount of bleeding is normal when the cord falls off.

☞ **Get medical help, if necessary.** If the cord

Your Baby's Soft Spots

The soft spots at the top and back of your baby's head are called the fontanels. They are spaces that exist because the surrounding bones in the skull have not yet grown together. The fontanels actually serve a useful function: They give your baby's head a little bit of flexibility so it can conform somewhat to the shape of the birth canal during labor. They also allow your baby's brain to grow easily without impediment.

The soft spot at the top of the head can make you a little nervous about handling your baby because it seems so vulnerable. After all, you can see the pulse beating there. You can, however, touch your baby's head, brush and shampoo your baby's hair, and go about your normal baby care routine without fear of damaging either the soft spot or the underlying brain.

Once again, recognize that your baby is tougher than he or she looks. A sturdy membrane covers the soft spot and protects it. That membrane is not exactly a batting helmet, however, so do be careful to protect your baby's head from sharp objects or blows.

or the area immediately around it becomes red, or if the cord starts to smell bad, call your doctor.

Bathing an Infant

After your baby's navel has healed, you can try a real bath, either in a little tub designed just for babies or in a basin. Even the kitchen sink will suffice, provided that it's absolutely clean and lined with a soft towel. You can bathe your baby every other day, or less frequently in dry climates. Here's how to do it:

☞ **Gather what you need.** Next to the tub lay out the usual supplies: cotton balls, washcloth, baby soap, towel. Add baby shampoo to the list.

☞ **Free your hands.** Take off any jewelry you're wearing that might scratch the baby.

☞ **Prepare the bath.** Fill the tub with about 2 inches of comfortably warm water. Test the temperature on the inside of your wrist. If your tub has a safety strap, use it.

☞ **Be gentle and patient.** Holding your infant's head in one hand, slide the baby into the water, toes first. Allow your baby a moment to enjoy this new (but somehow familiar?) sensation.

☞ **Start at the top.** The order of work is from cleanest to dirtiest. Start by washing the face with clear water. Wipe the eyes with a damp cotton ball. Wipe the ears with another.

Next, shampoo your baby's scalp and hair. Rinse carefully, keeping the flowing water out of your baby's eyes, ears, nose, and mouth. Make sure you test the rinse water for temperature before you allow it to touch your baby.

☞ **Move it on down.** Now wash the torso and legs and bottom. If you have a boy, lift his scrotum to clean underneath.

☞ **Cuddle and dry.** Wrap your baby in a soft towel and pat dry.

☞ **Share the fun.** Don't keep all the fun for yourself. Be sure Dad has a chance to bathe the baby, too. It's an opportunity for them to bond.

Speaking Your Baby's Language

If you want to have a heart-to-heart talk with your newborn, you'll first have to capture his or her attention. Cup your baby's head in your two hands. With your baby's back resting on your forearms, hold him or her up close to your face. (A newborn's eyes focus best on objects that are within 8 to 14 inches.) After a little bit, your baby's eyes will search out yours. Now talk in soothing tones. There's a good chance that your baby actually remembers your voice from before birth and will be enchanted to meet the person it belongs to.

Other than crying, a newborn doesn't vocalize much. A newborn baby's cry sounds very much like a cat's. And at 1 month of age, a baby may make some soft, throaty sounds.

At 2 months, these cat-like sounds may begin to develop into something that sounds more like a coo. At 3 months of age, your baby will finally begin to cry less..This may be due to nothing more than an increased "vocabulary." Your baby's vocalization now includes whimpers, chortles, squeals, chuckles, and lots of grunts.

And, you may ask, why does my baby grunt so often? Researchers say that, at about 3 months, babies will grunt with the effort of trying to hold up their heads.

As you and your baby get to know each other better, you'll be able to sort out the "I'm hungry!" cry from the "Hey, I'm bored" complaint.

You also will learn to read your child's body language: the contented snuggle, the tense body that announces a tummy ache, the flapping arms and kicking legs that cry out, "This is so much fun!" And, even in these early days of your baby's life, you may well be rewarded by a fleeting smile, that will leave you wondering whether it really happened.

Stimulating Baby's Mind

For now, *you* are your baby's best stimulation. So you should take any available opportunity to engage your baby's attention and interest.

Talk, talk, talk to your little one, or sing your favorite song and clap your hands in time. Your baby will watch, perhaps solemnly, but completely entranced with all your efforts at entertaining and communicating.

While you're bathing your infant, talk about "Rub-a-dub-dub, three men in a tub" or your theory on balancing the nation's budget. Your infant may not follow the intricacies of political debate, but he or she will be pleased to be included in the conversation.

Symptom Solver

The shorter hospital stays these days often send babies home early in their lives. To compensate, many hospitals routinely provide in-home visits from nurses or lactation consultants. If your hospital does not, you should discuss the matter with your pediatrician so that either a nurse will visit or an appointment will be set up for the baby two or three days after being discharged from the hospital.

In these intervening days, you may feel more confident if you know which symptoms may signal trouble and which may seem odd but are normal. **Doctors consider the following symptoms to be completely normal in most babies:**
- hiccups
- brief shaking of the arms and legs
- little snorting and gurgling noises
- breathing that stops for a few seconds, then resumes normally
- brief bluish color around the mouth or hands and feet

Here are the symptoms that mean you should call the doctor:

- **temperature higher than 100 degrees F** (normal is 96.7 to 99 degrees Fahrenheit)
- **fingernails that have a blue-gray tint**
- **blue-gray coloring inside the mouth**
- **yellow skin color**
- **weight loss of more than ½ pound** for an average 7- to 8-pound baby
- **failure to gain weight** after the fifth day of life
- **rapid breathing** (a breath every second) that lasts for more than 15 minutes
- **struggling to breathe,** with grunting upon exhaling
- **spitting up fluid that is yellow, red, brown, or green**
- **repeated forceful vomiting**
- **prolonged gagging and coughing when spitting up**

Enrich your child's environment with appropriate toys: a mobile, a crib mirror, a rattle, a music box. Wind up the music box frequently and watch your baby's face react to the familiar music.

Out and About

In your first forays into the great outdoors, be sure to protect your baby from danger.

In the summer, the biggest threat is direct sunlight. A baby's skin is more likely to sunburn than an adult's because it is thinner. But doctors recommend that you do not use sunscreen on a baby younger than 6 months. Instead, put up the stroller or carriage hood to protect your baby's face and cover your baby's legs with a light blanket. Walk on the shady side of the street. In fact, wander to the prettiest leafy glade in town. Both you and your baby will enjoy the experience.

In winter, be sure your baby is dressed warmly in a stretch suit with feet and a cap and is wrapped in a warm blanket. If you're traveling by car, turn on the heater and let the car warm up before you bring your baby outside. If you are walking, bundle your baby in a good warm quilt, put up the carriage or stroller hood, and stay out of the wind.

On extra-hot or extra-cold days, or if it's raining or windy, keep your baby indoors where he or she will be more comfortable and less vulnerable.

Common Problems

Even healthy newborns can run into a few glitches during their first couple weeks of life. You can handle most of the problems yourself. Here's a rundown of the most frequent problems and disorders found in newborns and what to do about them:

Baby Acne

Some infants develop a rash that's oily and pimply. It looks a lot like what the pizza delivery boy is suffering from, but is known as neonatal acne.

Traveling with Baby

On occasion, you may have to travel away from home, perhaps to visit the family to show them their newest relative. You shouldn't have any problems if you take some commonsense precautions.

If you are formula-feeding your baby, a switch in local water might cause an upset tummy. Therefore, consider using the more expensive, ready-to-feed canned formula or mixing up powdered formula with bottled water.

If you are traveling by air, offer the baby your breast, a bottle, or a pacifier to help ease ear discomfort during takeoff and landing. Try to get a bulkhead seat for more privacy and leg room.

If you are not visiting family, and you need infant care in a strange city, find out if your hotel offers child care services or ask the concierge to recommend a reputable agency. Ask whether the child care provider is licensed or bonded, and ask specifically whether the person has experience with newborns. Don't feel awkward about turning someone down, if you're even slightly uncomfortable. It's your baby who matters most.

☞ **Do nothing.** Fortunately, this condition will go away by itself in a few weeks, and it will not leave scars. All you can do is be patient. Do not even think about using an over-the-counter acne medicine. They are far too harsh for an infant's tender skin.

Jaundice

Jaundice is common, and most babies who develop it do so on or about their third day of life. It is so common, in fact, that the run-of-the-mill variety is called benign jaundice. It comes about because the baby's liver is immature, and it usually goes away in a week or two

Jaundice reveals itself when the baby's face, arms, torso, legs, and even fingernails turn yellow. The color comes from a yellow chemical, called bilirubin, that shows up in the blood when a baby's liver can't process it fast enough.

"You can judge whether jaundice is increasing," says Dr. Schiff, "not only by the intensity of the color, but also by the amount of body over which the jaundice extends.

"If it is limited to the head and upper chest, the jaundice is of less consequence than if the coloring extends to the lower body or legs."

If you suspect jaundice, here's what to do:

☞ **Get confirmation.** A visiting nurse should be able to spot any troublesome jaundice during a home visit your baby's first week of life. If you think you've noticed jaundice symptoms, be sure to bring this to the attention of the nurse. If your baby is not being examined in a home visit, call your baby's doctor and describe the symptoms.

If the color looks extremely yellow, or if it extends over most of the baby's body, the doctor may want to administer a blood test to check your baby's bilirubin level.

☞ **Be there for your baby.** If bilirubin levels are high, your baby will be treated by being placed in a clear plastic incubator under special fluorescent lights. His or her eyes will be covered to protect them. The lights help make the bilirubin water-soluble, so it can be excreted in bile and urine. Your baby will remain in the incubator for two or three days. The incubator has portholes, so you can reach inside to stroke and comfort your child.

Some hospitals offer a fiber-optic blanket instead of an incubator. The entire blanket becomes a light source. Parents usually prefer the blanket, if they can get it, because it allows them to hold and cuddle their baby during the treatment. In some parts of the country, hospitals allow parents to rent phototherapy equipment to use at home if it has been ordered by a pediatrician.

Colic

At least one in five babies suffers from colic, and nobody knows why. Why should a well-fed, well-rested, dry-diapered, dearly loved darling scream

The Colic Hold

H ere's one way that might comfort a colicky baby. Place your baby on your forearm, face down. His or her face should be resting on or near the palm of your hand. The tummy should be against your arm, and the legs should hang over either side of your elbow. Walk your baby in this position to see if it relieves the discomfort (and the crying).

like a banshee for up to 8 hours a day? And, more important, what can you do about it?

Edward Christophersen, Ph.D., head of behavioral pediatrics at Children's Mercy Hospital in Kansas City, Missouri, found that normal newborns cry for about 1½ to 2 hours every day. By the time a baby reaches 6 weeks old, the crying can increase to nearly 3 hours a day. That, dear parents, is normal. That is *not* colic. A colicky baby cries more than that. Way more.

The term colic refers to a behavioral syndrome rather than a condition with a specific cause. The chronic crying can begin when the baby is about 2 weeks old and can continue for three to six months. Usually, a baby will open with a salvo of wailing just before dinnertime. Some parents call it "piranha hour" or "arsenic hour." Most parents would like the baby to call it "quits."

If your baby screams as though in pain, draws his or her legs right up to the abdomen, and keeps at it for hours, your baby is probably colicky.

Colic is difficult, because there is no cure (except time) and has no proven cause. Parents need support and help during this difficult time. The two mistakes I made were to blame myself and to not ask for more help from family and friends who offered to watch my daughter so I could take a small break. If you have a colicky or very fussy baby, don't go it alone. Accept offers of help and get out and go for a walk or shopping. Even a small break can rejuvenate the "colic weary." Join a parent's support group to change your routine and, more importantly, find out that you are not alone.

Deb Furioni
Easthampton, Massachusetts

So what causes these extended and parent-aggravating crying jags? Some experts have suggested that chronic crying may be the result of poor digestion, malabsorption of certain proteins, or intolerance to formula, foods, and/or medications taken by the nursing mother.

Other experts have postulated that the cause is not intestinal, but is based on neurologic factors or even by a mom's uptight behavior

But, really, nobody knows. Therefore, there is no cure for colic. The best remedies are based on treating the symptoms of the condition and waiting for it to run its course.

☞ **Have a medical checkup.** "The important thing to do if you think your baby has colic is to have the baby checked by his or her doctor, because there are other reasons for crying," suggests Dr.

Schiff. "You don't want to miss another cause that can be alleviated or treated."

☞ **Don't blame yourself.** The first thing you have to know—and really *know*—is that the endless crying is not a signal that the baby is mad at you or dissatisfied with you. Colic is not a sign that you are doing a poor job of parenting. There is no medical formula that says: Colicky Baby = Inept Mother. You simply can't take colic personally, or it may interfere with bonding between you and your baby.

☞ **Don't blame your baby.** The second thing you need to know is that the baby is not "acting up" or being "bad" or "willful." Your baby doesn't want to scream and feel miserable. Your baby doesn't want to drive you out of your mind. What your baby wants is relief. So, muster up all the serenity and good humor you can and try the following

105

methods of colic control. Some methods work for some babies some of the time. If you're lucky, you'll find one that works for yours.

☞ **Try the colic hold.** Some parents swear by this method (see the illustration on page 104). It puts a little pressure on the baby's tummy, while allowing you to be comfortably near to each other.

☞ **Make a racket yourself.** It may help to turn on some white noise—a background hum like that provided by a vacuum cleaner or static on the radio.

Oddly enough, many parents have reported success with this particular technique. If the sound of a vacuum does calm your baby, you may want to make an audio tape of it. People have been known to burn out more than one vacuum motor during the colic period.

☞ **Fill up the baby tub.** Occasionally, a warm bath will soothe the baby or at least provide a distraction.

☞ **Sing.** It sounds simple, but don't forget the old standbys. Try rocking and singing or walking and singing.

☞ **Take your baby out for a drive.** You'll have peace and quiet as long as the gas tank doesn't run dry. Or, you may want to consider purchasing a product that mimics a car ride, with sound effects and everything. It's called SleepTight, and when tested in a study funded by the National Institute of Child Health and Human Development, it was found to resolve or reduce colic in 97 percent of babies..

SleepTight costs about $90, but because it has been approved by the FDA as a medical product, the expense may be covered by your health insurance. For more information, call 800-662-6542.

☞ **Ring the dinner bell.** If the crying has gone on for a while, your baby might have become hungry in the meantime.

Try offering your breast or a bottle. If your baby isn't hungry but seems happy to suck, offer a pacifier. Try shorter, more frequent feedings.

Handling a Bad Reaction To a Vaccination

It is possible for babies to experience a reaction to their vaccinations. There are two possible categories: a local reaction and a systemic reaction.

A local reaction shows up at the point where the injection was given. There might be a little redness, swelling, and discomfort at the site. Local reactions are rarely serious and go away in a day or so, and that's the end of it. If a local reaction persists longer than this, bring it to the attention of your baby's pediatrician.

A systemic reaction is more serious. With systemic reactions, a baby can develop a very high fever, prolonged crying periods, and even seizures. Should the baby develop a fever following a vaccination, or have a seizure, call the pediatrician immediately. A systemic reaction can be a medical emergency. Follow your doctor's instructions precisely. You can lower the fever by sponging the baby with cool water. When the seizure is over, you can give the baby some acetaminophen. (For the correct amount, see Dosage Chart on page 219.)

☞ **Check your own diet.** If you're breast-feeding, take stock of what you've been eating. Have you been eating vegetables that create a lot of gas, such as beans or broccoli? Give them up for a week and see if your baby improves. Are you a coffee fanatic? Your baby may have a case of coffee nerves from the caffeine in your breast milk. Try switching to decaf for a week and see what happens.

☞ **Take care of yourself.** After a few weeks of tending a colicky baby, you may feel edgy, frustrated, angry, depressed, and/or exasperated. Anyone would.

Many doctors recommend that while you are comforting your baby as much as you can, you also comfort yourself by building up a support network. Call your best friend, your mother, or your doctor, and vent your feelings. Plan ways to get out for a few hours on a regular basis. Call all your friends, too, for help.

☞ **Don't give in to anger.** Above all, if you begin to feel angry and feel as though your anger might get the best of you, walk away from the baby. Call someone right away. Take a deep breath and try to relax.

Starting Regular Medical Care

Before your baby left the hospital, doctors checked for PKU (phenylketonuria), which is a metabolic disorder that can cause mental retardation unless a special diet is followed. It's not a common problem (about 1 in 14,000), but it is one that can go undetected until damage has been done. Consequently, a PKU test is performed very soon after birth and rechecked at the baby's next visit to the doctor.

A baby who tests positive will be put on a special low-protein diet that prevents phenylalanine, a type of protein, from building up in the bloodstream and interfering with brain development.

A newborn also will be immunized for hepatitis B, usually in the first day of life.

"A baby whose mother has tested positive for hepatitis B will be immunized against the disease within the first twelve hours of life," says Dr. Schiff. "For others whose mothers have not had hepatitis B, we recommend immunization within the first twenty-four hours, but that's a matter of convenience more than anything else. Immunization for this disease can be started in the first or even second month of life."

Protection develops by fooling the body into believing it has already fought off a disease. Once you've had, say, chicken pox, your body has built up an immunity to it. It has developed an elite armed force of antibodies that "remember" the chicken pox virus, recognize it, then destroy it.

With vaccinations, it's possible to develop that "memory" without actually suffering through the disease. This happens when the doctor injects dead or weakened microorganisms, or the toxins produced by them, into the baby's body. This vaccination causes the baby to produce antibodies that are ready to fight off the disease that would have been caused by the bacteria or viruses had they been alive. Most of the antibodies will disappear, but a few will hang around, ever ready to recognize that particular disease and mount an immune response to it should it ever appear again.

Through immunization, your baby will be spared a great deal of suffering and pain. Your baby will never know smallpox, now eradicated because of immunization. Neither will your baby ever have to suffer diphtheria, tetanus, whooping cough, polio, measles, mumps, rubella, chicken pox, hemophilus influenza B, or hepatitis B.

Your grandmother would have walked through fire to have her baby immunized so thoroughly. If you don't even recognize the names of some of these diseases, thank your lucky stars. You also can thank the immunization programs that have made so many of them history.

Baby's First Checkup

Three to five days after being discharged from the hospital, your baby should be checked by a pediatrician or visiting nurse.

As part of the routine checkup, your baby will be weighed. Expect your baby to be lighter than he or she was at birth, especially if you are breast-feeding. The baby will be examined for jaundice. The doctor or nurse will assess your baby's urine, stools, breathing, heartbeat, and lungs. The baby's mouth will be examined for thrush.

My son is now 7 months old, but I vividly remember bringing him home and worrying about every decision—which diapers to use, how many layers of clothing to put him in, where he should sleep, etc. I was making myself crazy trying to sort through all the books, internet sites, and advice from others and finally decided that I would take my cues from my baby. I stopped thinking of him as "the baby" and started thinking of him as "the little person" who would find comfort in many of the same things I did—soft clothes, fresh air, a shoulder to lie on.

Sometimes I think doing too much research can be dangerous. I almost forgot he was a human, not a mysterious, knowing creature just waiting for me to make a mistake. When I realized this about myself, I could also stop feeling guilty for having moved him from his most comfortable space in my tummy and into the outside world.

Barbara Heathcote
Etobicoke, Ontario

The doctor or nurse will check that the baby's abdominal organs are all the proper size and in the proper location, listen for any heart murmurs that were not discovered earlier, and check to see that the kidneys are not unusually large.

Now is the perfect time to ask questions about breast-feeding, care of the umbilical cord, care of the circumcision wound, or anything else that has concerned you.

In two weeks, the baby will be checked again. At this point, the cord should have fallen off and the circumcision will have healed. The baby's PKU probably will be rechecked.

Now is the time to discuss your baby's sleep patterns. You should also remember to ask any questions you have about your little one's behavior, hearing, and vision.

Introducing Your Baby To Your Pets

Stefanie J. Lin, V.M.D., has a houseful of animals. A veterinarian in Sellersville, Pennsylvania, Dr. Lin is "mother" to 6-year-old Timber, a part-wolf, part-dog pet, who is part of the family. A dog named Maggie and two cats, Sammy and Ripple, complete the family menagerie.

When Dr. Lin was expecting her first baby, she started preparing her pets for the addition to the household weeks before her delivery. She says you can prevent a lot of unnecessary angst if you take the time to get your pet or pets ready.

For example, Dr. Lin likes to take her two dogs

everywhere she goes. She prepared Timber and Maggie for the baby by placing a car seat in her truck. They learned weeks before Avery was born that they were not allowed to jump on or around the seat.

Dr. Lin has experience training her animals and confidence they will follow her directions once they've learned what's expected of them. For others not so confident in their animals' behavior, she recommends installing a gate between the seats. (You also could hold off taking the baby and the animals out together at the same time until your child is older.)

Dr. Lin is taking her cue from animal behavior expert Karen L. Overall, VMD, Ph.D., and a diplomate of the American College of Veterinary Behavior. Dr. Overall runs the animal behavior clinic at the University of Pennsylvania and has developed a protocol for how to go about introducing your pet to your baby.

Introduce Changes Gradually

Pets like structure and consistency in their lives. It makes them feel safe. Change can upset them, and they will view the nursery as the epicenter of change. So, step one, says Dr. Overall, is to figure out what your pet's schedule is likely to be once the baby arrives, and begin to move the pet into its new feeding, walking, and playing schedule well in advance of the big day.

"It is best," she says, "if pets do not experience all the changes at once."

Be sure to figure into the schedule a 5- to 10-minute period each day for each pet. During this time you attend to only your pet's needs. Play, pet, or groom each one with undivided attention.

As for dogs, make sure they understand basic necessary commands: sit, stay, down, take it, and drop it.

"If your dog cannot follow these commands prior to the arrival of a baby, you are going to have serious management problems," Dr. Overall says.

Before the baby arrives, allow your pet to explore the nursery. Let your pet become familiar with the furniture and with the smells of baby and lotions.

Well before her delivery date, Dr. Lin allowed Timber and Maggie into the nursery, where they stretched out on the carpeted floor.

Be Cautious with Cats

Dr. Lin felt confident that her large, well-behaved dogs would pose no threat to the baby, but she was more concerned about introducing Sammy and Ripple to the new room. Cats gravitate to small cozy spots and are likely to think that a bassinet is made just for them.

Dr. Overall agrees that you can't let a cat get too comfy in the nursery, because once the baby arrives, you'll just have to toss him out on his whiskers, creating yet one more stressful change.

"It's not true that a cat will suck the breath from a baby," Dr. Lin says. (There is a folk myth to that effect.) "But a cat can accidentally suffocate a baby just by seeking a warm, snug spot to sleep."

Dr. Overall suggests keeping the door to the baby's room closed at night, barring both dogs and cats. If you're worried about being able to hear your baby's cries at night, you can always use a monitor.

While You're Away

Before your due date, arrange for someone to pet-sit in your home while you're at the hospital. Many animals become fearful and anxious in a kennel, and it would be helpful if you can prevent that added stress, she says.

While you are in the hospital, ask your husband to take home some clothing the baby has worn. Allow the pet to smell it.

Making Your Grand Entrance

Finally, when you and your infant arrive at your front door, ask your husband to hold the baby while you go in and say hello to your pet.

Your animal has missed you and will be delirious with joy that you are home. By greeting your pet alone, you won't have to worry about the animal jumping up and possibly harming the baby. Your first words of greeting will not have to be, "No! Get down!" Instead, you can offer a loving hello. Once the animal has calmed down, bring in your infant.

When you are ready to introduce them, sit down holding the baby. Give your pet a chance to sniff the baby and explore, while you pet the animal. Be calm and reassuring. This introduction, says Dr. Overall, may take anywhere from 15 minutes to half an hour.

She cautions you not to dangle the baby in front of the pet. "It is a wholly inappropriate and potentially dangerous behavior," she says. "It could cause the pet to lunge."

If your pet hisses or growls at the baby, correct him immediately. If the animal continues, put him in another room and try the introduction again at a later time.

Your pet is going to have to learn, says Dr. Overall, that if he wants favorable attention from you, he will have to behave in a favorable manner toward your baby.

Avoiding Future Trouble

From the first day back from the hospital, do not ever leave your pet alone with the baby—not even for "just a minute." Do, however, allow your pet to follow you around the house while you tend to the baby's needs.

Trust that everything will work out fine in your family, but be alert for signs of trouble. If your cat is urinating outside the litterbox or in a corner of the baby's room, the animal is expressing anxiety.

"Inappropriate urination and elimination in a cat is, indeed, one of the most common problems we hear about," says Dr. Lin. "Seek veterinary attention immediately to rule out a physical problem and to gain behavior modification advice. But don't punish the cat, because it will only make the problem worse," she adds.

If your dog is showing signs of what's known as predatory aggression—that is, if your dog appears to be hunting your baby as though it were his prey—you have a serious problem. It is so serious, you must take action immediately. Consult a veterinary behaviorist, who in turn may recommend finding the pet a new home or euthanasia.

Raising Healthy Children in a Toxic World

Infants and small children are tender and vulnerable little beings, we know. But we don't always realize how vulnerable!

Take, for example, children's response to environmental pollutants. Children, especially babies, are at significantly greater risk from pollutants than adults because they are in a dynamic state of growth. For their relative size, they breathe more air than adults do, eat more food, and drink more fluid. As a result, they consume a greater proportion of the pollutants found in air, food, and water.

To make matters even worse, kids often can't digest, detoxify, or excrete toxins as well as adults. Further compounding the problem is kids' habit of putting everything in their mouths. It greatly increases their exposure to toxins like lead or pesticides. So does crawling on the floor or on the ground outdoors.

At the same time the little ones are exposed to these environmental pollutants, they are growing their nervous, reproductive, immune, and respiratory systems. Not one of these systems is fully developed at birth.

So it's clear that parents need to protect their babies as much as possible from the toxic elements in our world.

Let's take a look at some of the most serious and most common problems and what you can do to protect your growing child.

Using Pesticides Wisely

Every year tens of thousands of children around the country are involved in household pesticide-related poisonings or exposures. In addition to flat-out poisoning, pesticides and herbicides (weed killers) have also been linked to cancer. One study, reported in the *American Journal of Public Health*, found the strongest cancer association with common weed killers—the kind used in suburban yards across the country.

Is there really cause for concern? Apparently, the answer is yes. The U.S. Environmental Protection Agency (EPA) did a survey on pesticides used in and around the house and found that almost half of all households with children under the age of 5 had at least one pesticide stored in an unlocked cabinet and less than four feet off the ground. That is definitely within the reach of children. (Of course, you don't have to worry about an infant getting into an unlocked cabinet, but just as you set up your baby's nursery with safety in mind, you'll want to start handling household poisons with your growing baby in mind.)

The survey also found that about three-quarters of households without children under the age of 5 also stored pesticides in an unlocked cabinet, less than 4 feet off the ground. The finding is significant because these households might include your best friend's place, your parents' home, or your next-door neighbor's.

Since 1981, federal law has required most pesticides manufactured for home use to be sold in child-resistent packaging. However, once the package is open, it's up to parents to protect their children from accidental pesticide poisonings or exposures both in their own home and in the homes of friends and acquaintances.

Remember, too, that pesticides are not limited to insect sprays, traps, or dips. Flea collars and pest strips also are sources of pesticide exposure. If your baby is going to use the dog for a big pillow, get rid of the flea collar. Consider asking your veterinarian about pills you can give your dog (or cat) to repel fleas and ticks. You might also go the organic route and buy a collar made with pennyroyal, a natural, herbal flea repellant.

Here are the basics for preventing a pesticide tragedy:

☞ **Keep pesticides out of reach.** Always store pesticides where children cannot get at them, in a locked cabinet or garden shed. You can install child-proof safety latches on your cabinets. They're available at the local hardware store.

☞ **Follow directions carefully.** When using pesticides, read the label before you open the package and follow the directions to the letter. Pay special attention to all the precautions and restrictions.

☞ **Don't offer temptation.** Never put pesticides in other containers, especially those that children may associate with food or drink.

☞ **Aim high.** Keep rodent or insect baits off the floor and out of the kids' sphere of activity.

☞ **Screw those tops down.** Use child-resistant packaging properly by closing the container tightly after each use.

☞ **Share your knowledge.** Alert baby-sitters, grandparents, and other caregivers to the potential hazard of pesticides.

In case of an emergency:

If the child is unconscious, having trouble breathing, or having convulsions, give appropriate first aid immediately. Call 911 or your local emergency service.

111

If the child does not have these symptoms, but you suspect pesticide exposure, contact your local Poison Control Center or your child's pediatrician, or call 911 or your local emergency service and follow their directions. Have the product container with you when you call for assistance so you can read the label over the phone.

For more information on poisoning and for general first aid guidelines, see Part 6, which begins on page 207.

Be Careful with Lawn Care

A rolling sward of emerald—that's the dream of many homeowners. And to achieve that velvety perfection, you need chemicals. You need herbicides to kill the dandelions, the clover, the crabgrass (even before it emerges from the ground!), and all the rest of the nongrass plants that nature tries to plant in your lawn. And you need pesticides to battle the beetles, the ants, the grasshoppers, and the other creepy-crawlies that threaten a dream lawn.

But perfection can come at a considerable price. The most popular lawn treatments are the weed-and-feed variety, which contain 2,4-dichlorophenoxyacetic acid (2,4-D). Researchers have found that farmers using herbicides, especially 2,4-D, have more cases of non-Hodgkins lymphoma (a kind of cancer) than farmers who do not use these chemicals. Further, the researchers found, the more the farmers use the chemicals, the greater their risk of developing cancer.

What does all this mean for you and your baby? If you use these chemicals, or if you employ a lawn service that does, follow label recommendations carefully. Before applying pesticides or herbicides, pick up the kids and their toys, round up your pets,

Lead Testing Centers And Hotlines

If you are concerned that your child may be exposed to lead in paint or ceramic ware, you may be tempted to buy one of the home test kits on the market. Resist that temptation. The U.S. Department of Housing and Urban Development (HUD) and other federal agencies have tested these kits and found them to be unreliable. Experts recommend instead that you save your money and call one of the following hotlines.

The National Safety Council Lead Information Center has a national list of laboratories that will test lead paint and can recommend one in your area. In addition, it can suggest a state laboratory to test a sample of your water for lead and a local health department that will do a blood test for lead. The call is free at 800-424-5323 (800-424-LEAD).

You also can receive information from the Alliance to End Childhood Lead Poisoning at 202-543-1147. Or, leave your name and number with a recording at the National Lead Information Center, 800-532-3394 (800-LEAD-FYI), and someone will return your call or mail information to you.

and keep them all away from the area until the pesticide has dried or for as long as is recommended by the label.

After applying the chemicals, immediately remove all the clothing you wore and take a shower. Do not touch or carry your baby while you're wearing the clothes that have been spattered with pesticides.

The Organic Alternative

Why take any chances when you have a baby in the house? If you are willing to settle for a slightly less than perfect lawn, consider organic lawn care. You can control bugs using a system called integrated pest management. That's a system in which you introduce so-called beneficial insects, such as lady bugs and praying mantises, to keep the bad bugs under control. And you use insecticidal soap spray to control insects on bushes and shrubs. Ask your county agricultural extension agent or someone at a local nursery for information about how to do integrated pest management in your own region of the country.

As for lawn weeds, you can grub them out. The job is not as grim as it sounds. Most weeds are annuals, so if you catch them before they go to seed, you're home-free for the rest of the growing season. Be sure to reseed the bare spots, so you limit the opportunity for a second crop of weeds to sprout.

Fertilize your lawn by leaving the grass clippings in place. As they decompose, they provide grass with an effective (and free!) fertilizer.

Avoiding Pesticides In Food

Until 1996, pesticides in processed foods and pesticide residue on fresh foods were significant problems. Under the old Food, Drug and Cosmetic Act, most pesticides were not banned in processed food, leaving infants and young children especially at risk.

Every day, about 1.3 percent of the nation's 2-year-olds (about 50,000 children) received in their food a dose of five pesticides in excess of the EPA's acceptable limits.

The situation started to improve in 1996 when President Bill Clinton signed a new law to improve the way pesticides are regulated in food.

Under the Food Safety Protection Act, all exposures to pesticides must be shown to be safe for infants and children, with a clear consideration of how sensitive the young are to these chemicals.

The central feature of the law is a set of safety regulations aimed specifically at protecting infants and children from pesticides in raw and processed foods. In addition, when the EPA sets about determining a safe level for a pesticide in foods, it must explicitly account for all other pesticides that an infant or child might be exposed to during the day, such as those found in drinking water.

So these days when you're buying fresh produce or prepared baby foods at the supermarket, you don't need to be as concerned about pesticides as you would have had to be just a few short years ago. If you are preparing your own baby foods from fruits and vegetables you've grown yourself, however, you need to remember to really scrub anything that was grown with pesticides.

Protecting Your Baby From Lead Poisoning

Lead exposure is harmful to the developing brain and nervous system of fetuses, babies, and young children. At high levels, lead can cause mental retardation and damage to kidneys, the central nervous system, and tissues that form blood. Lead poisoning in children is associated with behavioral problems, learning disabilities, hearing problems, and growth retardation.

This completely preventable condition is still "the most common and societally devastating environmental disease of young children," according to a Strategic Plan for the Elimination of Childhood Lead Poisoning developed for the U.S. Department of Health and Human Services.

As many as 4 million children around the nation may be exposed to enough lead in the environment to place them at risk, and as many as 200,000 actually may be poisoned.

In a case of lead poisoning, the human body treats the lead as though it were calcium, drawing it into the bone, where it can remain throughout an individual's lifetime.

In children, exposure to lead can have a devastating impact on their intellectual development. Children who ingest lead may end up with a lower IQ and suffer learning problems, as well as have problems with abstract thinking, concentration, motor skills, and vision.

What's more, extremely high levels of lead in the blood can cause a degenerative brain disease that can result in death if left untreated. They also can disrupt the body's manufacture of heme (the oxygen-carrying part of hemoglobin in red blood cells), thus depriving living cells of their much-needed oxygen.

How much lead are we talking about here? The bottom line is that children's exposure to lead should be limited as much a possible. You don't want to wait until symptoms develop to deal with this problem. Symptoms of elevated lead levels in the blood can include irritability, insomnia, colic, and anemia. Some medical researchers have gone so far as to say that lead ingested by children may be at the root of behavioral problems, such as hyperactivity, or even juvenile delinquency.

The Importance of Testing

By and large, the early stages of lead poisoning present few symptoms. Doctors at the Centers for Disease Control and Prevention say that a blood test is the only way parents can know for sure that their children are safe. The test takes only a few minutes, and results are ready within a week.

They suggest that all children younger than 6 should be screened by a doctor or by the local health department. Some community health fairs also offer screenings for lead poisoning.

If you think your child has been exposed to lead, have the child tested for the first time at the age of 6 to 12 months, then every year after that. This is especially important if your home contains lead-based paint or other lead hazards.

If you are not aware of any lead-based paint hazards, your child should have a blood test at age 1

and again at age 2, says Dr. Schiff.

Your child's pediatrician can prescribe a drug that removes lead from children by chemically binding to it in the bloodstream and escorting it out of the body along with urine. It has been approved for use only in children found to have high levels of lead in their blood.

Living Lead-Free

The best way of dealing with lead poisoning is prevention. But prevention can be difficult because lead can be almost anywhere. It's in water pipes and the solder in the joints. It's in housewares, pottery glazes, and lead crystal. It's in the dust on your old miniblinds. It's mixed into the soil, having been released from leaded gasoline years ago. And, it is in layers of old paint. But there are steps you can take to minimize your baby's exposure to this poison.

Handling a Paint Problem

How likely is it that your walls and woodwork are coated with lead-based paint? It's highly likely if your home was built before 1978. HUD estimates that there are about 57 million private homes built before 1978 that contain lead-based paint. Nearly 10 million of them are occupied by children younger than 7 years old.

If you are just now buying or renting an older property, ask about the paint. There is a federal law (the Lead-Based Paint Disclosure Rule) that requires owners to disclose any information they know about lead-based paint before the sale or lease of housing built before 1978.

Further, the EPA requires that sellers and lessors must give you a 10-day period in which to conduct an inspection or risk assessment for the presence of lead-based paint. Also, your sales contract or rental lease must include a Lead Warning Statement,

For three months after the birth of our son, my husband and I were absolutely delirious from sleep deprivation. We took turns getting up with him, but the interruptions were taking their toll. After one particularly disastrous night, when no one got any sleep, I finally put the baby in the bed with us. He looked at my sleepy husband and smiled that little toothless grin. Tears came to my eyes as I looked at the two of them together. I told my husband, "That makes it all worth it."

Lisa L. Moreno
Columbia, South Carolina

signed by both you and the seller or lessor. In addition, you must be given a lead hazard information pamphlet to help you determine how to protect your family from lead in the home.

Look for lead-based paint on window frames, walls, and the outside of the house. Surfaces in good condition are not usually a problem, except in places where they rub against each other and create dust. (Opening a window, for example.) The bigger problem is with peeling or chipping lead paint, because kids may decide to eat the chips.

Keep your walls and other painted areas in good repair so that lead-based paint chips do not come free. If you decide to get rid of the paint, do not strip or sand the old layers of paint yourself; you'll release lead particles into your household atmosphere. Instead, it's a good idea to call a professional, who will be able to remove the paint without contaminating your home.

Lead in Miniblinds

The Consumer Product Safety Commission (CPSC) has found a lead hazard in—of all things—miniblinds for windows. It recommends that you throw away any vinyl miniblinds purchased before July 1, 1996, that were imported from China, Taiwan, Mexico, or Indonesia. A good 25 million of these blinds were imported into the United States.

The source of the problem is the lead that was added to the vinyl to stabilize it. With exposure to sunlight and heat, the vinyl deteriorates. As a result, lead dust forms on the surface of the blinds.

The dust isn't much of a danger to adults, but young children (6 and younger) are in danger because they may wipe their hands on the blinds then put their fingers in their mouths.

The lead level in dust from some of the blinds was found to be so high, says the CPSC, that "a child ingesting dust from less than one square inch of blind a day for about 15 to 30 days" could have dangerously high blood levels of lead.

Washing the dust from the blinds isn't a viable option because it does not prevent the vinyl from further deterioration. You'll just have to bite the bullet and throw them away.

The good news is that lead-free blinds are now widely available. You'll find them in cartons or packages labeled "nonleaded formula," "no lead added," or "nonleaded vinyl formulation."

Lead on the Playground

Public playground equipment may also have chipping and peeling lead paint, the government warns. The CPSC has tested and analyzed the paint on playground equipment in 13 cities. It discovered that a lot of playground equipment is covered with paint that has lead levels "high enough to be recognized as a federal priority for lead hazard control measures." In a 1996 report, the commission said, "While deteriorating lead paint in homes is the leading cause of lead poisoning in children, the effects of ingesting lead are cumulative. Therefore, exposure to lead paint from playground equipment can contribute to the lead poisoning hazard."

The CPSC has urged cities and states to address this lead hazard and has provided information for them to use in their analyses.

In the meantime, the commission recommends that you do some inspecting on your own. Examine the paint on your children's playground equipment. If you find that it has deteriorated, contact your local officials and ask them to have the paint tested by an accredited laboratory.

If your children play on or near such equipment, make sure they don't put their hands in their mouths and be sure to wash their hands thoroughly after play.

Lead on the Table

Save that beautiful Mexican pitcher for decoration only. The problem with it—and with many imported ceramic products—is that its glaze can leach unhealthy amounts of lead into the beverages you serve. (Leaching is especially potent in acidic foods and beverages, such as lemonade and spaghetti sauce.)

In fact, shelve all imported ceramic dishes, pitchers, and other products. Standards for glazes are fairly strict in some of the countries that are famous for their lovely china—England and Japan, for example—but may be lax in countries such as Mexico and China.

When shopping for ceramic ware, check the bottom of each piece. Some are clearly labeled, "For decorative use only."

Heirloom dishes may also pose a lead problem because leaching limits were not established in the United States until about 1970.

Lead on Tap

If you live in an older home, particularly one built before 1930, your plumbing may be built out of lead pipes. These pipes can leach the heavy metal into your drinking water. Examine the plumbing; if the pipes are a dull gray (not shiny), and if you can scratch the surface easily with a house key, the pipes are lead. You will have to be particularly careful with your water supply.

Unfortunately, you are not off the hook if your house was built after 1930, because lead was used to solder copper plumbing until the mid 1980s.

To reduce or eliminate lead levels in your drinking water, cook only with cold water. Odds are, it will contain little lead because lead leaches more easily into hot water.

Also, run your tap water for a couple of minutes each morning to clear the lines of any lead that may have leached into it overnight from the plumbing. A cost-efficient way to do this is to take your shower before you begin the day's cooking.

Dealing with Indoor Air Pollution

You may think of air pollution as a problem in your city, something you have to be concerned about in the great outdoors. In fact, the EPA says indoor levels of many pollutants are "significantly higher than outdoor levels." And that's a real problem for infants and young children, who spend almost every minute of each day confined indoors.

The problem is so severe that comparative risk studies have consistently ranked indoor air pollution among the top five environmental risks to public health.

Secondhand Smoke

One of the worst indoor pollutants is secondhand smoke, which is a mixture of the smoke given off by the burning ends of cigarettes, pipes, or cigars and the smoke exhaled by smokers. This mixture contains more than 4,000 substances, more than 40 of which are known to cause cancer in humans and animals and many of which are strong irritants.

Secondhand smoke is a serious health risk to infants and children. If you smoke inside your home, you are increasing your child's risk of developing pneumonia, bronchitis, and other lower respiratory tract infections. In fact, passive smoking is responsible for between 150,000 and 300,000 lower respiratory tract infections in infants and children younger than 18 months of age annually, resulting in as many as 15,000 hospitalizations.

Children exposed to secondhand smoke are also more likely to have reduced lung function. They may show signs of respiratory irritation such as coughing, wheezing, or having excess phlegm.

Passive smoking also may cause thousands of healthy children to develop asthma each year. Children with asthma—and their ranks are growing worldwide—are especially at risk. Exposure to secondhand smoke increases both the number of episodes and severity of symptoms in hundreds of thousands of children who have this disease.

The government estimates that as many as 1 million kids with asthma have their condition made worse by exposure to secondhand smoke. Passive smoking also may cause thousands of healthy children to develop the condition each year.

Don't smoke in your house or permit others to do so, especially if children are present. To protect your child outside the home, find out about the smoking policies of the day-care providers, preschools, and other caregivers for your children.

Asbestos

Asbestos is a mineral fiber that has commonly been used for insulation and as a fire-retardant. You'll find it in pipe and furnace insulation materials, asbestos shingles, millboard, textured paints and other coating materials, and floor tiles.

Exposure to asbestos fibers produces no immediate health problems, but over time the fibers that have been inhaled can cause chest and abdominal cancer and lung diseases. (Smokers are at higher risk of developing asbestos-induced lung cancer.)

If asbestos products are not damaged or disturbed, they are fairly safe. Generally, material in good condition will not release asbestos fiber. Problems most frequently arise when asbestos is tinkered with. Elevated concentrations of airborne asbestos occur after materials are disturbed by cutting, sawing, or sanding, for example. Problems with asbestos fibers crop up most often in older homes.

Environmental health experts suggest that it is best to leave undamaged asbestos material alone if it is not likely to be disturbed. If you must remove it, rely on qualified contractors for cleanup.

Electromagnetic Fields

Over the past several years, there have been a number of reports in the media that the electromagnetic fields (EMFs) around electrical wires may pose hazards to children. EMFs are electric and magnetic fields created by electricity. They are produced not only by power lines and transmitters, but also by such everyday appliances as electric clocks, televisions, electric blankets, heated waterbeds, microwave ovens, and cell phones.

Many parents are now worried about their children's exposure to EMFs, especially the strong fields near power lines or microwave antennae. Is this really anything to be concerned about? The National Research Council attempted to determine, once and for all, whether exposure to EMFs can harm children's health.

In the autumn of 1996, the 16-member council issued a report on its three-year study. The council determined that there is an unexplained "weak but statistically significant" association between high levels of exposure to EMF and childhood leukemia.

No scientist has yet been able to determine exactly how EMFs affect our bodies, but the best research so far indicates that our cell membranes are sensitive to extremely weak, low-frequency magnetic fields.

Research scientists concerned about the health effects of EMF exposure have recommended a policy of "prudent avoidance."

If you plan to protect your child from EMF exposure, follow this rule of thumb: Keep your distance. Distance may well be your ally because the intensity of an electromagnetic field drops off as distance from the source increases.

Here are other prevention measures:

☞ **Watch where they play.** Keep your child from standing too close to television sets, microwave ovens, or computers. Forbid your child to play under high-power lines.

☞ **Reduce the time of exposure.** Instead of using an electric blanket, warm the bed with an electric blanket, then turn it off before you tuck your child in.

☞ **Draw a circle of protection.** Move any electric appliance (clock, baby monitor) away from the bed. Move your child's bed if there is a refrigerator or electric stove on the other side of the wall.

Chapter Seven

the working mother's survival guide

I f having a baby and dealing with a newborn are not flat-out hard labor, nothing is. But no matter how hard you're working, and no matter how much you're enjoying your baby, the day comes when most women—more than three-fourths, in fact—

have to go back to work after having a baby. You, too, may be having to pick up your briefcase, papers, or whatever, and head out the door to your regular job.

Some women's economic circumstances force them to return to work almost immediately after giving birth. Others take the traditional 6-week maternity leave. Still others opt to take the 12 weeks without pay that federal law made available in 1993. A few manage an even longer leave.

When the regular job does beckon, that transition is a tough one for a lot of mothers. "When I kiss the baby good-bye, I feel like I'm abandoning her," says one single mother who had to return to work as soon as possible for economic reasons. "Every day I feel that way."

Even mothers who really want to return to their careers can have ambivalent feelings. "I felt very conflicted about going back to work," says Eden Langford, a young mother in New York City who is also an account executive at an ad agency. "I loved being home and taking care of my baby, but sometimes I missed the fun and excitement of my job. I also missed the people I work with. But no matter where I am, I feel the stress of working, parenting, and running a home. I want to do all three things well—I've always been an overachiever—but there's just not enough time. At home, we rarely entertain anymore, and my husband misses it. At work, I sometimes get distracted. I'm always worrying about how the baby is doing at day care."

Ask almost any new mother what it's like to return to work, and you'll hear many of the same concerns: guilt, stress, and time pressure.

New mothers worry about not being the kind of mother they planned to be. They agonize about the quality of care their children are receiving in the

Share Your Job

If juggling job, child, and career seems daunting, consider investigating alternative or flexible work arrangements such as job sharing.

In job sharing two people basically share one full-time job, but the specific arrangements can vary. In one possible situation, two people split equally the 40-hour work week. In another, the pair alternates weeks on and weeks off. In yet another, two people customize their daily schedules, depending on their home situations.

What kind of employer would consider employing two people to share one job? The position is ripe for strife, given the possibility of unequal workloads, jealousy over recognition, and a lack of opportunity for advancement.

Reports published in *The Wall Street Journal*, however, suggest that job-sharing teams often forge a strong relationship that benefits both employer and employees.

These teams are motivated by a desire to balance personal or family activities with the status and career opportunity of a full-time job. The new breed of pairs is apparently surviving cutbacks, winning promotions, and even jumping ship for better jobs.

If you'd like to have a go at job sharing, point out to your employer that the company is getting two heads for the price of one. Promise that your team will resolve any disputes on its own. Finally, show that job sharing will allow you to master larger-than-life workloads without burning out.

---

hands of others. They feel the stress of juggling so many roles: worker, mother, homemaker, wife, and lover (perhaps also daughter, church or civic leader, neighbor, and friend.) And new mothers almost universally complain that they don't have enough time to do all the things they need to do. It seems there is no time at all for "want-to" activities, only time—and just barely—for "have-to" tasks.

The problems of a working mother are complex, and there are no easy solutions to them. However, it will help you to know the effects day care can have on a child and, partially as a result of that knowledge, how to choose the best day care you can afford. It will also ease the situation if you can prepare both your baby and yourself for the inevitable day when you must be separated. And it will help, on a purely practical level, to simplify your household by having reliable help when you need it.

Day Care's Effect On Children

It's only natural for a new mother returning to the workforce to worry that her absence will affect her baby in a negative way. The opinions of child-care experts also reflect real disagreement about whether an infant placed in day care will be helped or hindered by the experience.

Here's an overview of the pros and cons:

Good news: Children in day care learn academic and social skills earlier than stay-at-home kids, according to a survey done by the Child Care Action Campaign in New York City in conjunction with *Working Mother* magazine.

Good news: A Miami study of a model university day-care program found that children who entered full-time care as infants not only were more sociable, but also posted higher math scores than their peers in sixth grade.

Not-so-good news: Problem is, most child-care facilities in this country are not like model programs. A four-state study done by the Families and Work Institute found that most children get mediocre day care, and 10 to 20 percent get care so poor that it risks damaging their development.

Bad news: There are few studies of poor-quality day care, but those that have been done reveal that children in substandard day care score lower on tests that look at their ability to learn and understand. These children also are more resistant to guidance, the studies show. Researchers theorize that the negative effects may be the result of an ill-trained staff, inadequate materials, oversized groups, and high staff turnover.

Good news and bad news: Although kids in day care tend to be more self-reliant and confident, studies also show they are more boisterous, competitive, or likely to fight and argue. In a study of 589 children in average day-care facilities, John E. Bates, Ph.D., a psychology professor at Indiana University in Bloomington, found that those who had spent a lot of time in day care were more aggressive by the time they reached kindergarten.

Good news and bad news: Children in day care are more independent and determined to get their way, but they lack the social skills to accomplish that smoothly, says Alison Clarke-Stewart, Ph.D., a professor at the University of California–Irvine. Also, a North Carolina study found that this aggressiveness vanished after a few years in school.

Help from the Boss

As research seems to indicate, the better the child care, the better the child. And it logically follows that if your baby is happy, you will be happy, too. Selecting good day care will free you from residual guilt and allow you to concentrate on work when you are at work.

Your goal, then, is to find the very best child care your family can afford.

The first step is to determine how much you can spend. Your next step is to investigate whether your place of employment offers any benefits or programs that can help you. Nearly 8 out of 10 major U.S. employers offer some kind of child-care help, according to a report by Hewitt Associates, a national benefits consulting firm.

Referrals

Your employer may offer a resource and referral service for day-care options. This form of assistance

The Working Father

Some might snicker at the phrase "working father." Of course the father works. He's the breadwinner, after all. And he simply doesn't allow being a father to distract him from his career goals.

Or does he?

In a study entitled "Ozzie and Harriet Are Dead," researchers found that fathers are just as likely to bring family concerns to the office as are mothers. The study was conducted by Rosalind Barnett, Ph.D., a visiting scholar of psychology at Radcliffe College in Cambridge, Massachusetts. She says that her findings should reassure employers that mothers do make good, reliable employees and that men also have need of a humane corporate culture.

When it comes to issues such as getting paid leave to spend time with a newborn, dads typically have a harder time of it than moms. Even companies sensitive to mothers' needs often leave fathers completely out of the picture, according to *The Wall Street Journal*. One nationwide competition that names the best 100 companies for mothers is annually inundated with applications submitted by hundreds of companies. But an effort to select the best firms for fathers found only 30 companies in the entire country that actively supported men in parenting.

Today's fathers may face the daunting choice of "rat race" or "daddy track." Despite a growing focus on family values, it seems fathering is still largely devalued in the workplace. A University of Wisconsin study shows that 63 percent of men expect bosses to react negatively if they ask for paternity leave. Even at companies that offer family-friendly programs, the prevailing attitude among managers is that the men who use them are less than serious about their careers.

is commonly provided, usually in the form of a telephone hot line that offers parents referrals to child-care centers.

The best services employ trained counselors who give individualized advice on choosing care; others simply provide a list. Even a list can be helpful if you can find out which of your coworkers has used the center you are considering. You can talk to them about their experiences and learn a great deal. Also,

Mother's Separation Anxiety

Who suffers more when mothers and babies are separated? It's hard to say for sure, but studies have shown that a mother's guilt and anxiety about leaving her child for periods of time can have more of an impact on the child than the separation itself.

If you are overanxious about leaving, you may try to compensate for your absence by overmothering, according to a study done a few years ago by Cynthia A. Stifter, Ph.D., and Colleen M. Coulehan, both of Pennsylvania State University, and Margaret Fish, Ph.D. of Marshall University School of Medicine in Huntington, West Virginia.

Mothers who were very anxious about being separated from their infants, the study found, tended to be more intrusive and controlling with their infants than mothers who were less worried.

These worried mothers tended to stimulate their babies too much and had trouble picking up on cues that could have helped them interact better with their infants. In the anxious moms' earnest attempts to make up for lost time, they missed or ignored their babies' body language indicating the need for a break. They also missed other cues, perhaps putting away a toy the baby was still interested in.

A mother may feel she is lavishing her baby with positive attention: reading a story, playing a game, listening to music, dancing the baby around the room, winding up the jack-in-the-box, playing peekaboo. On her to-do list for baby, she can check off: Stimulation, Communication, Education. What could possibly be wrong with this interaction?

The baby may feel that there is a lot of noise, but not much satisfaction involved in this encounter. When the baby wanted to see the jack-in-the box pop up again, the little one tried to tell Mama by touching her arm. But she put the toy away without noticing. After a while, the baby showed signs of feeling a little overwhelmed. But that's when Mama picked the child up for a swooping waltz around the room. If a baby's subtle "I've had enough" signals are ignored too often, he or she may feel that Mama can't be relied upon.

The researchers say that these infants may become less secure rather than more secure in their attachment to mothers who are working so desperately to create something called "quality time."

There is no quick solution to extreme maternal separation anxiety, but if a woman becomes aware of her feelings she may be able to control her compulsion to overmother and also learn to tune in to her baby's cues.

---

the day-care centers that are listed are usually near the workplace—a big plus, because you and your baby can share commuting time.

If your employer doesn't offer a referral service, all is not lost. Just head for your local library. Ask the librarian if the library has a database with information on day care, social services, and community resources. (Don't let the word "database" intimidate you. If you are computer shy, the librarian will be pleased to set up the program for you and show you how to use it.) If your library doesn't have this information on a database, it should still have a number of other sources for this kind of information.

Dependent-Care Accounts

Does your employer (or your husband's) offer a dependent-care account? If so, you can put aside as much as $5,000 before taxes into it. (A few exceptionally generous companies partially match employee contributions.)

This kind of account can help you budget for day care. There is one serious drawback to these accounts, however. If you don't spend the money that you set aside for the year, you lose it.

On-Site Day Care

If you are lucky, your employer may offer on-site day-care. Fewer than 10 percent of the large companies in this country do, generally because of the high cost of insurance. If your company does, however, take full advantage of it. Just think, you'll be able to have lunch with your baby without leaving the office.

And here's a real plus: Because your company is

not expecting a profit from the enterprise, the cost to you is usually lower than that of most commercial child-care centers.

Big accounting firms routinely offer Saturday child-care services during tax season. Now many law firms also provide these services. Dewey Ballantine in Manhattan, for example, started an office baby-sitting service for full-time employees who need to work on Saturday. And if you must work late for some top-priority project, some firms even offer in-home child care.

Child-Care Choices

You have several day-care options, including care in someone else's home, a day-care center, care in your own home, and leaving your baby with a relative. No matter which one you decide to investigate, it helps to start by drawing up a list of absolutes. These are issues on which you absolutely will not compromise. For instance, the caregiver absolutely must pick up the baby whenever he or she cries. Surroundings absolutely must be clean and safe.

Your list of absolutes will serve as the backbone for your discussions with potential caregivers.

Care in Another's Home

Costs vary widely for having someone care for your baby in their home. A neighborhood stay-at-home mother might be happy to accept $100 a week to baby-sit your infant, but a licensed facility in a private home may charge $250 a week or more. Generally, however, these types of day-care arrangements are less expensive and more flexible than large day-care centers.

Make your initial selections based on family economics, then begin your investigation of the care-giver and the facility. Requirements for state certification vary from state to state, so start your research with your local health department to see what the standards are.

You can get some basic information from providers (payments, schedules, and the like) with a simple phone call, but the information you really need is available only by visiting the day-care home in person. It's important to spend some time with this potential caregiver who will be an important person in your baby's life. By all means, bring your baby to the meeting.

When you meet each potential caregiver, ask yourself these questions:
- **Does she seem** to enjoy my child?
- **Does she appear** to have the same beliefs and attitudes I have about discipline?
- **Is this a person** with whom I could have an open relationship?
- **Will she take** the time to regularly discuss my child with me?
- **Will she allow** me to drop in at any time to observe the group?

If your child is an infant, notice whether the caregiver does the following:
- **Enjoys holding and cuddling** a baby she' taking care of
- **Talks to and plays** with the baby
- **Feeds and diapers** the baby properly and washes her hands afterwards
- **Spends plenty of time** holding, talking, and playing with the baby
- **Helps the baby** find interesting things to see, touch, and hear

Walk around the home to see if there is:
- **A clean, safe place** to change diapers
- **A crib with firm** mattress covered with sturdy plastic
- **A separate crib** for each baby

Also look for:
- **Covered radiators**

On March 15, 1996, my beautiful son Zachary was born into this world. From that point on, I was, and still am, head over heels in love with him. I never knew it could be like this. He is my life and my entire world. It was very hard for me to go back to work, six weeks after his birth. I felt a hole in my heart. There is a place for him there that I feel every day. Now, almost a year later (where did that year go?), I still feel him in my heart, as I did those early weeks of his life. It is still difficult sometimes to head to work in the morning, rushing him and I out the door. But I know this is what has to be done, and we all must make the best of it.

Angela Wolpert
Dallastown, Pennsylvania

•**Safety equipment** (one or more smoke detectors and a first aid kit)
•**Bars on windows** above the first floor
•**Safety caps** on the electrical outlets
•**Baby gates** at the stairs

If your child is a toddler, also ask if the provider:
•**Will cooperate with you** in toilet training
•**Can guarantee a safe environment** for a child who is beginning to crawl and walk

Also determine whether the provider will:
•**Provide the right activities** and materials that will help your child develop both physically and intellectually
•**Set limits** in an age-appropriate way
•**Encourage good eating** and toilet habits
•**Have enough time** for each child in the group
•**Have enough room** for the children to move about freely

Most at-home day care maintains a good adult-to-child ratio, with usually no more than four children at one time in the care of one adult.

Ask the person directly:
•**Does she know** basic first aid and have regular medical exams for herself?
•**Will she care** for your child if the little one is ill?
•**If so,** is there a place away from the group where the baby can nap or rest?
•**Is the facility** licensed?

If you want to find an accredited child-care program in your area, call the National Association for Family Child Care (NAFCC). The association is an accreditation service rather than a referral service. However, it can direct you to an accredited child-care program in your area. Call 800-359-3817.

You also can call Child Care Aware, which works with local nonprofit agencies to train and accredit family child-care providers. It offers a consumer checklist to help you assess child-care providers, as well as a toll-free information line that can help you find resource and referral agencies in your community. Call 800-424-2246.

Day-Care Centers

Once you get out of day care offered in people's homes and into day-care centers, you're dealing with a much bigger arena. Some day-care centers are as big as small elementary schools, and you may worry that your little baby will get lost in such vast surroundings. But it's not the size of the building that matters so much as the size of the group your baby will become part of. If your baby's group is small, and if the same person cares for the babies each and every day, a big day-care center actually can feel quite homey.

The exceptionally good day-care centers are expensive, and many have waiting lists. On the plus side, however, the staff at these centers is usually well trained, and the center should offer programs that are designed to meet a growing child's developmental needs.

A community usually has several types of day-care centers, including the big chains such as KinderCare, independent for-profit day-care centers, and nonprofit centers. Ask your pediatrician what he or she knows about these programs and if any in your area stand out as particularly good.

Then pick up your baby and your list of concerns, and go on a tour to see what's out there. Call for an appointment. Reputable day-care centers welcome a visit from a potential client. They will allow you to observe and will have someone, most often the director, available to answer your questions.

As you visit each of the facilities, here's what to check into:

Day-Care Dynamics

How many children can a day-care center handle? Ideal adult-to-child ratios vary depending upon the age of the child:

- **For infants and toddlers up to age 2: There should be no more than three children per adult.**
- **For ages 2 to 3: The group should be limited to three or four children per adult.**
- **For those ages 3 to 6: The group can increase to eight children per adult.**

☞ **View the surroundings.** As you drive up, evaluate whether the outdoor play yard is adequately protected from sidewalk and road traffic. Note the age, quality, and quantity of outdoor equipment. Is the area nicely landscaped with grassy areas and trees?

☞ **Look over the indoor environment.** Determine whether the environment is safe and well lighted. Is it homelike and inviting?

☞ **Pay attention to how the babies are treated.** Are the babies in small groups with only one or two caregivers? Watch to see that the infants are cuddled, talked to, and played with. Watch especially to see what happens when a baby cries. Is he or she picked up right away and comforted?

☞ **Find out about the staff.** In your interview, ask the director of the center about the staff's education, experience, and turnover rate. In good programs, most caregivers are required to have two years of college, and the director usually is required to have a college degree.

☞ **Look into the child's future treatment.** Ask whether your baby will have one person as the primary caregiver. Ask about the center's philosophy on discipline.

☞ **Get information about specific programs.** Once you have established whether your baby will be safe and well-tended, ask about the programs offered at the center. Do the programs

Baby Signs

Don't worry if your baby seems tired when you first bring him or her home from day care. The environment can be extra stimulating, with lots of things to look at and listen to that are new to your child.

In addition, the unfamiliar surroundings may prevent your little one from taking naps as well as he or she does at home.

Here's the bottom line: Does your baby still smile a lot? Does your baby seem to be enjoying the experience? If so, your baby is probably doing just fine.

provide a variety of opportunities for both intellectual and physical growth? What are the goals of the programs?

Some centers are almost like schools in that they focus on teaching new skills and modifying behavior. Others are more laissez-faire, allowing the children to develop at their own pace. Many combine elements of both. Stay away from centers that are nothing but body-sitters, the ones that keep the children clean and fed but offer little stimulation for mind and body.

☞ **Find out about the application process.** The center should want to know about your child's developmental level, health status, and specific needs. It may ask you about your other children or about your outlook on raising your baby. Alarm bells should ring if these questions are not raised.

☞ **Ask how the center handles illness.** Under what circumstances will you have to keep your child home? What will the center do if your child becomes ill during the day? Will staff members administer medicine if your child needs it?

☞ **Get specific.** Ask not only about payments, but also about what items you will be expected to provide. Ask about what kinds of meals and snacks are served, and be sure serving times are always the same. Ask about holiday celebrations, field trips, and birthdays. In other words, find out all you can

before you make a decision and plunk down a substantial amount of money.

To find an accredited center near you, call the National Association for the Education of Young Children (NAEYC) for its list of more than 3,000 centers nationwide. Call 800-424-2460.

Care in Your Own Home

Possibly the best child-care option, albeit the most expensive, is a professionally trained nanny taking care of your baby in your own home. Under this arrangement, your baby remains in familiar surroundings and can develop a secure one-on-one relationship with the caregiver. You'll be free of worrying about commuting with your baby or agonizing about what will happen when your baby gets sick. And, if you pick your nanny well, you won't have to worry about the quality of care your child receives. You will, however, probably worry about how to pay for this Rolls Royce of child care.

The cost of hiring a nanny currently runs anywhere from $200 to $400 or more per week, depending on the nanny's age and experience. In addition, you will be responsible for paying Social Security and Medicare taxes at a rate of 15.3 percent (half of which is deducted from her pay), federal and state unemployment taxes, and, in some states, workers' compensation insurance.

You can hire a live-in nanny for whom you will have to provide room and board. Some live-ins are happy to share a hall bathroom with their charges, but others may not settle for anything less than a bedroom/bathroom suite. Live-in nannies also need either the occasional use of your car or a car of their own.

A second option is to hire someone who will commute to your home. She will work 50 hours a week and most likely have her own car. This type of nanny is paid more per week, usually $300 plus, but you are not responsible for room and board.

How do you go about hiring a nanny? You'll need to work with an agency, which will charge anywhere from $100 to $3,000 to find you a perfectly suited nanny and to check her references.

By contacting an agency, you are tapping into the expertise of people who know what they are doing. The more expertise they have, the more you can expect to spend.

The agency will investigate the nanny's background for motor vehicle accidents, child abuse, and any criminal charges. In addition, they will interview her personally if she is local. If she is relocating from another area, an agency there will have interviewed her.

"Each agency's style is different," says Wendy Sacks, president of the International Nanny Association. "Parents should ask questions and understand what exactly the agency does in a background check."

You might ask how many references the agency will check, for example. You'll also want to know whether the references submitted are meaningful.

"Two different agencies may say they check four references, but one may be checking the references of people who are friends and neighbors of the potential nanny, while the other may be checking former employers," cautions Sacks. "Know exactly what they are doing."

If a police report says that one M. Poppins does not have a criminal record in Dade County, Florida, Sacks warns, that doesn't mean that there isn't one in Cook County, Illinois. Be sure the search is thorough.

Interviewing a Nanny

Once a nanny has passed muster with the agency, she will be sent to your home for an interview with you. Consider how she will fit in with your household as well as with your baby. The primly starched Mary Poppins might be a disappointment if you and your children happen to be expecting someone more like TV's earthy Fran Drescher.

For more information about hiring a nanny, write the International Nanny Association, Station House, Suite 438, 900 Haddon Avenue, Collingswood, NJ 08108. This nonprofit organization will send you a free copy of "A Nanny for Your Family," a pamphlet that provides basic information as well as answers to commonly asked questions.

You also can pay for a preemployment screening on an individual caregiver by contacting The ChildCare Registry. It will confirm the individual's employment status and references, educational degree, date of birth, Social Security number, criminal and civil record, Department of Motor Vehicles record, and residence for the previous seven years.

The ChildCare Registry lists child-care providers who have submitted their own resumes for a background check. For $100, parents can obtain information on a provider who is registered. For $165 the registry will investigate an unregistered provider. Call 800-227-0033.

Once you've hired a nanny, you'll need to continue your evaluation of that person for some time. Spend time at home with the new nanny, suggests Sacks. "You can tell a lot about a person when you see them hands-on with your child or children," she says. And, she adds, make sure you take the time to train the nanny to meet your family's needs.

Imported Child Care

If you're considering one-on-one child care in your home, you might also want to look into hiring an *au pair* as part of a cultural exchange program. The program brings young adults into the United States and places them with families specifically to be child-care providers.

The organization running the program screens young adults, ages 18 through 26, who are experienced in providing child care, are proficient in

English, have a diploma from secondary school, have sound references, and have a driver's license. Most are young women, but some young men also apply and are accepted as au pairs.

Au pairs are selected from 17 European countries, ranging from Iceland and Great Britain to Switzerland and Turkey.

There are eight U.S. government-sanctioned au pair agencies under the umbrella of World Learning, a nonprofit organization that works with participating European offices.

The people at World Learning emphasize that "au pair" means "on par," and that this young adult should be treated as a family member. That means including him or her in family meals, activities, and even vacations. Au pairs can be given responsibility for feeding, bathing, diapering, and dressing infants. They can prepare meals for the children and assist with keeping their rooms and play areas clean and neat. Au pairs, however, do not do general house-cleaning or meal preparation. They will provide child-care services for 45 hours a week.

Your responsibility as a host family is to provide the au pair with meals, a private room, weekly spending money, one full weekend off every fourth week, and a day-and-a-half off the other weeks of the month.

In the year that the caregiver spends with you, you also are responsible for providing two weeks of paid vacation, an educational stipend, and up to six hours a week for study and to attend classes in accordance with U.S. government regulations, the full cost of U.S. domestic travel to and from the au pair's arrival point in this country, and time to meet with the local au pair coordinator. You'll also have to arrange for auto insurance if the au pair is to use the family car.

So what will all this cost you? At this writing, the total is a bit more than $10,000 for application and matching fees, spending money, and an educational stipend. That sum does not include the variables of domestic travel, car insurance, and room and board. The folks at World Learning say that au pairs are better than live-in baby-sitters or nannies in many ways. Remember, while the au pair is learning about America, he or she is also giving American children an opportunity to learn about another culture.

For more information about the program, contact World Learning in Washington, D.C. at 202-408-5420.

Preparing Your Baby

Once you've arranged for day care, it's time to ease your baby into this new life. Psychologists say that your return to work will be less stressful to your baby if the baby has already learned that he or she can get along just fine in the care of another person.

One of your first efforts to smooth the way back to work is to make a point of briefly separating from your child during the first few months. Hire a baby-sitter and go to the movies. Leave your baby with your parents while you shop. Trade off baby-sitting with your neighbor. Before long your baby will discover that, while the caregiver may not be Wonderful You, somehow those diapers got changed and that little tummy got filled.

When scheduling your return to the labor force, keep in mind that babies at certain ages have a harder time adjusting to a new person than at other times in their development.

Most babies between 7 and 10 months old, for instance, go through a period called "stranger anxiety," during which they are wary of anyone they don't see almost daily.

If your return to work coincides with this phase of your child's development, introduce your new sitter or caregiver with exquisite care. At their first meeting, hold your baby on your lap while you talk to the sitter. Encourage her to speak gently and to

My recommendation to new moms returning to work is this: Make sure you get up early enough to shower and dress before the baby wakes (unless you don't mind bringing him/her in with you). A moment of solitude is a good thing.

Completely dress—except for your blouse, which goes on right before you run out the door. I can guarantee that nothing your children deposit on your clothing will look like a fashion statement. And if you need to buy new clothes, it's easier to make quick changes in separates than in a dress—and you will need to make quick changes!

Diane Voie
Marysville, Washington

draw close to the baby gradually.

Next, schedule time to be at home with your sitter while your baby adjusts to her and while she learns your baby's routine and your baby's likes and dislikes. Even though you are still at home, let her do as much as possible.

Infants being left in child care outside your home are less likely to become upset if they have just eaten or taken a nap.

Older babies and toddlers can be a bit more difficult to leave. Here the key to success is to set aside plenty of time for your baby to adjust to this radical (to him or her) change. The process should take a full five days. It sounds like a lot of time, but if you invest this time up front, it will make the whole experience go a lot smoother for you and your baby. Here's the technique:

• **Day One:** Make the first day in day care just half a day. You should plan on staying there yourself the whole time. A morning in the new environment with you present will give your little one enough time to get the feel of the place. Then take your baby home with you and follow your usual routine.

• **Day Two:** The next day, again plan for half a day. This time, however, you should spend only an hour or so at the day-care center, then leave and come back at noon to take your baby home. Leaving and returning will demonstrate to your baby that he or she is not being dumped in some alien world—however friendly. Spending the rest of the day following your usual pattern will add to your baby's sense of security.

• **Day Three:** On the third morning, make sure you leave the day-care center a little sooner and return a little later—perhaps after lunch.

• **Day Four:** The next morning, again stretch the time that your baby is in child care without you.

• **Day Five:** Finally, on the fifth day, bring your baby to the center, then say a calm and steady good-bye. (And don't you dare get weepy in front of your little one.) Reassure your baby that you'll be back in a while. Then leave quickly. If your child is upset, ask the caregiver to provide comfort and reassurance. Almost all babies will cry for a few minutes, then settle into the routine that has become familiar over the previous few days.

One final note: Be sure to give the caregiver the phone numbers where you and your husband can be reached during the day, as well as the number of your doctor, pharmacy, and any other emergency numbers that are important. If you have family members or friends nearby, ask if they would be willing to help out in case of an emergency or serve as a backup if your regular caregiver becomes ill. Offer payment to make the arrangement fair and to make it formal.

Share and Simplify

No matter how well your child-care system works, if things aren't running smoothly at home, you'll be facing stress and frustration on a daily basis. So along with that contract you're working up for a caregiver, you might consider working out a written contract for you and your husband. This is a simple agreement as to who is responsible for different chores around the house.

To create this contract, you and your husband should make a complete list of household and baby-care chores. Your husband, just from helping you make such a long list, probably will understand why you need his help so badly. The next step is for the two of you to sign up for specific duties.

Gloss on the Go

Most mornings you'll be feeding and dressing the baby in the time you may once have spent on your hair and makeup. Yet, you still must look attractive and well-groomed at work, no matter what your job.

The way to generate a little gloss while you're on the go is to be prepared and to keep things simple. Here's what you need to do:

☞ **Check your clothing.** A few weeks before you start back to work, go over your wardrobe. Try everything on to see how the clothing fits. If some things are a bit tight, do not cram yourself into them. You won't look attractive. It's better to have a few outfits that fit well and look good and save the others until you lose the rest of the "baby fat."

☞ **Spruce up your wardrobe.** You probably haven't worn your work clothes since you were about five months pregnant, so they may be a bit limp and closet-wrinkled. Send these garments off to the cleaners or launder and iron them.

☞ **Consider your coif.** Get a really good haircut, one of the wash-and-go kinds that don't require curling irons and rollers. Or, get a perm.

☞ **Review your cosmetics.** Keep your makeup palette simple: one shade of foundation, one lipstick, and one blush from the warm red family, another set from the cool red family. These selections will harmonize with any colors in your wardrobe. Keep your eye makeup to a minimum, and if you use concealer for dark circles under your eyes, try to find one with a yellow hue to counteract the blue tones.

Keep all your cosmetics together in a zippered bag, so you can toss the entire collection into your purse.

If your husband would rather bathe the baby than do the dishes, fine. Encourage him to sign up for bath time.

If you don't mind swabbing the kitchen floor, then take on that task. Each of you choose the chores you find least onerous.

But let's face it, some chores will not be picked by either of you. Perhaps the best way to divide them between you is simply to take turns doing the the ones neither of you likes.

Part III

the baby blooms

adventures in eating

Your baby spends the first few months of life lustily yelling for milk. You hear those attention-compelling screams at 2 a.m., and perhaps again at 3:30, again at sunrise, and yet again at

noon. And that's only the first half of the day! Of course, you respond to these cries with all the love in your heart. Your reward is seeing your baby grow and grow and GROW.

The relentless pressure to be there with the next offering of milk soon eases off. By 3 months, a feeding schedule will begin to work itself out. And by 4 months, more or less, your baby will be on a fairly predictable schedule, probably wanting to nurse about every four hours.

Predictable feeding times make life so much easier. You can, for example, plan a trip to the supermarket between "lunch" and "dinner," so that you can cruise your contented baby up and down the aisles in relative tranquility.

If you have returned to your job, you may be able to manipulate both your schedule and the baby's so you, rather than the babysitter, are the one who provides most of the feedings.

Predictable feeding times are good for another reason: They lead to predictable nap times, which in turn afford you a measure of independence. You now will be able to count on having blocks of time to use as you need.

Your baby will seem a bit calmer and more independent, too. When your little one does feel hunger, the crying is less frantic. This means that your baby has finally begun to trust that breast milk or formula will be forthcoming on a regular basis and that you will be there to meet his or her needs.

And here's a nice aside: As feedings become more evenly spaced and less frequent, so do your baby's bowel movements.

Introducing New Foods

Most babies can thrive on nothing but breast milk or formula until they are about 6 months old. In fact, breast milk provides sufficient nutrition until a baby is about 6 months of age.

You will be bombarded by experienced mothers who want to share their wealth of knowledge with you about raising your child. Some of it is helpful, some very frustrating. Especially when their views are different than your own. Trust your instincts. You know your child better than anyone else. Even though you have never done this before, you will learn what's best for your little one. I had a mother-in-law who always wanted to know why my child wasn't reaching the "milestones" as fast as her son. One day (after hearing this for the hundredth time), I said, "Children develop at different rates, but I bet she will be able to do everything he could do by the time she turns 2 years old."

Dana Stone Sanders
Cartersville, Georgia

If you've been feeding your baby formula, at about 4 months of age, your little one may be ready to try some solid food. When a formula-fed baby is taking 32 ounces of formula a day and is still not satisfied, that's the time to start cereals.

Your baby may not be physically mature enough to begin eating solids, however, if he or she:
•**cannot hold up** his or her own head (necessary to prevent choking)
•**does not have control** of lips and tongue
•**hasn't yet outgrown** the tongue thrust reflex that automatically makes a baby expel food (Try touching the tip of your baby's tongue with the tiniest dab of cereal on a spoon. Watch to see if the tongue automatically thrusts the cereal out of the mouth. Try this a few times.)

When you decide to offer solid foods, look for a clue that the baby is ready. Is your baby looking around, noticing what you are eating? Does your baby seem interested in trying the food or at least mouthing it?

If the answer to these questions is yes, then the transition to solids should be easy. Most likely, your baby's doctor has suggested that you offer rice cereal as the baby's first food. The reason is that rice is the cereal least likely to cause an allergic reaction. Later your baby can progress to barley and oat cereal, and eventually to wheat and corn.

Watch for Allergies

What happens when your baby is allergic to a food? A baby's immune system can become sensitized to a particular food and produce antibodies. The result can be runny eyes and nose, wheezing, eczema, hives, diarrhea, even vomiting. A baby also may have a headache or a tummy ache, but these symptoms are not as likely to come to your attention.

When you start your child on a food, make sure it's just one food, and give it each day for about a week. Offer no other new foods during this time. Introduce the foods methodically: first cereal, then perhaps some pureed vegetables, and then pureed fruits. The reason for this approach is to identify allergies. By keeping the introduction of new foods widely spaced, it will be easy to determine which one is the culprit should an allergic reaction take place.

To prepare infant cereal, shake out a small amount into a dish. Stir breast milk or formula into the cereal. Feed your baby with a small spoon, such as a demitasse spoon or a special infant spoon. Serve your baby only one or two spoons of cereal. Allow your child plenty of time to feel, smell, and taste this extremely exotic (to him or her) dish. Some babies simply may want to touch the food. That's perfectly normal.

When your baby is 6 months old, you can try introducing some pureed fruit, according to the Children's Nutrition Research Center in Houston. They suggest pureed pears, bananas, and applesauce. Once your baby has learned to enjoy a couple dif-

ferent fruits, try introducing pureed vegetables.

Don't offer your baby meat until he or she is 7½ or 8 months old, says Suzanne LeBel Corrigan, M.D., a pediatrician in Irving, Texas, and an associate professor of clinical pediatrics at the University of Texas Southwestern Medical School. "It's difficult to digest, and the commercial baby food meats really don't taste very good," she says. "Besides, the baby doesn't really need the protein yet." That is because both breast milk and formula contain plenty of protein.

Buying Baby Food

If you are buying commercially made baby food, you'll want to select the best. Some baby food manufacturers add lots of starches, water, and sugar at the expense of more nutritious ingredients. To get the best, take the time to read the label on the jar. Ingredients are listed in order, with the main ingredient first. If you are buying pureed carrots, for example, carrot should be the first ingredient listed, not water.

You'll also notice as you read that single food items—a jar of yellow squash, for example—are less likely to contain fillers than mixtures such as carrots and peas.

Hold off on the baby desserts that have extra sugar. Your baby doesn't need calories from sugar when you can give him or her the nutritious sweetness of fresh fruit that you puree or mash yourself.

Avoid These Foods

Food should help your baby thrive and grow. The last thing you want to do is give anything to your child that might cause harm. Here are the foods to avoid during the first year (or longer, as directed by your child's pediatrician):

Might cause allergic reaction:
- cow's milk
- eggs (egg yolk is OK at 8 to 10 months)
- peanuts (wait until age 4)
- wheat products (wheat baby cereal OK after baby has successfully handled rice and barley)
- corn
- fish
- shellfish
- chocolate

Potential for choking:
- berries
- nuts
- peas and beans
- popcorn

When you feed your little one with commercial baby food, you may be tempted to spoon it out right from the handy little jar. Please don't. Spooning food from the jar introduces saliva into the uneaten portion, making it thin and watery. Instead, spoon a small amount into your baby's dish. Babies, you surely have noticed, are a drooly bunch.

A Weaning Team

If you've been worrying that weaning may be emotionally traumatic for your little one, don't. Leaving the breast or bottle behind is a big step, certainly, but many babies, in fact, are almost waiting to be weaned. Little smarties that they are, they have already noticed that Dad doesn't sit down to watch football with a nursing bottle full of lite beer. They've deduced that coffee is always served in a cup and never through a nipple. And when Big Sister packs her lunchbox, the juice is in a box with a straw, not a baby bottle with a cap. Because babies want to model their behavior after those they love, they usually are good sports about making the switch to a cup.

Weaning should be a gradual process. Remember, after all, that breast or bottle not only has been your baby's main source of nourishment, it also has pro-

Coping with the Veggie Hater

"Pah!" says your baby, scowling at the spoon containing a dab of pureed green beans. Your little one spits, expelling the single atom of green bean you just managed to insert between those tightly clenched lips. How does a concerned parent get a baby to eat vegetables such as green beans and squash when that baby has already known the heady flavor of pureed peaches?

A study done a few years ago at the University of Illinois at Urbana-Champaign found that babies are more willing to eat foods that have become familiar. Researchers asked mothers to try to feed their 4- to 6-month-old babies either pureed peas or green beans for 10 days. These babies, who had never tasted vegetables before, were offered either salted or unsalted varieties.

Each mother was told to put away the vegetable if her baby had refused the item three times in a day, but to try again the following day. The researchers found that after 10 days, the babies were eating more of the vegetable.

Even so, your baby—just like you—has individual taste preferences. If he or she doesn't like green beans, try pureed carrots or some other vegetable instead. Offer the green beans again in a month or so. Even a baby's tastes can change.

vided comfort and security since birth. Stopping abruptly will frighten and possibly anger your child. But if you slowly phase out nursing, your baby should wean with ease.

Begin the weaning process when your baby is happy and healthy, and when you can ensure plenty of interesting and diverting activities. Consider Mommy and Me exercise groups, Aqua-Baby classes, play dates with other toddlers, or visits to the grandparents. A baby who is having an adventure is not thinking about nursing. These activities are the perks of growing up, the rewards of being a big kid. In addition, the stimulation may help your baby sleep better at night, which is particularly helpful to a baby who is missing the bedtime bottle.

Weaning is a gradual process that will take several weeks. It's made easier if your baby has been drinking milk, formula, or water from a cup and has become familiar with it.

Weaning from The Breast

Some mothers are happy to breast-feed their babies for one, two, or even three years. Others figure they've done their duty after six weeks.

Homemade Baby Food

Sad to say, even the best of our commercial baby food products can be contaminated with pesticide residues. The companies manufacturing the products say that their foods are perfectly safe and prove it by showing that they have met or surpassed the Food and Drug Administration (FDA) guidelines.

Critics once argued that the guidelines for pesticide residues were based on the physical tolerances of adults, not of tiny babies. New laws are a lot stricter about the pesticide residues allowed in baby food, but the residues have not been eliminated completely.

While the debate ebbs and flows, a growing number of mothers have determined to take matters into their own hands, literally, and process their own baby food. If you have the time and inclination, here's how:

☞ **Buy organic fruits and vegetables.** You also can grow your own organically (without the use of pesticides or other potentially harmful chemicals).

☞ **Be scrupulously clean.** When you are working with baby food, be sure to keep all work areas spotless. Wash your hands before you begin. Wash the bowls, blender, pots, and food processor in hot, soapy water and rinse with extra-hot water. Or, run them through the dishwasher. It may be easier to remember which bowls and spoons need the super-clean treatment if you reserve a set just for making baby food.

Thoroughly wash any produce that you use in warm water, then peel.

☞ **Cook vegetables and fruits.** Vegetables such as green beans and peas can be steamed or simmered in a covered pot for 10 to 15 minutes. Most fresh fruits, except for bananas and avocados, must be cooked for a baby younger than 1 year old. Poach sliced fruit in a small amount of water until tender.

☞ **Puree.** You can use your food processor, fitted with the metal blade, to puree fruits and vegetables. You can puree as little as an ounce at a time, but processing a larger amount is more efficient. A blender also will puree well if you add a small amount of liquid (water, milk, broth) to the container.

☞ **Bake and mash.** Bake acorn squash, sweet potatoes, and white potatoes in the oven at 375º F for 1 hour. Remove the pulp and mash with milk or broth. No need to puree these vegetables.

☞ **Store for later use.** You can freeze cooked fruit, vegetables, even pureed meat, in ice cube trays. Transfer the cubes to a zippered bag.

☞ **Put safety first.** Do remember to label and date any food you freeze. When it becomes some anonymous frozen chunk, it's neither appealing nor safe.

When it's mealtime, select your cubes of squash, applesauce, or bananas and thaw them in the microwave. Voila! Dinner in a minute. Remember to give the food a good stir and to test the temperature before feeding it to your baby. It's important to stir well, because microwave ovens can leave dangerously hot spots in foods.

Any amount of time spent breast-feeding is beneficial, doctors say, but they do encourage mothers to continue breast-feeding until a baby is 1 year old.

But there comes a day when either you or both you and your baby know the end of nursing is near. Many factors play into the decision to wean. If you have returned to work, using a breast pump may have become burdensome and time-consuming. If your baby is still nursing off and on throughout the night, you may want to wean because you need the rest.

Perhaps it is your baby who is ready to move on. Most babies love and adore breast-feeding and work vigorously to satisfy their hunger. But at about 6 months, you may notice that your child is no longer as focused on nursing. With the introduction of several solid foods, your baby's dining horizons have dramatically expanded. Your breast milk is now merely one of several taste sensations.

By 9 or 10 months, when your child has become quite adept at hoisting a cup and when he or she is more interested in exploring the contents of your kitchen cabinets than in stopping to nurse, the time for weaning is upon you.

Once you know the time has come for weaning, here's how to go about it:

☞ **Take things slowly.** As a breast-feeding mother, you'll want to wean gradually for your own comfort as well as for your baby's. After several months of nursing, your breasts are providing a considerable amount of milk. In order to prevent engorgement or pain, you'll have to wean slowly in order to give your body plenty of time to decrease its production of milk.

☞ **Cut back the number of feedings.** Many experts suggest that the first step in weaning is to limit breast-feedings to four a day: morning, lunch, dinner, and bedtime. If your child seems to miss nursing, give him or her lots of cuddling and attention. Providing a cup of water or milk also can help put your baby at ease.

☞ **Give it time.** Give your baby and your body about a week to 10 days to adjust to this schedule of four feedings a day.

☞ **Shorten time at the breast.** Next reduce the amount of time you spend at each feeding. If you've been spending 20 minutes or so nursing, cut the time by 2 or 3 minutes for each feeding. Then, every 3 or 4 days, reduce the feeding time again by two or three minutes.

☞ **Offer your child alternatives.** As you cut down on the breast milk, offer your baby increasing amounts of formula in a cup. Do not give your child breast milk in a cup. (You want to slow down your milk production, and expressing milk will only encourage more production.

☞ **Try to relax throughout this process.** You're not trying to control air traffic over O'Hare International, so your timing doesn't have to be exact. And remember to be flexible. If your baby is extra tired or coming down with a cold, you can backslide a little bit and offer the breast to give him or her some extra comfort.

Making a slow, gradual transition will help prevent breast engorgement, plugged ducts, leaking, and other breast problems. If you feel that your breasts are engorging with milk, remember to wear your best support bra, apply ice packs, and take a mild pain reliever.

Weaning from The Bottle

If you have been bottle-feeding, you can wean your baby to a cup at about 8 months or so or whenever the little one has developed the coordination necessary to handle a cup. Continue with formula, postponing the switch to cow's milk until after the baby is a year old. (Cow's milk has been associated with the development of anemia.)

Here's how to wean your baby from the bottle:

☞ **Cut back feedings.** Begin by reducing the number of bottle feedings to four a day: breakfast, lunch, dinner, and bedtime. If your baby seems to be fretting over the lost bottles, give him or her plenty of cuddles and kisses.

☞ **Offer alternatives.** Next offer formula in a cup before each bottle feeding. Often a child who is used to drinking juice or water from a cup happily will swig a few ounces of formula and only then turn to the bottle. If the cup is something new for your baby, give him or her plenty of time to experiment and to get used to it.

In either case, don't allow your child to keep a bottle and carry it around the house. Offer a favorite toy instead or even a "blanky." Limit the availability of the bottle to feeding time.

☞ **Make those bottles disappear.** Once your baby is drinking well from the cup, the time has come to eliminate the bottles altogether, one feeding at a time. Begin with the bottle that seems the least important to your child, usually the one given at lunchtime.

After three or four days, cut out the dinnertime bottle. Remember to be flexible. If your baby seems upset, slow down the schedule so you eliminate a

Our son was very fond of his pacifiers. So before his third birthday, we explained to him we were going to have a party to celebrate that he was going to be a big boy. We told him he would have a cake and get big boy presents and he would put his pacifiers in a box because he wouldn't need them anymore. He could ask us anytime to let him see his "nunnies" in the box, but he couldn't use them once he had a party to say good-bye to them and celebrate becoming a big boy.

Would this really work? His birthday arrived, he said good-bye to his nunnies and put them in a box just like we'd talked about. He'd made it his decision, and he was fine with it. Of course, having the big boy toys to play with helped a lot.

Jane Stubbe
Annapolis, Maryland

bottle only once a week. Continue following the plan, eliminating the bedtime bottle last.

☞ **Be flexible about that final bottle.** This final bottle requires some special treatment. Many babies use the last bottle of the day as a means of throttling down the daytime motor and shifting into their sleep mode. For that reason, give your youngster a full week to adjust.

Make sure your baby has had enough milk in his or her cup at dinnertime. Each night, reduce the amount of milk you put into the bedtime bottle, until at the end of the week, you can completely eliminate that final bottle.

☞ **Be supportive.** If your baby fusses and has trouble sleeping, hold and rock the child, sing a lullaby or read a story, give your baby a back rub, or offer a clean pacifier.

Changing Appetite

In your baby's first year, he or she grows prodigiously, probably tripling birthweight and adding 8 to 9 inches in height. Wow!

Your baby needs a whole lot of fuel to grow that fast. After the first year, however, that phenomenal rate of growth slows down a bit and so does your baby's need for food.

You've seen the nearly constant demand for caloric intake during your baby's early months dwindle to four feedings (and several snacks) by the 12th month.

So don't be unduly alarmed if your child is no longer singularly focused on food. If you offer your baby lots of different kinds of foods to choose from

Coping with Food Jags

Every now and then a child gets stuck in a food rut. With vigorous head shaking and spoon waving, your baby will let you know that the little cubes of meat loaf you so carefully mashed for dinner are simply not acceptable. Nothing will do but breaded fish sticks, mashed just so.

It doesn't matter to your baby that they were served for yesterday's lunch and for dinner last night. Your baby wants fish sticks.

Such a jag usually wears off in a few days, so you can cater to a food preference for a little while, as long as your child is still eating a variety of other foods that includes cereal, fruit, vegetables, and milk.

But if your child will eat one thing, and one thing only, you'll have to take action. Keep the fish sticks in the freezer. Calmly set down the strips of turkey, serenely spoon out some sweet potato, garnish the plate with a bit of applesauce, and pour the milk. Nibble a spoonful of applesauce yourself to set a good example.

State matter-of-factly that dinner looks good. Then, without looking too concerned, wait to see what happens. Do not resort to coercion or bribery. If you must, you can tell your baby that a fish stick will be served at snack time.

every day, you'll be providing a sufficient and balanced diet.

Let's Do Lunch

During your baby's first year, his or her nutritional needs were taken care of primarily by either breast milk or formula. Feeding your baby correctly was, as they say, a no-brainer. Now, however, your baby is starting to eat regular food like a regular person, and you'll have to do some planning to see that his or her nutritional needs are met.

Basically, you will have to provide food from all the food groups in the proper proportions. The groups are grains (breads and cereals); fruits and vegetables;

meat, poultry, fish, and meat alternatives such as eggs, nuts, and beans; milk and other dairy products, such as cheese and yogurt; and fats and sweets.

Offer your little one little meals—a spoonful or two of yogurt, some sliced banana, a little chicken. The rule of thumb is to offer 1 tablespoon of food from each food group for each year of age. Give your child the opportunity to ask for more. Be sure also to offer between-meal snacks. These are not junk food snacks, but minimeals planned to provide added nutrition and an increased variety in your baby's diet.

Allow your baby to experience lots of different flavors and textures. Remember, a food that's refused one day may be accepted the next. Keep at it.

A typical menu for a 1- to 2-year-old might look like this:

Breakfast: ½ scrambled egg, ½ slice of whole wheat toast, two sliced strawberries, and 4 ounces of milk

Morning snack: ½ cup cereal with milk

Lunch: ¼ cup of brown rice, ¼ cup pureed carrots, a cube or slice of cheese, 2 ounces of milk

Afternoon snack: 2 ounces of yogurt with fruit and three crackers

Dinner: ½ ounce of pureed or mashed meat, ¼ cup of mashed potato, cubed or pureed winter squash, custard pudding, milk

Bedtime snack: zwieback and milk

Serve meals and snacks at the same time each day, making sure to offer the snacks at least two hours before meals.

Encourage a varied diet, offering whole-grain or enriched breads, cereals, and pasta. Provide poultry and fish, but limit red meats to no more than three servings a week. Offer fruit often, either as a snack or a dessert.

Try to get your baby to take at least one serving a day of a food high in beta-carotene such as sweet potatoes, yellow squash, and carrots, as well as one leafy green vegetable such as spinach and cabbage.

Food Pyramid

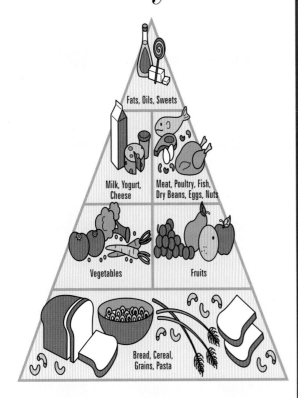

The U.S. Department of Agriculture (USDA) has devised The Food Guide Pyramid as a way to show which foods should be the foundation of the diet and which are least important. The same rules apply for babies as for adults.

- Grains. Provide 6 to 11 servings each day.
- Fruit. Offer 2 to 4 servings daily.
- Vegetables. Offer 3 to 5 servings daily.
- Meat, poultry, fish, dry beans, eggs, and nuts. Provide 2 to 3 servings a day.
- Dairy. Offer 2 to 3 servings a day.
- Fats and sweets. Use these sparingly.

Generally speaking, children like bland foods. They'll accept, say, mashed kidney beans, but balk at mashed turnips. Because they like bland-tasting foods, kids really don't need added salt or sugar. Without them your child will learn to appreciate the natural flavors in food.

Try not to be too upset if the applesauce becomes a medium for finger painting or the mashed potatoes are used as modeling clay. It's all part of the growing-up game.

The Question of Cow's Milk

When you are ready to switch your child to cow's milk at the age of 1 year, you'll face another question. What should you buy? Whole milk? Two-percent fat? One-percent? Skim?

Most doctors say that you shouldn't be too quick to answer "skim." Many health-conscious parents are vigilant about keeping fat out of their own diets, particularly fat from meat and dairy products with their attendant cholesterol. But adult nutritional standards and those for infants are different.

A child younger than 2 needs a certain amount of fat to grow and develop properly, and whole milk is generally thought to be just fine for a 1- to 2-year-old child. In determining which milk to choose, it's best to ask your child's own doctor. He or she will guide you to select the best option for your individual baby.

If your pediatrician advises whole milk (and he or she probably will), you might want to revisit the question again after your baby is 2 years old.

The Sophisticated Palate

As a child approaches the first anniversary of birth, he or she is often a willing subject for food experimentation. A 1-year-old will try new tastes and new textures. But if you serve only pureed baby food all through your child's

What to Feed Your Baby

One day you have a tiny newborn thriving on nothing but breast milk. A few short years later you have a young child begging for pizza instead of meat loaf and broccoli. Getting from point A to point B presents a challenge for both you and your little one. Here's an overview of the kinds of foods appropriate for each age group. If you're having problems getting your child to switch to more solid foods, talk to your pediatrician.

Admittedly, there's a bit of overlap in this table. That's because every child is different. As your child approaches each new plateau, you can begin experimenting with new textures. If your child does not seem to handle the new textures well, hold off for a couple weeks. After 15 months, you can begin introducing foods more rapidly. (Your child's curiosity about new tastes will make this happen almost automatically.)

Age	Texture	Foods
1–4 months	liquid	breast milk or formula with iron
4–6 months	pureed	infant cereal, pureed pears, pureed vegetables
6–7 months	pureed or mashed	infant cereal, pureed fruit and vegetables, mashed banana, applesauce
8–9 months	mashed, finely chopped	mashed potatoes or squash, mashed cooked fruits, pureed meats
10–12 months	finely chopped	macaroni and cheese, casseroles, dry toast without crust
12–15 months	chopped	serve any of the above in toddler portions

first year, you may miss the chance to help your little one get used to food with texture. You could end up with a baby who's stuck in the puree cycle—a baby who gags on lumps and can't seem to swallow even semisolid food.

To the left is a plan of introducing textures in food that will help your baby master the fine art of chewing and swallowing.

Making Mealtimes Happy

Sitting down to eat should be a pleasant occasion for your child, and it should be an opportunity to establish healthy eating habits that will last a lifetime.

Problem is, sometimes a parent's sincere concern over which foods the baby eats—and how much—can backfire. If you force a child to eat more than his or her appetite requires, you'll either have a rebellion in the high chair or an overly accommodating child who is learning to ignore the feeling of fullness, which leads to overeating.

Also consider this: What message are you sending when you tell your child that if he or she eats three green beans, the reward will be a cookie? You're implying that green beans are something to be tolerated, but that cookies are a rewarding treat. Even though it's important to keep mealtimes pleasant, don't fall into the trap of serving only foods that your baby seems to like. Continue to expand your child's food horizons by offering new fruits and vegetables or familiar foods served in a new way. Try French toast one day and corn muffins the next. Spread some mashed banana on a waffle square. Dice some tofu into the chicken soup.

Chapter Nine

Congratulations! It's a person

Was it really only a few months ago that you brought your baby home? And look what has happened since then. Your little bundle of joy (and bodily

fluids) has gone and turned into a person! Watching your baby develop during this first year is almost like watching the time-lapse photography on a TV nature show, where—in just about a minute—you see a little shoot spring from the earth, reach toward the sun, then develop a bud that swells, opens, and unfurls each petal to become an elegant dahlia.

Without the aid of any special effects photography, your little flower is speeding along, too, budding into the person he or she always will be. Happy, sassy, shy, wary, observant, silly, curious, loving—the traits emerge one by one, unfurling like the flower's petals.

A baby's brain grows faster than any other body part. And at the age of 2½ months, that brain undergoes what experts say is a major change. They call it the "two-and-a-half month shift." At this age, babies begin to spend more time awake. They become more aware of sounds, lights, and other outside stimuli, and they begin to react in slightly less random ways.

A Personality Shines Through

At 2½ months of age, your baby starts to remember the rattle or squeaky doll he or she encountered a few seconds before. Vision has improved to the point where your baby can maintain eye contact, and your baby definitely can recognize you.

As early as 6 weeks of age, your baby experiences the first stirrings of sociability and starts laying the groundwork for social interaction.

Here's how it happens: Your baby smiles at you.

Cleanliness Is Next To ... Impossible

I t's simply futile to try to keep everything out of your baby's mouth. Trying to keep every object around your baby clean, just in case he or she does pick it up, is equally futile.

On the other hand, you can't just ignore dirt and germs. To help you cope, here is some commonsense advice from the experts:

☞ **Wash a toy or other object after a play period.** Don't try to wash a rattle every time it bounces off the carpet. You'll drive yourself crazy.

☞ **Wash a toy or other object immediately if it has fallen on the ground outside.** Germs live in dirt. It's as simple as that.

☞ **Wash a toy or other object after it has fallen on the floor a number of times.** Don't worry about things that fall on a relatively clean floor, such as your own kitchen floor. A toy that falls to the floor in a public place, such as a crowded bus station, is another matter. You'll want to treat that as you would if it hit the ground outside.

☞ **Wash anything another child has played with.** This is not to imply that your own baby is cleaner and more germ-free. Fact is, a good number of colds get passed along this way.

Wonder of wonders, you smile back. Your baby coos. You respond with a coo of your own.

Something important has just occurred. Your baby has indulged in self-expression. Amazingly, you replied. A happy new world has just opened wide for exploration.

Your 3-month-old should frequently be placed right smack in the middle of family activities. Move the infant seat into the kitchen, for example, and allow your baby to experience all the sights, sounds, and smells of daily life. Watching the way you and other family members interact can help teach your little one a great deal about socializing.

You will be delighted to discover that your baby, at about 4 months of age, can laugh out loud. A month or so later, your little one will learn to squeal with delight. (And you will be delighted as well.)

You may be equally delighted to see that your baby now can take up objects. You won't be quite so thrilled at what happens to those objects: They frequently get crammed into the mouth.

Getting a Mouthful

Four-month-olds, according to child development experts, explore the world with their mouths. They use their lips, gums, and tongue, which is carpeted with both taste buds and sensitive nerve endings, to gain an understanding of the objects around them.

The nerves and muscles of a baby's mouth are highly developed at birth, unlike the eyes and hands. They are so developed, researchers have discovered, that infants can distinguish the shape of an object just by mouthing it.

Babies in one study were allowed to mouth an object that was hidden from their sight. Later the infants recognized by sight the ball or cube shape that they had experienced orally. They also could recognize by sight objects with different textures, such as ribbed or smooth pacifiers, after mouthing them.

Researchers were amazed to discover that the babies used the knowledge they gained orally to visually identify these various objects. Not too many years ago, it was generally held that the ability to integrate visual, oral, and tactile sensations into a unified perception developed slowly over several months. Now, however, some researchers have come to believe that even newborns may have this ability.

Oral experimentation actually has its beginnings before the fourth month, when a baby stretches out both arms, clasps his or her hands together, then jams all 10 fingers into the mouth at once. Fingers (and toes, too) are tasted and tested throughout the waking day.

Eventually, your baby's exploration expands so that by 4 months of age, anything your little one can reach will make its way into his or her mouth. For that reason, it's important to protect your child from all hard-edged objects. Also be really vigilant about keeping your child away from small toy parts, balloons, houseplants (some are poisonous), pills, and tablets.

Your baby's mouth remains his or her dominant tool for exploring until about 5 months of age. At that time, your baby's fine motor skills have developed to the point where hands can take up the task. At that point, your baby will first touch and inspect an object visually before putting it into the mouth.

A Developmental Yardstick

During the exciting time between 3 and 6 months, your baby will begin to express emotions by making a variety of vocalizations. Your baby will respond to the tone of your voice and actually begin to understand you. He or she won't get the exact meaning of your words, but your baby will understand your tone and the emotional content of what you are saying.

Given that, you will be able to let your baby know, for example, that you're thrilled with those baby smiles and you are madly in love with those little baby piggies. On a more practical level, you can reassure your little one you are not starving him or her, but merely taking a minute to warm the bottle.

If you think you've noticed your baby perking up at the sound of his or her own name, you may be right. Researchers at the State University of New York in Buffalo have determined that babies may be able to recognize their names at 4½ months of age, much earlier than previously thought by child development experts.

In one study, researchers 24 infants who were listening to a recording of four names. They noted that

Reading Your Baby's Body Language

Goo-goo," may be awfully cute when it comes out of your baby's mouth, but it's not really communicating. Make no mistake about it though. Your baby will tell you what he or she wants, if you just know how to interpret the language. We're talking body language here. The following cues will help you translate what your baby is telling you:

• **Looking away.** If you are showing your 2- to 4-month-old a rattle or a stuffed animal, and he or she looks away, your child is saying, "I've had enough stimulation for the moment." Put the toy out of sight once this happens. The two of you can take up the game again later.

• **Raising hands or touching you.** At 5 to 6 months, your baby may ask for your attention by raising his or her hand or by brushing your arm. Reflect on what you were just doing. Did you just sing a song? Maybe your baby would like to hear it again. Were you just babbling at each other? Perhaps your baby hadn't gotten to the punch line yet and would like to "talk" some more.

infants focused their attention on the stereo speaker playing their own name four seconds longer than when other names were played. Experts say that recognizing your own name is a big step in developing the sense of self.

Fear of Strangers

When your child is about 6 months old, you may notice him or her pulling back from new people. What you are seeing may be the beginning of stranger awareness, the growing recognition that there exists an "us" and a "them." Awareness of strangers, accompanied by anxiety, is probably your baby's first emotional milestone. It is both predictable and normal, and usually goes away shortly after the baby's first birthday.

In the meantime, if your baby seems upset by an unfamiliar person, you can help by staying close to your child and remaining calm. If you see someone about to swoop down upon your child for some friendly hugs that you know will be unwelcome, suggest that the individual approach gently and keep some distance.

Dropping Toys

As for play, babies approaching the half-year mark will enjoy grabbing objects, such as a rattle. They'll also enjoy a sense of accomplishment when they make a noise with it. ("Hey, Ma! Look what I can do!")

At 7 months, infants will begin to revel in their growing manual dexterity. They'll bang things together and pick up a toy in one hand, then transfer it to the other.

This stage of development culminates in the game all parents dread: Pick It Up, Drop It, and Yell.

You should understand that babies do not play this game to drive their parents crazy (insanity is just the side effect). What babies are doing is practicing their ability to grasp and release objects. And practice makes perfect.

Here's how the game is played: Your baby grasps a rattle, holds it for a second or two, then releases it over the side of the high chair. Then your baby wails because he or she really, truly wants to grab it again. As a kind parent, you retrieve the rattle, allowing it once more to be grasped. And, without fail, released. Followed by the yell. You retrieve it again. Your baby picks it up. Again. Drops it. Again. Yells. Again. You'll find your baby is capable of playing this game for a surprising length of time.

Thank goodness, your baby will soon be ready for more sociable games like peekaboo.

Separation Anxiety

If, at 9 months, your baby becomes a little clingy, you can suspect the onset of separation anxiety, a normal stage of development when your child is afraid to be separated from you. It will last until your baby is about 18 months old. It doesn't take a month-long cruise of the Greek Islands to trigger it.

More likely, it's you disappearing at bedtime or dropping your child off at day care.

Why all this anxiety? It's simply that your baby hasn't yet had the chance to develop a history of happy reunions with you. For all your child knows, when you walk out the door, you may never come back. No wonder he or she is frightened.

You can deal with this fear by being extra patient and kind. When you leave a room, tell your baby that you'll be right back. If your baby fusses when you are out of sight, talk from the other room. Eventually your child will come to understand that you have not fallen off the face of the Earth even though he or she cannot see you.

If you are leaving the baby for several hours, keep good-byes short and calm.

Getting into Things

At 10 months to 1 year, children are likely to begin exploring around the house. Children's early curiosity and desire for independence should be encouraged, so save the no-nos for those times that really are dangerous. Trying to lift a cup of scalding coffee warrants a no-no, but pulling a silk rose from the flower arrangement does not. In the latter situation, use your powers of distraction.

Real Communication Begins

Most children heading for their first birthday are little lovebugs, showing and seeking affection at every turn. In addition, they're catching on to language and probably will understand no-no and bye-bye. They may be able to point to familiar objects when you name them.

Games: A Baby's Work

s sociability and sense of self are emerging, your baby can begin to engage in some simple games. Now is the time to

Choosing the Family Pet

Many people don't consider their families complete without a pet to share their home. Children can learn a great deal about giving affection and receiving loyal devotion from a family pet. In fact, studies have shown that kids who live with a pet have an improved ability to interact with others. (To learn about how to introduce an established pet to a new baby, see pages 109–110.) You could, of course, wait until your child is a little older before introducing an animal to the house, but if you must have an animal now, there are a few things you should know.

☞ **Enlist the aid of a veterinarian.** Even before you start out for the pet store or pound, line up a veterinarian who will examine your new purchase before you take it home. Once you've selected an animal, you'll be able to take it directly to the vet. This initial checkup will uncover any health problems you might have missed. (Make sure you are dealing with a reputable pet dealer who will allow you to return an animal if it is found to be unhealthy.)

The vet is not just looking out for your new animal's health. Babies can pick up diseases and parasites from unhealthy animals, so he or she will schedule the pet for needed inoculations, wormings, and any other procedures that are necessary for the health of both your pet and your family.

☞ **Do your own checking.** When you've selected a likely pet for your household, don't go just by things like big, brown eyes or a friendly, wagging tail. Take a good look at the animal's appearance, checking for any signs of a health problem. Goopy eyes, a dull coat, moth-eaten feathers, and lethargic behavior are warning signs that all is not well.

☞ **Inspect the environment.** Take a careful look at the place where the pet has been raised or boarded. Are the cages and pens clean? Is animal waste removed promptly? Do other animals for sale look healthy and happy?

☞ **Clean up after puppies.** Once you install little Peaches in your home, keep the animal's living area clean and free of droppings. Roundworm is a parasite that is carried by almost every puppy. Although your vet is likely to treat the puppy for roundworm, cleanliness can help prevent its transfer. Because children often play on the ground, they are the most vulnerable family members to pick up roundworms. Symptoms of roundworm include fever, headache, cough, and poor appetite. (The condition can be treated with medications known as anthelmintics, which will work on both your child and your puppy.)

☞ **Carry out that kitty litter.** If Peaches is a cat, be sure to remove solid waste from the cat litter box every day to help prevent transmission of toxoplasmosis, a disease produced by *Toxoplasma gondii*, a one-celled parasite. Cats get the disease by killing and eating infected rodents. (And babies are perfectly capable of mistaking a litter box for a sand box meant for playing in.)

And be sure to keep your child's sandbox covered when not in use, so that it doesn't become an outdoor litter box for your cat.

Symptoms of toxoplasmosis infection may include fever, headache, swollen lymph glands, cough, sore throat, nasal congestion, loss of appetite, and skin rash. The disease, which can cause serious nervous system damage in infants, can be treated with antibacterial drugs.

☞ **Groom your pet.** Keep your dog or cat free of fleas, ticks, and mites. Watch out especially for deer ticks, tiny insects that have been associated with the transmission of Lyme disease. A lint remover that uses a roller of adhesive paper does a great job at picking up ticks that have not yet dug into the skin.

☞ **Practice personal hygiene.** Wash your child's hands after he or she has handled a pet. When your child is older, teach him or her to wash hands routinely after petting an animal. This habit may help prevent the transfer of ringworm, a skin disease caused by a fungus. Dogs, horses, cows, and most often cats—particularly long-haired cats—can pass the disease on to the people who pet them.

Ringworm usually shows up on exposed parts of the body, especially the scalp, appearing as a red, scaly sore. An anti-fungal drug can clear it up.

☞ **Keep a bird's cage clean.** If Peaches is a parrot or parakeet, guard against psittacosis (parrot fever), a bacterial disease. Babies and other family members can get the disease through contact with your pet bird's feces and the dust from the feathers.

Respiratory symptoms of psittacosis include cough and chest pain, but other symptoms may include fever, chills, fatigue, vomiting, and muscular pain. Your doctor can confirm the disease with a blood test and treat it with antibiotics.

Model the behavior you want your child to learn. If you argue a lot, so will your child. If you raise your voice, so will your child. If you treat your spouse with disrespect, so will your child. If you grumble about your chores, so will your child. Of course, the opposite is also true. Model the good behaviors, such as respect for others (especially your spouse), cheerful work habits, and quiet conversation.

Susan Kemmerer
Telford, Pennsylvania

start "Peekaboo! I see you!" You're guaranteed to get a squeal of delight when you reappear from behind your hands, a book, or a door frame. This game may not rank with Jeopardy as an intellectual challenge, but it's loads more fun.

What's more, the game encourages taking turns, which is a concept that is basic to conversation. There's something else you can do to help conversation skills develop: "Start singing or reading to your baby," advises Suzanne LeBel Corrigan, M.D., a pediatrician in Irving, Texas. "They love repetition."

Hold off on formal socializing, such as setting up dates for your child to play with others. Although babies may enjoy looking each other over, they won't really know how to play with each other for another year or two.

There's also a practical reason to downplay these kinds of situations. "I worry about the exposure to colds and viruses that comes with this kind of socializing," says Dr. Corrigan. "If your child easily gets colds or ear infections, play dates aren't worth it. Parents and siblings can provide the baby with just as much stimulation."

Choosing Appropriate Toys

To encourage the development of your baby's ability to understand things, the right kind of toys helps a great deal. Provide an infant with toys that have a variety of colors, shapes, and textures to stimulate the senses. For a 2-month-old, that might mean a mobile hanging above the crib. For a 6-month old, it may be a textured rattle to be explored with hands and mouth. Here are other suggestions:

☞ **Shake and rattle.** You can help a 2-month-old practice visual tracking by slowly moving a rattle across his or her field of vision, shaking the rattle as you go. In another month or so, your little one will be trying to grab the rattle. By 4 months, the child may be doing the moving and shaking without your help.

☞ **Be a cheapskate.** You don't have to spend a lot of money on toys to provide creative opportunities. Most young children enjoy playing with gift boxes and wrapping paper more than playing with the gifts themselves.

☞ **Open up the kitchen cabinets.** Make your pots and pans available. Banging on them with wooden spoons not only makes a lot of satisfying (to your baby) noise, but also shows the child that he or she can control when the "pan-demonium" starts and stops.

☞ **Save plastic containers.** Small containers from the deli and supermarket are fun for children to turn over and clap on the floor. Different sizes allow them to be nested into each other—a favorite activity of 1-year-olds.

☞ **Encourage creative scribbling.** For toddlers, recycle your mail and other correspondence by using the unused blank side as scribble paper. Buy your child big crayons, which are easier for a beginner to hold. Scribbling helps to teach eye-hand coordination, creativity, and self-expression.

☞ **Hold on to cardboard boxes of all sizes.** Big ones can become boats and houses. Shoe boxes serve as doll beds and clown shoes. Little boxes can be used as blocks, nested, or just clapped together.

☞ **Put safety first.** If you do buy toys, be sure they are simple, sturdy, and safe. More than 125,000 children a year are treated in hospital emergency rooms because of accidents related to toys, according to the U.S. Consumer Product Safety Commission. That figure does not include those children treated by doctors or clinics or at home. Some 40 percent of the injured children are younger than 5 years old.

Signs of Normal Hearing

In order to speak properly, children must be able to hear. To check on your baby's hearing, use these guidelines from the American Speech-Language-Hearing Association in Rockville, Maryland:

• **At birth,** a baby startles or cries at loud sounds.
• **From birth to 3 months,** a baby turns his or her head toward you when you speak.
• **At 4 to 6 months,** a baby looks around for the source of a new sound, such as a telephone ringing.
• **At 7 to 12 months,** a child listens when spoken to, looks up when his or her name is called, begins to respond to simple requests (wave bye-bye), and recognizes words for common objects.

If you suspect hearing difficulties, talk to your baby's doctor. You also can contact the following groups for information and support:

Beginnings for Parents of Hearing Impaired Children provides emotional support and information for parents. Write: 3900 Barrett Dr., Suite 100, Raleigh, NC 27609. Or, call: 800-541-4327.

The John Tracy Clinic offers a free correspondence course for families with a hearing-impaired child from birth to 5 years old. For information, write: 806 W. Adams Blvd., Los Angeles, CA 90007. Or, call the 24-hour help line at 800-522-4582.

Look for any safety warnings on the box, then look at the toy's parts to be sure they aren't so small they could be breathed in. (It has happened.) And make sure also that they can't be pulled loose and swallowed.

☞ **Buy with age in mind.** When making your selection, read the age recommendations carefully. A toy that is labeled for a child older than your own may require advanced motor skills or cognitive skills your baby has yet to develop.

☞ **Give your child some choices.** Babies like play telephones, stuffed toys and dolls, soft balls, toys with fingerholds, and toys that are large but light.

☞ **Encourage literacy.** Every baby should have

some books. Start reading aloud when your baby is 4 or 5 months old. Choose books with large, attractive pictures. Look for nursery rhymes and books that will be fun for you to read. (Think of it as performance art.)

If you are on a tight budget, then you can use old magazines or gift catalogs that have bright pictures. You will be able to point to and name lots of things your baby likes—cars, toys, and animals.

Let's Have a Little Talk

When babies are still very young, they are preparing themselves to speak. They may not utter a real word for many, many months, but at a very early age they're getting ready.

Babies can recognize words long before they can say them simply because more complicated neurological processes are required for speaking than for listening. In the meantime, they're starting to understand words from the context in which they are spoken. They also rely on your tone of voice, facial expression, and gestures for clues to meaning. Here's a scenario that probably happened in your own life that you most likely don't remember. It's the story of how you learned the word "book."

So, here we have Mother (your mother) reaching over to pick up a picture book. She smiles at you, settling you onto her lap. "Isn't this a nice book?" she asks. "Let's read this book together." Later she says, "It's time to put the book away." At the supermarket the next day, she stops at the rack of baby books and selects *The Happy Puppy*. She smiles while holding out the book so you can see the cover and asks, "Would you like to have this book?"

"Hmm," you say to yourself. "Using deductive reasoning, I'd say the probability is enormous that this particular object is called 'book.'" (Or words to that effect.)

Helping Baby Get the Word Out

If you want to help your baby learn to understand words and build a listening vocabulary, there are many ways to do it.

You can begin by showing your child that certain sounds mean specific things. Try this: Take your baby to the light switch and, as you turn on the light, say the word "light." Do this a few times a day, every day. Before long, when you say the word "light," your baby will turn to look at the light even before you turn it on.

That's when you'll know—really know—that your little one has made the giant intellectual leap of linking the spoken word to the object.

Don't limit yourself to a one-word vocabulary. It's important to talk to your baby in real conversation, just as if he or she understands every word you are saying. So make sure that you use real words rather than baby talk.

Face your child so he or she can see your lip movements. Use an engaged tone of voice, facial expressions, and even body language to make speech more expressive.

You may ask what conversational gambits will play well to a little one. You can always take a cue from your baby and talk about what he or she is looking at, such as "That's a nice bear. Your bear is brown." While you're at it, make the experience tactile as well as visual and add, "Touch your bear. She's so soft."

You can also talk about what you are doing together. When you're dressing your baby to go outdoors, talk about how you have to put on the shoes, the hat, and so forth. Clearly identify the pieces of clothing you are using.

At bathtime, name your child's body parts. In the supermarket, name the items as you take them off the shelf. Everyday activities offer tons of opportunities for learning to speak.

When your child does begin to speak, you can continue to help in language development by expanding on what he or she says. For instance, if your baby says, "doggy," you can expand the statement by saying, "Yes, that is a dog."

Expanding in that way provides an example of how the word your child just used can become part of a simple sentence. After hearing lots of examples, your child will be ready to start forming his or her own simple sentences.

As your child grows, play word games together. While you're driving, ask your child to point to a truck, a house, a car, a store, and other items. Put the child's response into words, saying, "Yes, that is a truck."

As you're enjoying the beginnings of what will become a lifetime of conversations with your child, here are three precautions to keep in mind:

☞ **Try not to hog the conversation.** Pause frequently to let your baby gurgle, coo, or babble. Allow your child to imitate your inflections and enthusiasm. Giving your little one a chance to chime in allows him or her to understand that in a conversation, people take turns. Before long, you'll be hearing real words.

☞ **Don't overdo it.** Be sensitive to your baby's signals about ending the conservation. You want to avoid baby-burnout. Babies who are beginning to fatigue often will tell you so by turning away from you as a way to avoid overload.

☞ **Don't worry about the timetable for talking.** Some experts think that the big development steps of talking and walking are sequential.

If your baby is not speaking but is active, crawling about, or actually beginning to toddle, that developmental step has taken precedence. Speaking is just waiting its turn in the wings. Keep in mind, too, that boys are generally more active than girls, so they may begin to speak later.

Raising a "Good Child"

Two teenage girls live on Elbow Lane, but they seem worlds apart.

Donna, 15, is very much a part of her community. She's a candy striper at the local hospital and spends Saturday mornings distributing newspapers, magazines, and games to patients. She's the kind of kid who, when she sees elderly Mrs. Fahey struggling to put out her heavy trash can, literally runs to help. She's in great demand as a babysitter because she's attentive, kind, and responsible. Quite simply, Donna is a good person.

Christine, 15, walks past Mrs. Fahey, too, but never notices her need for help. Chris is pretty and bright, but not especially happy. She worries a great deal about her looks and her clothes. She brags a little bit too much about good grades. She sulks if another classmate does better. She is so tied up in her own concerns that she cannot see the concerns of others. Christine certainly is far from being a "bad" girl. But somehow she seems to lack Donna's quality of obvious caring and concern for others.

We all would prefer to have a child like Donna. What is the secret to raising a big-hearted youngster who is sure to grow into a kind, generous, responsible, moral adult?

The first step is to take a look in the mirror and see the kind of person you are. Your child, in a large way, will be a reflection of you, says child psychiatrist Robert Coles, M.D. Dr. Coles is a professor of psychiatry and medical humanities at the Harvard Medical Center and the author of *The Moral Intelligence of Children: How to Raise a Moral Child.* Your child is a witness to the way you live your life. Your actions, basic values, desires, and assumptions will show your child how to be.

Dr. Coles suggests that you ask yourself: Who am I? What kind of a moral example do I offer? What do I hope for? What kind of a child do I want?

"Do you want a lonely genius, who is feared and envied?" he asks. "Or do you want someone who shares his brilliance and is admired for his tact and modesty?"

Dr. Coles emphasizes that instilling morality comes through shared daily experiences between parent and child. The best lessons are the off-the-cuff responses to everyday situations.

"We are blind to what children can see," maintains Dr. Coles. "The adult world is absorbed by children, and we are constantly educating them with our own behavior."

"Whether we know it or not," says Dr. Coles, "we are transmitting moral attitudes. Every day children learn lessons from us. They do. And slowly these lessons become absorbed in their minds, and they begin to develop the kinds of attitudes that they do."

Moral intelligence, he says, includes the ability to empathize with others, show concern for their welfare, and generously extend ourselves to them.

Balancing Affirmation With Restraint

We don't want our children to be so tied up with their own destiny that they don't care about anyone else, even their relatives or neighbors," says Dr. Coles. For parents, helping their children learn how to make that distinction involves striking a balance between affirming a child's individuality and teaching that child "certain restraints that have to do ultimately with consideration for others," he says.

It's best to start this kind of training at home, well before your child goes to school, "even before your child enters the world of language," advises Dr. Coles.

Psychologists' understanding of moral development is consistent: They know that empathy—the ability to see another's point of view—develops early. Many parents see evidence of this trait before their child can even sit up or walk. Their baby frets and kicks his or her feet and shows other unmistakable signs of distress when another child is crying.

"Even at a very early age, empathy is quite possible, quite available, and is ready to be developed in the mind and in the brain. Empathy is part of our inheritance as human beings," says Dr. Coles.

But hurt and pain also are part of our human experience, and that, too, is something even a young child can begin to accept. We can't bring up children without knowing some kind of hurt or pain. Take, for example, a 9-month-old baby who wants to be held all the time. Whenever the little one is put down, he or she cries and cries hard. That child needs to begin to understand the word "no."

"You can teach the child, with tact and dignity, that she has to share her mother with others in the family, and even with tasks—like preparing a meal," the doctor says. "Our job is to help the child to know 'no.' There will be tears, but there are tears in life. There is a needed and a normal aspect to moments of displeasure. We all must learn to bow to other forces and demands. That's why we stop at a red light, for example. That acceptance is the beginning of learning respect for legitimate authority."

As children grow older, they are taught by additional influences. Teachers, church or temple, even inspiring characters in great literature can help children learn how to be good people.

Translating Insights Into Actions

A sense of goodness or morality is taught through everyday actions, agrees psychologist Joseph A. Micucci, Ph.D., associate professor of psychology at Chestnut Hill College in Philadelphia. It's not so much any spe-

Children who are treated with gentle kindness are those who learn to display acts of tenderness and kindness. My tiny three-year-old son observed me bent over cleaning the bathroom, red-faced, perspiration beading on my forehead. He pulled me close to his face and said, "Mommy what's wrong? Let me help." And he gently kissed my face, taking a towel into his tiny hand to wipe over the counter. This is kindness and love personified.

Marscia Fleagle
St. Marys, Ohio

cific action that makes a difference, he says, but rather the general tone that is set by the parents' relationship with the child and with each other.

There are, nevertheless, certain beneficial attitudes we can foster within ourselves to help our children grow up to be good. Here's the lowdown:

☞ **Be attuned to your child's needs.** "A very young child is a world unto himself," says Dr. Micucci. The child responds to the outside world according to the way his or her needs are met. If the child's basic needs are satisfied, that child develops a sense of security, and that security is the absolute foundation for all other relationships.

You don't have to be a perfect parent, he says, but you do have to be attuned to your child's needs.

☞ **Allow for frustration.** Dr. Micucci cautions against being so responsive in meeting your child's needs that the little one never experiences frustration. Let's face it—a certain amount of frustration comes with being alive. If your child never feels frustrated, "the message you're sending is that frustration cannot be tolerated, and the child will never learn how to deal with it out in the world," says Dr. Micucci. "On balance, however, if you are going to err, go in the direction of overproviding, rather than underproviding."

☞ **Don't worry.** "It's important for parents to know," says Dr. Micucci, "that the way a child turns out is not strictly a result of parenting. Biology, genetics, and life experiences also help to determine how a child develops. It's also important to know that not everything is learned in the early years. As a child grows, there are many later opportunities for corrective (or destructive), formative experiences.

"It's normal for a new parent to be anxious, but an overflow of anxiety is not helpful, because your child will pick up on it as unease."

☞ **Be happy.** "Let your child develop a sense that he can make you and others feel good," says Dr. Micucci. Allowing your baby to see how his or her small acts and smiles give you pleasure—even joy—helps the baby to learn how to relate to others.

"The infant learns mutuality, a sense of 'we,' in helping someone else to feel good," he explains.

☞ **Deal with your own problems.** "It is not possible to separate how well we are parenting from how well we feel in general," says Dr. Micucci. "If you are unhappy, it will just naturally show."

The doctor especially urges parents who are unhappy in their marriage to deal with the problem for the sake of the children, if nothing else. "Ultimately, the tone of the family is set by the quality of the relationship between the mother and the father," he says.

"Discord and irritation will filter into the relationship with your children. The birth of a child, especially a first child, can become a distraction, keeping you from dealing with your problems. But this may be the very time when parents need to renegotiate certain aspects of their relationship in order to maintain a real connection."

☞ **Ban spanking.** For many people, discipline means spanking and nothing but spanking. And while most experts do not totally, utterly forbid it, they do not recommend it.

"What message are you sending when you spank?" asks Dr. Micucci. "The message is this: If you get caught, you'll experience pain, and then it's all over. You have not sent the message to your child that his or her actions have consequences."

☞ **Call for a time-out.** Instead of spanking your child, try what's known as a time-out. Child behavior experts maintain that this is a more effective form of discipline. It's a good way for a parent to respond to a child's inappropriate behavior.

To do a time-out, you simply remove the child from the sphere of activity and isolate him or her on the sidelines.

Explain to the child what behavior is unacceptable and tell him or her that this time is to be used to ponder the results of his or her actions.

"If your little girl is nasty to another child, you remove her. You give her a time-out. She learns the lesson, then, that if someone continues to be nasty, they will have no friends. They will be alone," says Dr. Micucci.

The rule of thumb for a time-out is five minutes until the age of 5 years.

"You can remove a toy or another favorite object as well," says Dr. Micucci, "to show that privileges depend on respecting others' needs."

☞ **Keep it simple.** Dr. Micucci warns against giving long dissertations to a child you are trying to discipline. "Children have a short attention span," he explains. "What they need is a clear objection, expressed with affection."

If you really feel a discussion is warranted, "wait until everything cools down, then talk about it," suggests Dr. Micucci.

Children first must feel secure that their own needs are met before they can relate to others. They need to learn how to handle frustration, so that later they will be able to control a hot temper and to follow the rules. They need to develop that sense of "we" that leads to sharing and giving. To learn to give love and affection, they need to see their parents interact lovingly with each other and with the rest of the family.

Part IV

your delightful toddler

your little
explorer

Christopher Columbus. Leif Eriksson. Marco Polo. Ponce de León. Amelia Earhart. Sally Ride. Neil Armstrong. Your baby.

It won't be long before your child will take "one small step" around the coffee table and "one giant leap" into a huge new world. He or she will explore every aspect of the immediate environment, from the feel of fresh grass between chubby little fingers to the taste of your bunny slippers under the bed.

Your baby has been working long and hard training for this transforming achievement. Vision had to sharpen. Hands and eyes needed a lot of training to work as a team. Muscles needed toughening. Balance had to be mastered.

Preparing the Niña, the Pinta, and the Santa Maria for the voyage to America was child's play compared to the work babies have to do to get ready for this great adventure of exploring their new world.

Let's trace that voyage, beginning at about 3 months of age.

Three to Five Months

At 3 to 5 months, your little explorer has made a great discovery. Hands! At about 3 months, your baby learns to open them. And taste them. Later, maybe at 3½ months, your baby begins to regard them intently. Look how the fingers can bend, how they wiggle, how they hold a rattle.

Also at about 3 months, your baby can lift his or her head for a few minutes. And—wonder of wonders—your baby can now see color.

At about 4 months, your baby should be taken in for another routine visit with the doctor, who will assess the little one's health and development.

"At that age, the baby's startle response should be gone," says pediatrician Suzanne LeBel Corrigan, M.D., associate clinical professor at the University

Save Your Aching Back

You reach into the back of the automobile to lift your baby from the car seat, and YOWWWW! There goes your back.

Every day and in every way you lift your baby countless times: in and out of the crib, the high chair, the car seat, the playpen, the stroller, the shopping cart. Every day your little one is a little bit heavier than the day before.

For some parents, particularly those who are no longer youngsters, frequently lifting a 15- or 20-pound child takes a serious toll on the back. Physical therapists say that by the time a person is 40, all kinds of accumulated muscle imbalances and postural problems make the spine more vulnerable to injury.

There are, however, a few actions you can take to reduce the risk of back pain.

☞ **Avoid bending over.** When taking your child out of the playpen, for example, lower yourself by bending your knees and keeping your back straight. Drop the side of the playpen and guide your baby toward you. Hold your baby close and stand up by straightening your knees, lifting with your leg muscles rather than your back.

☞ **Squat a lot.** Get in the habit of using a straight-backed squat to pick up everything: pots from the kitchen cabinet, the newspaper from the front step, whatever. This maneuver helps lessen the cumulative strain on your back.

☞ **Slide in from the side.** Choose a car seat for your baby that has left-side or right-side entry. It will help a great deal if you don't have to torque your back muscles by leaning over to place your baby into the seat from the front.

of Texas Southwestern Medical School in Dallas. (The startle response, which is also known as the Moro reflex, is a curious little set of actions that an infant does in response to a sudden change of position. He or she will act startled and cry out, flinging back the arms then rapidly bringing them back together again.)

This is the age when babies begin turning over on their own, rolling from their tummy to their back.

"They begin to reach for things," explains Dr. Corrigan. "They start smiling and trying to engage you. They have begun babbling. They like to be in a standing position and will clamp their little feet down if they are pulled upright.

"Babies this age are usually not frightened by their surroundings, but are interested in what's going on around them."

Here's what babies should be able to do by the end of the fifth month:

- **turn their heads** in all directions, from side to side, and up and down
- **be pulled** from a lying position into a sitting position by their arms
- **raise their arms** to be picked up
- **bear some weight** on their legs while being held in a standing position
- **reach for and grab** an object you offer
- **recognize you** and other family members
- **smile** at you
- **laugh, gurgle, and babble** at you and generally charm the living daylights out of everyone in the vicinity

Six Months

At 6 months," says Dr. Corrigan, "I expect babies to be able to hold their head and trunk straight when pulled from lying on their back to a sitting position. They should be reaching with both hands and rolling in at least one if not both directions. Their muscles should not be either stiff or floppy.

"Babies this age should be responding to sounds around them, turning their head to locate the sound. They should be able to follow objects both near and far with both eyes. They should be able to sit (with help) for a few seconds. They should be laughing and squealing."

Making the Best Tressed List

Whether a boy or a girl, born bald or with a mop of ringlets, at 7 to 10 months old, most babies will have grown enough hair to look a little shaggy and unkempt. It's now time for The First Haircut.

You might choose to do the trimming yourself. To record the event, take a "before" picture. Then, begin by dampening your baby's hair. Using a wide-tooth comb, remove any tangles. Start trimming, beginning at the nape of the neck. Use the comb to bring the hair away from the scalp, then grab each section with your left hand, holding the hair between your index and middle fingers. Holding the scissors level, trim off the excess. Work from back to sides, leaving the top and front for last.

If you choose to have a professional cut your baby's hair, look for a barber or beautician who is experienced in cutting children's hair. They often are listed in the *Yellow Pages* with ads saying "children welcome" or announcing they do "haircuts for the whole family." Some will have child-oriented chairs, such as little racing cars or Cinderella-type coaches. Such fancy extras aren't nearly as important as the stylist's patience.

Set up your appointment in person and bring your baby with you. The brief visit will allow your child to see the shop and perhaps witness other children getting a haircut.

On the day of the appointment, take a "before" picture, then give your baby a shampoo. Having hair washed at home is much less traumatic than having a stranger do it. Ask the stylist to just dampen your baby's hair with a mister or wet towel. After the hair cut, ask the stylist to skip the electric dryer; your baby will be happier without all that commotion.

No matter who cuts your baby's hair, remember to take an "after" picture. You'll later treasure these pictures of your baby's first haircut.

Seven to Nine Months

At any time between 7 and 9 months old, your baby will start to explore the house. This may well begin before your baby has even figured out how to crawl. The first movement along the floor may come when your baby figures out how to propel backward while lying on his or her tummy. (Your baby will shift out of reverse as soon as coordination is more developed.) Some babies use the bottom-bounce method. Sitting on the floor with one hand behind them and legs extended in front, they use their hand to push forward and their legs to pull forward. The motion achieved looks a little like a hop, but done with the posterior.

Eventually, most children begin to use crawling to get around on their own. A few daredevils skip the crawling stage entirely, preferring to simply stand up and walk.

The Big Step

Somewhere between 9 and 16 months old, most babies begin walking. Earlier, they practiced by cruising around holding onto the furniture, sometimes taking an unaided lone step from the coffee table to the sofa cushion. They also like you to "walk" them, a back-breaking endeavor that involves you standing behind them holding both their hands while they high-step to their destination.

Please do not be tempted to buy a walker to help your baby learn to walk. It's been found that walkers actually slow down the process. More important, they are dangerous. (See "Walker of Doom" on page 48.)

Instead, buy a toy that will help your baby practice walking. This toy should have a handle, wheels, and a center of gravity that is low to the ground. A baby-size shopping cart is ideal. With each stop, the

Baby-Proofing Your Home

When your little sweetheart is about 5 months old, it's time to look at your home with new eyes. Knee-level eyes. Before long, your baby will be creeping, then crawling, then getting into things—some of them potentially harmful. You can reduce any risk of accident by taking some commonsense precautions.

Perhaps the most important step is to reverse your thinking. Replace the notion "My baby can never reach that" with "Could my baby somehow reach that?"

It also might be helpful to actually get down on your hands and knees to do some exploring. Thinking like a baby, what do you see? I see some electric cords that might be good to taste. I might even use those cords as a way to pull myself up. And what are those interesting little holes in the wall where the cords plug in? Let's stick something into one to find out. Climbing the stairs looks like fun, but it might be even more fun to taste that lemon-scented liquid Mama keeps under the sink.

You get the picture. Here are some suggestions to keep your child from getting hurt:

☞ **Remove "steps."** If your baby has begun trying to climb out of the crib, remove the protective bumpers as well as any toys that could be used as steps.

☞ **Protect against shock.** Cover unused electrical outlets with safety caps.

☞ **Get cords out of the way.** Unplug and remove any lamp that could be pulled down on top of your baby should he or she yank the cord. If electrical wires are long, or if you are using extension cords, tack them to the baseboard and cover them with tape.

☞ **Forget your green thumb.** Some house plants are poisonous, so give your house plants to a foster home, especially those that live in big pots on the floor.

☞ **Block all stairways.** Install gates on all stairways, at the top and bottom. Keep cellar doors and doors to the outside closed.

☞ **Practice fire safety.** If someone in your house smokes (they shouldn't with a baby in the house), remove matches, lighters, ashtrays, and smoking materials. Keep the high chair, playpen, and other baby equipment away from the stove, heaters, fireplace, and furnace.

☞ **Empty lower cabinets.** Take all the cleaning supplies—yes, even the dish-washing soap—out of the cabinet under the sink and put them in a high place, completely out of your baby's reach. Take careful stock of what's in every floor-level cabinet. Remove shoe polishes, car wax, bug sprays, and weed killers. If you don't have a place to store these items, padlock the cabinets. Babies can and do taste just about anything.

☞ **Watch those sharp objects.** When you load cutlery into the dishwasher, place the knives, forks, and even the spoons into the basket facing downward.

☞ **Mind your pots.** When cooking, keep the pot handles turned toward the center or rear of the range, where they're positioned so your baby can't pull them down from the edge of the stove.

☞ **Take special care with medications.** Ask your pharmacist to put all medications in child-resistant containers. Keep all your medications, even aspirin and other nonprescription drugs, out of sight, preferably in a locked medicine cabinet.

☞ **Lock up toiletries.** Keep cosmetics and perfumes out of your baby's reach. Babies are especially tempted by items that smell good and come in pretty bottles.

☞ **Keep the toilet seat down and the lid closed.** Make sure the men in your house cooperate with this one.

☞ **Never drop your guard.** Don't assume that just because you've baby-proofed your house that it will stay that way. Continually scan for small objects that can be swallowed, sharp objects, and breakables.

---

child propels the toy forward, but always has something to hang onto if he or she starts to lose balance.

Your heart may swell with pride when you see your baby set off entirely unaided, but you may also want to laugh out loud. There goes Baby, reeling and teetering through the living room, arms held out for balance, knees turned a bit outward, a lurching shift of weight from one foot to another.

Often those first steps are taken on tiptoe, a walking technique that may last a few months. However, for some children, toe-walking becomes a long-term habit, one that should be called to your

Infant Swim Class

Swimming is a nice way for your baby to get some happy exercise and take a break from the rigors of toddling. Maybe that's why infant swim classes are all the rage.

Many parents would love to swim with their babies, but they have concerns about dunking their darlings into a pool that's ocean-deep to a little person who measures only 25 or 30 inches. Is it safe? Is it sanitary? Is it good for the child?

Yes, yes, and yes. But don't expect your baby to do any actual swimming. Most children can't learn to swim until they are about 4 years old.

Most aquatic classes for infants are designed for babies at least 6 months old. The classes involve parent and child working together (playing, really) over a course of about six lessons. The focus is family fun, an opportunity for quality time together, and a way for babies to get used to a pool.

A good program will require the baby to be accompanied by a parent and will employ instructors who are qualified lifeguards and are certified to give infant CPR. It will stress water play and developmental exercises such as kicking and dog paddling. You also can expect musical games and some water toys.

The program also should offer the parent some good advice about water safety: how to hold the child in the water, which kinds of flotation equipment work well and when to use them, and how to climb into and out of the pool holding the baby.

As for the pool itself, a well-maintained pool is clean enough for your child. A heated pool will be more readily accepted. You may be concerned about the effects of chlorine on your baby. It's not dangerous if it is present in normal concentrations, according to Donald Schiff, M.D., professor of pediatrics at the University of Colorado Health Sciences Center at the Denver Children's Hospital. If you don't notice a strong chlorine odor or feel that the water is stinging your own skin, the chlorine level is probably safe for your baby.

After you've had your swim, rinse your baby in fresh water, dry your baby, then apply hand lotion. Chlorine and water tend to dry out the skin.

If your baby vigorously resists going into the pool or if he or she is obviously frightened and miserable, don't force the issue. Perhaps your session is scheduled at a time when your baby usually takes a nap. If so, can you find a class held at a better time? Or, perhaps the little one simply isn't ready to take the plunge. Experts suggest that you wait six months, then try again.

For more information on child and infant swim classes, contact your local YMCA or the nearest chapter of the American Red Cross.

doctor's attention. The concern here is that if your baby's heels never meet the floor, the Achilles tendon can shorten. When that strip of sinew connecting the heel bone to the leg bone becomes too taut, your baby will have trouble putting his or her feet down flat on the floor. To break the habit, your doctor may recommend high-top shoes, which don't allow the child to walk on tiptoe.

Your Baby's First Shoes

Initially, your child will manage best by walking barefoot. Going shoeless allows the feet to flex easily, which helps your baby with balance. Plus, the toes need to clamp down on the floor in order to take those first steps. Once your baby begins walking outside, it's time for shoes.

It is possible to spend a small fortune on baby footwear. If you like, you can make a fashion statement with tiny Mary Janes, bitsy saddle shoes, or elegant footwear made of kid leather.

Or, you can simply buy sneakers, which is what many doctors recommend.

Sneakers are lightweight. They have nonskid soles. They are flexible. They can be machine-washed, if necessary. And they're often more affordable. (This aspect will become increasingly important to you as you see your child continually grow out of shoes that are barely scuffed.)

There is one drawback, however. Sneakers don't look that great bronzed.

The First Tooth

Teething can begin at almost any time in the first year. "Some babies begin to teethe at four months; others don't start until they are a year old," says Dr. Corrigan. "Either way is perfectly normal. Some babies get teeth without experiencing any problems, but others may be fussy or cranky.

"A child's basic temperament seems to have something to do with his response to teething. A fussy baby will be more fussy with teething. Other babies, however, don't seem to have any problems. You can see their gums are swollen and red, and it must be painful, but they seem content."

To treat teething pain, Dr. Corrigan suggests that you ignore the painkillers that are applied directly to the gums. "They just disappear as soon as the baby's saliva hits them," she explains.

Instead, she suggests giving acetaminophen (Tylenol) and offering the baby something hard and cold to chew on—"like a fat carrot from the fridge or a cold teething ring."

Visiting the Dentist

As soon as the first tooth erupts, it's time to start dental care, according to Theodore P. Croll, D.D.S., a pediatric dentist in Doylestown, Pennsylvania. "The most important thing a parent can do to prevent dental problems is to start early visits," he says. The first visit to the dentist may occur somewhere between 4 and 14 months of age.

The first several visits to the dentist should turn parents and dentists into partners who together care for the baby's oral health. "The job of the dentist and of the dental hygienist is teaching parents the

How Baby Teeth Come In

Your baby's first teeth begin to develop in the jaw about five or six months before birth. And your baby's first tooth will emerge when he or she is somewhere between 4 and 14 months of age. The baby teeth usually (but not always) debut in the following order: lower two front teeth, matching upper two front teeth, upper teeth at either side of the middle teeth, lower matching outer teeth, first molars, canines, and, finally, the second molars at about 2½ or 3 years.

tricks of prevention," explains Dr. Croll.

Don't wait for your baby's first examination to begin caring for his or her teeth, however. During the first year, babies are at risk for a condition known as nursing decay.

"If nursing sessions are prolonged," explains Dr. Croll, "and a nutritive fluid soaks the newly erupted baby teeth for excessive periods of time without being cleared from the tooth surfaces, bacteria in the mouth can convert the fluid to acid, leading to early tooth decay."

The potential for trouble with cavities exists for both bottle-fed and breast-fed babies. "I've had too many breast-fed babies with nursing decay," maintains Dr. Croll. "Two hours at the breast without a good brushing, repeated for many weeks, can really doom those little teeth."

It's not just milk that can do harm. The doctor has seen cases in which a 1-year-old's teeth have been completely destroyed as the result of nursing on a bottle of apple juice for extended periods.

"The inside surfaces of the upper front teeth are especially prone to decay because the nipple releases the fluid in that region," says Dr. Croll. He has examined a number of babies whose front teeth looked normal, only to discover that the inside surfaces if the teeth were decayed.

One of the most important tips that I received (being a new mom at home) from a friend was: Go out with just your husband once a week just for a couple hours. It was the best advice I received! At first it was hard to do. We probably went for one or two hours. Then I started really looking forward to that special night out. It gave me time to just think of my husband and him to think of just me! So find a baby-sitter soon and have a great time! It gives you a new energy level caring for your newborn baby and a nice thing to look forward to next time you go out.

Judith Newman
Buffalo Grove, Illinois

Your dentist or pediatrician will suggest that you take the following steps to avoid tooth decay:

☞ **Don't use food as a pacifier.** Avoid using a nursing bottle as a way to calm your baby and encourage sleep.

If you need a pacifier, use a pacifier. Letting your baby fall asleep with a bottle in his or her mouth can do serious damage to those tiny teeth.

☞ **Wake your baby up for feedings.** Avoid breast- or bottle-feeding while the child is asleep.

☞ **Ditch the bottle.** Change from a bottle to a cup when the child is about 1 year old.

☞ **Brush often.** You should brush, not wipe, your baby's teeth, using a soft-bristle toothbrush. Brush your baby's teeth after the morning feeding and before bedtime.

☞ **Don't be afraid to brush.** Concerned that using a toothbrush might be a bit much? Don't be.

"It's a pediatric myth that using a gauze square to wipe a child's gum tissue and teeth will adequately clean them," Dr. Croll says.

"Some people believe that you can damage a child's 'delicate' gum tissue by using a brush, but you should use a brush to do the job right.

" Don't worry about the gum tissue. It's like alligator hide. These babies are chewing on coffee tables, rocks, each other, and everything else in their reach. A toothbrush isn't going to hurt their gums!"

☞ **Don't use strong-arm tactics.** You should be gentle when brushing your baby's teeth.

Those baby gums might be tough, but you want the task to be pleasant enough that your child will be willing to continue it on his or her own when the time comes.

Stocking Your Medicine Cabinet

Many parents fill their medicine cabinets by picking up items as they are needed. That, however, is not the best approach. In the event of an emergency, you won't have the time to drive to the pharmacy for the items you need. The best approach is to stock the basic items. As your baby grows, you'll naturally accumulate a few more items. Here's our recommended list:

•**Acetaminophen**, such as Tylenol in liquid form, to reduce fever and ease pain.

•**Syrup of ipecac** for accidental poisoning. Call the baby's doctor or your local Poison Control Center before giving it to the baby. In fact, label the bottle with those two phone numbers and the admonition to call either of these numbers before administering ipecac. (The Poison Control Center is listed in your phone book.)

•**A thermometer.** The old-fashioned rectal thermometer is good and can be used under the arm. Avoid the plastic strips that show the temperature in a liquid crystal display. They are inexpensive but not accurate. There is also a relatively new thermometer shaped like a pacifier, in which the temperature registers on a digital liquid crystal strip. It, too, is unreliable.

•**A nasal bulb syringe.** This device is used to draw out mucus from a baby's nose when it is congested. Babies don't like the procedure much, but sometimes it's necessary because babies can't nurse when their nasal passages are blocked.

•**Plastic bandages** for small cuts and scrapes.

•**A topical antibiotic cream**, such as Bacitracin, to prevent cuts and scrapes from getting infected.

•**A topical cortisone cream**, such as Cortaid, for itchy rashes.

•**A penlight** for looking at sore throats.

•**Tweezers** for removing splinters or insect stingers.

•**A special measuring spoon** for giving liquid medications.

Get Flossing

As your child matures and becomes more independent, tooth brushing can become a bit of a tussle. The average 2-year-old, says Dr. Croll, will want to do the job alone. But a child that young simply can't.

"Most younger children do not possess the manual dexterity required to manipulate a toothbrush and dental floss in their own mouths," says Dr. Croll. And they need to have a certain amount of dexterity to properly remove plaque.

Is this plaque removal really so important at such a young age? Must you go through the daily struggle of brushing a 2-year-old's teeth? Do you *really* need this hassle? In a word: yes.

Dr. Croll refers to plaque as "a mouth menace." That's because this slimy material sticks to tooth surfaces. Left there, it hardens into a material called tartar that must be removed by a dentist or hygienist. Plaque and tartar promote tooth decay, infection of the gums, and bad breath.

The Fine Art of Taking Naps

Those first few months after coming home from the hospital, your brand-new baby slept most of the day, every day. At about 4 months, definite wake/sleep patterns begin to emerge. No longer does your baby slip in and out of sleep during the entire 24 hours. Instead, you'll see that your baby starts taking a morning nap and another in the afternoon, together totaling two to four hours of sleep. This napping pattern will continue until your baby is about a year old.

Naps are important. The human body is programmed so the temperature drops and the metabolism slows at specific intervals during the day and night. In order for these necessary processes to take place, a baby needs to get some real sleep at regular intervals. If you've been in the presence of a baby who has missed a nap, you know the loud and unhappy results.

How can you be sure your baby is napping sufficiently? Doctors say there is no specific formula for naps, because each baby has individual sleep needs. Most babies benefit from taking naps at the same time each day, however. Just like everyone else, babies fall into a routine. Watch your baby for sleepiness cues, then make that time nap time. Most babies seem to flourish with naps at midmorning and again at about 2 in the afternoon. (Napping any later than this can push back the bedtime hour.)

As your child grows and becomes more active, napping is even more important. It allows your baby to rest after hard physical activity and to lower stress levels. But getting your baby to nap can sometimes be a problem. A child who has been crawling, stretching, playing, or toddling can't simply hit the off switch and go to sleep. In addition to setting regular hours for naps, it becomes important to create a routine that enables your baby to wind down and relax. Reading a familiar story is an excellent way to help your baby decelerate.

Mastering the Challenge Of Bedtime

It may sound peculiar, but it is nevertheless true that your baby does reach a stage when he or she must learn how to fall asleep.

Often, a baby is tired and needs sleep, but is too fitful to nod off. The child is simply unable to relax and let go of the day. Research has shown that having an exciting, varied, novel, and responsive environment may make it hard for children to give themselves up to sleep.

What your baby needs, then, is a way to make the transition from wakefulness to sleep, and to learn to fall asleep alone.

Here are some suggestions that may help your child find comfort—and maybe even enjoyment—in bedtime:

☞ **Set the scene.** First, make sure no environ-

Head Banging and Crib Rocking

There's your little genius, bright as a summer sunrise. And what is your baby doing? Banging his or her head, slamming it down hard on the bed. It looks painful (and it probably is), but your baby keeps it up for some time before finally dropping off to sleep.

Or, maybe your little equestrian has begun to ride the crib across the room. Up on hands and knees, your baby pushes his or her bottom toward the feet, propelling the crib backward across the room with each lurch, until it finally bumps into something and stops. Then you can hear the squeak and creak as the rocking continues.

What accounts for this strange behavior? Should you be alarmed?

The experts say that head banging and crib rocking usually begin when the baby is between 6 and 12 months old. No one knows for sure why a healthy, well-cared-for infant would engage in this behavior, but the prevailing view is that it is simply the result of energy leftover at the end of the day.

Your baby spends that energy in a rhythmic way, and once it's all used up, he or she can fall asleep.

Eventually, the banging and rocking will stop on their own. In the meantime, look after your child's physical safety. You don't want that heavy crib collapsing on top of your baby.

Try putting the crib in a corner where it won't be quite as mobile. Tighten up all the screws. Buy some of those little plastic cups made to keep chair legs from putting permanent impressions in the rug, and put them under the crib legs to slow down the steeplechase.

mental problem is postponing or disturbing sleep. Is the crib comfortably padded? Are the sheet and blanket soft and clean? Does your baby have room to stretch and wiggle? (Your baby should be out of the bassinet and into a crib by the age of 6 months.) Have you plugged in a dim night-light? Is the room too warm or too cool?

☞ **Create a routine.** A bedtime routine serves two purposes. It lets your child know that bedtime is approaching. It also provides the opportunity for your child to unwind and disengage from the day.

Many parents have found success with the following approach: About an hour before bedtime, begin the countdown with a bath. Playing and splashing in the tub and batting at the rubber ducky will help use up some of the leftover energy.

After the bath, start slowing the pace. Pat your baby gently dry and apply lotion or powder if you use them. Spend some close, quiet time together. You can read a story while cuddling your baby. Or, you can say good night to Mr. Bear, Mrs. Clown, and all the other toys in a comforting ritual that prepares your baby for bed. Finally, put your little one gently into the crib and whisper your good night.

☞ **Keep trying.** If you hear a heartbreaking howl after you tiptoe away, do go back into the nursery and repeat your good night. Adjust the covers, pat your baby's back, tell your baby that you love him or her, and leave again. Your baby should be reassured enough to try to sleep. Sometimes it helps to leave the door open so the baby can hear reassuring family sounds while drifting off.

☞ **Don't give rewards for crying.** Rewards will only encourage a repeat performance. Do not pick up the baby, do not rock and cuddle the little one, do not offer a bottle. Just let your baby know that you're still nearby, but that it's time to sleep.

☞ **Provide a little support.** Some babies seem to need a little extra help going to sleep. That's where a "blanky" or a stuffed toy comes in handy. These transitional items can provide enough comfort and security so the baby can soothe himself or herself to sleep.

☞ **Be reassuring.** The crux of the bedtime blues is probably separation anxiety, a perfectly normal phase of development that kicks in at about 8 months. To a baby in the throes of this anxiety, your good nights sound like "Good-bye forever."

So be consistent in using the bedtime routine, performing the same steps in the same order at the same time each night. Before too long, your child will respond to the routine by relaxing and allowing sleep to come.

Awake at the Midnight Hour

Even though your child may be sleeping 8, 10, or even 12 hours at night, awakenings in the middle of the night are common.

What happens is that when baby awakens, all is quiet. There's no familiar clatter from the kitchen. No drone from the television set. No lights. "Oh, no!" thinks Baby. "They left me. I'm all alone in this strange new world!" It's at that point that Mom and Dad hear the wailing.

Your instincts may tell you to rush right to the nursery. Instead, wait a minute or two to see if your baby quiets down on his or her own. Sometimes all that's needed is a little night-light, so that when your baby's eyes open, the familiar surroundings offer some reassurance that everything is OK.

If the crying continues, go in to reassure your baby (and yourself) that everything is OK. Do not, however, make this simple act of comforting a big event: no feeding, no singing, no taking your baby out of the crib.

To do any of these things will encourage more midnight raids on your sleep. Instead, simply say a few soft words and go back to bed.

so *grown up*

Board up the windows and batten down the hatches, because Hurricane Baby is headed right for the center of your life. The forecast is for whirling winds of activity, accompanied by howling protests and gales of laughter.

What's the cause of all this bluster? You might call it a start of life challenge that your baby meets head on with every ounce of exuberant enthusiasm available in that growing body.

A child between 18 months and 3 years old is not an infant anymore, but certainly is not a preschooler. This period constitutes a time of transition between the two stages, a passage from one of relative helplessness to one of some independence and self-control.

You know from your own times of transition—such as from student to worker and footloose single to responsible parent—that transition periods can be tough. They're exciting and rewarding, but at the same time they demand a great deal of energy and emotional flexibility.

In the transition from babyhood to childhood, your little one also will test his or her physical and emotional limits, pushing them time and time again, in an effort to expand them. All this activity means your baby is starting to grow up.

Turning Two: The High-Energy Vortex

The centerpiece of this period is the so-called terrible twos, when your child undergoes a burst of verbal, intellectual, emotional, and social change. You can witness your little one passing into a new phase of life as the rates of physical growth and motor development slow their frantic speed and at the same time the growth of the intellect and emotions begin their rapid surge.

One product of these changes is that your child is extremely curious. Perhaps some of the curiosity always was there, but the child's newly enhanced physical development now allows for constant experimentation. Sometimes watching that curiosity in action is simply wonderful; sometimes it is simply maddening.

Here's a real-life story: Little Samantha used her small wooden mallet on the bright-colored pegs in her board. She exulted as they went down through the board. "This is wonderful! I wonder what else I can do with my hammer?" she might have thought. She next hammered on the lowest of a flight of wood steps, making a grand noise that caused the cat to jump up and run. "Hmm," she may have wondered, "will this hammer make all animals jump?"

Taking her mallet to the next level of scientific research, she pounded it against the front of the fish tank. Sure enough, the fish darted to the corners. She banged again. Oops! Samantha was surprised by shattering glass, 20 gallons of tropics-warm water, and two dozen flopping fish crashing down around her. End of experiment.

Two-year-olds will poke, prod, bang on, lift, or push almost anything they encounter. If the object is big enough, they'll try to climb on it, sit on it, crawl into it, or burrow under it. They are driven to know: How does it work? What does it do? Why is it here? All these urgent questions need answers. That's why 2-year-olds are always fiddling with things. They'll take almost anything apart to see what's inside. (Of course, they can't put it back together, because they don't yet have the necessary physical skill.)

Sometimes, instead of experimenting alone, a 2-year-old will come to you for the answer. Typically, when you give it, your child will summarize the information in a two- or three-word sentence (as in, "Fish go bye-bye").

As the year progresses, you'll see a subtle change.

The Blanky

It's not called a "security blanket" for nothing. That worn piece of cloth really does provide security and comfort, especially when a child is not feeling well or is in a stressful situation.

Toddlers often call these pieces of cloth "blankies" or "bankies." Experts know them as "transitional objects." In a toddler's struggle for autonomy and independence, he or she is more able to separate from Mama—at least for a short time—if there is something on hand to hold on to. The object (it's as often a stuffed toy as a blanket) is a symbol of comfort and security. Some experts say it's even a symbol of mother.

As long as your child seems to need a blanky, allow it—no matter how grungy and tattered it looks.

You'll notice that your child is doing less lone exploring and more socializing. Your child will enjoy some give-and-take games, laugh at your silliness, and even come up with a few jokes, although they'll be of the pie-in-the-face variety.

Somewhere along Route 2, your child will completely master feeding himself or herself and will figure out how to get dressed (with supervision). During this time, your child may also learn to use a potty. And you'll be so proud. Your little one also will discover and frequently use the words "my," "mine," and "no." Your child may have tantrums and even bite. And you'll be so concerned.

This period provokes an emotional tug-of-war, for parents and child. In the quest for selfhood, in trying to establish some independence, your child will stake out a personal territory. (My! Mine!)

One minute your child will be running away from you as fast as possible; the next moment he or she will be back, clinging to your knees and whining for attention. Children in transition rejoice in their growing independence. At the same time, they require a framework of stability, support, and security. Life is a balancing act, and the 2-year-old teeters between the two needs.

Let's take a look at how parents can best guide babies in transition so that life remains reasonably calm and happy.

Just Saying No

The answer is "no." Whatever the question, your child's answer is "no." You know, for example, that your little Keesha is starving. She hasn't eaten for hours. But if you ask her, "Do you want to eat lunch?" the answer will be, "No."

"Are you hungry?"

"No!"

"Would you like a cookie?"

"No."

And no, No, NO.

Well, you're the mother, and you know best, so you prepare some sandwich triangles, fill up the plastic cup, and place them on Keesha's tray. In response, she rather dramatically drops the cup over the side, screaming, "No! No! No!" The pieces of sandwich are shoved off the tray after the cup.

What is happening to your baby? She's hungry and miserable and acting like a brat. You know she really wants to eat, so why is she behaving in this upsetting way?

It's a phase all toddlers go through, and it's called negativism. Many experts believe that negativism is a tool a child uses to differentiate self from his or her mother and to enhance the sense of self.

Establishing a Sense of Self

Children start out in life feeling they are extensions of their mothers. But sometime between 12 and 18 months of age, they develop a growing awareness that they are not part

Mystery Solved

Your child is a perfect angel for Grandma. The baby-sitter says your baby is sooooo good, a pleasure to watch. So why is your baby a little prince or princess for everyone else, but a wicked little demon when you're the one doing the baby-sitting?

Simple. Your baby doesn't trust these other people the way he or she trusts you. Your baby doesn't trust them enough to feel free to test limits. They may not be there to save the day if he or she goes too far. But when you are there, your baby knows that—no matter what—you'll come to the rescue.

of their mothers at all, but totally separate beings. In other words, they develop a sense of self. As individuals, they try to establish some control over their surroundings. But first they have to confirm the theory that, indeed, they are individuals.

Mama wants Bobby to take a nap. Indeed, Bobby feels hot and tired, but getting ready for bed is not at the top of his agenda. In order to demonstrate to himself that he is not Mama, he will refuse to cooperate. He may be tired and miserable, but, by golly, he's Bobby. Not Mama.

For parents, this tempest in a high chair becomes frustrating. You can save yourself some trouble if you simply don't ask your toddler many questions. For example, instead of asking Bobby if he wants to take his nap, you can say something like, "I'm sure you're tired, so let's get ready for bed now." Period. No discussion.

A parent also can ask questions that elicit something other than "No," such as, "Do you want to sit on Daddy's lap or in your high chair?"

Avoid escalating a "no" answer into a confrontation or you'll be battling all day. Also forget trying to reason with your child. A lot of the negative answers are just an automatic response, and your child may not really mean "no" at all. Besides, you know there's no point in arguing about some things. So why bother? Instead, allow your child a minute to reconsider your request and calmly begin anew.

There are times when you cannot and should not take no for an answer. In matters of safety—sitting in the car seat, holding hands while walking across the parking lot, not stepping into the street, and the like—you will have to exert your authority even if it displeases and upsets your child.

The fact is that from time to time you will have to insist on certain behaviors, whether your child likes it or not. At times like these, it helps to have laid a groundwork of good feelings. Throughout the day, do your best to recognize and reward your child's good behavior as a way of generating some positive feelings to balance the negativity. As your child wends his or her way through the "No" phase, try to keep your sense of humor. This, too, shall pass.

Surviving a Temper Tantrum

Everyone is staring at you. Let's see, there are 10 checkout lanes in the supermarket, each with about five people standing in line. That makes approximately 50 people glowering at you because you are a Bad Mother Who Cannot Control Her Own Child. A child whose red, wet face is contorted in a piercing howl. A child who has flung himself to the floor, kicking both feet, in the aisle between the AAA batteries and the sugar-free gum. A child who is clearly out of control and in great distress. You get the picture.

Temper tantrums are not fun. They are also not at all unusual. And they certainly are not a sign of poor parenting. What they are is a way for a young child—often a tired or hungry child—to deal with his or her frustration.

In this theoretical tantrum at the supermarket, our young mother was in a hurry to pick up a few things for dinner. She wanted to make it a quick and easy trip—just zipping in and out of the store.

Mom wanted to sprint through the market, but Kevin wanted to dawdle, to poke at the eye-level cans and boxes. Besides, Kevin was too worn out to rush. You can guess what happened. Mom, losing patience with Kevin's poky ways, asked him to move along and got no response. She then asked him to sit in the cart, and when she still got no response, she attempted to pick him up and put him in the cart. "No, no, no, no!" screamed Kevin, bursting into horrendous sobs.

What do you do when your child is having a tantrum? How do you respond to such a primal force of toddler nature?

When your child is having a tantrum, there are several steps you can take to minimize the trauma for everyone.

☞ **First and most important, remain calm.** Don't raise your voice. Even if you are flustered, embarrassed, or overwrought, stay calm. If you respond with "Stop that!" or "Behave yourself!" you'll just crank up the tension level.

☞ **Don't get angry yourself.** Remind yourself that your child is not being or trying to be manipulative. Your child is emotionally overwhelmed and simply too young to know how to handle frustration or anger. Yelling at your child just adds to the burden and makes everything harder.

☞ **Pick up your baby and hold him or her tight.** Restrain the flailing arms and legs, if you can, and move to another location. Carry your child out of the supermarket, away from the playground, or even from one room to another at home. Remain in that new spot until your child begins to pull himself or herself together.

☞ **Offer your love.** As the screams become small, shuddering sobs, continue to comfort your sweet, tired, upset baby with kind words and soft kisses. Right now, when many would say your baby least deserves it, is when he or she needs your love and caring.

Being a mom is a true blessing ... in disguise. I have a 33-month-old daughter. At times, I am furious and frustrated with her persistent ways of testing the world and me. But underneath my exhausted and resilient layers of being her mother—the nurturer, disciplinarian, teacher, doctor, entertainer, provider, and protector—I love being with Jade. She constantly reminds me that I am loved, no matter how many mistakes I make as a parent. I've become a better person.

Jill Schuman
Honolulu, Hawaii

☞ **Inform your doctor, if necessary.** Some children having a tantrum become so upset they hold their breath and even faint. The American Academy of Pediatrics says that if your child has fainted, you should call your pediatrician. The problem is not that any physical damage was done during the fainting spell, but that the doctor may want to check to be sure there is no medical problem that caused it.

Setting Limits

Some parents shrink from the concept of discipline, conjuring visions of the British boarding school, complete with headmasters wielding switches and rapping knuckles. But that's not discipline—that's punishment. There's a big difference.

If you look into the origins of the word "discipline," you'll discover that it comes from the Latin word *disciplina*, which means teaching or learning. The dictionary definition is "training that perfects, molds, or corrects the mental faculties or moral character," and "to train or develop by instruction and exercise, especially in self-control."

Simply put, discipline is a method of teaching your child self-control. It is never, ever an exercise in vindictiveness.

Testing the Limits

Children between the ages of 18 months and 3 years are always testing to see what's allowed and what they can get away with. It's a rare child who simply absorbs a restriction and forever obeys it.

Most children test a rule to find its parameters. Does the prohibition against throwing things in the house include throwing things at or through windows and doors (not technically in the house, you see)? Some children live more recklessly, testing to see what happens when two rules are broken at the same time. Or, children test to see what happens, when caught breaking a rule, if they blatantly lie.

Sometimes a child will outright break a rule for reasons other than testing what you say. Take Courtney, for example, who just dumped her new shoes into the toilet after you've made it clear that she's not to put clothing or toys there. She's usually not a naughty child, so what's up?

Maybe Courtney could use a little extra attention. She played quietly for quite some time while you were busy paying the monthly bills. After a while, she got bored and lonesome, but you were still busy. So, she tried the shoes-in-the-toilet trick. It's a sad truth that good behavior usually goes unrecognized but bad behavior is noticed immediately. Courtney broke a rule, and suddenly you were right there in the bathroom beside her. She got your attention, even though it meant being scolded.

Here's an exercise that might prove helpful: Whenever you feel your child has indulged in particularly naughty behavior, ask yourself if you have been giving the child all the attention that he or she really needs.

Don't reward bad behavior with your loving attention. But do take the opportunity to question whether you need to pay more attention to your child's needs in the coming days.

Praise the Good

If you understand that discipline is a method of teaching self-control, you'll see that more than just punishment must be involved. In fact, it may be the least important part. You want to enhance your child's self-control by encouraging good behavior as well as discouraging bad behavior.

The Pointing Game

Your child can understand a lot of words. You can take advantage of this listening vocabulary by communicating through pointing. Here's how the game is played:

You ask, "Where is William's nose?" William puts his finger on his nose.

"Where is William's belly button?" William touches his belly button.

And so on, with ears, eyes, toes, and hair.

You can make the game as complex or as simple as you like. For example, you could ask, "Where is William's patella?" and teach William to point to his kneecap.

Make a point of noticing good behavior and commenting favorably on it. No normal parent goes around saying, "Thank you for not putting your new shoes in the toilet. And, by the way, it was kind of you not to maim the dog today."

On the other hand, you can compliment your child on eating neatly, putting away toys, petting the dog gently, and lots of other acts of goodness that might be overlooked.

If you hit a rough spot, where your child seems caught in the trap of disobedience, remember this: Children respond better to positive suggestions than to negative instructions.

In practical terms, that means you'll have greater success by saying, "Walk close to Mama," than by saying, "Don't run away."

If you and your little one have come to an impasse, employ a technique called time-out. This is done by removing your child from whatever situation is creating the problem and putting him or her in a separate place. (Picture Dennis the Menace sitting in his little chair, facing the corner.) Leave your child there for two or three minutes, while he or she ponders the nature of the misdeed.

Growth of the Mind

Toddlers, even the best and the brightest among them, are not schoolchildren, or even preschool children. They are former babies on the way to becoming children. For that reason, it's usually counterproductive to begin lessons, use flash cards, or engage in other formal methods of instilling knowledge.

That is not to say that you should ignore the growth of the mind. Experts say the best ways for you to encourage your child's intellect is to allow your child to explore the environment and have many experiences. As your child moves through an experience, listen to his or her comments and questions and respond.

Here are a number of intellect-stimulating activities you and your child might have together:

- **planting radishes** (they're foolproof to grow), harvesting them, and eating them
- **collecting autumn leaves**
- **baking apples**
- **listening to different kinds of music**
- **watching ants** work in the soil
- **eating snow**
- **visiting a petting zoo**
- **playing with wet sand** or mud
- **scattering crumbs** for the ducks in the park
- **visiting your neighbor** and her baby
- **browsing through a children's bookstore**

Let your child's curiosity lead the way. You'll undoubtedly find yourself enjoying these experiences with new eyes and a childlike delight in the freshness of the world.

It will be obvious that your 2-year-old loves to learn. Encourage that natural enthusiasm. Then relax and enjoy the ride, being careful not to push your child. Keep in mind that every single human being (yourself included) works and learns at his or

Toys That Help The Mind Grow

Toys look like fun. And they are. But toys also have some important work to do. They help encourage a child's intellectual exploration and development. You can help by selecting toys that work best. Consider putting together a dress-up box of old clothes: hats, ties, blouses and shirts, shawls, and the like. Simple toys such as clay can help develop finger dexterity. When you're buying toys, look for ones that:

- **come with objects to hide, stack, sort, match, or manipulate.** The traditional stacking rings are always good, as are blocks and boards that pegs fit into. A more advanced toy is a set of foam stars, circles, tubes, pegs, and other shapes in bright colors that can be twisted and shaped into an endless variety of costumes, crowns, and creative creatures.
- **children can play with by themselves.** An excellent example is a toy phone that makes a realistic dial tone and actually records messages your child can play back. You can leave the messages, or, better yet, you can record your child saying, "Hello," "Bye-bye," and other selected phrases.
- **have parts that pop up when the child presses a button.** You'll be amazed at how many times your child can press a button without boredom.
- **kids can climb, slide down, or crawl through.** There's nothing like that sense of physical adventure to keep an inquiring mind stimulated.

her own pace. Don't pressure your child to learn the ABCs just because Amanda down the street can recite them. If you make learning a chore, you risk making it a turn-off.

The Growth of Language

The average 2-year-old can say anywhere from 50 to 300 words, but can understand many, many more. Those who speak fewer words are still well within the range of normal and

If your new baby is a "good" baby who eats well, sleeps often, cries seldom, and has small ears, thank God. You have been blessed.

If your new baby is a "difficult" baby who spits up everything, seldom sleeps, often cries, and has large ears, thank God. You have been blessed.

Eva L. Langley
Langley, Arkansas

also have a much larger listening vocabulary.

Two-year-olds speak in sentences composed of two or three words, usually just nouns and verbs. They can understand simple commands.

Some are Chatty Cathys early in life; others seem more like the strong, silent type. Children really, really want to speak. As soon as they can, they will. Accept your child's level of ability and continue to supply him or her with the kind of stimulation that encourages talking.

One way to do this is to talk a lot yourself. You can talk about lots of different ideas, and chances are your child will be able to follow you. Again, let your child be your guide. His or her curiosity may lead you down some strange roads, but the trip will be fun. If, for example, you see your child watching the dog scratch himself, share the information that the dog is scratching because he's dirty and needs a bath. If you were so inclined, you could follow up with a plug for cleanliness.

Because the child can understand a lot of what you say, it's best not to slip into baby talk (unless you do want to be called Mummy-Wummy).

As they move toward their third birthday, children will begin to use "I" and "me" in place of their names. A girl who might have said, "Fiona kiss dolly," now will say, "I kiss my dolly." This shift in language is one more sign that the concept of self has taken hold.

Practicing New Words

Your child's spoken vocabulary grows because every day he or she attempts to say new words. It's a tough task, and some words don't come out quite right the first few times. Don't correct pronunciation at this point. You want to encourage these attempts, not stifle them. Instead, respond to your child's statement. Repeat the word that was mispronounced, but say it correctly. For example, you can respond to the question, "See yite, Mama?" with, "Yes, I do see the light."

Encouraging the Body

Regular exercise will help your toddler grow in strength, grace, and agility. The goal is not to develop some little toddler triathlete, but to achieve the ancient Greek ideal of a sound mind in a sound body.

To that end, try to build some exercise into each day's schedule. Because it's way too easy to succumb to the temptation of using the television set as an electronic baby-sitter, make it a point to do physical activities.

When you're providing opportunities for physical play, you don't need any fancy equipment, but you do need to keep safety in mind. Here are some suggestions for encouraging exercise:

☞ **Provide something to push or pull.** Toddlers who have just learned to walk enjoy playing with push-and-pull toys. The classic is the push toy that "pops corn" as it rolls.

☞ **Bring on the balls.** Provide several kinds of balls to help your child develop eye/hand coordination. Big, bright-colored balls are good for rolling on the floor. Light balls or those made of foam are good for children to play catch with.

☞ **Provide things for climbing in or through.** Big boxes or fabric "tunnels" are great props for the crawling games that foster a child's large muscle development.

☞ **Provide some transportation.** When your child is old enough, purchase a tricycle for him or her. The challenge of riding a tricycle helps both

The Child Who Bites

Just like children who have tantrums, children who bite are responding to feelings of frustration or anger. In this case, however, they are taking it out on other children.

If your child bites someone, here's how to deal with it:

☞ **Make it clear that biting won't be tolerated.** Tell the child you understand that he or she must be feeling angry or upset, but that biting is not acceptable. State the rule strongly.

☞ **Suggest alternatives.** Let your child know that the next time he or she is feeling mad or upset it's OK to jump up and down or stamp feet.

☞ **Behave like an adult yourself.** Whatever you do, do not bite the child to show how much it hurts. You'll be giving the message that it's OK for grown-ups to bite, and that it is indeed a painful and powerful thing to do. That's not the message you want to deliver.

☞ **Check out the scene of the crime.** If your child has bitten another child in day care, inquire whether there are enough toys that kids don't have to fight over them and enough adults to supervise or intervene quickly.

☞ **Be patient.** This, too, shall pass. Most children stop biting by the age of 3 years, when they are better able to put their feelings of frustration, anger, or jealousy into words.

coordination and development of the leg muscles.

☞ **Know when to call it quits.** Play only for as long as your child seems to be having a good time.

Playing Alone and With Others

If your child is not in day care, where learning to play with other children comes with the territory, you may want to help your child learn to share and be social by asking a few children about the same age to your house to play.

It's a good idea to limit the number of kids to three or four and set aside a play period of no more than 60 to 90 minutes. Aim for a time when the children will have been fed and have had a nap.

When the little ones arrive, they probably will stare intently at each other. Then each one will head for a toy, grab it, and retreat to a neutral corner. Suddenly there is no group, only four kids playing with four different toys. Does this mean you're a dud as a play group hostess? Nope. Everything is going smoothly.

Playing solo is the norm for most children 18 to 30 months old. Toddlers are just so busy exploring the world, they may even ignore other children entirely. Put in a room with other toddlers, each will enjoy being near the others but will play alone. This is called parallel play.

Learning to Share

At some point, however, there will be interaction. Perhaps your own sweetheart, who has been loading and unloading the little circus train, will get bored. Your child will look up and discover another child playing with a musical bear. Your child will make a swipe for it, shouting, "Mine!"

The experts say that at this age children don't understand the concept of sharing, and they will not understand it until they are 3 or 4 years old. Further, they are naturally selfish and self-centered. So, what's a parent to do?

You can begin to foster the concept of sharing, but until it sinks in, you will need a short-term plan to keep the group happy. One practical step is to buy a few toys that are kept out of sight and brought out only for the play group. These particular toys belong to no one in particular, so the children won't feel too possessive about them.

If one child snatches a toy from another, step in and return the toy to the first child. Don't let the aggressive child keep the toy that's been taken. If the behavior continues, give the little tiger a time-out away from other children.

There are other ways you can help your child learn to share. Make a point of sharing with your child: Offer half of your sandwich, a sip of your cold drink, a turn at holding the kitten. Talk about how nice it is when people share their things with other people. Promote the idea that if you share with someone, that person is likely to share with you.

Don't forget: When your child does share, reward the act with sincere appreciation.

Fostering Empathy

To help your child evolve from being a self-centered baby to being a member of society who is aware of the feelings of others, be a role model yourself. You can do that by showing respect and concern for others.

You can teach empathetic behavior during play time by pointing out to your own child the way others are feeling and suggesting ways to help them feel better if they're upset. Suppose little Jeffrey across the room has just stepped on and broken the crayon he was using. You might point out that Jeffrey looks sad and suggest that the two of you help him find another crayon.

If Katy is crying, suggest that your child bring her a toy or go give her a hug.

When Your Child Hits

Kids get angry, just as you do. But where you might count to 10 or leave the room, a child might hit or shove. That is a child's way of expressing negative emotions. All children have to be taught how to handle these feelings in an appropriate way.

If your child has just hurt another, immediately step between them and comfort the hurt child. Tell your child that people do not hit each other. Next, help your child to express his or her emotions: "Were you angry with Katy?" "Are you feeling angry because Katy took your toy?"

Help your child recognize that Katy was crying

because hitting hurt, and remind your child that "we do not hurt other people; we talk to them." Make it clear that if your child hits again, he or she be will be given a time-out.

Toilet Training

Every mother yearns for the day when her child is out of diapers. Just like the Fourth of July, it's Independence Day!

Before you can celebrate a victory, however, you have a significant challenge ahead of you. When you're ready to tackle this, put any other plans on the back burner for the duration.

Some children are ready to be toilet-trained at 18 months of age, and many are ready by their second birthday. According to a survey of parents done by *Parenting* magazine, 16 percent of first children were potty-trained at 18 months or younger, 21 percent at 19 months to 2 years, 6 percent at 2 to 2½ years, 15 percent at 2½ to 3 years, and 25 percent at 3 years or older.

Experts in child development have found that the older your child is when you begin potty training (within limits), the easier it will be. Toilet training is a gradual process that can take anywhere from two weeks to many months.

How can you tell if your child is ready? First, there are physical considerations:

•**Can the child easily walk** to a toilet and easily sit on the toilet?

•**Can he or she pull down clothing** and pull it back up again by himself or herself?

•**Does he or she urinate** at specific times in the day, rather than dribbling throughout the day?

There are emotional considerations as well. Training often goes better when the child has passed through that stage of negativism from 18 to 24 months when every other word is "No!"

A child will likely want to be trained if he or she has a stronger sense of self and has shown a great desire for independence.

Buying the Potty-Chair

Most doctors and psychologists agree that your child will be happier and learn more quickly if you use a separate potty-chair rather than the toilet. For one thing, toilets are scary for little kids. They are too high, and the flushing makes too much noise. In addition, children worry about weird things like falling in and getting flushed down the drain.

Generally, toddlers are more accepting of a small potty-chair. This nifty little piece of furniture has the advantage of allowing your child's feet to remain on the floor while he or she sits on the chair. This helps during a bowel movement.

When you set out to buy the potty-chair, it may be a good idea to take your toddler along. Encourage him or her to participate and plant the idea that this is a special chair. This way your toddler will understand that the chair is his or her very own and no one else's. That sense of ownership can be helpful during the learning period.

Here's what to look for:

•**The best kind of potty-chair** to buy is one that looks as much like a toilet as possible (to make the next transition easier).

•**The chair should have a sturdy base** and a nonskid bottom.

•**Potty-chairs with arms** may look appealing, but they occasionally cause problems, because your child might lean on the arms getting in and out of the chair and tip it over.

•**Avoid seats with straps** or seat belts.

Beginning Training

Once you've selected the right chair and brought it home, you're ready for basic toilet training. Here's what to do:

☞ **Have a plan.** The general idea is to teach daytime bowel control first. Next, and a little more difficult, teach urinating in the potty. Finally, work toward nighttime control.

☞ **Be happy.** Be relaxed. Simply explain to your child that the chair is his or her own. Perhaps you can paint your child's name on it. Talk about how the potty-chair is just like a small toilet, and that's where bowel movements and urine (substitute your family's terms) will go.

☞ **Get your child used to the chair.** If and when your child is interested in trying out the chair, sit him or her down on it. Since we're still in the talking stage, have your child stay fully clothed. The point of this stage of training is to eliminate any sense of strangeness about the chair and make it familiar and unthreatening.

☞ **Be consistent.** Sit your child on the chair at about the same time every day. When the procedure has become routine, plan a second seating.

☞ **Talk about the process.** These sessions should be fairly brief. Talk about how "pretty soon" you'll be taking off the diaper so he or she can use the chair—the same way Daddy and Mommy use the toilet.

☞ **Have a trial run.** After talking comes practicing. When it seems to you that your child is about to have a bowel movement, encourage trying the potty. If your child goes in his or her diaper before you can get to the potty, do not even hint at disappointment or disapproval. Just say something like, "We'll have better luck next time."

Some parents turn an accident like this one into an opportunity to demonstrate how the potty is used by shaking the diaper's contents right into the bowl of the potty-chair.

☞ **Move on to the real thing.** Next comes doing. At this point, you should have a pretty good idea of when your child needs to use the potty. Remove your child's diapers and encourage him or her to sit on the potty-chair at what seem to be the appropriate times. Your approach should be one of gentle persistence. When your child is successful, especially for the first time, make a big fuss. Call Daddy at work to let him know of the triumph achieved at home. Give hugs and kisses and maybe even a small prize or treat.

☞ **Graduate from diapers.** Once your little one seems to have caught on to using the chair, you can switch from diapers to training pants. These will allow your child more independent access to the potty, because he or she will be able to push the training pants down and pull them back up without your assistance.

☞ **Continue to offer assistance.** Your help still will be needed for wiping. For a while, your child's arms will be too short to effectively wipe. (Remember, always wipe girls from front to back.)

☞ **Flush and wash.** Once your child has finished sitting on the potty, deposit the potty's contents into the toilet and allow your child to flush it. Follow up with washing hands, which always should be incorporated into the routine.

Hint: Potty-chair cleanup after a bowel movement is easier if you line the container with toilet paper, a paper napkin, or even a coffee filter. Just be sure that whatever you use won't clog the toilet. Remove the liner and flush.

Part V

The Encyclopedia of Common Illnesses and Diseases

common illnesses and diseases

From allergies to vision problems, this encyclopedia provides concise information about how you can help your baby get through a variety of everyday health problems.

Each entry will tell you:
- **what the condition is**
- **what the symptoms are**
- **whether or not it is serious**
- **if and how you can treat it at home**
- **when to call the doctor**

Allergies

A child with an allergy has an abnormal response to a substance, such as pollen, that is ordinarily harmless. That substance is called an allergen if it causes an allergic response. The allergen activates the immune system in much the same way that a disease-causing virus would. The result is generally inflammation, irritation, and discomfort. More rarely, a serious allergic reaction can be life-threatening.

Respiratory Allergies

If your baby has a respiratory allergy, you'll notice red, runny eyes, bouts of sneezing, a runny nose, and/or wheezing.

When either parent suffers from allergies, their baby is twice as likely as an infant in the general population to develop an allergic condition. If both parents have allergies, the baby's risk increases about four times.

Even so, medical research suggests that, by taking aggressive action during a baby's first year, you may prevent some allergies from developing. Here's how:

☞ **Limit exposure to potential allergens.** This is particularly important in the case of respiratory allergies. By keeping a high-risk infant's living area meticulously free of dust and other potential allergens, you can lessen your child's chance of becoming allergic.

☞ **Think Spartan.** To achieve an appropriate standard of cleanliness, the baby's surroundings will have to be fairly sparse: no plush rugs, no curtains (if you can get away without them), no cute teddy bears propped on the shelves.

Whatever is in the nursery will have to be damp-mopped, dusted, or laundered frequently. It's a lot of tedious work, but—you already know this if you suffer with allergies—it's worth it. If you can prevent your child from developing allergies in the first place, you've given him or her a real gift.

Dust Mites

Your major allergen enemy indoors is the ubiquitous dust mite. These tiny members of the spider family thrive in warm, humid indoor environments. They can settle in nicely if you provide them with comfy curtains, carpets, and mattresses.

Actually, it's not the mite itself that causes trouble, it is the microscopic mite's even more microscopic waste products. Even after you have vanquished the mites, the allergen may linger until all their waste products have been cleaned from the environment.

Don't become discouraged, just keep after the problem until it clears up.

To make your baby's room inhospitable to mites:

☞ **Avoid wall-to-wall carpeting.** Instead, opt for flooring you can easily mop clean.

☞ **Toss throw rugs in the washer.** You should vacuum or launder any short-pile throw rugs once every week.

☞ **Keep things dry.** Reduce the humidity in the room to below 50 percent by plugging in an air-conditioner or dehumidifier.

☞ **Opt for washables.** Avoid feather pillows, down comforters, quilts, wool blankets, and other bed linens that are not easily laundered in hot (130 degrees) water. Buy only machine-washable stuffed animals (warn the relatives), and machine-wash them every two weeks. When they aren't being cud-

Allergy-Proofing Stuffed Toys

If your baby has latched on to a stuffed toy that can't be washed in hot water, put it in the dryer for five minutes. The heat and the extra-dry air in the machine can kill the dust mites that have been dwelling in Pooh's plush fur.

dled, stash the stuffed animals in a drawer or closet.

☞ **Change the linens often.** Wash bed linens (including blankets) every week.

☞ **Don't forget the window treatments.** If you must use curtains, wash them every two weeks in 130-degree water.

☞ **Use plastic sealers.** It's best to seal the mattress (and pillows when baby is old enough to use one) in plastic cases.

A sealed-in-plastic bed doesn't have to feel cold and sound crunchy. Some mattresses and pillowcases, for example, come with soft cotton on the outer surface. So shop around to find outfittings that appeal to you.

The Family Pet

Another source of a year-round allergy is animal dander. And what, you may well ask, is dander? It's the scales that are shed from an animal's skin or hair or from a bird's feathers. You'll have to take some strong measures to keep animal dander from being a problem.

☞ **Banish the offender.** If you can bring yourself to do it, your sweet kitty ideally will either have to become an outside cat or go reside with friends and relatives.

The same goes for the dog. (If your baby already is experiencing serious respiratory allergy symptoms, you definitely will have to get the animals out of the house. If your doctor tells you this is neces-

Allergy Resources to Help at Home

Wheezing, sneezing, stuffy nose, red eyes—parents can feel so helpless when dealing with a baby's allergy symptoms. In addition to your doctor, there a number of other helpful resources:

• **The Johns Hopkins University** Dermatology, Allergy, and Immunology Reference Laboratory will assess the allergens in your air, testing for such items as mold spores, dust mites, cat dander, or cockroach waste products. Call 800-882-4110 for information about the tests.

• **The Environmental Protection Agency** in Washington, D.C., can provide you with a list of recommended air-filtering devices. Call 800-222-5864 (800-222-LUNG). Consider using room air cleaners with high efficiency air (HEPA) filters.

• **Allergy Publications,** Box 640, Menlo Park, CA 94026, will send you a free listing of products and services compiled by the American Allergy Association. The list will include information on how to obtain special items. One available product is a special dust spray with a tannic acid solution that deactivates allergens created by house dust mites and cats; a quart treats up to 600 square feet.

• **Allerpet.** If you aren't yet ready to give up your pet, you can try out this product. It comes in three formulations, a spray for birds, a solution for cats and other small, furry animals, and another for dogs. You rub it on the animal's fur about once a week.

• **The Asthma and Allergy Foundation of America** will send you a pollen map to help you determine the seasons in which allergens are a particular problem in your area of the country. Call 800-727-8462 (800-7-ASTHMA).

---

sary for the baby's sake, compliance must be considered mandatory.)

☞ **Make baby off-limits.** If you simply can't part with your pet, keep it out of the baby's room. Even if the pet is confined to a part of the house, it still helps to shampoo and brush the animal often.

Smoke

Some babies are extremely sensitive to tobacco smoke. You'll have to be particularly vigilant about keeping cigarettes, cigars, and pipes out of your home. Keep your child away from smoke in other places as well.

Trees, Grasses, and Flowers

Pollen is not quite a year-round allergen, but in some parts of the country it comes close. Trees release pollen in spring, grasses release it in summer, and ragweed goes into full production in late summer and early fall. Here's how to protect your baby:

☞ **Become a clock watcher.** Keep your baby indoors before noon, if possible, because pollen is released in the morning.

☞ **Put up some barriers.** It helps to keep your windows and doors closed. (Here's a good excuse to use your air-conditioner.)

☞ **Banish the buds.** Sorry, you simply can't have cut flowers in the house.

Mold

You thought mold was just gunky stuff that attached to your shower curtain? Not so. It's a major league allergen. Fight mildew and mold with hot, soapy water, chlorine bleach, or special commercial products that kill mold.

Food Allergies

If you or your spouse has food allergies, there are some steps you should take to protect your baby:

☞ **Ban the bottle.** Ideally, your baby should be breast-fed for at least the first year. Research has shown that gastrointestinal allergies—which can cause cramping, diarrhea, vomiting, and rashes—are uncommon in babies who are fed nothing but breast milk.

Breast milk protects babies in two ways. First, by

nursing, you prevent the baby from being exposed to food substances that might provoke an allergy. If you breast-feed long enough, the baby's immune system has a chance to mature and may be able to handle a food that might have become an allergen if introduced earlier.

The other protective factor in breast milk is that it provides certain kinds of antibodies known as immunoglobulins that often are deficient in the immune systems of newborns. Some researchers believe that these immunoglobulins can offer some protection against the formation of food allergies.

These immunoglobulins, according to some researchers, also seem to protect the baby's intestinal lining, thus reducing the likelihood of an adverse reaction to a food. So even when your baby is old enough to try some juice or solid food, it may pay to continue to breast-feed for a few more months.

Eventually your baby will be weaned from the breast or bottle and introduced to the wide world of fruits, vegetables, and meats. If your child eats a new food then develops a rash, wheezing, or diarrhea or other intestinal upset, consult your doctor, who may suggest that you eliminate the problem food from your child's diet. The most common offenders are cow's milk, eggs, corn, citrus fruit, wheat, barley or rye gluten, nuts, chocolate, and seafood.

Food allergies, although uncommon, are tricky. Your baby may not have a bad reaction the first time he or she eats, say, a chocolate cookie. But having once eaten it, your baby can develop antibodies against it.

Those antibodies will create an allergic reaction the next time the food is eaten. Then, when you offer the same kind of cookie a week later, you will be amazed when the hives pop out all over that little face. Because allergies are so tricky, you should consult your doctor whenever you suspect an allergic reaction.

Preventing and Treating Allergies

Allergies can be remarkably difficult to deal with:

☞ **Sidestep the problem.** The best treatment for both respiratory and food allergies is avoidance. Whenever possible, keep your baby away from those items that clearly make him or her sick.

☞ **Medicate.** Sometimes, however, avoidance is nearly impossible. Your doctor will be able to suggest or prescribe medications that help keep allergic reactions under control

Asthma

 sthma is a disease of the airways. A person with asthma has overly sensitive airways that narrow down and produce mucus in response to items such as pollen, dust, animal dander, and molds—the same kinds of items that cause respiratory allergies. The result is impaired breathing.

You'll suspect your child is having an asthma attack if he or she is experiencing labored or restricted breathing, a tight feeling in the chest, and coughing and wheezing.

Here's a brief look at what happens during an asthma attack: When those with asthma breathe in, they expand their chests, and the airways open up. During inhalation, air can move around any obstructions that may be in the airways. But, when they stop breathing in and try to breathe out, these obstructions trap the air in the lungs. As a result, people with asthma have to take shallow breaths at the top of their lungs.

The condition can develop quickly, but its severity varies widely. Many cases of asthma are so mild they go undiagnosed, and sometimes a chronic cough is the only symptom. Other people can experience life-threatening attacks in which breathing stops altogether.

About 15 million people—that's about 7 percent of the nation's population—have asthma. It's the number one cause for school absenteeism among all children with chronic diseases and the major reason that children are hospitalized. Cases of asthma also are on the increase.

A common cause of asthma is allergies. However, the disease also can follow on the heels of an infection such as bronchiolitis, a wheezing disease that affects children younger than 2 years old and is caused by a viral infection of the airways.

Most babies haven't been around long enough to develop asthma. They can, however, develop allergies that lead to asthma. Therefore, it's important for parents who have allergies to protect their children from potential allergens as much as possible and for as long as possible. (See Allergies on pages 181–184 and Food Allergies on pages 183–184.)

Birthmarks

It's common for a newborn to arrive on the scene wearing a birthmark somewhere on his or her face or body. These come in all kinds of colors, shapes, and sizes, but the most common include stork bites, strawberry marks, Mongolian spots, and moles.

Stork Bites

These birthmarks appear as pink patches on the newborn's neck, eyelids, or upper lip. Some people call them angel kisses.

How serious are they? Not serious at all. In fact, most don't even need treatment and usually disappear by the time the child is 2 years old.

Strawberry Marks

One out of ten babies has a strawberry mark at birth; others develop one sometime in the first week of life.

These birthmark look a lot like a strawberries. They range in size from a tiny red spot to one nearly as big as the palm of your hand.

Most do not require any treatment. They are harmless and will go away by themselves. A strawberry mark may grow a little as your child grows but usually is gone by the time your child is 10 years old.

If a strawberry mark seems to be getting larger, your doctor may suggest a new treatment with a laser that can completely remove the mark.

Occasionally, a strawberry mark bleeds. Should that happen, apply pressure to stop the bleeding. And do make sure you let your doctor know about the bleeding.

Mongolian Spots

Mongolian spots are blue marks that can develop on babies that have African, Asian, Hispanic, or

Mediterranean ancestry.

The spots are normal and can appear anywhere on the face or body, especially the buttocks and back. They do not require treatment, and they usually fade by late childhood.

Moles

The moles a baby is born with are called nevi. They usually are brown or black and may sprout hair at the center. There is a danger that at some point in the future some nevi may develop into melanoma, a serious form of skin cancer.

Because of the risk of melanoma, large moles should be removed. Smaller nevi should be observed carefully by a doctor throughout your child's life.

Boils

A boil is a painful red lump in the skin, measuring ½ to 1 inch across. It's caused by a bacterial infection of a hair root or skin pore. A few days after appearing, a boil fills with pus, then comes to a head. When it comes to a head, it will have a white spot in the center that looks as though it's about to burst.

To help the boil come to a head more quickly, apply warm compresses to the skin for 20 to 30 minutes several times a day.

You'll have to use the compresses for several days—maybe even a week—before you get results. When the boil looks ready, see your doctor to have it lanced.

Car Sickness

The symptoms of car sickness are light-headedness, pallor, and sweating, then queasiness, nausea, and vomiting.

Motion sickness can happen to anyone (just ask any astronaut), but it's more likely to happen to children because their developing brains are more susceptible to conflicting signals. Children with chronic ear problems are the ones most likely to have this problem.

Preventing and Treating Car Sickness

Many children outgrow motion sickness. In the meantime, you can:

- ☞ **Keep the car well ventilated.** Open the window if you can, and never, ever smoke with your child in the car.
- ☞ **Make frequent stops.** Motion sickness is more likely to develop during longer drives.
- ☞ **Provide a pleasant diversion.** Bring along an audiocassette for your child. Tell your child to close his or her eyes while listening. (At the very least, the cassette will be a distraction.)
- ☞ **Medicate.** If your child is 2 years or older and your doctor approves, you can try giving liquid antinausea medicine such as Dramamine. (Younger children may find some relief from eating something. Try offering the child a couple of crackers or a piece of zwieback.)

Common Cold

A cold is caused by viruses that are spread from one person to another, usually by handling something recently touched by somebody who has a cold. Your child touches that toy, that doorknob, that whatever, then touches his or her nose. That lets the virus in.

The viruses move into the nasal passages, where they are fruitful and multiply. Then they wander down to the throat, sandpapering mucus membranes along the way.

Eventually the viruses come upon the windpipe, where they tickle, tickle, tickle until your child coughs and sneezes.

Whether you treat it or not, a cold normally lasts seven to 10 days. An associated fever may last about three days, and a cough can hang on for two to three weeks.

Both you and your child will be much happier if you do treat the cold, however.

Preventing and Treating the Common Cold

Here's what to do for a common cold in an infant or young child:

☞ **Humidify.** Make your baby's breathing easier by humidifying the nursery.

☞ **Try nose drops.** If your baby can't breathe to eat well or sleep, use saline nose drops before feedings and bed.

As always, you should get your doctor's permission before using any medication for the first time.

You can buy nose drops suitable for infants and children at your local pharmacy. You can also make your own nose drops by stirring a level ¼ teaspoon of table salt into an 8-ounce glass of warm water

To use your homemade drops, dip a cotton ball into the solution and allow just a few drops to flow into the baby's nostrils. Wait a minute for the salt water to soften any dried mucus before using a nasal aspirator to remove the mucus.

☞ **Unstop that little nose.** If your baby still can't breathe, use a nasal aspirator to suction out the thick mucus. First, squeeze the bulb, then insert the tip gently into one nostril. Release the bulb to suction out the mucus.

Repeat with the other nostril. Release the mucus into a tissue and wash the aspirator thoroughly after each use.

Chances are your baby will really hate this procedure, but do it anyway. A baby who can't breathe

---

When to Call the Doctor

How can you be sure that the cold your tiny, vulnerable baby has is just a cold? At what point should you stop trying to treat the problem yourself and get in touch with your family doctor? Most babies with a cold sleep poorly and are irritable. Call the doctor when you see any of these other changes in your baby:

• **marked differences in behavior**
• **a fever that lasts** for more than three days or that rises abruptly
• **labored or difficult breathing,** even after the nose has been cleared, accompanied by rasping or heaving of the chest
• **gooey (not just watery) eyes** that look red and irritated
• **swollen glands** in the neck, armpit, or groin
• **presence of cold symptoms** beyond the usual 10 to 14 days
• **signs of an ear infection** (earache, signs of discomfort when lying down, discharge from the ear)
• **persistent crying**

One final note: If your mother's intuition tells you that something isn't right, or if you feel concerned about your baby's health, go ahead and call your pediatrician. That's what he or she is there for.

---

through the nose is not able to nurse at either the breast or bottle.

☞ **Keep track of your baby's temperature.** The most comfortable way to take a temperature is in the armpit.

Place the bulb end of a thermometer (oral or rectal) under the armpit and hold that arm snugly against the body for three to four minutes. You'll have to withdraw the thermometer in order to read the temperature.

(See also Fever on paged 194–195 and Sore Throat on pages 200–201.)

Constipation

There are few hard and fast guidelines to help you determine whether your child is constipated. It's important, however, to first consider the baby's pattern of elimination. Some babies have a bowel movement three times a day, every day. Others babies may have a bowel movement only once in three days. Your job, then, is to determine whether your child is deviating from his or her usual pattern. Then, if the stools are hard and compact, or if there is blood in the stool, you know that your baby is constipated.

Don't become too upset if you see blood. The cause is usually a small tear in the anus. The tear, which is known as an anal fissure, most likely occurred when your child had difficulty passing a bowel movement.

Put away all thoughts of ulcers and internal bleeding and set about fixing the constipation. You should, however, always mention bloody stools to your child's pediatrician. Although it's unlikely that this signifies a problem, your pediatrician is the best one to make that judgment.

Preventing and Treating Constipation

It's important to pay attention to constipation, because it can make a bowel movement difficult or even painful to pass. As a result, the child may try to hold it in for as long as possible, thus compounding the problem.

Here are several things you can do at home to help deal with this problem.

☞ **Try a little juice.** If your baby is younger than 6 months of age, you can—with your doctor's approval—give him or her a little prune juice mixed with water. The recipe is one part prune juice (about a ½ ounce) to two parts water (1 ounce).

The Day-Care Cold

Young babies get sick more frequently than older children because their immune systems are not as well developed. As a result, a child younger than 1 year of age may have four to six respiratory infections. Being in day care can often double or triple that number.

Short of keeping your child in a bubble—and perhaps not even then—there is no way to prevent the spread of a cold. Contagion can be minimized a bit if the day-care facility frequently cleans toys and strictly enforces a hand-washing policy.

Most day-care centers will expect you to keep your baby at home when he or she has a fever or breathing difficulties. Provided your child seems to feel OK, he or she can return to day care despite a runny nose and sore throat. But check with the center, which probably has its own rules. A few places have a wing set aside to isolate and care for sick children, but such facilities are few and far between.

☞ **Check in with the doctor.** If your baby is breast-feeding, he or she probably is not constipated, or the constipation is caused by something other than diet. Breast-fed babies normally go six or seven days without a bowel movement.

If your baby goes a few days longer, check in with the doctor. He or she will examine your baby to be sure there is no physical problem, such as a tight anal sphincter.

☞ **Say no to cows.** Pediatricians say that a child younger than 1 year is too young for the switch to cow's milk. If your baby has just started cow's milk, return to the formula.

☞ **Reach for the fiber.** If your child is already eating solid foods, bulk up the diet with fiber foods. Try adding some stewed dry fruits, such as prunes or raisins. Switch to whole-grain cereal and bread.

☞ **Consider using a laxative.** If the constipation doesn't clear up, your baby's doctor may well suggest using either a stool softener or a laxative. Never give your child a laxative without first asking the doctor.

Cradle Cap

Cradle cap is a common scalp condition infants have. (The medical name is seborrheic dermatitis.) It results from the baby's skin producing too much of a waxy, oily substance called sebum.

With cradle cap, the baby has oily scales on the scalp and perhaps around the eyebrows. In severe cases, you'll see yellow crustiness or tannish spots on the baby's scalp.

Most cases of cradle cap are more bothersome than serious, but the condition can persist for months. Other cases, however, can be severe, spreading to the face, neck, and even the buttocks.

Treating Cradle Cap

Here's how to deal with the problem:

☞ **Oil thoroughly and follow with a good shampoo.** You can start to eliminate cradle cap by massaging the baby's scalp briskly with mineral oil to loosen the scales, then shampooing.

☞ **Remove the scales.** Following the shampoo, remove the scales from the scalp and hair using a soft brush.

☞ **Ask the doctor for help.** If the cradle cap gets worse, your pediatrician can suggest a special shampoo to dissolve scales. If the condition spreads to the face, neck, or elsewhere, your doctor also may prescribe a cortisone ointment. Rarely, the area with cradle cap develops a yeast infection. Should that happen, the skin will be extremely red and itchy. Your doctor may prescribe a specific antiyeast cream.

Croup

Croup is an inflammation of the throat, windpipe, and airways that is caused by some of the same viruses that cause the common cold. Children between 6 months and 3 years are most often afflicted with croup. The condition often follows on the heels of a cold. The child will wake up (probably in the middle of the night) with a terrible cough—like a bark—that continues for an hour or longer. Sometimes the baby may have difficulty breathing in addition to the cough.

Treating Croup

Your baby may well be frightened by the awful cough and perhaps panicky if he or she can't breathe easily.

Humidifier Dos and Don'ts

Babies benefit from a little extra moisture in the air, especially when they have a cold. Consider buying a cool-mist humidifier, which is not too expensive ($15 to $45) and widely available. One type uses a simple propeller to shoot moisture into the air. Another type, the ultrasonic humidifier, uses high-frequency vibrations to project small particles of water into the air. The ultrasonic unit is quiet and won't dampen your baby's blankets if it's placed near the crib.

Whichever one you choose, keep the humidifier clean. Wash it out, according to the manufacturer's directions, with hot, soapy water and chlorine bleach to keep mold from growing. Rinse it thoroughly.

If you use plain tap water in the humidifier, it will leave a white film on surfaces in the room. This is even more of a problem if you have hard water. You can avoid this problem by using distilled water or by cleaning the humidifier thoroughly after each use to eliminate the mineral residue from tap water.

You'll also find warm-mist humidifiers on the market ($30 to $70) that release steam. They have controls that help regulate the humidity in the room and an automatic shut-off feature.

Although an old-fashioned steam vaporizer is inexpensive ($8 to $20), it's not recommended. It produces steam that moisturizes the air, but has the potential to scald if it should tip over.

Keep your cool. It's important for you to swing into action quickly. But you also need to remain calm and steady so you don't cause your child to become frightened.

Humidify. Run your cool-mist humidifier, aiming it right at the child. Moist air will make breathing easier and help calm the cough. You can use a blanket to make a tent over the crib or bed so that the moist air is trapped around the baby. Prop your baby up into a sitting position to further help breathing. Stay with your child, monitoring his or her breathing.

Create a steam room. If you don't have a humidifier, take your baby into the bathroom. Turn on the shower and the taps in the tub or sink using hot water. Close the door and make a steam cabinet out of the room. Stay there for 15 to 20 minutes. Encourage your child to relax.

Try some cold air. Some children also get relief from breathing cold air. Hold your child near an open freezer door and allow him or her to take in the cold air for a few minutes. Do make sure that you keep your child warm for the duration of this treatment.

Offer warm fluids. You also can try giving your child some warm water (or other warm, clear liquid such as tea or broth) to help break up mucus in the throat.

Be vigilant. If your child seems to be breathing better and the cough has subsided, you probably are in the clear for the rest of the night. Do keep the humidifier on and do stay near.

Talk to the doctor. Croup can linger for several days, so call your doctor in the morning to let him or her know that an attack has occurred. You may feel more secure if you schedule an office visit. Be sure to use the humidifier for the next several days (all 24 hours) to keep the air moist.

Seek immediate medical help, if necessary. Call your doctor at once and go to the hospital if your child doesn't respond to moist or cold air,

if the muscles below his or her breastbone and between the ribs are visibly sucking in and out with each breath, if your child prefers not to speak (and normally does), and/or if your child's temperature is more than 101 degrees.

Head for the emergency room or call 911 if your baby has no cough, but is having real trouble breathing, exhibited by high-pitched, noisy inhalation; arching his or her neck to breathe; poor color; bluish lips; drooling; or difficulty swallowing.

The doctor will use medication to open up the airways. Your child also may be placed in a croup tent, where he or she will receive plenty of moist air and oxygen.

Diaper Rash

Diaper rash is an inflammation of the baby's skin around the genitals and buttocks. It can be caused by any number of irritants, including moisture, simple chafing, and naturally occurring chemicals, such as urea in the urine and enzymes in the baby's stool.

If a wet diaper isn't changed right away, bacteria break down the urea so it becomes ammonia, another irritant. In addition, diapers that have not been rinsed thoroughly when they were laundered can retain a detergent residue that may irritate your baby's skin.

On rare occasions, diaper rash reappears when the baby begins to crawl. In this case, it's caused by too much friction of cloth against sensitive skin.

Treatment Options

Here's how to deal with diaper rash:

Wash your hands. You should do this before diapering the baby, as well as after, so you don't introduce bacteria into a vulnerable area.

Change and toss. Change your baby's diapers more frequently than normal. If you have been using cloth diapers, you may want to switch to disposables until the rash clears up. Disposables contain a gel that keeps urine away from the skin.

Be gentle when cleaning. Wash your baby's bottom gently with lukewarm water. Don't use a washcloth (it's too rough); just use your hands. If your child has had a bowel movement, use a soft cloth and mild soap to clean up. You can dry your baby's bottom by blotting gently.

Blow dry. If your baby's skin is extra sore, spare him or her the potential pain that blotting might cause and try drying the skin with a blow-dryer set on low.

Set up some protection. Create a barrier between your baby's skin and the irritants that can cause diaper rash. You can do this by coating his or her bottom with an ointment such as zinc oxide, A&D Ointment, or Desitin.

Allow for some southern exposure. Let your baby go bare-bottomed as much as possible. Skip the plastic pants or diaper wraps at night, because dusk to dawn is a long time to keep moisture trapped against a baby's sore and sensitive skin.

Remove irritants from diapers. If you are using cloth diapers, wash them with mild soap. Then rinse them two or three times.

A severe diaper rash may become raw and ooze. Under these circumstances, the skin is open to secondary infection, usually a yeast infection. A yeast infection produces patches of bright red skin. The patches are marked with well-defined edges composed of bumps.

You should call the doctor if the rash is raw, pus-filled, bloody, or blistered. Your baby may need either an antibiotic ointment or a treatment for yeast infection.

Medicate. If your baby appears to have a yeast infection, you can try treating it with an over-the-counter ointment containing either clotrimazole or miconazole. (Check the labels.) You might also ask your pharmacist for a recommendation.

Be a sleuth. In most cases, diaper rash will clear up in three or four days. If the rash continues to reassert itself, ask yourself whether the baby has been introduced to any new foods, or if the baby is taking any new medications—say, for ear infections. Perhaps your baby is sensitive to the new substances. If you suspect this might be the case, let your doctor know.

Diarrhea

When your baby is having bowel movements more often than usual, and they are loose and watery, the cause is probably diarrhea.

Simple diarrhea is a messy business, to be sure. But in and of itself, it is not a big problem. The big problem is the dehydration that often accompanies a bout of diarrhea.

During diarrhea the inner lining of the intestine leaks fluid, flushing salt and minerals (electrolytes) out of the body. The lining also fails to properly absorb the nutrients in food.

A child can become dangerously dehydrated when too much water and salt are lost. The younger the child, the more quickly and easily he or she can become dehydrated and experience serious complications from diahrrea.

Preventing and Treating Diarrhea

Treatment at home generally relies on diet. If your baby has a good appetite and seems to be his or her usual, lovable self, the problem is simple diarrhea with no dehydration. Here's how to get the problem under control.

Choose fluids wisely. If you're treating an infant and are breast-feeding, continue to breast-feed or offer formula. You should, however, eliminate apple juice, because fruit sugars tend to make diarrhea worse.

☞ **Use special formula.** If you're treating an infant on formula and the child is vomiting, replace the formula with an electrolyte solution, such as Pedialyte or Rehydralyte. These are available at your local pharmacy.

☞ **Back off solid foods.** If your child has been eating solid foods, limit him or her to the electrolyte solution for a couple of feedings, so your child's bowel can rest. Then gradually introduce (one at a time) bananas, rice, applesauce, and toast. (Although it's best to avoid apple juice, applesauce can be helpful in treating diarrhea.)

☞ **Seek help when needed.** If the diarrhea has not responded in two or three days, call the pediatrician. Diarrhea that lasts longer than two weeks may lead to serious malnutrition. Your doctor will want to examine the child and do tests to discover the cause of the problem.

☞ **Consider antibiotics.** When a baby has diarrhea, it's usually caused by a viral infection, the kind of infection antibiotics can't counter. Antibiotics do, however, work on diarrhea caused by bacterial or parasitic infections. Let your doctor make the decision about whether to use antiobiotics.

☞ **Beware of over-the-counter medications.** Those over-the-counter "stopper-uppers" are not recommended for babies younger than 2 years old. If you're treating a child older than 2, read the label carefully before using any medication and follow directions to the letter.

☞ **Keep future bouts at bay.** To prevent diarrhea and other infections, wash your hands after using the toilet or changing diapers and before preparing food. Wash your baby's hands often, too.

Ear Infections

Ear infections usually occur in the middle ear, a complex and delicate bit of anatomy located just behind the eardrum. The middle ear is almost enclosed, with just one opening in the form of a tiny tube (the Eustachian tube) that leads to the back of the throat. It's this area that causes most of the problems.

A baby's Eustachian tube is still soft and tends to collapse frequently. When that happens, the middle ear cannot drain through its only opening, and it receives no ventilation. Given those conditions, the middle ear is ripe for infection. The infection most commonly arrives on the heels of a cold.

The medical name for this condition is otitis media. It's estimated that nearly half of all babies will have at least one such ear infection before they blow out the candle on their first birthday cake.

Preventing and Treating Ear Infection

Otitis media requires a visit to the doctor, who will examine the baby's ear with an otoscope. The eardrum usually will be red and swollen. Sometimes the pressure is so great against the eardrum that it rips. A torn eardrum allows pus to drain into the ear canal.

The doctor will treat otitis media by prescribing antibiotics for the infection and perhaps suggesting acetaminophen for pain relief. Here's what you can do to help:

☞ **Use antibiotics appropriately.** It's important to give your child the full course of antibiotics, even if he or she seems better, to be sure that all the bacteria lurking in the ear's warm, damp recesses have been wiped out. If any remain, you can expect another bout of otitis media.

☞ **Consider surgery, when appropriate.** Sometimes a child has such persistent or recurring problems with the middle ear that a doctor may recommend that an ear specialist insert little tubes in the eardrum to prevent the buildup of fluid. This recommendation usually is made when both of the child's ears have been involved and the infections have caused a documented hearing loss and/or a related delay in speaking, among other factors.

☞ **Do not give a bottle to a baby who is lying down.** The fluid that the baby is drinking can collect in the Eustachian tubes and drain back into the ears, creating the conditions favorable to ear infections. Instead, hold your baby in a semi-upright position while giving a bottle.

Eczema

Eczema is an inflammation of the skin that causes the affected area to turn red and ooze moisture. One of the most common types of eczema is atopic dermatitis (AD), a condition that causes patches of the skin to thicken, dry out, and become scaly.

Eczema tends to run in families and seems to be an allergic reaction. It can appear in babies as young as 1 month of age. It often shows up on the baby's cheeks, forehead, scalp, or limbs as a red area with blisters that ooze to form crusts, or as a thick, scaly area with well-defined, clear edges.

Sometimes eczema erupts when the baby has been introduced to foods such as cow's milk, eggs, wheat, or oranges. But factors unrelated to food allergies—such as dry air, too frequent bathing, and scratching—can make the condition worse.

Preventing and Treating Eczema

The rash sometimes goes away by itself, but that can take months or even years.

Once your pediatrician has made the diagnosis, and you know for sure what you're dealing with, here's what to do:

☞ **Moisturize.** Use a hypoallergenic moisturizer daily to keep your baby's skin from becoming dry and itchy. Ask your doctor to recommend an appropriate product.

☞ **Medicate.** Apply an over-the-counter 0.5 percent hydrocortisone cream to the trouble spots, provided you get your doctor's approval. Ask your pharmacist to suggest creams that contain this ingredient and that are appropriate for infants.

☞ **Cut down on bathing.** Alternate short baths with sponge baths. And when you give your baby a sponge bath, it's necessary to wash only the body parts that actually need it, probably just the face and bottom.

☞ **Don't let bathing time be drying time.** Use moisturizing soap. Pat, don't rub, when drying your baby. Apply moisturizer while your baby's skin is still damp.

☞ **Avoid wool.** Don't dress your baby in woolen clothing, which can irritate sensitive skin.

☞ **Avoid harsh chemicals.** When laundering your baby's clothes, use soap, not a detergent, and skip the fabric softener or dryer sheets.

☞ **Avoid dry air.** Humidify your baby's room to keep his or her skin from drying out.

☞ **Consult with your doctor.** If the condition doesn't improve, your doctor may prescribe a corticosteroid cream to help reduce inflammation and swelling. Ask about using antihistamines at bedtime to relieve your baby's itching and allow for a more peaceful sleep.

☞ **Seek comfort from others.** You can find support and detailed information from the Eczema Association for Science and Education, 1221 SW Yamhill #303, Portland, Oregon 97205. The group publishes a quarterly newsletter.

Fever

Most doctors define a fever as an oral temperature above 99.5 degrees, a rectal temperature above 100.4, or an armpit temperature of more than 98.6 degrees. (The rectal temperature is considered to be the most accurate indicator of the three.)

A fever is not a disease. Rather, it is a symptom that an infection is present somewhere in the body. Fever usually appears early in an illness, especially with a viral infection. It often appears well before any other symptoms have developed.

In fact, not only is fever not a disease, it serves a good purpose—provided it's not too extreme—by kick-starting the body's immune system.

For that reason, it may be a good idea to wait 24 hours before calling the doctor. For one reason, the fever simply may go away. In addition, the day's wait will allow other symptoms to develop, making a diagnosis easier and more accurate.

How to Take a Baby's Temperature

Forget about taking a baby's temperature orally. Your baby just doesn't have enough control to keep a thermometer in the right spot under the tongue for a long enough time. Your best choices, then, are to take the temperature rectally or in the armpit.

Taking a rectal temperature. Use a rectal glass and mercury thermometer. Begin by shaking the mercury down to below 96 degrees Fahrenheit. Lubricate the bulb end of the thermometer with petroleum jelly.

Place your baby, tummy down, on your lap. Gently separate the buttocks and insert the thermometer about 1 inch into the rectum. Never force the thermometer. Leave it in place for one or two minutes, or until you see that the mercury has stopped rising.

Taking an armpit temperature. Use either an oral or a rectal glass and mercury thermometer. Shake the mercury down to below 96 degrees Fahrenheit. Place the bulb end of a thermometer (oral or rectal) under the child's armpit and hold that arm snugly against the child's body for three to four minutes. Withdraw the thermometer to read the temperature.

Warning: Do not wait 24 hours if your child is 3 months old or younger, or if your child looks and acts sick.

Treating Fever

Here's how to deal with a fever:

☞ **Use medication.** You can help lower a fever by giving your baby the appropriate amount of acetaminophen every four hours. You can determine what's appropriate by reading the label or by asking your pediatrician.

☞ **Do not give aspirin to children.** Aspirin has been associated with Reye's syndrome, a rare but potentially fatal neurological illness.

☞ **Hydrate.** Get your baby to drink plenty of water or juice to replace fluids lost through sweating.

☞ **Use some cool strategy.** Your baby may welcome a cool compress spread across the forehead or the eyes. Use a clean cloth, soak it in water, and wring it out before applying. A sponging with lukewarm water also helps dissipate the heat. Do not use cold water or alcohol.

☞ **Let out some heat.** Dress your baby in light, loose clothing so heat can escape.

Hernias

Two forms of hernias are fairly common among infants, the inguinal (groin) hernia and the umbilical hernia.

Inguinal Hernia

An inguinal hernia develops when the intestine protrudes through an opening in the lower abdominal wall. Most inguinal hernias don't hurt. You'll probably first notice one when you're changing a diaper. In boys, it will look like a lump alongside the penis or in the scrotum. Girls do not develop inguinal hernias as often as boys do, but if one exists it will look like a bulge in the groin.

An inguinal hernia that does not hurt is not an emergency, but you should talk to your doctor about it. He or she will want to examine the child and plan a surgical repair of the hernia at some point in the not-too-distant future.

If the hernia does hurt, it may indicate that the intestine has become trapped and requires immediate surgical care.

The Umbilical Hernia

With an umbilical hernia, the baby's navel pops out when he or she is crying or straining. It is popping out through a space between the vertical muscles in the abdomen. When you were pregnant, that space allowed the blood vessels of the umbilical cord to pass inside the baby.

An umbilical hernia doesn't hurt and usually closes by itself as the child grows. In the meantime, the baby has an "outey"—a belly button that pops out rather than being indented.

There's nothing you can do to make this kind of hernia go away. Tape, belly bands, and coins will not speed the process.

If, for some reason, the umbilical hernia does not close, however, it can be repaired surgically.

Hiccups

Hiccups are involuntary spasms of the diaphragm that cause your baby (or you, for that matter) to draw in a gulp of air. The squeaky noise is the result of the rush of air pushing through closed vocal cords.

When babies hiccup after a meal, it's probably just a sign that their tummies are full. Here's what you can do:

☞ **Wait them out.** Hiccups are usually not a problem. In time, they'll go away.

☞ **Have your child relax.** Sometimes it helps

Hydrocele: Common in Baby Boys

Many boys are born with what's known as a hydrocele. It comes about because fluid ("hydro") that normally surrounds the abdominal organs flows into the scrotum. It's often associated with an inguinal hernia.

You can suspect a hydrocele if one side of your son's scrotum is swollen, and the swelling increases when he's crying, but decreases when he's quiet or sleeping.

Often, the hydrocele simply goes away without any treatment by the baby's first birthday.

Your doctor will examine your son at routine checkups. If the hydrocele persists or is extra large, the doctor may recommend surgery to remove the fluid and close the opening that allows fluid to drain into the scrotum.)

Call the doctor if your child appears to have discomfort in the area, and if he is nauseous or vomiting. These symptoms may signal a hernia, which will require immediate surgery to release the part of the intestine that has been trapped in the scrotum.

your child to lie down, a position that relaxes the abdominal muscles.

☞ **Check with the doctor.** Don't worry about hiccups unless they last more than three hours. At that point, give your pediatrician a call.

Insect Bites

An insect bite is exactly what its name implies; a bite of an insect that breaks the skin and possibly draws blood. (See Part Six for information about insect stings; that is, when an insect uses a stinger to inject venom.)

The most common insect bites are from mosquitoes, fleas, bedbugs, chiggers, biting flies, blister beetles, fire ants, centipedes, and ticks.

With the exception of tick bites, insect bites are not a serious matter unless they become infected.

Some spider bites can be serious, however.

Preventing and Treating Insect Bites

Here's how to deal with insect bites:

☞ **Keep bugs at bay.** The best way to protect your child from insects that bite is to repel them, particularly if your little one is still too young to run from the bugs or swat them away. Spritz your baby's clothing and shoes with an insect repellent; most will work for about four hours. Don't apply the repellent directly to a child's skin, because it can be absorbed into the body. (Always read labels carefully before using insect repellent on or anywhere near a child.)

☞ **Neutralize the itch.** If your child has been bitten, apply a little underarm deodorant that contains aluminum salts directly to the bite sites. Sounds nutty, but it does ease the itch. Or, shake some meat tenderizer into a little water and dab the solution onto the bites. That relieves itching, too.

Out of deodorant and meat tenderizer? Try a drop of ammonia (not near the eyes or mouth) or apply an ice cube. Or, you can buy a package of Burrow's solution, that tried-and-true skin soother, at the drugstore and use that to ease the itch.

☞ **Get medical help when necessary.** If your child has a bad reaction to a bite—excessive redness or swelling, a discolored area around the sore, muscle stiffness, fever, or difficulty breathing—call your doctor for emergency treatment. You may be dealing with a poisonous spider bite.

Watch Out for Lyme Disease

If you know that your child has been bitten by a deer tick, you'll have to be alert for the signs of Lyme disease. Although there are regional variations in the frequency of Lyme disease, the problem seems to be spreading.

This disease is caused by bacteria that are transferred to the human body via ticks. The ticks suck the blood of wild animals that is awash with this bacteria and become infected themselves. When a tick bites you, you can become infected.

Adults can pick up these ticks by walking in the woods or in thick, high grass. But where would a child encounter them? Perhaps by curling up with Rover, who, in his rovings, may have brought home a couple of six-legged hitchhikers.

The first sign of the disease is usually a rash that looks like a bull's-eye surrounding a small red pimple. Other symptoms appear later and include achy joints, fatigue, dizziness, shortness of breath, and a more general rash. If you see any of these symptoms, take your child to the doctor, who may be able to confirm the presence of the disease with a blood test.

Treatment with antibiotics in the early stages of Lyme disease is imperative to prevent the disease from turning into a serious disorder.

Lead Poisoning

This completely preventable condition is unfortunately still quite common. When the human body is exposed to lead, which is poisonous, it treats the lead as though it were calcium, drawing it into the bone. Once in the bone, it stays there. In fact, lead can accumulate steadily for as long as you live. Extremely high levels of lead can cause a degenerative brain disease that can result in death if left untreated.

Children who are exposed to lead may end up with a lower IQ and suffer learning problems, as well as have problems with abstract thinking, concentration, motor skills, and vision.

Some medical researchers have gone so far as to say that lead ingested by children may be at the root of behavioral problems, including hyperactivity or even juvenile delinquency.

An accumulation of lead levels also can disrupt the body's manufacture of heme. Heme is the oxygen-carrying part of hemoglobin in red blood cells, and lack of it can deprive living cells of their much-needed oxygen.

Subtle symptoms of elevated lead levels in the blood can include irritability, insomnia, colic, and anemia. But, by and large, the early stages of lead poisoning present few symptoms.

For details on how to deal with this problem, please see "Living Lead Free," which begins on page 114.

Pinworms

Pinworms are tiny worms that live in the lower part of the large intestine and are attached to the intestinal wall. The major symptom of pinworms is intense itching in a spot that's not polite to scratch. Sometimes the rectum becomes painful. Girls may experience vaginal pain as well.

Polite or not, infected children are driven to scratch. In the process they pick up some almost microscopic worm eggs. The worms deposit their

How to Remove a Tick

If you see a tick attached to your child, what do you do? You need to remove it quickly and carefully. The longer a tick remains embedded, feeding on your child's blood, the greater the chance of an infection.

To remove the tick, you'll need some tweezers. Use them to grab the tick as near to the skin as you can get. With a firm and steady motion, pull the tick away from the skin. Do not twist or turn the tick, because you might break off the head, which will remain in the skin.

When the tick is out, wash the site of the bite with soap and water, and wash your own hands.

eggs just outside the body, on the anus. So when children indulge in scratching, they pick up the tiny eggs on their fingers and under their nails.

Later, the unsuspecting child puts his or her hands in the mouth and swallows the eggs, causing a reinfection.

The eggs travel to the small intestine, where they hatch. They move down to the large intestine and begin the cycle again. The itching reappears in about a month.

Preventing and Treating Pinworms

A pinworms infection sounds gross, but it is actually fairly easy to control:

☞ **Collect the evidence.** In order to diagnose pinworms, the doctor may ask you to collect some eggs by pressing a piece of cellophane tape to your child's anus. The best time to do this is when the child first wakes up, before having a bowel movement or a bath. The doctor will probably give you a glass slide on which to stick the tape or a pinworm lab packet.

☞ **Participate in treatment.** If pinworm eggs are found, the doctor will prescribe medication not only for your child, but also for you and all the other members of your family. That's because pinworms are so easily passed from one person to another on towels and bed linens as well as fingers and hands.

☞ **Stop all that sharing.** You need to take steps to keep pinworms from traveling from one family member to another. You can help prevent reinfection by having your child wear a diaper or underpants overnight, by washing his or her hands first thing in the morning, and by keeping everyone's nails short and clean. Wash the infected child's sheets and clothing every day in hot water for the duration of the infection. Try to keep your child from scratching.

Rocky Mountain Spotted Fever

Despite its name, this disease is found all over the country, not just in the mountanous West. It's transmitted by the American dog tick.

One of the main symptoms of this disease is (no big surprise) a rash. It usually begins on the extremities and moves toward the trunk. Other symptoms include an extremely bad headache and high fever.

If you suspect Rocky Mountain spotted fever, call your baby's doctor. Early diagnosis and treatment with antibiotics is essential to prevent serious consequences, including inflammation of the lungs, heart, and liver.

Poison Ivy

When your child breaks out in a rash of weeping blisters and searing itching, he or she has probably been in contact with poison ivy (or its cousins poison oak and poison sumac). Your child is experiencing an allergic reaction.

The rash itself is called contact dermatitis. A child gets the rash by brushing up against the plant. The plant component that causes the reaction is an ingredient in its resin known as urushiol. Even very small amounts of this chemical can cause a whole lot of rash.

Generally, a child encounters the plant when playing outdoors. For that reason, most cases occur in the summer. But you also can come in contact with urushiol via smoke particles when one of the plants that contains it is burned.

Even worse, urushiol can get passed around. Dogs and cats, for example, can carry the chemical home on their fur and pass it along when they climb onto your child's lap.

Once your child has been exposed to poison ivy,

a rash will appear, usually the next day. The skin where your child touched the plant will become red, then itchy bumps and blisters form. The rash lasts about a week to 10 days.

Treating Poison Ivy

Here's what to do if you know you or your child has been exposed to poison ivy:

☞ **Wash away the poison.** Head to the nearest sink and wash your child's skin thoroughly with soap and water. If you can wash off the urushiol within five minutes or so, you may prevent the rash totally, or at least lessen its severity

Also, make sure you wash the clothing your child was wearing, then wash it again.

☞ **Cool the inflammation.** If a rash does develop, apply cold, wet compresses to the inflamed area. To do this, soak a cloth in either water or Burrow's solution, which you can buy in any drugstore without a prescription.

When to See the Doctor

You need take your child to the doctor only if the rash is severe, covering more than 10 percent of the body, or if it is on the face or genitals. The doctor may prescribe antihistamines to reduce the itching and a corticosteroid lotion, cream, or tablet to reduce the inflammation.

☞ **Try to keep your child from scratching the blisters.** Contrary to common belief, liquid from the blisters does not spread the rash to other parts of the body. Scratching, however, can introduce bacteria to any open spots on the skin, setting the stage for an infection.

☞ **Reach for the calamine lotion.** The pink stuff that's been around for years can, indeed, provide a measure of relief.

☞ **Be patient.** The sores will generally heal without any further treatment. If they seem to be get-

ting worse over a period of several days, call the doctor for treatment.

Sore Throat

Minor sore throats often accompany the common cold or even alert you to the fact that one is on the way. They come, and they go. If the sore throat strikes during the winter—the most likely time—it helps to keep your child's room humidified. You can also use acetaminophen to ease discomfort.

If your child complains of a sore throat that just won't quit, however, you're dealing with something more serious that needs a doctor's attention. One of the most common causes of a more serious sore throat is an infection with streptococcus bacteria, known as a strep throat.

A doctor must prescribe antibiotics to clear it up. Strep infection symptoms include an extremely red and painful sore throat, fever, enlarged and tender lymph nodes in the neck, white spots on the tonsils, and dark red spots on the soft palate.

Preventing and Treating Strep Infection

Here's how to deal with the problem:

☞ **Get a proper diagnosis.** Antibiotics do work to clear up strep throat, but these medications will not work on a sore throat caused by a viral infection such as influenza.

For that reason, the doctor will want to swab your child's throat to get a sample, and then do tests to make sure the troublemakers are, indeed, strep bacteria. The most recent tests may allow the doctor to have results in just a few minutes and hand you an appropriate prescription as you walk out the door.

☞ **Watch those siblings.** Strep throat is known to be moderately contagious among children who

Scarlet Fever

Scarlet fever is a strep throat accompanied by a crimson tongue and a bright scarlet rash as well as a flushed face, sore throat, and fever.

School-age children are the most likely people to experience scarlet fever. Fortunately, the infection is quickly cleared up with antibiotics. Any child with the above symptoms should see a doctor promptly.

are in close contact with one another.

The incubation period for strep throat is two to five days. The brother or sister of a child with strep throat has a one-in-four chance of getting it, too. If one child has strep throat, it's a good idea to have all the children tested for this condition.

☞ **Do other parents a favor.** Children with strep throat should be kept at home until their temperature returns to normal and they've had at least a day's worth of antibiotics.

Sunburn

Babies have sensitive skin and can sunburn quickly. What may seem to you like little time in the sun can be too long for your baby.

If your child has been in the sun too long, the burn will bloom 6 to 12 hours later. Aside from turning red, a serious sunburn will blister and may even lead to dehydration.

Worse, research has shown that if your child has a serious sunburn before the age of 10, the chance of developing a melanoma, a deadly form of skin cancer, much later in life can double or even triple.

Preventing and Treating Sunburn

Your best bet is prevention:

☞ **Keep infants out of the sun.** Please note that sunscreen is not recommended for babies younger than 6 months of age, because babies this young may have problems handling and excreting any sunscreen chemicals absorbed by the skin. In any case, babies younger than 6 months should not be in direct sunlight.

☞ **Set up a barrier.** Slather your baby with a PABA-free sunscreen half an hour before going out. Use one with an SPF of at least 15. Use a higher SPF sunscreen if your child is extra fair. Don't forget the back of the neck, the tips of the ears, the nose and cheeks, and the hands and feet.

☞ **Be conservative.** Keep your baby out of direct sunlight between 10 a.m. and 2 p.m., when ultraviolet radiation is greatest.

Dress your baby in a cute sun hat with a brim and in loose, cotton clothing with long sleeves and pants. If your baby's play area is in a sunny spot, provide some shade with a patio umbrella or rig up a tarp.

If your child has been in the sun too long and develops a burn, you'll need to provide relief.

☞ **Cool the flames.** Treat a mild sunburn by bathing the baby in cool water or applying a cool, damp cloth to the area.

☞ **Ease the pain.** You also can give your baby acetaminophen to ease the discomfort.

☞ **Get medical attention.** Call the doctor for a serious sunburn—one in which the skin blisters and the child develops chills, fever, or a headache.

Thrush

Thrush is a fungus infection caused by a yeast organism, *Candida albicans*. It's responsible for the formation of white patches in the mouth, on the inside of the cheeks, and on the tongue, gums, and roof of the mouth. If you scrape away one of the patches, the skin underneath will be red and may bleed.

This fungus lives in both the mouth and the vagina, and your baby may have picked it up during

Bye-Bye Tonsils

At one time, most American children had their tonsils surgically removed. Known as a tonsillectomy, this procedure was thought to help prevent throat infections.

However, scientific studies eventually showed that these operations didn't help. Children had nearly as many throat infections after a tonsillectomy as before. Today, the operation is not routinely done.

It's been found, however, that the operation provides real benefits in three particular instances:
• when an abscess has formed in the tonsils that can't be cured with antibiotics or opened without removal of the tonsils
• when the tonsils remain permanently swollen and thus cause problems swallowing
• when the adenoids (lymph glands next to the tonsils) are so swollen that they block the tubes that drain the ears, thus increasing the risk of middle ear infections

If your physician recommends this surgery for your child, talk to your medical insurance carrier.

Because of the large number of ineffective tonsillectomies done in the past, many insurance policies will not pay for the surgery unless it has been preapproved.

birth. Thrush is most common in newborns, but can develop later if your baby has to take antibiotics.

It's not a serious problem, but, because it's painful, it can interfere with eating. Your doctor may suggest using an antifungal medicine to get rid of the infection.

A word to nursing mothers: If you are breast-feeding, you and your baby may be passing the infection back and forth through contact with your nipples. If so, put a few drops of the baby's medicine on your nipples after you finish nursing.

Vision Problems

The American Academy of Pediatrics recommends that pediatricians check a baby's eyes at birth and at each subsequent visit.

Vision tests start at 3 years of age. Most pediatricians also do a subjective check at each routine visit.

Why so early? There is at least one condition—strabismus—that if caught and treated early can prevent a lifelong vision problem. Strabismus, or crossed eyes, is caused by an imbalance in the way the two eyes work together.

A child who has crossed eyes that are left untreated is in danger of developing lazy eye. With lazy eye, the child's brain will begin to ignore the blurred picture it is receiving from the weaker eye and rely entirely on signals it receives from the stronger one. When that happens, binocular vision is lost and with it depth perception, as well as peripheral vision on the side of the weak eye.

Don't be concerned if you notice crossed eyes in an infant younger than 3 months. A young infant's eyes occasionally may wander or cross simply because the baby is still learning to focus two eyes together. Crossed eyes in a baby older than 3 months should be mentioned to your pediatrician.

If strabismus is treated early, it is often reversible. Different causes of strabismus dictate the method of treatment. Generally speaking, the earlier the treatment, the simpler and less expensive it can be. Sometimes all that's needed is an eye patch over the good eye, which forces the weaker eye to develop. Another possible treatment is a pair of eyeglasses with one filmed lens over the good eye and one corrective lens over the weaker eye. Sometimes a doc-

Eye Tests for Tots

A 3-year-old doesn't know the letter E from the number 8, so how can a little tot take an eye test? Easy. Doctors use pictures of cats, dogs, birds, sailboats, or other objects a child can identify.
In addition to testing for clarity of vision, the doctor observes how well your child's eyes work together and how they react to changes in light. The doctor also examines the eye itself for signs of injury or disease.

tor has to surgically adjust the muscles of the lazy eye before a child can use both eyes in tandem.

Strabismus is not the only possible vision problem in infants and young children; it is simply the most likely.

If any other problems develop, you're likely to get clues that your child's eyes need to be checked. If your child does a lot of eye rubbing or covering of one eye, for example, it may be time to see an eye doctor. Ask your pediatrician for a recommendation. He or she probably will suggest an ophthalmologist, a doctor who specializes in diagnosing and treating problems and diseases of the eyes. (An optometrist specializes in testing the keenness of your sight and determining the proper prescription for corrective lenses. An optician grinds the lenses to fill the prescription.)

Remember that your child can't tell you about experiencing blurry vision, about seeing double, or about any other kind of vision problem. When a child always has seen the world that way, that way seems normal. It's up to you to be on the alert for any problems.

Symptoms of Possible Vision Problems

According to the Lighthouse National Center for Vision and Child Development, you should check with your pediatrician if your child has any of these symptoms:

- frequent blinking
- frequent eye rubbing
- excessive tearing
- redness that lasts for days
- extreme light sensitivity
- frequent squinting or frowning
- holding objects close to the eyes
- avoiding tasks involving small objects
- tilting the head to use only one eye
- covering one eye to see
- occasionally crossing eyes
- recurring eyelid infections
- rapid movement of eyes from side to side
- recurring headaches or dizziness, especially in combination with any of the above symptoms
- double vision
- bulging eyes

Immunizations: A Lifetime of Protection

Children should be immunized against a number of specific diseases. The American Academy of Pediatrics, the American Academy of Family Physicians, and the Advisory Committee on Immunization Practices agree that the following immunizations are necessary: hepatitis B, diphtheria, tetanus, pertussis, Hemophilus influenzae type B, polio, measles, mumps, rubella, and chicken pox.

Immunization involves a series of approximately 15 injections given during the first two years of your child's life. Your pediatrician will let you know when your child should receive each of these injections. Seeing that your child gets all the protection against disease that modern science has to offer is one good reason for you to schedule your child for routine visits to the pediatrician.

These diseases are most dangerous during your baby's first two years of life. If some dire emergency prevents you from keeping to the schedule, however, doctors say the situation is correctable. You do not have to start the inoculation program again from the beginning, as once was believed. Doctors now advise simply picking up whenever you can and moving on.

Because of routine childhood immunizations, the number of cases of infectious diseases has plummeted in the United States. Measles, for example, struck nearly half a million children in 1962; but 25 years later, after the introduction of the measles vaccine, only 3,655 cases were reported.

Whooping Cough Protection Made Easy

In the mid 1990s, a new vaccine was introduced for whooping cough (pertussis). This was good news, because this vaccine provides immunity against the disease with fewer side effects than the older version. If you don't know what whooping cough is (and many young parents don't), that's because the earlier vaccine worked so well at eradicating the disease that there are few cases of it in America these days.

Although the original vaccine did the job, it worried some doctors and parents because about half of all children who were inoculated experienced unpleasant side effects, such as swelling and soreness at the site of the shot, fever, and inconsolable crying. On rare occasions, the side effects escalated to more serious levels, including shock, convulsions, and seizures.

Why would anyone take the risk of having a child experience these kinds of symptoms? The answer is simple. Whooping cough is a disease that can lead to serious respiratory problems, including pneumonia, and can even be fatal.

Back before the 1940s, when the original vaccine was developed in this country, whooping cough was at epidemic proportions. More than 265,000 children a year became ill, and 7,500 died. When concerns about the vaccine's safety led health authorities in Great Britain, Sweden, and Japan to either suspend pertussis inoculations or slow them down in the 1970s, the disease quickly reached epidemic levels again.

The new vaccine, however, is considered to be safer because it is made up of only parts of the pertussis bacteria, rather than being made from whole pertussis cells, as was the old vaccine.

Ask your pediatrician about this new vaccine. (It is more expensive than the older one.)

Part VI

emergencies and first aid

emergencies
and first aid

Accidents can happen, but if you are prepared, you can prevent them from turning into tragedies. This section of the book provides you with detailed information on

how to respond to a number of common accidents and medical emergencies. They are arranged in an easy A-to-Z format, so you can find help fast.

In the meantime, the best piece of advice we can give you for handling any emergency is this: Be prepared. Do not wait until you have a medical emergency on your hands to decide how you're going to deal with it.

Here are several simple steps you can take well ahead of time to help protect your family from grave harm.

☞ **Take an infant first-aid course.** In this class, you will learn ways to help your child in the event of a serious accident. Such skills may even help you keep your child alive until you can get professional medical help. Especially valuable is instruction in infant cardiopulmonary resuscitation

(CPR). To find such a class in your neighborhood, contact any chapter of the American Red Cross or the American Heart Association.

☞ **Turn your telephone into a life line.** Post the Poison Control Center number and your doctor's number on each phone in the house. (You'll find the Poison Control Center or the Poison Information Center number listed with other emergency numbers in the phone book, probably on the inside cover or first page.) If your region of the country does not use 911, display your emergency number on each phone, too.

☞ **Post emergency information.** To help baby-sitters and other caregivers, compile key information about each of your children and keep it near your telephone or post it in a central location, perhaps magnetized to the refrigerator.

Here's what to include:

- **each child's name** and birth date
- **your address** and home phone number
- **a neighbor's or a relative's name** and phone number
- **your pediatrician's name,** phone number, and address
- **directions** to the nearest hospital
- **the name of your insurance carrier,** your group number, and the children's identification numbers, if any

And for each child note the following:

- **any allergies**
- **regular medications**
- **date of last tetanus booster**
- **dietary restrictions, if any**
- **medical history of any serious illness,** surgery, or injury

☞ **Purchase or prepare a First Aid Kit.** Please see the list to the right for details on what needs to be in such a kit.

☞ **Baby-proof the nursery.** Please see page 39 for a list of items and procedures to which you need to pay special attention.

☞ **Take steps to prevent burns.** There are a number of things you can do in terms of fire and burn safety:

- **Set your hot water heater** no higher than 120 degrees Fahrenheit to prevent scalding.
- **Keep all flammable liquids** locked up.
- **Don't overload electrical wiring** by using extension cords or multiple plugs in one outlet.
- **Install smoke detectors** on each floor of your home, including all sleeping areas or hallways outside sleeping areas. Test the batteries regularly.
- **Purchase a safety ladder** if your home has a second floor.
- **Install a fire extinguisher** where it can be easily reached from the kitchen, the basement, and the garage.

☞ **Take steps to prevent drowning.** Never

Your First-Aid Kit

To put together your own first-aid kit, gather the following items and always keep them together in the same place in your home. Clearly label the box FIRST AID, so that others can recognize it. Or, you can purchase a first-aid kit, which is clearly marked with a red cross.

Items to include:

10	individual ½-inch adhesive bandages
10	individual ¾-inch adhesive bandages
10	individual 1-inch adhesive bandages
10	individual adhesive round spots
Box of 12	2×2-inch sterile first-aid dressings, individually packed
Box of 12	4×4-inch sterile first-aid dressings, individually packed
Box of 12	Nonstick sterile dressings, individually packed
1 roll	gauze bandage, 1 inch by 5 yards
1 roll	gauze bandage, 2 inches by 5 yards
1 roll each	adhesive tape, 1- and 2-inch widths
2	cloth squares, 36×36 inches, to use as a sling or to hold dressings
1	tourniquet (long, wide strip of cloth)
1 bottle	rubbing alcohol
1 bottle	acetaminophen, adult strength*
1 bottle	acetaminophen, children's strength*
1 tube	antibacterial ointment
20	paper cups
1	bottle syrup of ipecac
1	bottle activated charcoal capsules
6	diaper pins
1	flashlight
1	pair scissors
1 bar	strong (deodorant) soap
1	pair tweezers

* Periodically check expiration dates

leave standing water (even in a scrub bucket) where a toddler could reach it. Tip over wading pools when they're not in use.

Animal Bites

Animals can be unpredictable around children. In an instant, that kitty that seems so gentle and innocent can reach back into its primal nature and bring forth the claws of a tiger. Your beloved pup may snap out or bite, having had enough of a toddler's petting.

To prevent this type of accident, never leave your baby or toddler alone with the family pet, no matter how well-trained or docile you may think the animal is. Also, never allow your toddler to approach a strange dog or cat.

Cat bites and dog bites each present their own set of problems.

Cat bites puncture the flesh deeply, but leave a fairly small opening in the skin. These bites are hard to clean and therefore are much more likely to become infected.

Babies younger than 4 months old can be especially vulnerable to the bacteria that cause cat bite infections (and also to an unpleasant infection known as cat scratch fever), so make it a practice to keep your cat away from your baby.

Dog bites, on the other hand, tear flesh open, so the wound may require stitches.

If you are concerned about your child getting rabies from a domestic pet, you probably don't have to be. The danger of contracting rabies from a dog or cat has dramatically lessened in recent years. The Centers for Disease Control have reported only one case a year since the 1980s. The reason? Pet owners have prevented the spread of rabies by vaccinating their family pets.

Wild animal bites are always cause for concern. The wild animals most frequently found to have rabies are skunks and raccoons, but the disease also has been found in a number of other animals, including bats, foxes, groundhogs, and rodents.

If you see a wild animal that is extremely aggressive or lethargic or seemingly unafraid of you, you are seeing signs that may indicate rabies. Also be concerned if you see a nocturnal creature such as a skunk or bat active during the day. If you encounter such an animal, do everyone a favor and call your health department, animal control officer, or even the police.

Rabies is usually spread by the saliva of a rabid animal via a bite or even a scratch that breaks the skin. Symptoms are slow to develop, taking anywhere from three weeks to two months.

First Aid for Animal Bites

☞ **Reach for soap and water.** If your child has been bitten by a cat or dog, wash the area immediately with soap and warm water. If your child has been bitten by a dog, apply pressure to the wound to stop the bleeding, then wash the bitten area with soap and warm water. Finally, apply a loose bandage.

☞ **Do damage control.** If the bite is large, stop the bleeding with pressure, then get medical help. If the animal bite has not broken the skin, simply apply ice to reduce the swelling and bruising.

☞ **Prevent rabies.** Your doctor will determine whether your child needs a series of rabies vaccinations (consisting of five shots) based on whether the animal was domestic or wild. If the animal was domestic, no problem exists if that animal has had a recent rabies shot. If possible, check with the owner.

If the animal's immunization history is unknown, the doctor will determine whether the animal appears healthy and is available for confinement and observation, and also whether any cases of rabies have been recently reported in your area. If the biting animal was wild, the doctor will determine whether it was one of the species in which rabies has been reported. He or she will recommend the full rabies treatment if there's a possibility that the animal might carry rabies.

☞ **Watch for infection.** Over the next few days, be on the alert for any sign of infection at the site of the wound.

If an infection does develop, your doctor may prescribe an antibiotic to help it clear up.

Breathing Stops

If you think your child has stopped breathing, here is how to check: Place your child on a table or other firm surface. Open the airway in the throat by tilting his or her head back and lifting the chin. Place your ear very close to your child's mouth and listen for air going in and out, while at the same time watching the chest to see if it rises and falls. Listen and watch for a count of five (One-Mississippi, Two-Mississippi, etc.). If you don't see, hear, or feel signs of breathing during that time, begin to resuscitate your child.

Mouth-to-Mouth Resuscitation

If your child has stopped breathing, you must work quickly. Keep your head, ask someone to call for emergency medical help, then do the following:

☞ **Tilt your baby's head back slightly.** This will help open the airway.

☞ **Seal your lips over your baby's nose and mouth.** You are going to use the force of your own breath to help your child's lungs do their work.

☞ **Start blowing, gently.** Breathe slowly into your child's nose and mouth once or twice. Blow just hard enough to make the chest rise.

If the chest hasn't moved, you should then tilt your child's head to the side and try giving the two breaths again.

If the air still won't raise the chest, assume that the airway is blocked and follow the instructions for choking on pages 213–214.

☞ **Feel for a pulse.** If the air has gone in, firmly press three fingers (not your thumb) against the inside of your child's arm just below the armpit. Take about five seconds to feel for a pulse.

☞ **Continue blowing.** If you find a pulse, but your baby still isn't breathing, continue giving one slow breath about every three seconds. Once a minute, recheck both breathing and pulse.

As long as your child has a pulse, repeat this step until he or she begins to breathe alone or until help arrives.

☞ **Help the heart pump.** If you can't find a pulse and your baby still isn't breathing, place two fingers in the center of your baby's chest, approximately a finger's width below an imaginary line between the nipples.

For children older than one, use the heel of your hand placed two fingers' width below the imaginary line between the nipples.

Once your hand is in the proper position, you should give five quick compressions (within about three seconds), gently depressing the breastbone with your fingers about an inch each time. Then give one slow breath.

☞ **Repeat the procedure until help arrives.** Over the next minute, repeat this cycle—five gentle compressions every three seconds followed by one slow breath.

Continue until you feel a pulse or until help arrives. Check both pulse and breathing every few minutes.

Just a reminder: Infant CPR classes are available in your region. Call the American Red Cross or the American Heart Association for information on how you can attend these classes.

Instruction in the proper technique is important, because failure to perform CPR correctly can lead to internal injuries or, even worse, might be completely ineffective.

Is It Broken?

It may not be easy to tell whether your child has a broken bone or some other problem, such as a sprain. Suspect a fracture if:

- **You see swelling.**
- **You see bluish discoloration.**
- **The child is unwilling or unable to move the affected limb.**
- **The child is unwilling to put weight on the affected limb.**

Suspect a broken collarbone if:

- **The child's shoulders look uneven— one slumping lower than the other.**
- **The child supports one arm by cupping a hand under that elbow.**

Broken Bones

Broken bones are fairly common among children. Most are caused by falls. Although a broken bone is a serious matter, it is not as serious as an adult bone fracture.

Why? Because children's bones are still a bit pliable. They have a little give, so they don't snap as easily as older bones. For that reason, children's breaks are often called "green stick fractures." The odd term refers to the way green wood will bend, then break only on one side. In a green stick fracture, the bone also bends before it breaks, snapping only part-way through.

Children also can experience what's known as a bend fracture, which technically isn't a broken bone at all. In this condition, the bone may be bent or even twisted, but it isn't actually broken.

Sometimes a break is complete. The bone may shatter or splinter, and a porttion of it may even push through the skin.

First Aid for Broken Bones

Dealing with a possible broken bone in a safe and gentle manner until help arrives or until you can get the child to the doctor is vital:

☞ **Use a splint.** If you think your child has fractured an arm or a wrist, you can prevent further damage by putting a splint on the injured part as you travel to your doctor's office or the nearest emergency room. Using a splint simply means immobilizing the injured area against a hard, straight surface.

You can create a splint by using a rolled-up newspaper or magazine, or a board. If possible, apply an ice bag to the injured area at the same time in order to reduce swelling.

☞ **Get to the doctor's office.** If you suspect a collarbone fracture, take your child to the doctor's office immediately.

☞ **Call for help.** If your child's leg is broken, call an ambulance. Do not attempt to move him or her to the hospital yourself, or you could risk further damage to the bone.

The same precautions apply if you suspect a back or neck injury: Do not move the child yourself; call an ambulance.

☞ **Stop the bleeding.** If the injury is bleeding, stop the bleeding by placing firm pressure on the wound, using a clean cloth or pad (a sanitary napkin will work).

If the bone has pushed through the skin, do not try to reposition it under the skin. You could cause further damage.

Medical Treatment for Broken Bones

After X-rays to determine the exact nature and location of the fracture, the doctor will put the bone in a cast. A cast usually eases the pain right away. Your child will have to have periodic X-rays to check how well the bone is mending.

If your child has a fractured femur (thigh bone), he or she probably will be hospitalized and require traction.

The cast for a fractured femur will cover your child's back, hips, and abdomen as well as the injured leg and the upper part of the other leg. (An opening is left for urinating and defecating.)

In the case of a broken collarbone, the doctor may simply place the limb on the affected side into a sling to make the child more comfortable. Or the doctor might place the child in a brace to hold the shoulder stable.

The doctor will instruct you about how to lift, bathe, dress, and otherwise handle your child until the break has healed.

A fracture in which the bone has broken through the skin usually requires surgery.

Bruises and Bumps

A bruise is a black and blue mark that is caused by bleeding under the skin. A bump is the result of swelling. Bruises and bumps usually travel together.

To ease pain and lessen swelling, apply ice to constrict the blood vessels. Use an ice bag or a cold, wet cloth.

When to See the Doctor

Call the doctor if:

• **The bump or bruise** continues to grow after a day or two.

• **The child vomits,** becomes drowsy, or loses consciousness.

• **The bruise appears** on soft areas such as the cheeks or abdomen.

• **The bruise interferes** with motion.

• **The child has recurrent bruises** or bruises unexplained by activity or trauma.

Burns

The most common type of burn injury in children is scalding, so it's no surprise that most burns happen in the kitchen and the bathroom. But your child can be burned almost anywhere in and around your home. The main culprits are hot liquids, electricity, chemicals, and, of course, open flames.

You've probably heard these injuries referred to as first-, second-, and third-degree burns. The degree indicates the severity of the burn, with the first degree being the least severe and third the most serious. (In determining how serious a burn is, a doctor will consider both the degree of the burn and the area of the body surface that was burned.)

•**A first-degree burn looks red.**

•**A second-degree burn blisters** or shows ruptured blisters.

•**A third-degree burn reaches a deeper level** of the skin and may appear black.

First Aid for Burns

First-degree burns are the only kind you can safely treat at home:

☞ **Cool the burned area.** Immerse the injured area in cool water for about 10 minutes. The cool water will draw the heat out of the skin, lessen the extent of the injury, and dramatically decrease the pain. Don't make the mistake of reaching for ice, thinking that if cold is good, colder must be better. Ice is too hard on fragile, injured skin.

☞ **Ban the butter.** Although applying butter to the burn is an often-used home treatment, it's not a good idea, because it will hold in the damaging heat. The same is true for any other lotions and ointments.

☞ **Protect the injured area.** After a cool soak, cover the burn with a sterile, nonadhesive dressing.

☞ **Relieve the pain.** If your child is still in pain,

you should give him or her some acetaminophen.

☞ **Leave blisters be.** If the burn forms a blister, don't break it. Opening up the skin that covers a burn (even the blistered layer) is like inviting the local bacteria in for a sit-down dinner.

☞ **Get emergency help for electrical or chemical burns.** A burn caused by electricity shouldn't be treated at home. The appearance of electrical burns can fool you, because they sometimes are more serious than they look. For that reason, they need medical evaluation. Go directly to your doctor or to an emergency room.

If the burn was caused by chemicals, flush the area with cool, clean water for about 10 minutes, then seek medical help. Put your child in the shower, use a garden hose, or find some other source of water you can use to flood the burned area.

When to See the Doctor

To help prevent possible scarring, nerve damage, infection, loss of bodily fluids, or even shock and potential disability, the following types of burns should get immediate medical attention:

• **burns on a baby** as big or bigger than the palm of his or her hand

• **burns with blisters** or broken blisters

• **burns on the hands,** face, feet, or genitals

• **burns that look either white** or charred

Choking

Choking is caused by an actual obstruction of the airway and shouldn't be confused with coughing or spluttering. Choking occurs when food or a small object becomes lodged in a child's windpipe. Common food offenders include grapes, hot dog slices, hard candy, pieces of hard fruits and vegetables, chunks of meat, and gobs of peanut butter.

If your baby is coughing and can breathe, he or she is not choking. Chances are, if you allow your baby to cough for a minute or so, the offending tidbit will be safely expelled. Do stay near and keep close watch.

If your baby isn't making any noise—except maybe a high-pitched wheeze—the windpipe is clogged, and you have to help.

Have someone call your local emergency number while you perform the following steps. If you are alone, try the treatment below for one minute. If it doesn't work, call the emergency number yourself.

First Aid for Choking

Follow this choking-relief technique for a child younger than 12 months:

☞ **Let gravity help.** Turn your baby face down over your arm, holding his or her head in your hand, with your arm supporting the chest and stomach. Your baby's head should be slightly lower than his or her body.

☞ **Try a few slaps.** Using the heel of your other hand, try to dislodge the object by rapping the baby smartly between the shoulder blades a few times.

☞ **Try the other side.** If your baby is still choking, turn him or her over onto the back. Place your middle and index fingers on the center of the breastbone just below an imaginary line between the nipples. Give five quick downward thrusts.

☞ **Scoop it out.** If your baby is still choking, turn him or her back over and look down the throat. If you can see the object, and you think you can reach it without probing deeply, turn the child face down. The best position for this maneuver is to have the child lying on a table or counter, while you work from below in a kneeling or crouching position. Make a hook with your index finger and try to scoop it out, being careful not to push it back into the windpipe.

☞ **Keep trying.** If the child still can't breathe, continue to alternate back blows and chest thrusts until the object is coughed up.

☞ **Help with breathing.** If your baby is not breathing even after the airway has been cleared, seal your lips over the little one's nose and mouth and blow gently. If the chest rises, continue giving one breath every three seconds until your baby recovers or until help arrives.

☞ **Follow up with a medical check.** Once your baby is breathing, pay a visit to the emergency room to confirm that no foreign bodies have entered the lungs.

You can use the Heimlich maneuver on a child 12 months or older. Here's how:

☞ **Get into position.** Place your child on the floor on his or her back. Kneel at your child's feet.

☞ **Position your hand properly.** Place the heel of one hand in the center of your child's body, between the navel and the rib cage. Your second hand should be placed on top of your first.

☞ **Thrust rapidly in an inward and upward direction.** Be gentle. You don't want to cause damage. Six to ten thrusts should do it.

Cuts and Scrapes

You usually can judge the severity of a cut from its depth and by the amount of bleeding. Some cuts bleed more than others simply because of their location. For example, cuts on the scalp, face, and lips tend to bleed profusely because those areas contain many small blood vessels.

Scrapes are abrasions of the skin and look as though the surface has been sandpapered away. Most scrapes need to be cleaned with soap and water, then left alone to form nature's own bandage, a scab.

If, however, the scrape is large and oozing, it needs a sterile dressing. You can buy nonstick pads. You also can keep a sterile gauze pad from sticking to the wound by first applying an antibiotic cream. In either case, change the dressing at least every day,

Picking at Scabs

A scab is irresistible to a child: Pull the knee up almost to the chin—all the better to see it—then try to lift the scab's outer edge. Break off a little piece; bend another piece. Ouch! The scrape is bleeding once again.

How can you help your child leave that scab alone? Try applying an over-the-counter antibacterial ointment that will soften the scab and make it less itchy. It will also, of course, kill germs. It may also help to keep the scab covered during the day with a bandage. If picking at the scab has resulted in redness, swelling, or pus, the wound under the scab may have become infected. Give your doctor a call.

or even more frequently if it gets wet or dirty.

Hint: If a bandage sticks to the skin, you can soak it off with warm water.

First Aid for Cuts

Cuts that are still bleeding need treatment.

☞ **Stop the bleeding.** Apply pressure with gauze or a sterile compress to stop bleeding.

☞ **Wash the wound.** Once the bleeding has stopped, remove the gauze so you can wash away any dirt with soap and warm water.

☞ **Dry the area.** Blot with sterile gauze.

☞ **Prevent infection.** Apply an over-the-counter antibacterial ointment, spray, or cream. Then bandage the area.

When to See a Doctor

Get medical help quickly if:

•**Bright red blood** is spurting or flowing profusely from a wound.

•**The cut is gaping** or has ragged edges.

•**The wound looks as if it may** leave a scar on the face.

Medical Treatment for Cuts

A doctor will stitch deep or jagged cuts, drawing together the skin and the underlying tissue. Stitches will help a cut heal with a minimum of scarring.

The doctor may use either dissolving or nondissolving stitches (or both on the same wound), depending on the type of cut. If the doctor is treating a deep cut where muscle needs to be rejoined, he or she might use dissolving stitches that will disappear in about two months. If the doctor uses nondissolving stitches on the surface, they can be removed in about a week.

Dental Injuries

Toddlers are unsteady on their feet. It's not unusual for a toddler to chip a tooth or even knock one out. There are all kinds of ways to lose a tooth: falling, hitting it against a coffee table, banging it on the crib rail.

If your child has had an injury to the teeth or gums, seek professional advice right away. Dental experts say that injuries to primary (baby) teeth can adversely affect the developing permanent teeth that lie just below the gum line. A dentist will save a primary tooth if possible, but not if doing so will endanger a permanent tooth.

First Aid for Dental Injuries

If your child has knocked out a baby tooth:

☞ **Stop the bleeding.** Gently press a sterile gauze pad to the gum.

☞ **Call your dentist.** Your dentist should assess the damage in case it is possible to save the tooth. Baby teeth usually are not replaced in the jaws, however, for fear of damaging the underlying permanent teeth.

If your child has knocked out a permanent tooth, here is how to save it:

☞ **Act quickly.** If the tooth is still partly attached to the gum, gently press it back into the socket.

☞ **Safeguard the tooth.** If the tooth is totally unattached, pick it up carefully by the crown, not the root. Treat the tooth extra gently. If the tooth is dirty, run a soft stream of cold water over it. Do not wash away any attached tissue, because if enough live tissue remains and is kept alive, there is a chance the tooth can be reattached. Or, you can place the tooth in a cup of cold milk (best) or ice water to keep the tissues from drying out.

☞ **See the dentist immediately.** Get to the dentist's office within 30 minutes, if you can.

Medical Care for Dental Injuries

If the tooth has been chipped, your child's dentist probably will smooth any rough edges to make the child more comfortable. Larger chips, however, may require restoration.

If the tooth has been knocked loose, the dentist might stabilize the tooth with wires (a procedure called splinting) and prescribe an antibiotic to keep an infection from developing.

Ear Pain on Airplanes

Ever wonder why little kids scream their heads off on airplanes? It's because takeoffs and landings can cause them excruciating pain. The pain is caused by changing air pressure in the cabin, which causes the eardrum to be either stretched outward or sucked inward. Most adults are never aware of changing air pressure, but children are more sensitive to the change in pressure and to the stretching in their ears.

First Aid for Ear Pain on Airplanes

Swallowing or sucking can help relieve pain because it equalizes the pressure across the eardrum. So, to help this problem, here are some things to try:

☞ **Provide something to chew.** Give an older child chewing gum or hard candy.

☞ **Encourage yawning.** If your child is old enough to understand your request, this technique can be quite helpful in relieving excess pressure on the eardrum.

☞ **Offer something to suck on.** Nurse a baby or offer a pacifier or a bottle during both takeoffs and landings.

Electric Shock

A jolt of electricity can result in anything from minor discomfort to death, depending on how much electricity is involved. Most commonly, shocks happen when a child either bites an electrical wire or pushes a metal object into an electrical outlet. Sometimes children stumble onto live wires broken loose by storms or automobile accidents.

First Aid for Electric Shock

Before you offer assistance, you'll need to make sure the electricity is not still flowing.

☞ **Turn off the power.** Pull the plug or turn off the switch.

☞ **Get live wires out of the way.** Never touch a live wire directly. Move the wire with a rolled-up newspaper or any thick, dry object such as a piece of wood, heavy cloth, or sturdy plastic that won't conduct electricity. (Do not use metal.)

☞ **Resist the urge to touch your child until it's safe**. If your child is being shocked, your first impulse will be to pull the child to safety. Do not touch the child while he or she is still in contact with the current, or you will be shocked, too.

☞ **Assess the situation.** When the electricity has been turned off, check your child's breathing, pulse, skin color, and ability to respond. Also look for burned skin, especially in or around the mouth.

If your child is not breathing, begin CPR. For instructions on how to do this, see "Breathing Stops" on page 210.

☞ **Seek professional emergency help right away.** A serious shock can do damage to the internal organs.

Insect Stings

You think your baby is soo-oo-oo sweet. Well, so do those bees and yellow jackets that make their home outside your door. Bee stings usually are not serious, causing only minor swelling at the site of the sting. Some people who are allergic to bee venom, however, can experience severe reactions.

Severe reactions are unusual in a baby younger than 1 year old, but they can happen. (It's usually not the first sting but the ensuing ones that provoke allergic reactions.)

Warning: If, after a bee sting, your child has difficulty breathing or begins to vomit, get emergency medical help immediately. Also watch for:

• **major swelling**
• **hives**
• **all-over itching**
• **dizziness**

First Aid for Insect Stings

The first step in treating an insect sting is to remove the stinger.

☞ **Don't squeeze.** Do not grab the stinger with tweezers or between your fingernails. Squeezing the stinger in that way may just release more venom into your child's bloodstream.

☞ **Do scrape.** Scrape off the stinger using your finger, a credit card, or a playing card.

☞ **Provide pain relief.** Reduce the pain, itching, and swelling by applying an ice bag or a cold compress to the sting.

Nosebleeds

Nosebleeds are pretty common among children and often can be prevented by placing a humidifier in the nursery. Children whose nasal passages are dried out are more likely to have the problem, and the humidifier can be a big help.

First Aid for Nosebleeds

If your child is having a nosebleed, here's how you can help:

☞ **Change the angle.** Tilt the child's head forward to prevent gagging.

☞ **Focus on breathing.** If your child is old enough to understand your instructions, ask him or her to breathe through the mouth.

☞ **Apply a little pressure.** Gently squeeze the soft tissue part of your child's nose together between your thumb and first two fingers, closing off the nostrils.

☞ **Be patient.** Hold your child's nose in this position, maintaining the gentle pressure, for 10 full minutes.

☞ **Wait it out.** If the bleeding hasn't stopped, continue holding the nose for as long as 30 minutes, stopping every 5 minutes to see if bleeding has stopped.

☞ **Get help, if necessary.** If the nosebleed lasts more than half an hour, or if the bleeding seems unusually heavy, call your doctor or take your child to the emergency room.

Medical Treatment for Nosebleeds

The doctor may need to pack the nose in order to help stop the bleeding. Later, the doctor may want to follow up by cauterizing (sealing) the problem blood vessels.

Consult your doctor if your child is having nosebleeds every day or every other day. Such frequency may indicate that a blood vessel needs to be cauterized. The doctor may ask for blood tests to try to find out why your child is bleeding so frequently.

Poisoning

Your home may be completely baby-proofed, but visits to relatives and neighbors, vacation homes, and public places still present opportunities for the ever-curious child to cram something dangerous into his or her mouth.

Signs of trouble include:

- **a child holding an open container of a toxic substance**
- **burns on the lips or mouth**
- **excessive drooling**
- **off-smelling breath**
- **nausea or vomiting**
- **abdominal cramps without a fever**
- **difficulty breathing**
- **unusual sleepiness or irritability**
- **convulsions or unconsciousness**

First Aid for Poisoning

If you suspect that your child has ingested poison, be calm and act quickly.

☞ **Gather evidence.** Take away the poison and set it aside for later identification.

☞ **Force your child to spit.** The idea is to get rid of any poison remaining in his or her mouth. Save this spit as a sample for the doctor.

☞ **Assess the damage.** Get emergency help immediately if your child has:

- **severe throat pain**
- **excessive drooling**
- **difficulty breathing**
- **convulsions**
- **excessive drowsiness**

Common Household Poisons

You'd be amazed at just how many poisons you have lurking in and around your house. This list is not all-inclusive, but it covers the household items that most frequently cause problems.

Houseplants
Chinese evergreen
dieffenbachia
English ivy
jasmine
Jerusalem cherry
lantana
mistletoe
philodendron
poinsettia
Garden plants
autumn crocus
azalea
belladonna
bird-of-paradise (seed pod)
buttercup
castor bean

daffodil (bulb)
deadly nightshade
delphinium
foxglove
holly (berry)
horse chestnut
hyacinth (bulb)
hydrangea
iris
larkspur
lily-of-the-valley
mountain laurel
oleander
pokeberry
potato (sprout, root, vine)
rhododendron
rhubarb leaf

sweet pea
tomato plant (leaf)
wisteria (seed)
yew
Cleaning supplies
ammonia
disinfectant
cleaning fluid
dishwashing detergent
drain cleaner
floor wax
window cleaner
laundry bleach and detergent
metal polish
rug cleaner

sodium bicarbonate
spot remover
Miscellaneous
antifreeze
car wax
gasoline
glue
kerosene and lighter fluid
liquor
paint and paint thinner
prescription and over-the-counter medication
shoe polish
vitamin pill
weed killer and insect killer

☞ **Call for help.** If you don't think you have an immediate emergency on your hands, call the Poison Control Center or Poison Information Center.

The number should be posted on each telephone in your house. If you have not yet taken this precaution, you'll find the number listed on the inside cover or first page of your local phone book with other emergency numbers.

☞ **Be as specific as you can be.** Tell the people at the Poison Control Center what poison you think the baby ate. They will tell you what to do.

The treatment will be dependent on the type of poison, so it's important for you to be as specific as you can possibly be. And if you're not sure, you need to say that, too.

☞ **Be prepared to answer the following questions:**

•**What is your child's age** and weight?

•**Does he or she** have a serious medical condition of any kind?

•**What is the name** of the substance swallowed? (Read the name on the container label out loud to them. If the ingredients are listed, read those as well.)

•**What time** did your child swallow the poison?

•**How much poison** did your child swallow?

☞ **Follow directions to the letter.** If you are advised to make your child vomit, give syrup of ipecac and a drink of water. You may be advised to give your child activated charcoal capsules to prevent absorption of the substance.

☞ **Watch for results.** If your child doesn't vomit in 20 minutes, repeat the dose once.

Catch the vomit in a basin so it can be inspected. If your child is still vomiting after one hour, you should call the doctor.

☞ **Don't induce vomiting unless you're told to.** Some poisons burn the throat, and vomiting will only increase the damage. Such caustic poisons include strong acids such as toilet bowl cleaners or strong alkalis such as drain cleaners.

When the poison is such a caustic, you may be advised to have your child drink milk or water.

Splinters

Here are some good tricks for removing splinters without causing too much pain or discomfort.

☞ **Always wash the area first.** You'll be able to see better, and you'll remove bacteria that could enter the wound once the splinter is removed.

☞ **Use the tape trick.** For a small surface splinter (or even a cactus needle), try putting a piece of tape over the splinter, gently press down the tape, then pull the tape off. The splinter may come off with the tape.

☞ **Let liquid do the job.** Soak the affected part in Epsom salts or soapy water for half an hour. Soaking may bring the splinter to the surface of the skin so it can be removed more easily.

☞ **Clean your tools.** Sterilize the tweezers or needle you'll be using to remove the splinter with rubbing alcohol or a flame.

☞ **Disinfect the sight.** Pour some alcohol over the splinter's entry point to disinfect it.

☞ **Get physical.** If the splinter is sticking out, simply grab it with your tweezers and draw it from the skin. If the splinter is under the skin, use a needle to gently lift up the skin, then use the tweezers to remove the splinter.

Sprains and Strains

A sprain is simply stretched or torn ligaments, the "cables" that attach muscles to bones. Sprains happen in the joints, most commonly the ankle. A strain, on the other hand, is an injury to muscles or tendons caused by excessive stretching.

If your child gets either a sprain or a strain, he or she may experience pain, swelling, and bruising in the affected area.

Treat a strain or sprain by applying cold compresses the first day, then warm compresses the next. You also can give acetaminophen to relieve the pain.

Medical Treatment for Sprains and Strains

If your child is experiencing a lot of pain and swelling, or cannot bear any weight, call the doctor. The doctor will investigate the possibility of a fracture and possibly X-ray the joint. The doctor may apply an elastic bandage or splint. A severe sprain may even require a cast.

Pain Relief Warning

Never give aspirin to a child. If a child has a fever, aspirin can cause Reye's syndrome, a rare, but potentially fatal, condition. Instead, doctors recommend acetaminophen. It's really important to get the dosage right, however, because overdose can cause liver damage and can even be fatal. You need to be aware that infants' formulas of acetaminophen are quite concentrated, so even a little extra can cause overdose. Complicating the matter is that acetaminophen is found in lots of other children's medications—cold preparations, for example. So it's best to read the package label before giving _any_ over-the-counter medication to your child. (If a medication contains acetaminophen, you should not be giving more acetaminohen.) When in doubt, talk to your doctor. Here's the typical dosage for acetaminophen:

Age	2*–3 months	4–11 months	12–23 months	2–3 years
Weight	6–11 pounds	12–17 pounds	18–23 pounds	24–35 pounds
Dose	½ dropper	1 dropper	1½ droppers	2 droppers

*If your infant is younger than 2 months old and has a fever, call your doctor right away. **Note:** If your child's weight is lower or higher than the indicated average—say, 25 pounds at 12 months—base the dosage on the baby's weight.

Part VII

letters from mothers to mothers

Letters from Mothers To Mothers

As this book was being created, editors at Better Homes and Gardens® books invited mothers across the nation to share their wisdom with the new mothers who would be buying this book. After all, who is more qualified to offer advice about being pregnant, having a baby, and raising children in today's world than women who have done just that?

Mothers throughout America came through with hundreds of letters and e-mail postings on the Better Homes and Gardens magazine website, offering everything from practical tips to deeply moving stories of what it feels like to be a mother. They told us what we should include in this book (and what to leave out). They wrote about the pain and joy and the awesome responsibility of being a mother. They told us about feeling humbled and privileged by being entrusted with the gift of new life.

You'll find many of the letters we received from mothers scattered throughout this book. Here are some more of the best.

Becoming a Mother

The Greatest Gift

Today a doctor confirmed what my heart already knew: I am carrying a child. This is a joy unlike any other. It is too amazing for science and too wonderful for words.

Today a stranger in an elevator confirmed what my body already knew: My child is becoming obvious. "When are you due?" As I answer, maternal pride wells up from within. It is too complex for science and too new for words.

Today a strong kick confirmed what my mind already knew: I hold within my womb a human

Childbearing is painful, but I've never felt so much a woman, never so strong or fulfilled in my life. The reward of holding your beautiful baby erases all the pain. I remember crying and saying, "I did it." I did it all by myself, no painkillers, just the support of God, my husband, and friends.

Jessica L. Brown
Prescott, Arizona

being. Another kick follows as if to say, "I am a real, live person." It is too spiritual for science and too precious for words.

Sally A. Powell
Downers Grove, Illinois

Enjoy the Moment

If there is one thing I have learned in my 27 years, it's that life is fleeting. Moments come and go so quickly. Only four months ago, my baby was still a dream I held inside of me. Now his little hands grasp my fingers, and he stares at them intently, turning them gently back and forth as if he is making a great discovery. That moment will soon pass, and one day I will hardly remember there was a time when my fingers could entertain him.

Tina Smith
Houston, Texas

Cycles of Life

To me, giving birth brings your life full-circle. It is the most awe-inspiring event you'll experience as a woman. It is the first time in your life you could imagine giving your life for someone without hesitation. The love you receive from your child is love in its purest and most soul-connecting form.

Lori Stark Zarbock
Harrisburg, North Carolina

No Complaints

When I first found out I was pregnant, I was over-joyed. Then came all of the advice, old wives' tales, and horror stories. I grew more and more afraid of the unknown. The one thing that no one ever bothered to tell me is how truly overwhelming a mother's love could be. Not once have I complained about a fussy baby, midnight feedings, and soiled diapers. After all, it's my sweet baby I am caring for. I don't mind nurturing my precious baby boy, even after a 9½-hour workday. In fact, I look forward to it.

Melissa Rose Colar

Baton Rouge, Louisiana

Seeing Husband as Father

My husband cried at the first sight of his daughter, and he continued to sniffle as he accompanied her to the nursery to be weighed and clothed. A videotape of the nursery experience made by a friend captured one moment I will always treasure: When the nurse asked him what we were naming our daughter, a full minute passed before he was able to say her name between sniffles.

That love continues to this day. I had never seen this side of my husband, and his transformation from friend to husband to father has been the greatest blessing of our marriage.

Pam Lewis

Cheyenne, Wyoming

Life's Major Accomplishment

Like all new mothers, I couldn't wait to hold my baby. I knew I'd be excited to see the beautiful face for which I had waited 9 long months. Emotion flowed so wildly those first few minutes I held my little miracle. Everything I had worked for in my life—graduating from college with honors, establishing a successful career—was suddenly so futile. I was holding the most important thing I had ever accomplished. I had brought a miracle into this world. For the first time in my life, I truly felt important.

Kate Spruill

Virginia Beach, Virginia

Can This Be Real?

When my first baby was born, I kept waiting for the wonder of it all to die away. "Nothing can possibly be as wonderful as I think this baby is," I kept telling myself. But, while it has cooled from a painful intensity to a quiet certainty, the wonder has never gone away, and the world is a different place. I have never gone back to "normal." One thing I do know: Although a new mother looking at her baby is widely regarded as a stereotype of infatuated delusion, she is one of the few people with an unobstructed view of human life in all its fragility and grandeur—the whole world in one small, astounding bundle.

Penny Downing

Scarborough, Ontario

Nothing Will Be the Same

Sitting in my hospital room awaiting my little boy to be wheeled in from the nursery was like being a little kid again, running to the Christmas tree to see what Santa left. This is when I bonded with him. I let him know that I would always love him and would take care of him for the rest of his life. I love him more and more each day. My son has changed my life not only in routine, but also in my beliefs and basic philosophy of life. He has definitely made my life complete, and I thank God every day!

Jane Scelta

Monroe, New York

Greatest Job on Earth

Becoming a mother has been the most incredible experience for me, and I am so grateful to have been given the gift of motherhood. There are so many things that I have had the opportunity to experience from motherhood, but the most special ones to me are those feelings of love. There is nothing more intense than the love for a child. I knew that I would love my children with all my heart, but I had no idea how intense the feeling would truly be. It is so intense at times that it almost hurts.

I try to describe the feelings I am experiencing to friends, but as I tell them, it is indescribable. It is as if there is a door, and behind this door are feelings and emotions that can only be experienced when the door is opened, and the only way to open the door is to become a parent. If you never became a parent, then you will never open the door to these wonderful feelings. I know parenthood is not for everyone, but, for those people who do wish to have children, enjoy and savor every moment of parenthood because it is truly the most heartfelt, rewarding job a person will have.

Kelly Gonzalez

Pacific Grove, California

Be Kind to Yourself

The best thing you can do for your baby is to schedule time for yourself into your week. Give yourself two hours to play alone. Moms need play time also. What will you do? Soak in a tub of bubble bath, nap, get a facial or haircut, visit a friend, pray, read a book, garden, exercise. Do whatever it is that nurtures you. That simple treat on a weekly basis will keep you centered and help you give your best to your baby.

Don't wait for it to happen automatically. You have to be intentional about planning for your two-hour treat. It's a gift of love to yourself and to your baby.

Sandra J. Woodard

Charlotte, North Carolina

Keeping a Journal

I remember when they placed my daughter in my arms, I felt absolute conflict. Immediately, I was elated. How gorgeous this little wonder was. I told myself I would cherish every second of mothering this miracle. Seconds later, I was overcome with the realization that I had a finite amount of time on this earth with her, and I remember whispering to her, "One lifetime with you is one thousand too few."

Those words are the first that appear in a journal I keep for her. I record little victories and special moments. I use a journal as opposed to a baby book because I can impart what my husband and I are thinking, because as much as you swear you will never forget some toothless smile or tearless doctor visit—you do!

Melanie Braun

Sterling Virginia

Cherishing the Memories

I find that I forget all the important things—like how it felt the first time my baby was glad to see me, or when my son gently rocked his baby sister and sang her the same lullaby that I sang to him—if I don't write them down. So I keep a journal of the everyday experiences, because every day is extraordinary with children. I look back on my journals for inspiration, because each phase passes quickly and is gone forever.

Dany Burns

Silver Spring, Maryland

Think Prevention

Enough can't be said about babyproofing a home. We have all the standards: cabinet locks, gates at stairs, and outlet covers. We have gone a step further by adding hook-and-eye locks to tops of doors that are off-limits. We have them on bathrooms, the master bedroom, an office, and some closets. We've even attached the china cabinet, grandfather clock, and large TV to the wall with hidden anchor rods. The more prevention you take, the less time you spend saying no and causing frustration for you and the kids.

Lori Stark Zarbock

Harrisburg, North Carolina

Listen to Your Heart

New mothers are inundated with information from an incredible number of sources. We have so many philosophical choices to make, and those choices mark us as being politically correct—or not.

> My method for coping with childbirth pain was to listen to my favorite music via a Walkman. I increased the volume of the music as the intensity of the pain increased. At one point, the doctor asked me if Madonna were listening to me sing when she was in labor.
>
> Mary Hansen
> Roswell, Georgia

One of the most delightful gifts Sara has given to me is a sense of my own voice. My intuition as a mother is good. I believe many of us have good instincts with our children. We have to strive to filter out the noise of others—take the best they have to offer and throw out the rest. Listen to your own soul, and you will find a wisdom there.

Brenda Glasure
Lorain, Ohio

Relaxing Helps

As I look back at the two years that have passed since I held Dane for the first time, I am flooded with memories. I was the mom-to-be who thought she was so prepared. I read all the books and talked to everyone I could. The truth was, when he was born, I quickly realized how unprepared I was.

During those first six weeks I learned more than in the nine months it took to form Dane's life. I learned that to combat total exhaustion you must nap. The most important bit of advice I can give is to relax. When I look back, I think I was not relaxed enough, and that caused a cycle of tension.

Amy Dunigan
Mt. Joy, Pennsylvania

Motherhood: A Spiritual Experience

Giving Thanks

I thank God every day for blessing me with a baby girl and a man who cherishes our daughter. Every day seems so much brighter, fuller, and more worthwhile. Sometimes my heart feels as if it will burst when I look upon her as she's sleeping. She's my little angel. Parenthood is the best thing that has ever happened to me, and I hope this feeling never goes away.

Ronnetta Maldonado

Killeen, Texas

Special Needs, Special Responses

What an incredible feeling to have this new life growing inside of me. I never felt so whole, so beautiful, and so full of life. At about 25 weeks we found out that the baby had spina bifida and hydrocephalus. We had no idea what to expect, and so we tried to become quickly educated. I remember saying to my husband, "We don't know how to raise a child with special needs." He said, "Honey, we don't know how to raise a child."

This was our first, and he was correct. I remember thinking that I wanted this baby to stay inside me forever. If it could stay inside of me, it would always be with me, and I could always protect it. My spiritual life began to grow at that time. I didn't pray that God would take away my baby's problems, but that He would help us handle them and give us strength and knowledge to help our child.

Sean Patrick Grady was born June 27, 1995. He has had seven surgeries in his short 20-month life. Eventually, he will walk with braces and crutches. Sean has the most incredible disposition, a beautiful personality, and a great sense of humor. We truly have been blessed.

Tracey Grady

Palatine, Illinois

Learning about Love

I came to comprehend the love of God more completely when I became a mother. I experienced the preciousness of my babies, and I recognized the shallowness of my love as compared to God's love. "Nothing could tempt me to release my children from the bonds of my love," I thought as a young mother.

I grew in my understanding of God's grace to me and my children. I grew in my expression of love for them. I learned to let them go. It has been in small steps over a lifetime. I allowed them to walk alone, to ride a bicycle, express their thoughts, attend school, drive cars, attain difficult goals, fall in love, and marry. They are now free to learn the same lessons as they become parents.

Respecting them not as extensions of myself but as unique persons frees them to continue to discover their way to God through life experiences. Daily they will have opportunities to deny self and love one another.

This is the bottom line in faith and parenting.

Sandra J. Woodard

Charlotte, North Carolina

Falling in Love

Thank you for the opportunity to share a little bit about life as a new mother. First, I have never felt more fulfilled in my life. It took us three years to conceive our daughter, Abigail. As the pregnancy progressed, my husband, Gord, and I became increasingly filled with joyful anticipation. Abby's birth was so incredible. I was terrified, like all women, but it was such an invigorating experience.

Abby was so odd-looking and didn't even look like she could be our baby. But during our first night together in the hospital, I kept her in bed with me. She had a long period of wakefulness, and in my dazed state, I kept drifting off but felt her stare. I opened my eyes to see her gazing intently into my eyes, however limited her vision, for about an hour. I just fell so deeply in love with her.

Now Abby is 6 months old and continues to be a daily joy. Seeing the world through her eyes (even simply playing with blocks and cups), feeling her blind faith in and dependence on her daddy and me, and watching her take baby steps toward independence has helped both Gord and me to have a clearer picture of how much God loves us as His children.

Anne Bell

Oshawa, Ontario

Baby's Angel Aunt

I know that God was watching over me when he sent Annie to me just weeks before my younger sister was murdered. On the frantic, 16-hour drive home to be with my family, I distinctly remember Annie being suddenly alert, and I bent over her in her car seat, with my face close to hers. Her eyes were as blue as my sister's eyes—for minutes it seemed neither of us blinked—and I saw my sister's eyes in Annie's. It was almost as if God gave me one more chance to look into my sister's eyes, the eyes I would never see again in this world. It was sad and strangely beautiful and comforting all at once. I'll never forget it.

Since then, Annie has continued to be, I feel, the conduit to my sister, Sharon, whenever we need it. When Annie was about 20 months old, we traveled home again to celebrate Christmas with Grandma. When we walked in the door, Annie immediately rushed to the small living room table upon which my mother has put several photos of Sharon. She saw them, picked them up, and said, "Sharon." My daughter, only 8 weeks old at the time of my sister's death, had never met her aunt.

In later months, out of the blue, she would mention Sharon's name in ways such as, "I'm going to tell Sharon," if she was angry about something. Once, I gently pressed her further when she mentioned Sharon's name. "Do you see her?" I asked. Annie quietly nodded. "What does she look like?" I said. "Kind of like an angel," came the reply.

Although I know I can't make such moments happen, I long for them. As Annie grows, and her infant innocence begins to fade into knowing toddlerhood, I wonder if her spirit will remain as open to such miracles being done through her. Perhaps I will need to let go of these comforts as I had to let my sister go. I will release them unwillingly and sadly, yet will be grateful for the gift.

Nancy Casey

Winona, Minnesota

Gratitude for the Gift of Life

My husband and I began trying to have a baby more than three years ago. For months, we were not successful. Those months turned into two years. My son, Timmy, was born on May 1, 1996, which happened to be our eighth wedding anniversary. He has brought us so much joy. I can't clearly remember the discomfort of labor or the weeks leading up to it. I have only one delivery memory. I held my crying newborn to my face and whispered, "It's OK. Mommy is here," and he immediately stopped crying. I still cannot believe this beautiful child is mine. Thank you, God, for this perfect gift!

Jennifer Franks

Robbinsville, New Jersey

A Prebirth Visitation

The birth of my third child (a son named Carter) was a special blessing to me. I have two other children, but had lost two babies in the process of trying for a third. When I found out I was pregnant again, I was scared. My doctor immediately did a sonogram to check for a heartbeat, and there it was, big as day. He was actually alive. Now the trick was to keep him alive. The next few months were like walking on eggshells.

I spent many months worrying about this baby. Was he growing right? Did he have any diseases? There was no foundation for these worries, but it seemed like I was always praying for the baby to be healthy. As patient as I believe God to be, I'm sure He got rather tired of my supplications.

When I was about seven months' pregnant, a

I just wanted to share the feelings I had when holding my newborn daughter. My husband was with me through the whole delivery, and we were able to spend some time with our daughter before my husband needed to leave for the evening. The quiet time with my daughter after that was precious. I nursed her, and when looking down at her, I had the strange but wonderful feeling that she was my mother. It made me cry. I love my mother very much, and I love that I see her in my daughter.

Kelly Roth
Madison, Wisconsin

miraculous event happened. I don't remember what I was doing at the time, but I had a vision of my baby. It was only a flash, but I remember every detail. I saw him from the waist up through the amniotic fluid. At the time, my son was breach, and that is how I saw him, with his head up! He looked to me to be content. I thought he was a little thin, but at seven months, babies are a little thin. I couldn't get over how happy he seemed to be. Through the rest of my pregnancy, I didn't worry about him at all. When he was born, I saw him for the second time. He looked exactly the same, only plumper and healthy. He also has proved to be a contented baby. All the pain I suffered during the loss of the others has been made up by the joy Carter brings to my life now.

Misti Norton
Oklahoma City, Oklahoma

Asking God for Help

I entered the final month of my pregnancy with great anticipation. The first eight months had passed quickly with no complications, and my doctor classified me as a textbook pregnancy. Just days after my nine-month checkup, the contractions began. I still had four weeks until my due date. We rushed to the hospital, where I was diagnosed with preterm labor and put on bedrest for two weeks.

The contractions continued throughout that period, sometimes soft and barely noticeable, but often strong and close together. As nervous new parents, we visited the emergency room three times during those two weeks, only to be sent back home to bed.

The contractions grew stronger each evening when the baby was more active, and every night I endured the frustrating task of trying to sleep in five-minute intervals between contractions. Many nights I retreated to the couch completely exhausted, all attempts at sleep defeated.

Two weeks before my due date, I lay in bed awake waiting for the next contraction and feeling incapable of continuing this evening ritual for another two weeks. I rose from the bed and slowly walked to the couch. My frustration level was high, and I began to cry as I sat down. I tried to weigh my options: Go to the hospital again and refuse to go home? I realized then that the only realistic thing I hadn't done yet was pray.

As I cried, I prayed to God to help me get through this situation. I tried reasoning that if I were exhausted, I wouldn't be able to properly care for my baby or even make it through the delivery. I asked him to give me the strength to endure the contractions and the sleepless nights for another two weeks until my due date. And I asked him to help me understand why this was happening.

As I rose from the couch and walked back into my bedroom, a calmness filled me. I realized I wasn't going through this ordeal alone. We were both going through this, and I had to be strong for my child. As I slowly sat on the edge of my bed, a smile crossed my face just as my water broke.

Suzy Feine
Prior Lake, Minnesota

Vision of Comfort

My baby was due February 5, 1996. I had him on December 20, 1995. The baby weighed 3 pounds, 9 ounces. I only got to see him for a second. After he was delivered, they swept him away to take care of him. It wasn't until the next day that I got to see him. The night he was born I couldn't see him, and it was upsetting to me. So, all I could do was pray.

I knew there was nothing I could do physically for him. It was all up to God now. While lying on the bed all alone, I looked over, and on the trash can (of all things!), I saw a vision of Jesus holding a baby in his hands looking at him. I got up and walked all around the room trying to see if the vision would still be there. No matter where I went, it was!

It was comforting. I knew at that time that Jesus was watching over my baby. I told my husband this story, and he thought I was a little crazy. I know that I had so much faith and had said so many prayers, that God truly was there with me. I will never forget this. I now have a healthy 17-month-old son.

Chana McGinnis
Bowling Green, Kentucky

Giving Birth

Knowledge Combats Fear

When I told my Mom that I was pregnant, she was thrilled but added, "I hope you know what you are getting into, because Grandmother never told me how much it would hurt." We are so fortunate today to have so many resources to prepare us for the big day of labor and delivery. Knowledge can be one of the best weapons against fear, and fear is best conquered when you go into labor, as it can be one of the most incredible experiences of your life. Try to keep your mind open and don't let anyone, be it a friend, an instructor, or a book, convince you that labor should happen in a certain way or that there is a "good" or "bad" way, because each person and each experience is one and its own.

Jan Borreil
Tacoma, Washington

Mind over Pain

My daughter celebrated her 22nd birthday today, but I remember the day she was born just as if it were yesterday.

When I was pregnant, all I kept hearing was how painful labor was going to be, but that after the baby was born and I held my new bundle of joy, I would soon forget the pain. I was still scared. I

Being a mother is the greatest gift one could ever receive. I am a blessed mother of two adopted boys, and for me, the gift is so powerful. Not being able to give birth to my own children was difficult, but that no longer matters. When you adopt children, they instantly become yours, and it does not matter if you gave birth or not. I am so lucky to have these beautiful boys to love. Adoption is a wonderful thing. Maybe you could put some things in your baby book about adoption. Adopted parents are lucky.

Lori Ratigan
Maple Valley, Washington

wasn't sure if I was going to be able to endure it. But then a few weeks before my daughter was born, I read something that said to focus on pleasant thoughts for the duration of the pain. So, when my labor began, I focused. I focused so intently that I never felt the pain. Instead, I thought about lying on a beach with the sun beating down on me and the waves lapping at my feet. The nurses came in periodically to see how I was doing. Things were going great. The labor pains were beginning to come more often, but I remained focused.

Then the nurse came in to check on me. After checking to see how much I had dilated, she rushed to the door and called to get the doctor immediately. Then she came back to me and said, "My God, you're completely dilated and about to have this baby! Why didn't you call me?" I told her I was waiting for the pain to get bad. I didn't know I was about to deliver. I was quickly moved to a stretcher and whisked to delivery. Within five minutes, my daughter was born.

I've always thought the Lamaze breathing method seemed kind of funny, but now I realize the purpose of it is to get the mom to focus on something other than the pain. I never took Lamaze classes. I don't know if Lamaze was an option back then. But I remained focused without the funny breathing—and it worked.

Glenda Linzel
Vancouver, Washington

Inspiration from Nature

I am sure it is hard to understand how a cow could be my inspiration for giving birth. My husband,

Michael, and I had just moved to a farm after being city slickers all of our lives. When I was 7 or 8 months' pregnant, we went to help his grandfather with some of his cows, which were calving. There was one cow that needed to have her calf pulled. This is the first time I ever witnessed a creature being born. It was a hard labor for the cow and calf. The calf was breach, and its legs were split apart. The cow was being exceptionally calm. She didn't bellow or move about. We watched as Michael's grandfather pulled the calf out. I looked over at the cow, and she had one tear running down the side of her face. I must admit, I cried, too, when my daughter Sara was born.

Lynn Bournia
Iliff, Colorado

Singing Her Song

I used to sing "Twinkle, Twinkle, Little Star," to my daughter while I was pregnant. A moment I will treasure forever is after giving birth. They wrapped my daughter up and placed her beside me. I sang her the "Twinkle, Twinkle" song, and her little head turned toward me. That, for me, was the best day of my life.

Angie Perrazzino
St. Leonard, Quebec

A Tidal Wave of Love

The most powerful emotions wash over a new mother when she holds her newborn for the first time. My daughter waited until the exact due date to be born, but she came in only 20 minutes! When I held her in my arms it was as if a tidal wave hit me. No one can imagine how much or to what depths they can love until they hold their own newborn. As you look into that tiny wrinkled face, you see a future of dreams and possibilities as endless as the sea. You want this moment to last forever.

Angie Freeman
Ridgeland, Mississippi

Hard Work, Big Pay-Off

Having a baby is tough. When I went into labor, I refused to take any drugs or have an epidural because I wanted to have a completely natural childbirth. I wanted to accomplish something. After seven hours I gave in and took the Demerol. It helped a lot.

I named my baby Christopher, and he was the most beautiful sight I'd ever seen. I had never felt such warmth inside. I had definitely accomplished something and, even though having a baby is so tough, I would do it all over again to see my newborn baby. It was the best day of my life!

Kimberly Woo
Thornhill, Ontario

Mental Vacation from Pain

I remember using techniques taught in our childbirth classes to deal with the pain. I just imagined I was somewhere far away on a beach, and I could feel the breeze and mist from the water. My concentration was so intense that I would not even speak to my husband, and I didn't want him to touch me either. Afterward, he told me how worried he was that I would not talk to him. I explained that I was so far away that whenever he spoke to me or touched me, it brought me back to the pain. It was easier for me to block him out than the pain.

Looking back on the whole experience, I actually remember feeling as if I were on the beach. I highly recommend childbirth classes of any kind to everyone. Nothing will prepare you for the pain, but going into labor with some knowledge of ways to cope with the pain is absolutely invaluable.

Renee M. Picking
Bristol, Indiana

Speak Your Mind

This is my advice for new parents: Let the nurses and doctors know what you want when you get to the hospital. Don't just tell them that you would like to hold your baby when he/she is born. Tell them that you want to hold the baby until you say they can take him/her. You really need to be specific and write down your expectations, even if they sound unattainable. The nursing staff will tell you if what you want is out of this world, and you may be pleasantly surprised.

Laura Benkovich
Minneapolis, Minnesota

Bonding with Babies

The Smile Factor

I didn't fall in love with my babies at first sight. When my firstborn arrived, I didn't even recognize her. She was wearing a veritable wig of jet-black hair, and I wondered where she came from. Certainly not from me. I watched as they placed her under the warming lights. Exhausted and in pain, I stared, motionless, as my doctor gathered a needle and thread to sew back the opening her 8-pound-body needed to push through my size-2 frame.

She had entered the world wide-eyed and wonderfully perfect, silently watching the world around her. After the doctor finished, and while he and my husband exchanged handshakes and congratulations, a nurse busied herself with my newborn daughter. "What is her name?" she asked. I hesitated. Was this real? For nine months, my husband and I guarded our choices from those we knew and those who asked. "Caroline," I answered. In that moment, she became mine. Suddenly, wholly, and irrevocably, she entered my heart.

Two-and-a-half years later, I found myself once again in the delivery room, but my little boy was quick to remind me that this was a whole new ballgame. Far from the quiet observation his sister had shown, he was screaming in indignation before he was fully born. Once again, I wondered, who is this child that has come from within me? This time, the pain was excruciating, and I admit that it took me a few minutes to recover from my own experience and concentrate on his. Poor little fellow. His transition from womb to world was a hard one, and as the weeks went by, his fussy days and wakeful nights continued unabated, leaving me tired, frazzled, and unable to find the time or energy to truly enjoy this precious infant.

But then he began to smile. A start-with-a-twitch-at-the-corner-and-move-ear-to-ear kind of smile. A light-up-your-face-and-put-a-twinkle-in-your-eyes kind of smile. A look-at-that-smile! kind of smile. And when my little boy breaks into one of those, it sends a river of mother love to dance through my veins. Forget the sleepless nights and fussy days. This little guy has found his way so deep into my heart there's no way out.

Stephanie Winter
Bloomington, Indiana

Pain, Passion, and Responsibility

Every day I have the honor of being called Mom. Attendant to this honor is the, at times, overwhelming and unparalleled sense of responsibility of two little people to be nurtured and looked after in so many ways.

Nothing could have prepared me for the emotional deluge that started with pregnancy and intensified with the birth—the physical reality—of my baby. My baby.

I remember cradling my 1-day-old baby daughter in my arms, slowly focusing on the indefinable miracle that she was. Her fingers, her toes, her pert little mouth, button nose, and pixie ears. Out of seemingly nowhere, I was overcome by a deep sense of enormous responsibility. This was my baby. Forever a being of my very body. Was I up to the task?

The pain and passion of being a mother are visceral. The infinite love is juxtaposed with the demands, frustrations, worries, and often-times dislike of one's very own child. The child of my body. How can I feel this?

Being a mother is for me an experience so varied, so rich, so powerful, and so valued. The oft-heard, "I love you, Mom," are words I will forever treasure and embrace. They are the words that say it all.

Sue Tasker
Oakville, Ontario

Crying: A Baby's Way of Saying I Love You

Even with a clean diaper, fully fed and burped, and adequate stimulation, sometimes babies cry. And cry. And cry …

Somehow I had missed the information about crying babies. I blamed myself. Maybe I am making him cry? Does my baby not like me?

That is ludicrous! Imagine leaving a dark, warm, watery world to be thrust out into a bright, cold, antiseptic environment and not be able to say in words, "Hey, it's cold!" or "Turn down the lights!" I would scream, too. And scream. And scream …

Once in this new world, the only form of communication that gets results, lies within the scream. "Waaa …"—a warm, loving body responds with food. "Waaa …"—the wetness down below becomes warm and dry. "Waaa …"—the pressure is relieved by being put over a shoulder and burped.

As a new parent learning how to understand this tiny being with the lungs of steel, I am often shaken up by this primitive form of communication. I began viewing these crying episodes and fussy moments differently: My child was telling me how much he loved me. He was describing how much he appreciates my efforts to accommodate him. "Waaa" is my child's way of saying, "I love you, Mom."

Cori Costello
Wood Dale, Illinois

Survival Tips From Mothers

Document the Memories

One of the best pieces of advice I can offer to expectant mothers is to take some pictures of yourself while pregnant. My daughter was born prematurely at 28 weeks of gestation, and I did not have a chance to get even one picture of myself pregnant. During my second pregnancy, I made sure I took pictures at different stages of my pregnancy. My son was also born prematurely, at 32 weeks of gestation, but I have something to show him later.

Beatrice Ducharme
Toronto, Ontario

Getting Acquainted With the Help of Music

The baby is in the womb, duly attached and floating. You and a portion of the psychiatric world would think it's oblivious, too. From my experience, I don't think so. You and your husband or partner will sing to it, talk to it—directly—down there. Or, you'll play soft, melodious music loud enough so it can penetrate the lining of your pregnant belly. Soon your baby starts dancing around every time it hears parents or others. There is a little discomfort as it grows, and the protruding limbs appear to dance all over the lower part of your body. Yes, it's uncomfortable but awe-inspiring.

You can continue to explore music together after your baby is born. Music is a universal language. A lot of the world's music is great for babies. New rhythms and languages offer opportunities for them to explore their own tongues, voices, and bodies. For example, African and South American instrumental music was a favorite in my home, as well as classical and rock—from the Beatles, to Mozart, to South African

I never thought my darling angel would become the monster described by other parents of 2-year-olds. The perfect child was Hannah. Sweet, loving, compliant, obedient. I could go on and on about the little dear. She slept 10 hours a night since she was 6 weeks old. Recited nursery rhymes at 19 months. Was completely potty-trained at 22 months. The perfect child—until three weeks before her second birthday.

She threw herself down in the grocery store. The produce boy saw her. The Mexican family with quiet children was curious. The lady behind the deli counter turned away, embarrassed. A little, old grandmother gave me a stern look. My first reaction was shock. Was this my darling angel? My second reaction was anger. My darling was on the dirty floor in the produce section. My third reaction was embarrassment. Everyone was staring and somehow I had failed. But finally I just laughed.

All those emotions in that instant just burst out of me in the form of a big belly laugh. To my amazement, Hannah froze. She looked up at me, confused by my reaction. Wasn't Mommy supposed to be mad? I was still laughing so hard that tears rolled down my face. Hannah laughed, too. I picked her up and put her back in the child seat in the basket and finished my shopping. I learned a valuable lesson. Keep your sense of humor. Anger and frustration only perpetuate the problem. If you laugh at the minor conflicts, you can buy more time to figure out how to deal with the problem constructively.

Melissa Ka
Indianapolis, Indiana

rhythms. After all was said and done, my child's favorite cassette turned out to be Little Richard's rendition of old tunes such as "Itsy-Bitsy Spider."

Ines Jeffrey
Toronto, Ontario

Take Help When It Comes

After my son was born, I realized that the best thing I could do in those few days of instability and transition was to have people around me I felt close to. Just to have your friend, spouse, or parent there, to cry on someone's shoulder when things get to be too much, can make a gigantic difference in the way you feel. You need someone there who you aren't ashamed to show how difficult all these new experiences are to deal with.

This is not the time to try to act stalwart and strong. You have enough things to do without trying to make a good impression. Most of all, realize that this phase will be over with soon enough, and in time you will be able to survive an evening without a box of tissues by your side.

Cheryl Day
Anacortes, Washington

Taking the Adoption Option

Adoption: The Hardest Labor

I would like to share a moment that will live forever in my heart. The moment was the first time I saw my daughter. She was 5 months old. Her thick, pitch-black hair was standing straight up on the top of her sweet little head, her dark eyes were sparkling, and her toothless smile was framed by the deepest dimples I had ever seen.

My "pregnancy" with her was two years long, since my husband and I had gone through extensive background checking, preparatory classes, VISA applications, and on and on, just so we could be approved as adoptive parents of this adorable Korean baby. She was born in January, and we received her picture in February, but we couldn't hold her in our arms until June.

I have three children, two sons by birth and one daughter by adoption. Each is special and loved. As difficult as the physical pain can be in having a baby, by far the hardest labor I experienced was the 5½ months of labor between January and June waiting for Kari to come.

Barb Witschen
White Bear Lake, Minnesota

Child of the Heart

My husband and I are adopting our son from South Korea. We have been through many emotional highs and lows during the entire adoption process. My advice to others who have chosen this route is to remember that each step is one step closer to your child. When it seems like it will be forever until your little one is with you, don't despair.

There are so many things to do to get ready, both psychologically and physically: Read books on children, the country (if it's an international adoption), plan the nursery, enjoy the time you have left alone with your spouse while it's still just the two of you, because that is precious also.

I know when we started the adoption, we wanted a child. As the paperwork piled up, the home study was done, and classes were attended, my heart felt different. I realized that although this child was not from my body, it would be from my heart. Now my heart feels about two times its old size because of the love for my son. Some people have said my husband and I took the easy route to parenthood, but they are so wrong. Adoption is difficult on the psyche. It is the most painful and wonderful experience I've had the pleasure to be part of. I look forward to my next child.

Susan Ambrose
Meriden, Connecticut

What to Do About Siblings

Creating Brotherly Love

On January 1, 1997, we welcomed our second child into the family. As our firstborn was a little older than 3, we were concerned for how he would react after being the only child for so long. We checked out a number of books from the library on this subject (there were a lot!) and not only read them but discussed them in light of my growing tummy.

So, our son was full of anticipation when the time came. When gifts came for his sister, he opened them, and I had collected a number of small gifts for him over the 9-month waiting period so he would feel special, too.

We took them to get pictures together right away and took our son out to pick out a special frame for the photo and put it on his dresser.

Most of all, we try to let him be involved with her so a natural bond can occur. We praise him for helping get her diapers at changing time, winding up her swing, rattling her rattle, and playing with her. He especially enjoys being allowed to be a part of her bath time. We got him a squirt bottle to help rinse her off, which is fun for both of them. (Of course, during this time and always, they are under adult supervision.)

My husband is also sensitive to the fact that our 3-year-old needs a little more one-on-one time with him and me. When he gets home, he divides his time to play with our 3-year-old, then to spend time with the baby so I can also have some one-on-one time with our 3-year-old.

This has worked so far for us, and we're thrilled, especially the first 3 months when it's all so new to our son to have another child in the house vying for our attention. Hopefully, this will help someone else.

Wanda Taylore

Richmond Hill, Ontario

Double Trouble

I remember months running around the house, shirt half open, balancing my baby on my hip and trying to catch up with my toddler, checking to see if she had to try the potty. I remember trying, really trying, to keep up with current events by reading *The Wall Street Journal* while I ate some breakfast, my little girl watched *Sesame Street*, and my baby slept. For those of you who have ever tried to read *The Wall Street Journal* to the tunes of *Sesame Street*, you know it doesn't work. The child watching interrupts with requests for juice, Cheerios, and help in the bathroom, and the baby wakes up. So much for breakfast or the newspaper.

For now, my days—and, unfortunately, all too many of my nights—revolve around my children. They have to. And though many days may pass before I have time to make my own, I know that it is up to me to carve out those moments and remember who I am and what it is I want my future to be.

Some days are simply overwhelming. It would be easy—and often is—to become so inundated with the drudgery of housework and child work that I forget not only about myself but also about the little miracles that occur every day in front of my eyes. My babies won't be babies long. Soon they will be out in the world at play dates, preschool, and the various programs we will jointly choose. The more I remember and appreciate this, the more enjoyable my days become, the less overwhelmed I am, and the more confident and comfortable I feel about myself and my role as a mother. I owe it to myself and to my children.

Stephanie Winter

Bloomington, Indiana

A Job for Life

Here is how the job description read: Wanted: Dynamic, energetic individual for full-time position. Must be able to withstand extreme pressure and demands, will require on-call availability 24 hours a day. Benefits are excellent and can be matched by no other position. Plan on retaining the position for life—not many positions on the market today can offer that guarantee. Approximately 40 weeks of training required.

So my husband and I discussed the career change. Can I do it? Will it be good for us? Will I be good at it? What are the pros; what are the cons? It's a whole change in thought process. We concluded, "Yes, it's time to make the change!"

I began training for my new career in August, and there was oh-so-much to learn. Numerous books to read and classes to attend. Several physical exams to make sure my body was up to the demands it would have to meet. I was up all hours of the night. Each day brought me closer and closer to the day that I would begin this new career.

The anticipation was unbearable, but finally the day arrived, and I have never once looked back. Here is how my first day on the job went: My heart

After delivering a baby four months ago, the labor part is still fresh in my mind. This is what my doctor told me, and it really helped when I was in the pushing stage: Try not to scream when feeling painful contractions. Instead, put all that energy into pushing the baby. Because I held to this philosophy, it took only 35 minutes to push the baby out.

Colleen Collins-Moreno
Sacramento, California

soared to a level I never knew existed. The tears came like a river swelling after a flood. The camera flashed—the red eyes were captured and the feelings of joy were explosive.

Every second of my life and my husband's has changed in a way that is indescribable. The decor in my living room has expanded to include anything that either rocks, bounces, swings, or has four wheels. Forget the best-selling novels in the bookstore; let me go to that special section in the back, the section where the Golden Books rule.

All of these emotions because of that job that I accepted.

By now I am sure some of you have figured it out. I'm a mom—that's my job!

Lynn B. Behan
Oakland Park, Florida

A Member of the Club

At the age of 42, I married a wonderful, loving man who completed my life. I always thought that I would have children, but long had accepted the fact that I would not, and Bob and his teenage son, Ricky, became the family I never had. We had taken the approach that if there were any miracles left in our lives, then we would have a child. Even so, it came as an incredible surprise when, a month after the wedding, I found out I was pregnant.

What has surprised me the most about being pregnant was that all of a sudden in my early 40s, I became a member of a club I did not know existed. The understanding that came with being a member of that club was surprising, too. The club I refer to is the unique relationship that exists between you and all other women who have ever been or are

239

I was euphoric each time I held one of my babies for the first time. My babies weren't even very pretty. They were squashed, wrinkled, bruised, with misshapen heads—but oh-so beautiful to me. I'm sure that's where the saying "the fruits of your labor" must have originated. The sweetness of the result is in direct proportion to the agony of the labor.

Susan Kemmerer
Telford, Pennsylvania

---

pregnant. Everyone relates stories now that they never would have told me before, perhaps sensing that I would not have understood.

I now know what it means to have morning sickness (and understood better my cousin's intense motion sickness), and I understand the tiredness, the ability to lay on a couch and do nothing, the fears of miscarriage, the fear of loss, and the challenge and responsibility of this creature growing inside me. I now understand the bodily changes women go through and wonder why I used to know so very little.

I was a student, and my teachers were often friends half my age. I cried when I heard the heartbeat and when I found out it was a son. I have been moved by my husband's care and tenderness. I am truly blessed, and as I wait the next 4½ months for the arrival of our child, I am certain that more wondrous changes will occur. Membership in the club and the life experience that is unfolding each day make the miracle all the more worthwhile.

Marji Clark
Chantilly, Virginia

Laughter Forever

Where do I begin? Seven months ago, our son was born. On the way home from the hospital, we stopped at a store, and my husband went in to pick up a prescription while the baby and I waited in the car. Everything was quiet, until there was a wee sound from the back seat. I laughed to myself and realized my husband and I were no longer just two, we were now three.

Since then, he has been a joy to watch.

Everything is a curiosity. And so, we are reminded to marvel at details. Those first few weeks we wondered what we had gotten ourselves into, and now we know: tickle bugs, giggles, silly games, and singing those nursery rhymes we thought we had forgotten.

Laura Dahdouh
Vancouver, WA

The Best Career Choice

I was still working as a hairdresser while I was pregnant with my first child. About eight weeks before I was due to give birth, I let all my clients know that I would no longer be working at the salon once my baby arrived. Although they were disappointed to lose me as their stylist, many commented, "Good for you! You will never regret staying home to take care of your child."

It has been a drastic change of lifestyle, but I wouldn't trade these moments and experiences I have shared with my daughter for any position or amount of money. This is something priceless that no parent should miss, and every baby needs the bonding, nurturing attention from family.

Gina M. Irving
Burke, Virginia

Twin Gifts

Double Expectations

"Congratulations, Janet—this is great news," announced my fertility specialist. "I have twins; they're just great. I know you're going to love them, too."

After waiting for 2½ years, enduring surgery, injections, and numerous doctor appointments, I was expecting a wave of euphoria if I ever became pregnant. Instead, I was calm and perplexed. After the years of praying, bargaining, and begging God, I was curious as to why my dream had been granted at this particular time. And why I had been given the gift of twins. I thought it might be a mistake—especially since we were so used to monthly disappointments—so I took more than one pregnancy test. Then came the wave of anxiety: Was I really up to the challenge? Would they be healthy, and if they weren't, would I be able to maintain my sanity?

I was perplexed. I should be dancing in the clouds. I couldn't understand my reaction. Life was developing inside my flat belly. As time passed, and the morning, afternoon, and night sickness kicked in, however, I knew it was no mistake. I began dreaming of all the magical wonders I would be able to show my children.

More questions began to pile up. How do I show two babies equal amounts of love? How do I breastfeed two babies at once—I'll feel like a cow. How do I get two babies out of the car at same time or shop for groceries?

As the pregnancy progresses, however, I imagine my twins playing together in the womb, creating adventures to experience upon their arrival, wondering who the voices are that speak to their mother's tummy. I smile and thank God for the miraculous gift of life—or lives—and think what a wonderful gift for my babies to have another being to bond with, even before their birth.

Janet Golden
Philadelphia, Pennsylvania

Special Delivery

Cesarean Love

From the time I was 16 or so, I knew what I wanted to do with my life. My career was to be a mom and wife. Like every young woman, I thought that time would never come fast enough, or perhaps that I would never find the man with whom I would achieve that dream. I am happy to say that I did find him, and we just celebrated our third year of marriage and have a beautiful 13½-month-old son.I found out I was pregnant on June 1, 1995. It was the third test I had taken, and I fully expected it to come out negative as the first two had. The unbelief and pure joy I felt were just—WOW! My sister was in the waiting room, and I burst out of the exam room laughing, unable to contain the news, which I yelled from about 20 feet away. After that, there was no stopping me. I called or personally delivered the news to everyone I could think of.

I got home before my husband was off work, so I freshened up from my drive and grabbed the bib that I had been saving for just this day. It said, "I Love My Daddy." I drove to my husband's workplace, and he was just getting back in from his field work. He didn't ask me anything, so I just went in and put the bib on his desk and waited. At first, he didn't seem to get it, then I think shock set in. He led me around the office, announcing it to all his coworkers. I think he kept his shocked look for about 4 months!

I had a relatively easy, uneventful pregnancy. A 10-hour labor ended in Cesarean section. I first saw our son in a Polaroid my husband and mom brought up to the recovery room. He was about 2 hours old when I got back to my room, and they brought him to me immediately. I was instantly in love!

I was groggy, but I remember every bit of that first meeting. It was so amazing. Throughout my difficult labor, the one thing that had kept me going was my mom telling me to "breathe for the baby." Now I was holding that baby. I have read a number of stories from women who have also had C-sections. They talk about how they felt like less of a woman or like a failure for not vaginally delivering their child. As a result, they couldn't bond with their baby for awhile.

A few months after he was born, I had some feelings something like that, but I got over it. The end result is what matters, and I wouldn't change one bit of the process that got our son safely into this world. So, I guess I would tell moms and moms-to-be to enjoy every moment, whether it's your first or fifth child. I look back on my pregnancy so fondly; it was such a wonderful time. I am so thankful that the Lord allowed me the experience and the privilege of carrying and birthing a child. I will never take it—or my son—for granted.

Tami Pelles
Pendleton, Oregon

Early Arrival

Since the birth of my son, Taylor, 10 months ago, I have learned a lot of things—from basic parenting to unconditional love of a child. Though he is a very healthy and active baby now, his entrance into the world got off to a rough start. While pregnant, I read everything I could get my hands on about childbirth, took all the birthing classes that were offered in my area, talked to friends and other people about their experience. I felt like I was prepared for anything. But nobody told me about what to do about having a premature child.

I had a very uneventful pregnancy, and there was no indication that anything was wrong. Between my 34th and 35th week, my water broke suddenly, and I delivered a 5-pound, 4-ounce boy within 3 hours. Although he was a good weight, he was still 6 weeks early and his lungs were not quite developed yet and had premature lung disease. He was rushed into the neonatal intensive care unit at the hospital, and there he would stay for the next 3 weeks. His stay at the hospital was hard on my husband and I, as anyone could imagine.

The hardest thing that we have ever had to do was leave the hospital the day after he was born, without him. Of course, nobody can ever be prepared enough for that. Even though we were excited about his birth, and we knew that everything would be okay, we went home with a big empty feeling in our hearts. The bassinet remained empty beside our bed, and all the images I had in my mind about walking through the front door with our new child … none of that happened.

Months after he came home from the hospital, I still have people asking me how I was able to leave the hospital without my brand new baby. I have even had people say that they would never have left and would have gotten a bed for themselves placed next to the baby. Of course, that is not an option.

Expectant parents should be ready to expect anything, so my advice would be for them to check with the hospital where they will be delivering and make sure that they have a neonatal intensive care unit. People need to be aware of what their options are and how to make the most of a difficult situation.

Kristin Penny
Sugar Land, Texas

Cesarean for Safety

Nineteen years ago, when my husband and I were taking a course in Lamaze, our instructor included information on Cesarean sections. Out of 10 couples in our class, statistics said that at least one of us would probably have a C-section. No one in our class was anticipating this type of delivery. At the time, I told myself that it probably would not be me, but I paid close attention anyway.

During one of my scheduled appointments, I even mentioned this possibility to my doctor, and he did not think it likely that I would need one. Nevertheless, after 21 hours of labor, including 2 hours of pushing, the decision was made to do a C-section. During the 2 hours of pushing, I still had only dilated to 9 centimeters, but my doctor wanted me to try everything I could so we could avoid surgery.

When the time came to make the decision, I told my husband to read the release papers to me and show me where to sign. At no time—not before, during, or since the Cesarean section—did I feel I had failed in any way. I did everything humanly possible, and the important thing here was to deliver this baby safely. The surgery went well, delivering a healthy

baby boy to a pair of overjoyed, if exhausted, parents. There were, by the way, two Cesarean sections performed from the couples of our Lamaze class.

I would advise any expectant mother to learn about Cesarean-sections just in case she may need one. Knowledge and preparation help take some of the fear out of the unknown.

Debbie Sternfeld
Schaumburg, Illinois

Overcoming Depression
Getting Professional Help

I was thrilled when I heard the cry of my second baby, a girl. The birth and delivery process is truly a miracle, and it can all be so overwhelming. Once home, everything was wonderful. About five months later, I was at the point where I didn't want to hold my daughter anymore. I didn't want to hear her cry or even laugh. I couldn't cope with the thought of getting up in the morning, for I was up all night. I cried all the time. I thought I was going crazy. Well, I wasn't.

I found out I was experiencing postpartum depression. It is a not-so-publicized illness (yes, an illness that is treatable). I was lucky enough to find an OB-GYN also specializes in psychiatry. I was referred to a psychologist, was put on medication to help with the metabolic imbalance causing the depression, and also attended a support group for postpartum depression. It was a terrifying experience. I felt so alone until I attended the group. Everyone understood exactly what I was going through; they had either been there or were there at that time. We all cried together, and I think we were even able to laugh at times.

If you are having problems coping, or things just don't feel right, please speak up. Share your thoughts with someone you trust: a spouse, parent, friend, or doctor. Don't be afraid! This is a treatable illness, and once everything is back on track, you can enjoy that precious little gift from above. I encourage everyone who is a victim of postpartum depression to gain knowledge. There are books available and people to talk to and help you.

Don't go through it alone. I tried, and it wasn't until I reached out for help that it got better. I'm even considering a third child. (Now I think I really am crazy!)

Pam Vermeulen
Sterling Heights, Michigan

Recovery through Sharing

After I had my first child, I was extremely depressed. I had quit my job of 5½ years to stay home and take care of my new daughter. All of my friends worked, and none had young children. It was a difficult time of adjustment for me. What helped me the most was finding a parent/child play group. I got to meet lots of mothers with young children. I got the chance to share frustrations and interests with others who could relate. They have been lifesavers. I don't know what I would have done without them.

Joanna Simpson
Dallas, Oregon

Minding the Marriage

The one thing I wish people had told me before the birth of my first daughter was the impact the experience has on your marriage. My daughter was born in 1991, and all of the books I read discussed how wonderful the experience was and what a great bonding experience it was for the parents. No one explicitly discussed how the stress and sleeplessness can effect your marriage. Thus, when I was home, depressed, stressed, and tired, my husband and I fought all of the time.

One time (which we remember humorously now), we both screamed about who was going to file the divorce papers first (we are both attorneys). The period of adjustment ends (thank God), but it

was hard when all of the books depicted the period as a completely wonderful time, when I was experiencing just the opposite. My solution was to search every bookstore for some book that would say that the marital friction was normal. I also polled every one of my friends who had given birth. Lucky for me, most of my friends and relatives confirmed that marital friction is indeed normal and no cause for alarm (or instant divorce). And, we now can look back upon the period and laugh.

Anne Tozier Teleisha
Hempstead, New York

The Clouds Do Lift

I had read about postpartum depression, but I really thought it was an excuse to lie in bed and an excuse to act like you wanted. However, I quickly found out that postpartum depression was real. Every day it was a challenge to get out of bed. I didn't want to shower. I didn't want to get dressed. I didn't want to eat. I felt lost and alone, and I cried at the drop of a hat. Nothing made me feel better. I thought, I am going to be this way for the rest of my life.

But after about two months, I started to feel better. I wasn't as depressed, and life didn't seem as hopeless. It's now four months later, and I can just now say I am mentally starting to feel myself. Motherhood, whether the first time or second, shouldn't be a race to be the best mother in the world. Never set your expectations too high, because you're coping with your body changing and the responsibility of a baby.

Staci McCormick
Tulsa, Oklahoma

Help from the Baby

In the first couple of months after giving birth to my first child, Jacob, I experienced on-and-off bouts with the blues. I was sleep-deprived, sore, flabby, and completely worn out with his feeding schedule. Although I knew breast-feeding was best for him, I couldn't help getting frustrated when he wouldn't latch on right, or he'd want to nurse when I'd want to sleep, or he'd be hungry an hour after I'd fed him. Some days I'd just cry, and other days, although it sounds horrible, I'd just want to go away and leave him with anybody else but me.

Then came a morning when he was about 7 weeks old that I went in to get him at 6 a.m. after three hours of sleep. I was thinking, "Why can't you just sleep a little longer?!" Frustrated, I stooped over his crib and said in a tone of mock anger, "Well? What do you want?" I was greeted by the sweetest smile (his first smile) I'd ever seen. It was then I realized all my hard work had paid off. Every day since then I've been greeted by that sweet smile in the morning, and it makes me realize how lucky I am to be a mom.

Christine Damon
North Little Rock, Arkansas

Comfort in Numbers

Postpartum depression hit me four days after Spencer was born. I felt as if I were being swallowed alive, even though I was so in love with my son. I didn't understand what was happening to me. I turned for advice to everyone I knew who had given birth. Everyone said it was "the baby blues," and it would go away within a week or two. Week after week passed, and the depression continued. I spent my days crying and calling my husband frantically on the phone while he was at work. The depression was indescribable. I couldn't eat, sleep, or speak to people.

Finally, I found answers for what was happening to me. I realized I wasn't alone, but postpartum depression and it's harsher sister, postpartum psychosis, are kept in the closet by women. They're taboo. I found out about a meeting of professional women who were suffering or had suffered from this awful condition, women who knew how I felt. It was so reassuring. The worst of my condition lasted about 3½ months.

My husband and I want to try for a second child soon again. I've done my research and have a game plan for what may happen the second time. (Postpartum depression is generally more severe in subsequent pregnancies). I'm a little nervous, but the joys of motherhood I've experienced in the last 11 months outweigh anything else.

Karen Neapoltan
Sherman Oaks, California

Nursing a Baby: What It's Like

The Real Thing

If a Ph.D. were offered for knowledge of breast-feeding, I think I would have one. During my pregnancy, I attended a breast-feeding class, read all sorts of literature on nursing, and even "surfed the Net," reading on the subject. I learned about all of the best positions or "holds" for nursing; I learned how I was supposed to express and store milk.

My first nursing experience was like the first bicycle ride without training wheels. The first few times I nursed my daughter were less than perfect. I had to get used to holding a swaddled newborn as well as figure out how to hold my breast like the diagrams in the book. Nothing seemed to feel comfortable for both of us. One time I even broke down and started crying with her. I felt inadequate in meeting her needs.

Just as those bike rides became more enjoyable with time and experience, so has nursing my daughter. Ashley is now 6 months old. While she is nursing, she looks up at me with such beautiful, innocent eyes. Sometimes she stops to "talk" to me or her daddy. She will sometimes kick her legs and nurse at the same time. (Maybe I should try exercising while I eat, too.) I am glad I have continued nursing. I can see from her weight gain and her behavior that she is content with nursing. I feel privileged to be able to provide her source of nourishment as well as get to know her like no one else can.

One cannot learn to ride a bicycle by reading books on the subject; the same applies to nursing a child. The books are helpful, but nothing comes close to the experience itself. The books cannot tell a mother what is right for her and her baby. The two have to discover that together. The books cannot describe what a wonderful bond nursing brings. The books will never express what beautiful, intimate moments are shared between a mom and her precious child. The best thing to do is to experience it for yourself.

Rhonda Williams
Lake Charles, Louisiana

Formula Wins Out

My first nursing experience was painful and a little humiliating. It was close to 3 in the morning, and a nurse came in with my squalling baby. It took a while to get my milk down and involved the nurse grabbing my nipple and shaking vigorously. I keenly remember that I then knew how a cow felt when she needed milking and the "farmer" had cold hands. (Not to mention the indignity of the whole exercise.)

Nevertheless, we kept at it and were successful. After three weeks of providing my innocent little one with nourishment—and huge breasts that leaked like nothing I'd ever seen, coupled with feeding every few minutes (it seemed)—we moved on to formula. Welcome to the world of sterilizing bottles, nipples, pots, and pans … I learned a lot. Who knew that my breasts could be thought of in a whole new way?!

Helene Casey
Toronto, Ontario

Third-Time Winner

I am the mother of three, and I wish I knew with the first what I now know with the third. I was so "aware" of myself nursing with my firstborn that I made myself a nervous wreck. I wouldn't nurse in front of anyone (including family), meaning I sent myself off to a back room or to a bathroom to nurse. Needless to say, I wasn't very successful at nursing. My milk quit producing enough to satisfy my son within the first two months. I wasn't quite as shy and embarrassed the second time around, but I still wouldn't feed at friends' houses or at restaurants, so I supplemented with bottles. My second son chose the bottle over me.

Heartbroken, I decided never again would I let other people do this to me. I had my third (and last) child in October 1996, and can say we are still successfully nursing. She and I bonded immediately, and I have nursed her everywhere from the birthing room to conventions. I am discreet, and no one around me is even aware of the baby nursing. I just want everyone to know it can work, and it is worth it. Relax and go with it.

Kellye Pickens
Greenville, Texas

The Ultimate Fast Food

I think that the most important decision I made was to breast-feed. I had read during my pregnancy about breast-feeding and knew the many benefits, both physical and emotional, to my baby and to me. I was also starting to learn the basics of good nutrition for myself. It seemed obvious that the only choice was breast-feeding. How could I give my child the best crib, the best toys, and the best room decorations, and not provide the best nutrition?

Since good nutrition is important to overall health, I knew I wanted the best for my baby. Once my daughter was born, I was in awe. I couldn't believe this beautiful baby was mine. The feeling of seeing my baby for the first time was incredible, but seeing her nurse was incredible, too. Breast-feeding seemed the natural continuation of pregnancy and childbirth.

My husband and I were able to pick up and go whenever we wanted. Travel was so easy, too. We never had to worry about packing food for the baby, keeping the food cool, or heating it up. As long as we took diapers and a blanket, we were set.

I nursed my daughter more than two years. She was not ill until her first cold when she was almost 2 years old. By breast-feeding, we saved money that would have been spent on food, bottles, medicine, and doctor visits. To us, it was a win-win situation. Breast-feeding was the best decision I made as a mother. I have four children now, and I have nursed all of them.

Susan Vicknair Theall
Kenner, Louisiana

Focus on Safety

Voice of Experience

I recently experienced a terrible accident with my 5-month-old daughter that could have cost her life. Although I am diligent regarding her safety, I made the terrible mistake of not rebuckling the belt of her car seat following a diaper change in a store restroom.

When we reached the car, and I pulled the car seat out of the shopping cart, it tipped forward just enough to pitch her out. She fell 3 or 4 feet to the concrete and landed right on her head. I knew instantly this was more than an average fall, so we did the whole 911-and-ambulance-ride-to-the-hospital thing. Elizabeth sustained a nasty skull fracture. Fortunately, there was no bleeding in the brain and no brain damage. She is expected to make a full recovery in eight to nine months. There are several comments I have for new moms regarding infant safety:

1. There is nothing like the feeling that your child may die because of a careless accident you could have prevented.

2. Never allow your child to sit in a car seat even for a second without the belt securely buckled.

3. Accidents can happen to the best of us. Nobody can be perfect all of the time. Everyone gets distracted from time to time. No one intends for a child to get hurt.

4. If an accident does occur, at some point, you need to be able to forgive yourself. I am still working on that.

Beth A. Leonard
Southlake, Texas

Looking to the Future

Grandmother to Be

I first envisioned myself as a grandmother when my ten-month-old daughter took her first steps. At that second, I realized that every step from now on will take her a little farther from my arms.

Oh, I know she will come running back into my arms for bruised knees, bruised egos, and a bruised heart, but never again will she be so innocently dependent.

I know in my heart that each step I take on the road to becoming a grandmother will be a journey like no other, a one-way ticket to life. And on that journey, thanks to my little girl, I will look at every leaf, every flower, every bird, and even the moon way up high, like I have never before seen them—through the eyes of innocence.

As she learns to master the art of feeding herself, her ABCs and counting, I realize she will quickly proceed from kindergarten through college. Someday she will marry, and I will be holding her child—my grandchild.

Along this journey we will laugh together and cry together, experiencing all the joys of being a toddler, a teenager, and a young woman ... together. I accept the fact that each of these stages will bring their own exciting milestones to be shared.

Lynn B. Behan
Oakland Park, Florida

Love the Moment

As a mother of three preschool boys and expecting my fourth child, I would tell a new mom to wake up each morning and remind yourself that your baby—and this day with your baby—is a gift. Never forget this even when you have been up all night nursing, or comforting a sick or teething baby, or when that precious baby spills spaghetti all over your freshly mopped floor.

As you always hear from older women, "Enjoy this time with your kids while you can. They grow up before you know it." This is not just a cliché— it is true wisdom. Please do not waste away these precious years with your baby, feeling frustrated at all of the time and energy he takes. This is a passing season—one that will pass all too quickly. Enjoy your precious gifts while you can.

Alisa Harris
Jonesboro, Georgia

Late Baby, Lasting Love

I am the mother of five children, grandmother of one, and with another grandchild due in August. I had my first child at 21, and my last at 38. Some people thought I was crazy to have a baby at 38, but I had been recently reunited with and married to my childhood sweetheart, and having this baby was very important to us.

She is now 8 years old, and I couldn't imagine life without her. She's made our family one, because she's as related to my husband's kids from his first marriage, as she is to mine.

The advice I give to young moms (who ask,) is to thoroughly enjoy each stage their child goes through. All too soon, they're on to the next one.

My favorite time with all my kids was at 2 a.m., when it was just the two of us with no distractions or interruptions. I remember just taking in their sweet baby scent, like it was perfume.

When my youngest was an infant, Phil Collins' song, "Groovy Kind of Love" was out, and we'd listen to it at 2 a.m. together. It reminded me so much of her, it's become "our song."

Sure, having a baby later in life will mean having children around longer, but I think my daughter keeps me young. I'm 46, and during her three-week spring break from school, we went bowling and roller skating. Probably wouldn't have been doing that without her!

Valerie T. Misch
Camino, California

Part VII

questions parents ask

Appendix

Questions parents ask

ew parents always have questions. After all, you're now responsible for the total well-being of a brand new human being. And this child does not come with an instruction manual. Here are the answers to some often asked questions.

Q How can I tell whether my child is deaf?

A Deafness is sometimes difficult to detect. Signs of deafness such as late talking or slow intellectual development are occasionally misdiagnosed as autism or retardation. Certainly, testing a child for the awareness of sounds is not hard. For infants, ring a bell or shake a rattle. For toddlers, check their reactions when you slam a door. For older children, observe their responses to telephone conversations to see whether they are hearing well. If in doubt, consult your doctor.

Q What are some of the major developmental milestones I should look for in my child?

A Children mature at different rates. Generally, however, babies smile at about 6 weeks (plus or minus 2 weeks), roll over at 3 or 4 months, and notice that a stranger is not Mom or Dad at about 5 months. Most babies can sit with support at 6 months, without support at 7 months; they stand between 10 and 12 months, and take their first steps between 12 and 15 months.

Many babies speak a few words—Dada, bye-bye, go, no—when they are 10 to 12 months old. By 18 months, they put together sentences of two or three words: "I go bye-bye," for instance.

Q What should I do if my baby doesn't reach a milestone on schedule?

A Don't be too worried at first, because the

timetables for developmental milestones are tremendously flexible. Be reminded, for example, that Albert Einstein didn't talk until he was 4½ years old. But he probably gestured more brilliantly at 8 months than most youngsters do at age 2.

Q Should I help my child achieve milestones?

A Absolutely. That's what parenting is all about. Toddlers want to know how to go up and down steps. Youngsters want to know how to swim or ride a bicycle.

You should have some sense for which milestones occur at what ages, but don't push your child. Let the child take the initiative. When a milestone is reached, dramatize the moment. When your child takes those first steps, for example, reward him or her with hugs and love, showing how happy you are.

Q What are the best kinds of games and toys for children, and at what ages are they most appropriate?

A Anything that a youngster can make noise with is good. One of the best toys for a 1-or 2-year-old may still be a pot or pan and a wooden spoon. A set of metal keys that can't be swallowed is just as effective as, if not more attractive than, the plastic ones the store sells. Also, blocks and balls are as good as ever. Incidentally, crib mobiles are an excellent purchase, too. Infants are capable of learning a lot more than people once thought, and crib mobiles provide color, design, and motion to stimulate babies' minds. But look for ones that have a seal of approval for safety.

Toy manufacturers are starting to print age ranges on their boxes and, generally speaking, those ranges are correct. But manufacturers still are clever enough to promote toys that parents will think their youngsters should have as opposed to toys that the youngsters may actually want and need for development.

Q How can I tell whether my child is "gifted" o "slow"?

A A gifted child is always experimenting and ha an excellent memory. The gifted youngster con stantly analyzes, eyeing situations from all angles Finally, the gifted child is creative, forever coming up with new questions or solutions.

The child who is slow or who is retarded constantly repeats himself or herself, and doesn't play curiously. Such children play repetitively and can only think in terms of the concrete or specific rather than in generalizations.

Q My child is reading at age 3. Does this mean she's a genius?

A She certainly is showing evidence of giftedness in a particular area, but that doesn't mean she's necessarily a genius.

And don't push the reading just because of her apparent gift. Instead, enjoy reading with her. As a matter of fact, don't push her into anything. You may feel pressured by friends, family, and society in general to push your child into growing up more quickly than is best. Ignore this pressure, because pushing will do the youngster no good.

Q How soon can I tell whether my child is right- or left-handed?

A At age 4 months, see which hand the baby uses to reach for an object. Another simple test is to note, at about age six months, which ear your child first tugs. If your 6 month-old tugs his or her left ear, chances are you've got a southpaw. If the right ear is the first to be tugged, you're likely to have a right-handed child. Later, at age 9 to 10 months, observe which hand the child transfers objects to.

None of these methods is foolproof. Some children do not develop a consistent hand preference until they are between ages 4 and 7.

Q I want my child to be the best she can be, but I

don't want to put undue pressure on her. Where should I draw the line?

A That's a tough question. Recognizing the difference between you and your child is essential. You can't ask her to live out your unfulfilled ambitions, a type of pressure that is all too common. Parents usually don't realize they're pushing too hard, although sometimes the pressure comes knowingly. One of the best barometers to gauge whether your prodding is excessive is the opinions of the people around you—grandparents, neighbors, friends. They often can perceive a problem before you can.

Q Should I rock my newborn to sleep, or is it better just to put him in the crib?

A There is no such thing as loving a baby too much, and rocking is a great way to show your baby love. Don't worry that he will get so used to being rocked that he can't or won't fall asleep without it. Your baby actually began rocking in the womb, floating in rhythm to your movements. Eventually, the baby who is used to rocking will grow accustomed to not always having mother around to rock him. You can help this transition by offering the baby a favorite blanket.

Q Do children learn language by imitating or by being corrected?

A They learn by both imitation and correction. There is nothing wrong with correcting a youngster's speech if done in a constructive rather than an aggressive fashion. Suggest the proper pronunciation and ask the youngster to try to say it after you. Do not scold the child for speaking incorrectly.

Q When does a baby become a toddler?

A A baby becomes a toddler on the first birthday. A child is considered a newborn or neonate until he or she is a month old, an infant until age 1, and a toddler from ages 1 to 3.

Q How can I teach my child to properly express anger?

A Anger is a normal part of being human. It helps adults stake their territories, and it helps 2 and 3-year-olds establish identities separate from their parents. Later, by age 4 or 5, a youngster may use anger to say to a sibling that certain things are "mine."

When you teach your child the proper ways to express anger, you certainly want to stress that he or she shouldn't be cruel. At the same time, though, you don't want your child so worried about how to express anger that he or she is unable to vent it in any way.

One way a child learns to express anger is by watching how you and your spouse argue. When Mom and Dad quarrel, the youngster watches. And if violence is part of your relationship, it's likely to be a part of your child's relationships.

How you handle being angry at your child is important, too. Again through example, you can show your child that it is OK to be angry sometimes, but not to use physical violence.

Finally, the best way to help children handle anger among themselves is to let them try to settle their differences on their own.

Q My youngster kicks and bites to express anger. How should I handle the situation?

A The child who kicks or bites playmates should be removed from the other children and not be allowed to play with them for a while. Unless the offense was serious, the separation need only be brief.

Some biters and kickers may be showing the first symptoms of depression; in children under age 11, depression may manifest itself in aggression, not sadness. If the kicking and biting persist, have a mental-health professional see your child.

Q My child is a bully. What can I do about it?

253

A Your first step should be to love your child even more than you already do, because bullying usually is a sign of low self-confidence. The typical bully feels like everyone else is better than he or she is, and by hurting others, the child is trying to make himself or herself feel important. You also should try, if possible, to pin down the source of your child's insecurity. The worst step you can take is to bully the bully. Your youngster will only interpret that as further reason to bully other people.

Q My 2-year-old picks out clothes in the store, but then wears the same old outfits day after day. How can I get her interested in her new clothes?
A Your youngster enjoys the experience of shopping with you, not the experience of wearing new clothes. A little girl (or boy) needs only a few outfits, so the advice is simple: Don't buy her all of those new clothes. Two-year-olds want sameness, and you may actually be contributing to the problem by giving her all of those choices.

Q How can I get my youngster through the grocery-store checkout lane without having him throw a fit because I won't buy him candy or other unnecessary items?
A With some youngsters, you need only explain why you won't buy them the candy or other tempting items. You may have to offer the explanation every time you go to the store for a while, but the child will eventually accept it.

Such simple explanations won't work with every youngster, though. If your child falls into this category, plan on one trip to the store when you will have to take a stand and suffer the consequences. After the inevitable tantrum begins, turn to the checkout person and say, "Excuse me, but my child and I are going to have a moment of meditation." Then take off to a quiet part of the store for a disciplining session, explaining to the child why the behavior is not acceptable. Some situations may

require further punishment—say, time in a chair—once you get home. The important thing to remember is that you should not be so embarrassed by your child's behavior that you give in. Having gone through one such trip, the child probably will not act that way again.

Q I feel as if I'm always nagging, always saying "don't, don't, don't." How can I avoid appearing negative to my children?
A Saying "yes" to reinforce appropriate behavior is very effective, but parents should not feel guilty when they need to say "no" or "don't." Try taking a little more time to explain the "don't" to your child instead of taking the easier way out by saying "yes."

If you can anticipate a situation, you may be able to avoid saying "don't." For instance, if you see your youngster eyeing a butcher knife on the kitchen counter, remove the knife.

One reason you may repeat so many "don'ts" is that *you don't* follow through and make your child pay a consequence when he or she disobeys your initial "don't." Finally, think about whether you're saying "don't" because it's really necessary, or because it's an automatic reaction.

Q Is there a way I can show disapproval and still seem loving?
A Actually, one way of loving is to say no and to show disapproval.

When saying no, though, always make clear that what you disapprove of is the act, not the child. For instance, you might say to your child, "I love you, but I am angry that you took away Sally's toy. You'll have to give it back to her." A comment like that is much more effective than one that loads your youngster with guilt: "You are acting so bad that you are giving Mommy a heart attack."

Comments that make a distinction between being angry with what a child did and being angry with the child himself or herself may be difficult for any youngster under age 6 to understand. Just be sure that your anger is always eventually followed by hugs. Your behavior, not what you say, will make the difference.

Q How useful is ordering a misbehaving child to sit in a chair?

A Very useful, if it means your child will lose something. Time spent in a chair in front of the television is ridiculous.

Actually, sitting in a chair provides youngsters who are overstimulated with a time-out of sorts. Many children misbehave simply because they're overwhelmed by all that's going on around them; they merely need an opportunity to get away from the hubbub.

Q How should I handle my 2 year-old's negative attitude?

A Most 2-year-olds say no to everything. Nothing tastes right. You can't do anything right for them. That attitude is part of normal development. In some instances, you can avoid hearing no by giving your youngster two choices or by phrasing the question so that it can't be answered with a yes or no. But consistently trying to avoid situations where your child will say no is not a good idea. Youngsters who don't resolve this negative phase may be handicapped emotionally later on.

Q What can I do to calm my 3-year-old's fear of doctors?

A For most youngsters, fear of the doctor is actually fear of getting a shot. Find a pediatrician who is sensitive to your child's anxiety. Shots, of course, are inevitable, but children usually accept them better when doctors explain why the shots are necessary.

Q Is thumb-sucking harmful?

A Active thumb-sucking may have an influence on the upper front teeth. If the habit is causing signifi-

cant bite problems, you might have to encourage your child to break the habit. Check with your child's dentist or pediatrician for tips.

Generally, however, when the child wants to quit sucking the thumb, he or she will. There's little you can do about it. Parents who worry about this may only be creating more problems.

Q Should I take the pacifier away from my child?

A No. Children will let go of their pacifiers when they're ready. Parents get too alarmed by oral behavior.

Q Our youngster, who's an only child, seems very jealous when I pay attention to visiting children. Any suggestions?

A Only children often tend to be lonely. When they act jealous of other youngsters, they may actually be sending a reverse message—that they would like to have companions. The best solution to the only child's loneliness is to get him or her involved in a group activity.

Q How should I handle the embarrassing questions my youngster asks in front of people who appear different to him—the handicapped, smokers, people of different races?

A Openly. The other person will feel more comfortable if you answer your child rather than telling him to be quiet. The parents' reactions, not the innocent questions, are what tend to cause hurt.

Q How should I deal with my child's fear of being too far away from me? Our 3-year-old needs to be wherever I am all day long.

A Such behavior is not unusual for 3-year-olds. They're continually playing, then going back to check on Mom, then going off to play again. If your youngster, however, does seem truly anxious about losing you, you may want to take him or her to a mental-health professional. Other family issues may be causing the clinging..

There also is the possibility that you want your child to be too dependent on you. You may need to be loved too much, and perceive the child's independence as a rejection, as an insult. This makes you do something to sabotage efforts at independence, which in turn causes your child to feel anxious about being away from you.

Q How can I prepare my youngster for the arrival of a sibling?

A Educate the child about your pregnancy, allowing him or her to participate in it, if at all possible. For example, if the hospital or birthing center in your community will allow it (and you think your child can handle the experience), let your child attend the birth. And by all means, before the new baby arrives, discuss with your child what will be different at home after the birth.

Q Is it normal for the first child to regress after the second child is born?

A It's normal every time a new baby arrives. An excellent example is the youngster who is potty-trained, then starts to mess the pants again when the sibling is born. Skills that are lost when a sibling is born, however, are usually regained in a short period of time.

One way to ease the older sibling's concerns is to let him or her sleep in the crib a couple of nights and offer her a bottle again. If your child has easy access to these baby things, rather than being denied them, he or she will quickly discover that they are boring and will become uninterested.

Even better, however, is to emphasize the specialness of being a "big sister" or "big brother". Point out all the things your child can do that the new baby can't do.

Q How can I get my 2- and 4-year-old children to stop fighting at bedtime?

A Sometimes, a 4-year-old fights with a younger child because he or she doesn't like being treated the same as the sibling. And rightly so. Put the younger child to bed earlier. Then let the older youngster do something special before going to bed.

Q My 3- and 5-year-old children constantly ask me to settle their disputes. What should I do?

A Unless the dispute is causing harm or injury to one of the youngsters, stay out of it. To intervene in children's arguments is one of the most unrewarding acts parents can undertake. Just as disciplining two youngsters in a car while you're driving is impossible, so too is settling children's disagreements. Indeed, children need to learn to settle their own disputes as part of growing up.

Q When will my child begin to understand that his actions have an effect on other people?

A Such understanding comes with socialization, which starts at age 3 and takes hold about age 4. Only then can you talk meaningfully with him about how a particular kind of behavior will not win friends.

Q How can I teach my child not to interrupt when someone else is speaking?

A Interruptions are inevitable—and, indeed, natural—because children, especially around age 2 or 3, need to be at center stage.

Even so, there are times when such interruptions should not be tolerated. Mealtime is a good example. If Mom and Dad are talking about something important, the children should expect a severe consequence if they interrupt. That could mean removing the offender from the room, or sending the child to a chair or to his or her room.

But children also need to have their turns at talking. Observe their right to join in the conversation at certain times, and watch that you aren't interrupting them.

Glossary of Terms

Abrupto placentae: separation of the placenta from the uterine wall.

Active phase: the second phase of the first stage of labor. In the active phase, contractions last about one minute and occur every two to five minutes. These contractions gradually dilate the cervix to 10 centimeters.

Adhesions: the abnormal union of separate tissues during healing.

Afterpains: abdominal cramps caused when the uterus contracts during the first days after birth as it returns to normal size.

Alpha fetoprotein (AFP): a protein produced by the unborn baby's liver and passed through the placenta into the mother's blood. A higher than normal amount of AFP indicates neural tube defects, such as spina bifida, in the fetus.

Amniocentesis: a test to determine genetic or other defects in the fetus by examining amniotic fluid taken from the mother's uterus.

Amnion: the bag of waters (also called the amniotic sacthat surrounds the fetus in the uterus.

Amniotomy: breaking the amnion—the bag of waters surrounding the fetus.

Amniotic fluid: the fluid inside the amniotic sac that surrounds and protects the developing fetus.

Anemia: a deficiency in the number of red blood cells, or hemoglobin.

Ancephaly: a fatal, congenital defect in which most of the brain has failed to develop as it should.

Anesthesia: loss of sensation. See General anesthesia and Epidural anesthesia.

Antepartum: before labor or giving birth.

Anterior position: the most common position for the baby's head during birth, where it is facing the mother's back.

Apgar score: a system to rate a newborn's well-being on a scale of 1 to 10 by evaluating the heart rate, respiration, muscle tone, reflexes, and color. The total of the ratings is called the Apgar score.

Areola: the darker-colored area around the nipple of the breast.

Aspiration: suctioning or siphoning fluid from a body cavity.

Asthma: a respiratory disorder in which bronchial spasms cause difficulty in breathing.

Basal temperature: the body's lowest temperature during the course of the day.

Bilirubin: a pigment formed by the destruction of red blood cells. See also Jaundice.

Birthing room: a homey alternative to the traditional labor and delivery rooms.

Blood cholesterol: cholesterol absorbed from food and manufactured by the liver. It is carried in the blood for all parts of the body to use.

Bloody show: a vaginal discharge of mucous

tinged with blood; a sign of oncoming labor.

Braxton-Hicks contractions: mild, irregular uterine contractions occurring any time during the final trimester. Each lasts 20 to 30 seconds, and the contractions stop after a few hours.

Cephalopelvic disproportion: a condition in which the mother's pelvis is too small for the baby's head to pass through at birth.

Cesarean section: surgical incision of the walls of both the abdomen and uterus as a means of delivering a baby.

Cholesterol: A soft, waxy substance needed for normal body functions. Too much cholesterol can lead to hardening of the arteries, coronary heart disease, and stroke. See also Blood cholesterol and Dietary cholesterol.

Chorion: the outermost membrane enclosing the fetus, part of which becomes the placenta.

Chorionic villus sampling (CVS): a test to detect genetic abnormalities in the fetus by examining a small fragment of the chorion—the tissue that later develops into the early placenta.

Chromosome: a rod-shaped body in the nucleus of a cell that carries hereditary factors.

Classical incision: a vertical incision made in the upper part of the uterus to deliver a child by Cesarean section.

Colostrum: a thin fluid secreted by the breasts before the production of breast milk.

Congenital: a condition that exists either at or before birth.

Crowning: the appearance of the baby's head in the vagina during the second stage of labor.

Dietary cholesterol: a waxy substance that is in foods of animal origin, but not in fruits, vegetables,

or grains. Too much dietary cholesterol raises blood cholesterol levels, raising the risk of heart disease.

Down's syndrome: a congenital condition, formerly called mongolism, that often includes mental and physical retardation.

Dystocia: difficult labor.

Eclampsia: sudden convulsions that occur during pregnancy caused by toxemia or poisonous compounds in the bloodstream.

Ectopic pregnancy: a condition in which the fertilized egg begins to grow in the fallopian tube or elsewhere outside the uterus.

Edema: swelling caused by excessive fluid buildup in the body.

Effacement: thinning of the cervix.

Embryo: an unborn baby from conception until eight weeks following conception.

Endoscopy: examination of an internal body space using a lighted optical instrument.

Epidural anesthesia: a local anesthetic (also called a regional anesthetic) that numbs just the lower body.

Episiotomy: an incision made from the vagina toward the anus to ease a vaginal delivery.

External cephalic version: manipulating the fetus from outside the uterus to position so that the head is down.

External rotation: a baby's spontaneous turning of the head when he or she exits the birth canal.

Fetal alcohol syndrome (FAS): numerous physical and mental defects caused by a mother drinking alcohol during pregnancy.

Fetal hemolytic disease: the destruction of the

etus's red blood cells by a mother's antibodies when mother and child have incompatible blood cell factors.

Fetal monitor: an instrument used to measure the fetal heart rate and uterine contractions during labor.

Fetus: an unborn baby from eight weeks after conception until birth.

Forceps: an instrument used to grasp a baby's head to help guide the baby's body during birth.

General anesthesia: a state of unconsciousness, along with loss of feeling and sensation, usually as the result of administering gas.

Genetic counseling: an analysis of family medical history combined with medical tests for the purpose of helping couples plan their families in the face of possible inheritable problems.

Gestation: pregnancy.

Gestational hypertension: a condition in which a mother develops high blood pressure 20 weeks after conception.

Glucose challenge test (GCT): a test for gestational diabetes.

Human chorionic gonadotrophin (HCG): a hormone that indicates pregnancy.

Incompetent cervix: a cervix unable to remain closed; can lead to premature labor.

Jaundice: yellowing of the skin and eyes caused by excessive amounts of bile pigments (bilirubin) in the bloodstream.

Lactation: milk production in the breasts.

Lamaze method: a way of preparing for childbirth, developed by Dr. Fernand Lamaze, that emphasizes exercises and breathing patterns to help a woman through labor.

Lanugo: the fine hair that covers the fetus.

Latent phase: the first phase of the first stage of labor, where contractions occur every five to 15 minutes and last for about one minute.

Leboyer delivery: a technique that aims to reduce the pain of birth for the baby by providing a soothing environment and by postponing or avoiding certain traditional procedures.

Leopold's maneuvers: an examination to determine a baby's position in the uterus.

Lochia: discharge of blood, mucus, and tissue after giving birth.

Mastitis: a breast infection.

Meconium: the newborn's first bowel movement, usually greenish black.

Miscarriage: spontaneous abortion, usually before the 20th week of pregnancy.

Neonatal: a word referring to a newborn baby up to 1 month old.

Neural tube defects: a faulty formation of the spinal column during pregnancy.

Oxytocin: a pituitary hormone excreted during childbirth. A synthetic form (Pitocin) can be given to induce or speed labor.

Placenta: the structure through which the fetus receives nourishment and oxygen and eliminates waste. It develops on the uterine wall in the third month of pregnancy and is expelled after childbirth.

Placenta previa: a condition in which the placenta becomes implanted in the lower part of the uterus and extends over the opening of the cervix.

Posterior position: a condition in which the

unborn baby's head is turned toward the front of the mother's body.

Postpartum: after childbirth.

Preeclampsia: a condition in which a pregnant woman experiences high blood pressure, edema, and protein in the urine.

Prepared childbirth: an instructional program to teach expectant parents about the physiological changes of pregnancy, the stages of labor, and pain management during childbirth.

Presentation: the part of the baby's body first to emerge. A breech presentation means the buttocks emerge first; a cephalic presentation means the head emerges first.

Prodromal labor: the earliest stage, when contractions are 20 to 30 minutes apart.

Pudendal block: a local anesthetic injected into the vaginal wall to numb the entire pelvic area.

Quickening: the stage of pregnancy where the mother first feels the baby move.

Rh factor: a group of substances in the blood that can cause an allergic reaction. Those who lack the factor are Rh negative. An Rh positive infant born to an Rh negative mother may develop serious problems, including anemia.

Sickle-cell anemia: a hereditary anemia caused by crescent-shaped (sickle-shaped) red blood cells.

Silver nitrate: an antiseptic used to prevent gonorrheal eye infections in newborns.

Spina bifida: a defect in which some of the vertebrae fail to close, exposing the contents of the spinal canal.

Station: a system using numbers to describe the progress of the baby's head through the pelvis during labor. Station ranges from -4, where the descent has not yet begun, to +4, where the descent has been accomplished.

Tay-Sachs disease: a disease that affects both fat metabolism and the brain and causes progressive weakness, blindness, and, ultimately, death.

Thalassemia (or Beta thalassemia): a genetic blood disorder found in people of Mediterranean origin that causes severe anemia, enlargement of the liver and spleen, and frequent infections.

Toxemia: a condition involving toxic substances in the blood.

Transition: the final phase of the first stage of labor, during which the cervix reaches its full dilation of 10 centimeters.

Trimester: one of the three-month periods during pregnancy.

Ultrasound: sound waves directed into the uterus and bounced off the baby used to create a picture for diagnostic purposes.

Uterus: the hollow, pear-shaped organ in which the baby develops during pregnancy.

Vulva: a woman's external genitalia, including clitoris and labia.

Index

scrubbing, 28
vitamins in, 22
Vegetarians, 23
Vernix, 65
Vinyl flooring, 38
Viruses, 186–187
Vision
color, 157
problems, 202–203
Visual stimulation, 37–38
Vitamins
fat-soluble, 25
good food sources of, 24
for preventing stretch marks, 19
RDA for pregnant women, 24
water-soluble, 25
Vocabulary, building, 150–151
with pointing game, 172
practicing new words, 174–175
Vomiting
as symptom of motion sickness,
186
as symptom of poisoning, 217
as symptom signaling trouble in
newborn, 102

W

Walkers, 48, 159
Walking, 159–161
Walking epidural, 58
Wallpaper, nursery, 37–38
Walls, nursery, 38
Wardrobe
nursing, 83
nursing bras, 85, 87
work, *129*–130
Water, drinking
exercise and, 20
lead in, 29, 116–117
for prevention of hemorrhoids,
17
Water birthing, 63
Water breaking, 15
Water safety, 161
Water-soluble vitamins, 21, 25
Weaning
from the bottle, 138–139
from the breast, 136–138
Weight gain
baby's appetite and, 139
during pregnancy, 17–19

stretch marks and, 19
Whole milk, 141
Whooping cough, 204
Windows, nursery, 39
blinds with safety tassels, 40
lead in miniblinds, 115–116
Wood smoke, 29
Word games, 151
pointing game, 172
Working fathers, 121
Working mothers, 119–130
back-to-work wardrobe, *129*–
130
breast-feeding and, 89–90
child-care options for, 123–128
compensation for time away, 257
dependent-care accounts, 122
flexible schedules for, 34–35
guilt of, 119, 122
job sharing positions for, 34, 120
maternity leave, 33–34
separation anxiety, 122, *124*
Worrying, excessive, *108,* 153–154